HARVARD DISSERTATIONS IN AMERICAN HISTORY AND POLITICAL SCIENCE

EDITED BY
FRANK FREIDEL
HARVARD UNIVERSITY
AND
ERNEST MAY
HARVARD UNIVERSITY

A GARLAND SERIES

CONFINES OF CONCEPT

AMERICAN STRATEGY IN WORLD WAR II

IN TWO VOLUMES
VOLUME ONE

JOHN ELLIS VAN COURTLAND MOON

GARLAND PUBLISHING, INC.
NEW YORK & LONDON 1988

Library of Congress Cataloging-in-Publication Data

Moon, John Ellis van Courtland.
Confines of concept : American strategy in World War II / John
Ellis van Courtland Moon.
p. cm. — (Harvard dissertations in American history and political
science)
Originally presented as the author's thesis (doctoral—Harvard
University, 1968).
Bibliography: p.
ISBN 0-8240-5140-8 (set : alk. paper)
1. World War, 1939-1945—United States. 2. Strategy. I. Title II.
Series.
D769.M65 1988
940.54'0973—dc19
88-21965

Printed on acid-free, 250-year-life paper
Manufactured in the United States of America

NA

To the Memory of My Parents,
Marie Edmée [Choisy] van Courtland
Moon (1898-1979) and
Carlyle van Courtland Moon
(1897-1972):
To whom I owe more than
I can ever acknowledge

Introduction:

My first impression on returning after twenty years
to my former work is a feeling of strangeness. What was
so thoroughly mine has now taken on independent life.
This feeling of change goes far beyond the impact of
reading recently released documents from the National
Archives of the United States, the Public Record Office
of the United Kingdom, the Franklin D. Roosevelt Library,
the Library of Congress and the numerous other depositories
of private and public documents. It does not merely come
from the new insights provided by the recent multi-volume
biographies of Eisenhower, Churchill, Roosevelt, Patton,
Montgomery and other leading figures. Nor is this feeling
merely a reflection of the re-examination of America's
role in the war provoked by such excellent scholars as
Christopher Thorne and John W. Dower. Finally, this
sense does not merely mirror the views of a scholar
now blessed with the published texts of the Eisenhower
papers and with the complete Churchill-Roosevelt
correspondence.

No, above all, this feeling of strangeness reflects
travel in time. I am a different man living in a different
world. As we move through time, the past is ineluctably
transformed. I am far more conscious today of the ways
in which relations between individuals, organizations
and nations are bound by the threads of power, more aware

of the compulsive force of security which often translates
itself into an obsession with survival, more perceptive of
the ways in which power undercuts as it uses ideology.
It is our fortune to grow with age into complexity.

And the world around us as it changes makes us reflect
back upon the world we leave behind. The way in which
I now see World War II is inevitably conditioned by the
Vietnam War, the final decline of colonialism and the
development of the Third World, the nuclear revolution
and the growing danger of proliferation, the threat of
terrorism, the sobering realization that great power
carries severe limitations and vulnerabilities. Although
some of these developments were apparent twenty years ago,
their consequences are far clearer now and will be even
clearer two decades from now.

There are things I know about now that I didn't know
then: ULTRA, the efforts of certain members of the
British government to reach accommodation with the
Germans after the fall of France, the shameful "abandonment
of the Jews" by the Western Allies, the volume and
complexity of American strategic planning after the
Casablanca Conference. There are things that I inferred
which are now documented: the British plans to use gas
to repel a German invasion of the United Kingdom, the
disingenuous handling of the Greer incident by President
Roosevelt who was fully informed of the facts before he
delivered his "shoot on sight" speech.

There are things that I knew but that I now see

differently: the relocation of loyal Japanese-Americans
into concentration camps, the conflict, much sharper
than I once thought, between United States and United
Kingdom interests which reveals that America was a hard
bargainer in pressing its post-war interests against
those of the British Commonwealth.

There are things that I knew in one way and not in
another: emotionally, not intellectually. Growing up
during the war years, I saw propaganda films as truth
rather than myth. I was blind to the racist theme
which now casts a shadow on the American conduct of
the Pacific War.

This essay is a meditation on the concepts and
preconceptions of American strategy studied in the
accompanying work, and an attempt to reflect on the
afterlife of these strategic beliefs in the nuclear
age. The concepts and preconceptions which molded
American strategy in World War II (the defensive-offensive
complex, the direct approach, the autonomous war, the
righteous war and the temporal imperative) were all
affected by the onset of the nuclear age. The post-war
period saw the continuation of some strategic beliefs,
the culmination of some and the contradiction and
reversal of others. Forming the traditional American
approach to war, these concepts and preconceptions
emphasize the maximum use of force in the minimum amount
of time. Therefore, if uncontrolled by policy, they
prefigure Absolute War which Clausewitz used as an

an effective standard with which to measure historical
conflicts. The major task of deterrence in the post-
World War II world would be to keep the use of force
within the limits set by policy. Therefore, this essay
will conclude with a brief analysis of the conflicting
logic of warfare and deterrence and with the author's
reflections on the realities and possibilities of
warfare in the nuclear age: limited, total, absolute.

The Defensive-Offensive Complex:

In the final decade between the two World Wars, the
United States moved its defensive line forward towards
its future enemies: stonewall defense to hemispheric
defense to global defense. President Roosevelt sought
to draw the forward line at an advanced point, covering
the approaches to the New World, shielding the security
of the United States. That forward line, once defined
and established, also guarded the bases from which
future offensives against the Axis coalition would be
launched. The ambiguity inherent in any advanced
geographical position lies in perception and intention.
Is the purpose of the occupier defensive or offensive?
Is he merely trying to cover his country or is he
preparing to strike at the enemy's homeland?

The paradox of the defensive-offensive complex is
maintained in post-war American thinking and planning
for conventional and nuclear war.

Since 1945, the forward line of global defense is

the geographical embodiment of the policy of containment.
In the first decade of the Cold War, this line, defined
and extended under Communist challenge, was seen as a
defensive perimeter drawn around the Soviet Union, its
satellites and its allies, a wall constructed to prevent
an aggressive foe from staging a breakout. Ideally, by
1955, the line protected Western Europe, the Mediterranean,
the Middle East, the Indian sub-continent, southeast Asia
and the western Pacific including Japan, Formosa and
South Korea. This geographical shield comfortably
covered all approaches to the Western Hemisphere. Even
then, however, it had its irregularities. West Berlin
stood deep within Communist territory. Moreover, emerging
Third World nations did not see themselves as fitting
comfortably behind this defensive line nor did they
identify their national interests with those of the
United States and its allies.

The domino theory, evoked in Europe before it was
defined in Asia, was an inheritance of the 1930s. The
Nazi march of conquest from the reoccupation of the
Rhineland to the attack on Poland was held up as a clear
warning to the future defenders of the free world.
That parallel, remembered by President Truman in 1950
when North Korea invaded South Korea, later was unimag-
inatively applied to southeast Asia when the resistance
of the South Vietnamese government began to erode under
the pressure of the Vietcong insurgency.

Tragically, a linear concept was repeatedly forced

upon a fluid and complex challenge. The geographical embodiment of the front line was far better suited to meeting a conventional external invasion than to stopping an insurgency. Vietnam serves as a warning against the rigid definition and application of a forward line of defense.

By the 1960s, the line was more difficult to define in clear-cut geographical terms than it had been in the late 1940s and early 1950s. The accession of Cuba to the Communist camp (1958) placed a hostile state within the Western Hemisphere. This process accelerated throughout the 1970s with the triumph of the Sandanistas in Nicaragua (1979) and the accession of Marxist regimes in a number of African states: Ethiopia (1974), Angola (1975), Mozambique (1975).

Today, the concept of the forward line of defense holds especially tenaciously on the Central European Front. Since Western Germany cannot be defended in depth, since political considerations militate against the sacrifice of territory for time, NATO's declaratory policy commits its forces to forward deployment for defense. Other areas of primary United States interest (Japan, the Western Pacific and the Persian Gulf) are also conceived as advanced points against potential attack. However, the concept of a geographical line encircling the enemy bastion has been seriously modified. Strategically, the globe has now assumed a checkerboard pattern.

By the 1980s, however, a new frontier had emerged as a potential forward line of defense: space. The debate over the Strategic Defense Initiative (SDI) highlights the defensive-offensive complex. Ideally, SDI would function as a series of layered defenses which would begin by destroying launched missiles at the booster stage. Envisioned by President Reagan as a purely defensive system, it is seen by the Soviets as a technological shield which, if it functioned perfectly, would give America a first strike capability. Once the shield had shattered the Soviet sword, the American sword could descend with overwhelming force upon a helpless enemy. Moreover, as critics have pointed out, the technologies inherent in the Strategic Defense Initiative could also be adopted directly to offensive purpose. Again, we have a compelling example of how the terms "defense" and "offense" can interchange according to the perceptions and intentions of the antagonists.

The ultimate expression of the defensive-offensive complex in the post-war world is the nuclear force. Peacekeepers, the missiles standing on alert in their underground silos or moving underseas are the minutemen of instant destruction. In the doctrine of deterrence, the strength of defense stands on the capacity for immediate offense. The protection of United States security interests depends upon the ability of its nuclear forces to deliver a swift and utterly destructive

blow against enemy targets. Deterrence weds defensive
purpose to offensive means.

Moreover, the nuclear umbrella is extended to cover
regions of vital interest within the American advanced
line of defense: Western Europe, Japan, the Persian
Gulf. The concept of extended defense covers not merely
the Western Hemisphere but also regions that, beginning
with the 1940s, President Roosevelt and his successors
have considered essential to United States security.
Not surprisingly, therefore, NATO planning against a
Soviet advance does not rule out the first use of nuclear
weapons by the West to halt Warsaw Pact aggression.
For Western Europe, the nuclear sword is the shield.

From the beginning of military history, sword and
shield have performed different functions in a single
action. The shield wards off the enemy's blow while
the sword kills or cripples him. Ultimately, weapons
escape classification because the intentions with which
they are wielded remain invisible until translated into
action. Even then, motives often remain mysterious.

The Direct Approach:

In World War II, the direct approach to victory was
the axle upon which United States strategic plans turned.
It was the basis for the invasion plans against Northwestern
Europe which culminated in Operation OVERLORD and for the
Central Pacific thrust towards the Japanese homeland.
It was premised upon the belief that only a direct ground
offensive against the enemy's center of power would

force a confrontation in which the enemy's army could be
annihilated. The direct approach was also the theoretical
foundation for the hopes of the air planners that victory
could be achieved solely through air power by destructive
blows delivered against the sources of enemy power: his
economy and his morale.

In the nuclear age, however, the direct approach has
become too dangerous as a course of action. Nuclear
warfare is the ultimate Napoleonic battle of annihilation:
a direct approach to the destruction of the enemy's will
in a single battle. The World War II debates between
strategic and tactical bombing, between precision and area
attacks, are continued in nuclear war planning. Should
the objective be the enemy's forces, his economy or
his morale? Counterforce or countervalue? The advocates
of targeting the enemy's military forces, his economy,
his leadership or his capacity for post-war recovery
are the descendants of those who placed their faith in
precision bombing during World War II. The proponents
of city busting are the disciples of Bomber Harris and
Curtis Le May. Indeed, the latter bridges the transition
given his prediction that a future nuclear war would be
an all-out assault. Of course, the direct blow as
envisioned by the Air Force is better suited to hypothetical
planning than to implementation. It is a strategy of last
resort suited to deterrence but of doubtful value in
action.

Defensive concepts, however, go against the grain

in American military doctrine. The Navy and the Army have
also sought to restore offensive priority to strategy.

Under the leadership of Secretary John Lehman, the
Navy has adopted a strategy designed to confront Soviet
naval power in the Barents and Norwegian Seas, pushing
the defensive-offensive frontier towards the enemy's
naval bastions. This strategy, questionable on geo-
strategic and deployment grounds, has raised serious
concerns about the threat it could pose, in case of
conventional war, to the maintenance of nuclear deterrence.
The primary objective of Mahanian strategy, the direct
confrontation and destruction of the main enemy fleet,
now embodied in the Soviet Navy's Submarine-Launched
Ballistic Missile Force, may no longer be feasible in
the atomic age.

There have also been attempts by the Army to adopt
mobile offensive tactics, combining firepower and speed,
to the conventional or nuclear battlefield: the concepts
of Follow-on Forces Attack and the Deep Strike favored
by the advocates of the Land/Air Battle. The proposed
strategy (defined in Field Manual 100-5: 1982 edition)
would carry the battle far behind the enemy's lines,
disrupting his communications, impeding his follow-up
forces and possibly seizing valuable assets for bargaining
war termination. Even this resurrection of the offensive,
however, is not tied to any direct approach towards the
heart of the enemy's power. Such an approach has become
too dangerous.

Ultimately, the execution of either the Arctic
strategy or the Land/Air Battle strategy, like the
Air Force's strategic nuclear strike against the U.S.S.R.,
would depend upon presidential approval. In any
conventional conflict, policy considerations could
rule out the execution of either strategy. In a nuclear
war, the synchronization of the command and control
essential to success on the maritime or land battlefields
would be almost impossible to maintain.

In post-war planning, the direct approach remains
mainly an Air Force concept. The Army's newly declared
strategy is partly a reaction to America's experience in
its two post-1945 wars where the abandonment of an
offensive strategy tied to a direct approach proved
deeply frustrating.

In Korea, after General MacArthur's Inchon landing,
the United States momentarily returned to the direct
approach when it moved northward, seeking to destroy
the demoralized North Korean Army and to reunify the
country. After the Chinese intervention and the American
repulse from the Yalu, however, the United States
returned to the policy of holding the aggressor along
a defensive perimeter and bringing him to reasonable
terms through massive attrition. It denied General
Van Fleet the opportunity to smash the enemy forces
when they were vulnerable to amphibious envelopment.
No drive into North Korea, let alone into Manchuria
or northern China, was contemplated once the painfully

protracted negotiations began at Panmunjon.

In the Vietnam War, conventional battle lines did not exist. The direct approach had nowhere to go because an invasion of the north aimed against the center of enemy power in the Hanoi-Haiphong area and the Red River delta was precluded. In a war which lacked conventional battle lines and in which the enemy enjoyed sanctuaries beyond military conquest, United States ground forces were deprived of the foundation of the direct approach for land warfare: movement from a definite starting point towards a decisive objective. So they were forced to wage a battle of annihilation within the territory of the people they were defending.

To conclude, in Korea and Vietnam, political leaders forbade the application of the traditional American approach in warfare. Ironically, the United States, whose military planners had scorned British strategy in World War II as "indirect" and "indecisive", was now condemned to wage two attritional wars under restraints which foreclosed decisive results. Korea and Vietnam raised serious questions about the ability of the United States to wage successful local wars in the nuclear age.

The Autonomous War:

Even twenty years ago, I was skeptical of the prevailing stereotype of United States political innocence opposed to European sophistication. Now, I am even more sharply conscious of the ubiquity of power relations.

The concept of the autonomous war, the belief that the
military should be allowed to conduct operations untrammeled
by close political control, that the target of these
operations is solely the enemy's army, not diverting
political objectives or territorial prizes, that belief
seems quaint today in the aftermath of Korea and Vietnam.
But it was as political as the belief that military
operations must be carefully controlled and monitored
by the civilian leadership so as to safeguard national
policy aims. For the belief in the autonomy of war
guarded the military services against what they considered
unwarranted and unprofessional meddling by their political
chiefs.

Furthermore, it was protected by the President's
tolerance. As pointed out in my work, it conformed
with President Roosevelt's policy objectives and his
vision of the post-war world. His earlier direction
of the war, when he educated the Joint Chiefs of Staff,
ran counter to his later approach.

The constant in F.D.R.'s control was his emphasis
upon the maintenance of the anti-Axis coalition. He
never allowed his military chiefs to take any operational
decision which would threaten the Grand Alliance. His
emphasis, over the objections of the Joint Chiefs of
Staff, on aid to the United Kingdom was clearly evident
twenty years ago. His emphasis on aiding the U.S.S.R.,
his impatience with the slowness of Lend-Lease deliveries
to Russia, his reluctance to use American military aid

as a political bargaining chip, were also evident. They led
his critics to charge him with political naivete, with the
failure to settle post-war problems while he had the
leverage of conditional aid. This impression of political
innocence was reinforced, in the critics' minds, by his
failure to support a strategy that would contain Russian
expansion in Eastern and Central Europe.

Reflection convinces me that either of the above
courses would have been politically foolish and could
have been militarily catastrophic. Given the number of
German divisions (varying between 130 and 200) that were
deployed on the Eastern Front, the President could not
afford to alienate his suspicious ally by carrying out
military operations clearly designed to forestall Soviet
advances in Central and Eastern Europe or by using aid
as a bargaining tool, especially since before the summer
of 1944 the Allies had little else to offer to the
Russians.

The emphasis of the Joint Chiefs of Staff on the
creation of a Second Front was keyed to the maintenance
of Russian resistance; it answered a long standing
Soviet demand. It insured, therefore, when it was
finally executed in June 1944, the maintenance of the
coalition while it kept Western forces away from areas
of primary Soviet interest.

Before the execution of OVERLORD, the policy of
unconditional aid, often complicated by the limitations
and hazards of shipping and by the scarcity of resources

in the earlier stages of the war, allayed Soviet irritation
over the postponment of the Second Front. Any other policy
would have exacerbated relations to an extent that
could have threatened the coalition.

The President's "permissiveness", therefore, eminently
suited his political objectives. The emphasis upon
winning the war in Europe as rapidly as possible with
as few political complications as possible, so as to
redeploy American forces for the defeat of Japan, was
emphatically political. Another strategy (an invasion
of the Balkans or a thrust through the Ljubljana Gap
towards Austria and Central Europe) would have weakened
or threatened the President's policy.

Moreover, it would have been politically unacceptable
to the American public. President Roosevelt never forgot
what some of his successors have ignored: the boundaries
of military and political action are defined by public
support. The direction of his policy before Pearl Harbor,
detailed in Part II of this work, shows his caution to
a marked degree. Because of his sensitivity to public
attitudes, he often preferred an indirect approach to
a direct confrontation. But, if he had been more Lion
than Fox, he might have failed in justifying his course
of action to the American public.

In the closing year of the European war, he showed
that same caution in reacting to the counsel of some of
of his advisers like Averell Harriman and towards the
urging of his chief ally Winston Churchill when they

proposed a bolder and harder line towards the Soviet Union.
He would not endorse any course of action that could
threaten a coalition which he may have sensed was far
more fragile than he could admit.

President Roosevelt's administrative style, his
informality, has also been targeted by his critics.
They charge that his notoriously sloppy administrative procedures
and his dislike of formal lines of command led to a lack
of coordination between policy and strategy. That
"failure" is usually identified as the failure to devise
a strategy which would frustrate Russian designs on
Eastern and Central Europe. Except for the closing
months of the war, when the State-War-Navy Coordinating
Committee (SWNCC) was established, there was no agency
empowered to harmonize diplomacy and war. The unproven
assumption behind this criticism is that the creation
of an agency like the National Security Council would
in itself have led to a different management of the
European War. Given President Roosevelt's administrative
style and the degree to which his aims and his vision of
the post-war world were shared by his chief advisors,
it is doubtful that such an administrative mechanism
would have made much difference in the definition of
policy or the direction of strategy.

In a post-war world, overshadowed by the threat of
nuclear war, a tighter system of coordination and control
was necessary. The National Security Council, created by
the National Security Act of 1947, was designed to advise

the President on all security issues, acting as a forum
for political, diplomatic and military viewpoints.
Although not designed as a decision-making body, it would
presumably provide a means for the coordination of policy
and strategy.

Moreover, presidential control over military operations
in Korea and Vietnam strikes a dramatic contrast to
F.D.R.'s relaxed hold in the concluding years of World
War II. President Truman specifically limited General
MacArthur's operations against the Chinese Communists.
At least at the beginning of Operation ROLLING THUNDER,
a graduated bombing capaign, President Johnson kept a tight
hand over bombing operations against North Vietnam.
Even President Nixon's more permissive bombing and
mining campaign against the Hanoi-Haiphong area and
other targets (Operation LINEBACKER) was hedged with
precautions to prevent the destruction of Soviet shipping.
Such direct management of military operations stands
opposite to the loose Rooseveltian control.

In the post-war period, the compartmentalization of
policy and strategy has vanished. The mutually accepted
frontier between the realm of the statesman and the
soldier has disappeared. Now policy and strategy
penetrate and interpenetrate one another more closely
than ever before. We could easily come to the conclusion,
therefore, that the United States has now achieved the
coordination between policy and strategy that it failed
to achieve in World War II. Such a conclusion, however,

is too stark. It ignores the fundamental transformation in
the relation between United States policy and strategy
since the invention of nuclear weapons. It ignores the
revolution in American foreign and domestic policy, a
revolution which occurred in the five years following
the end of World War II. That revolution has brought
an indefinite American commitment to the defense of
Western Europe and other vital sections of the world
which could not be foreseen in early 1945. Instead of
being neglected in peacetime, the American military,
for the first time in United States history, were
encouraged to develop and maintain forces in being
even in the absence of hostilities.

The older, more permissive system was ideally suited
to an America disarmed in peacetime, a relatively isolated
America which could rely upon the mobilization of its
considerable manpower and its unparalleled industrial
resources when confronted by a serious threat, an America
whose military tasks were limited in time and foreclosed
by victory. In a world armed with nuclear weapons, where
the boundaries between peace and war are no longer distinct,
where the conduct of local military operations could
escalate into a confrontation which could unlock an
annihilating war, the older approach, suited to a safer
time, would be fatally dangerous. So we have a world in
which weapons are widely deployed while their possible
use is tightly controlled from the top. Such a system
has apparently functioned well in maintaining deterrence

and preventing the outbreak of World War III. It is
questionable, however, how it would function in the
direction of actual operations even in a non-nuclear war.
Given the imprecision of air bombardment, totally controlled
and surgical operations against North Vietnamese targets
were operationally impossible until the closing phase
of the bombing war. Lyndon Johnson was haunted by the
nightmare of an air strike igniting a confrontation with
the Chinese or the Russians. Will "smart bombs" and
electronic warfare make the difference? The 1986
air strike against Libya gives pause.

It is certainly doubtful that control would function
efficiently in the conduct of a full-scale nuclear war
between the United States and the Soviet Union. As
communications were disrupted, operations would command
policy and strategy. War would become truly autonomous.

The Righteous War:

When I wrote Confines of Concept, I started from the
conviction that World War II, unlike most conflicts, was
a righteous war, that the Western Allies fought against a
monstrously evil system in Europe and against a cruel
militaristic empire in the Pacific. Having grown up
in Europe and the United States during the Second World
War, I still hold firmly to that belief. However, the
American conduct of the "good war", raises many questions
which cannot be answered by the simple antithesis of
good vs. evil. War is above all, especially as reflected
in propaganda, the great simplifier. But there are

shades and complexities, undertones and currents, which
are also part of the truth.

The Nazi enemy was as evil a foe as any propagandist
could wish for. And the Japanese, who attacked the
United States without a declaration of war, who mistreated
and killed their prisoners and who savagely ravaged
China, were cruel and barbarous in their conduct of war.
But these images of the enemy were expanded to encompass
all. American propaganda came perilously close to
identifying every German and Japanese with the image of
the fiendish enemy. This process of dehumanization was
part of pyschological mobilization for war. The enemy
had to be turned into an alien, uniform in trait and
character. Individuality was obliterated as he became
merely the Other. The process was a necessary preliminary
to killing.

Western leaders saw the Nazis as master conspirators
bent upon world conquest and the Japanese, and to a
lesser extent, the Italians as their partners in crime.
The degree to which the individual Axis nations fought
separate and uncoordinated wars, the degree to which
their ambitions and their plans conflicted and crossed
one another was not recognized. The conspiracy theory
cast the course of aggression as a plot which began at
a distinct point in time and then proceeded step by step
towards world conquest. In Asia, the first move was
the annexation of Manchuria; in Europe, the reoccupation
of the Rhineland and the re-armament of Germany. The

long term historical context was often ignored: the impact
of Western imperialism in East Asia, especially on Japan;
the impact of the Versailles Treaty and the post-war
inflation on Germany. If propagandists touched on the
further recesses of the past, they simply sought antecedents
and analogues for the present: German and Japanese authori-
tarianism and militarism. The complexities of the enemy's
history, culture and traditions were ignored or denigrated.

The plot, in the sense of a conspiracy and in
the sense of the action of a story, unfolded move by
move. The enemy's evil intent was finally proven by
the ultimate act of aggression: the firing of the
first shot. Once that ritualistic act had been enacted,
once the United States was attacked at Pearl Harbor,
the war became a crusade whose only fit denouement was
the destruction of the evil foe. History became
melodrama.

The destruction of the evil foe justified measures
which are normally regarded as abhorrent and uncivilized.
Again, war acts as the great simplifier, nationalizing
ethics while casting values into universal terms.
Although the United States and its Western Allies
observed certain codes and restraints during World
War II (regarding the use of poison gas) and honored
certain conventions (regarding the treatment of prisoners
and helpless civilians once the battle was ended), it
waged war with ruthlessness against Germany and Japan.
As long as they could be justified, as long as they

were seen as accelerating the defeat of the enemy, weapons
and tactics were used without remorse. Enemy cities
were blasted and incinerated causing thousands of civilian
casualties; unrestricted submarine warfare was waged
against Japanese shipping in the Pacific; Japanese soldiers
in their cave defenses were exterminated by flame throwers
and grenades as thoroughly as rat warrens are fumigated.
The decision to use the atomic bomb, often denounced as
a special horror, has to be viewed within the context
of a war waged with almost every available weapon. To
fight a ruthless foe, Americans hardened themselves
with the zeal of crusaders. The cause justified the
means.

Crusaders are blind to irony, the enemy of the
rhetoric of justification. Today, we can see numerous
ironies in the justifications used by the Allies in World
War II. First, the war was fought against the vicious
racism of the Hitler regime. Yet the United States
government, responding easily to the West Coast hysteria
that followed Pearl Harbor, victimized its loyal Japanese-
American citizens, uprooting them from their jobs and
homes and relocating them in concentration camps. Racism
inflamed American propaganda on the Pacific War and
helped to intensify the tactical ferocity with which
that conflict was conducted. As John W. Dower summarizes:
"War without mercy." It did not, however, determine
the major strategic decisions of that conflict which
were made on professional military grounds.

Moreover, despite its denunciations of Nazi pogroms against the Jews, the United States did little to offer sanctuary to the victims of Hitler's anti-Semitism or to impede the ghastly extermination programs at Auschwitz and the other death camps once it became obvious that Hitler was systematically attempting to destroy an entire race.

To American blacks, especially to those serving in the segregated armed forces of the United States, the anti-racist rhetoric of war must have seemed bitterly ironic. Did the image of the enemy reflect the shadow of a subterranean self?

In the American and British view, the Second World War was also waged for the preservation and the extension of human freedom to all peoples. That claim, although compelling to the captive populations of occupied Europe, must have seemed hypocritical to the natives of the European colonial empires, especially to their future national leaders.

These ironies were obvious to perceptive contemporaries, even to some who supported the Allied cause. Other ironies arise out of the aftermath of the war. Although the United States tried to maintain its anti-colonial stance throughout the war, its chief ally Great Britain, especially its leader Winston Churchill, was determined to maintain the empire. Great Britain fought for the imperial status quo which the war destroyed.

The instrument of that destruction was another

imperial power: Japan whose main achievement was to
discredit the western powers by ignominiously defeating
them at Singapore, Hong Kong, the Netherlands East Indies
and throughout the Western Pacific. Japan claimed that
it was waging war to free Asia for the Asians. Although
that claim encouraged some nationalistic leaders, like
Subhas Chandra Bose of India, and although it led to the
creation of the Indian National Army and the Burma
Independence Army, the ruthlessness of Japanese rule
ignited a nationalism which they could not control and
which triumphed only after their defeat.

There are two deeper ironies. The Allied crusade
also accelerated the process which challenged the pre-war
status quo. For the Allied war aims, as defined in
the Atlantic Charter and in the United Nations Charter,
had a dynamism that escaped any control their authors
sought to place upon them. The ideology for which the
Allies fought had a revolutionary impact beyond prediction.
It awakened more than its evokers sought to awaken.

The ultimate irony, however, is that a war fought
to establish an enduring peace ended in the use of
weapons of mass destruction, weapons which heralded
an age of continuing insecurity overcast by the threat
of annihilation. The bombs dropped to end the war were
the progenitors of the nuclear arsenals in whose shadow
we live.

Power undercuts while it uses ideology.

The American image of the enemy in the Cold War was

a direct inheritance from World War II. Nazi dictatorship was replaced by the Soviet totalitarian state. Each was characterized as a conspiratorial aggressor who sought world domination. The transfer of the image of the enemy from Nazi Germany to Soviet Russia was natural given the ruthless nature of Stalin's dictatorship, the establishment of oppressive Communist regimes under Soviet bayonets in "liberated" Eastern Europe, the Russian pressure in the eastern Mediterranean, the coup in Czechoslovakia (1948), the Berlin Blockade of 1948-1949, the fall of China to the Communists in 1949 and the outbreak of the Korean War in 1950. Once more, the pattern seemed clear: a repetition of the road to disaster from Manchuria and the Rhineland to the invasion of Poland and the attack on Pearl Harbor. Moreover, the enemy was again seen as monolithic: a single power operating from one ideological command post: Moscow. Against this single minded foe, the entire free world must unite while time remained.

The perception of the enemy, however, depends upon the reading of invisible intentions. As the Cold War continued into the 1960s and 1970s, the rigid Manichaean concept of the two blocks fragmented. The breakup of the colonial empires which created a multitude of nations where single powers had once dominated ended the bilateral world that had emerged briefly in the Second World War and that had persisted in its immediate aftermath. The United States could no longer credibly maintain that

those who were not for us were against us or that neutralism
was immoral.

Moreover, the image of a monolithic Communist empire
also fragmented. Despite the spread of Communist regimes
to the Caribbean and to the African continent, Moscow has
been unable to keep firm control over its ideological
confederates. Its clients have often turned the game
against the U.S.S.R., servants becoming masters in the
bargaining for aid and arms. Beginning with the defection
of Yugoslavia in 1948 and climaxing with the estrangement
of Russia and China in the early 1960s, the monolithic
image shattered. Even in the Warsaw Pact, Russia, which
asserted its primacy by military intervention in the
1950s and 1960s, now moves more cautiously.

Finally, the image of the U.S.S.R. has split. The
older Cold War image, which persists in conservative
circles, projects an adventuristic and expansionist
power. The newer image, reflecting nuclear stalemate,
the hopes of detente and the need of the super powers
to accomodate to one another, sees Soviet policy as
cautious and conservative. In the latter view, national
self-interest is more important than ideological fervor.

The Manichaean view, which envisions the Cold War
as a conflict between a conspiratorial "evil empire" and
the freedom fighters of the world, is increasingly
unconvincing given four decades of peace, despite a
number of close confrontations, between the super
powers. A Manichaean view of a world conflict can be

more easily maintained in the short run and in a world at war than in an indefinite period of uneasy peace. Belief in a plot cannot be maintained firmly if the story runs on without a foreseeable future.

Moreover, understanding of conditions in countries plagued by Communist insurgency strongly suggests that leftist revolutions are ignited largely by local poverty and instability rather than by the outside conspiratorial agitators who seek to encourage them. This more complex perception of revolution in the post-war world militates against the view that turmoil is directed from a remote center. At the least, instead of a single-minded plotter, we have inherited a multitude of conspirators.

The pattern of the plot has been complicated by the invention of nuclear weapons. In the pre-Hiroshima age, the conclusive evidence of the evil conspirator's intent was that he fired the "first shot." In planning for World War III, the United States has axiomatically assumed that its natural antagonist, the U.S.S.R., will fire the "first shot", thereby confirming its aggressive intentions.

Moreover, having rejected the option of preventive war in the 1950s, the United States would not fire until fired upon. Since in nuclear war, the first strike may be decisive, only a secure retaliatory force, a second strike force, insures that the United States can honor the tradition of the first shot without being mortally wounded.

But, in the nuclear age, what does the "first shot" mean? A nuclear Pearl Harbor against the United States? A conventional attack against Europe? A Soviet invasion of the Persian Gulf? A Soviet backed Arab jihiad against Israel? The scenario possibilities are endless.

And how do you react to it? The United States has foregone the option of preventive war. It has not, however, foregone the option of first use: especially, the use of tactical nuclear weapons to halt a Soviet conventional attack in Central Europe or in other vital security regions to whose defense it is committed.

Moreover, although launch under attack safeguards the traditional ritual in its purest form, launch on warning (pre-emptive war) is a compelling option which no American president can foreclose. It is, however, problematic. What does warning mean: the evacuation of the enemy cities, the mobilization of his forces or the jamming of United States intelligence gathering devices? Although urban evacuation or mobilization would signal rising tensions between the super powers, would they automatically herald a Soviet attack? Remembering 1914, would the leaders of the major powers hesitate to interpret mobilization as a certain signal of impending general war? If the Soviets released their strategic nuclear strike, would the United States know in time to launch on warning? Or would it await certain confirmation, deterred by incredulity, even after its satellites and radars were jammed, that the Soviets had actually launched their missiles?

Although there are many scenarios for the conduct of
conventional warfare between the super powers and although
there are some scenarios (like that of General Hackett in
The Third World War) for limited nuclear exchanges,
scenarios for full-scale nuclear war become fuzzier
after the first act. Since it is hard to perceive what
would happen after a Soviet-United States nuclear exchange,
since the weapons of a future war are largely unproven
by battle, it is difficult to envision a protracted
nuclear war. The traditional course of a total conflict
for the Allied powers in World War I and World War II,
from defeat to triumph, from unpreparedness to full
mobilization, seems inapplicable and irrelevant.

Essentially, how would the United States conduct a
nuclear war? Its military tradition since the Civil War
has favored a concentration upon the destruction of the
enemy's power and has emphasized the need for total
victory. Nuclear war is the culmination of the Napoleonic
battle of annhilation. Moreover, American military policy
has generally regarded weapons as morally neutral. Almost
any weapon is justifiable if its use furthers military
operations. If war is evil, all the better reason for
bringing it to an expeditious end by the use of all
means at hand.

But, in total war, what are the sources of the enemy's
power: his military forces, his leadership structure,
his economy or his population? In the first Single

Integrated Operational Plan (SIOP) drawn up in 1960 by
the Eisenhower administration, there was no question.
Everything was cast in a single annihilative blow against
the enemy's heartland. Any distinction between counterforce
and countervalue targets would become academic. It
was Bomber Harris' area bombing carried into the nuclear
age.

However, the American attitude towards city busting
has always been ambiguous. On the one hand, democratic
nations are more likely than totalitarian nations, who
still emphasize the destruction of the enemy's military
forces, to believe in the efficacy of morale bombing.
The national will is identified as the ultimate source
of power. Destroy it and the war will end. On the other
hand, American leaders and planners have felt uncomfortable
about targeting civilian populations. Some of the newer
SIOP targeting plans which concentrate on military,
economic or leadership targets harken back to the
American belief that war should not be waged directly
against innocent civilians. They are an attempt to restore
the primacy of innocent intent.

These attempts to use weapons of mass destruction
in a more surgical fashion are not convincing. The
process of traditional justification broke down after
World War II because future wars could no longer by
judged by the criteria of the past. (Indeed, it can
be argued that it began to break down during World War II.)
Innocent intent cannot win suit against the effects of

the massive destruction involved in nuclear war. As
George Kennan summarizes so eloquently in The Nuclear
Delusion: "...there is no issue at stake in our political
relations with the Soviet Union - no hope, no fear, nothing
to which we aspire, nothing we would like to avoid - which
could conceivably be worth a nuclear war."

No nuclear war can be blessed into righteousness.

The Temporal Imperative:

In the total wars of the twentieth century, the
temporal imperative was geared to the military, industrial
and psychological mobilization of the nations at war.
For the United States in World War II, its rhythm moved
from general unpreparedness and defeat to deployment
for victory. As long as the war lasted long enough,
the United States and its allies would succeed in
mustering their great potential strength to overwhelm
their enemies. As long as the war did not last too
long, the American leadership would succeed in maintaining a high level of public commitment in waging the war
to total victory. As this study shows, the pressure
for the achievement of a rapid victory assumed in
World War II a force that transcended military logic.

In the nuclear age, the temporal imperative underwent
significant modification. Earlier strategic plans,
devised before the attainment of nuclear parity between
the U.S. and the U.S.S.R. and before the integration
of tactical nuclear weapons into the armed forces,

foresaw a war evolving along the familiar temporal pattern.
A Soviet sweep over Western Europe would be followed by a
buildup for counter attack: the United States and its allies
would fight for time until their resources were fully
mobilized for a victorious offensive against the U.S.S.R.

Even after the American loss of atomic supremacy,
the temporal imperative could operate in the traditional
manner if the war remained conventional. Then mobilization
could play its role and could bring victory to a nation
temporarily weaker but potentially stronger than its
foe. Possibly, this logic could also operate in a
slowly unwinding, protracted, nuclear conflict if such
a war could be fought.

But the limits of psychological mobilization cannot
be forgotten even for an immensely powerful nation.
In the Vietnam War, policy leaders forgot General
Marshall's injunction that "a democracy cannot fight a
Seven Years War." Its apparent endlessness, an impression
emphasized by the lack of definable battle lines which
could be identified with the successful forward movement
of the war, made it an open ended conflict without apparent
progress. Ultimately, the collapse of public support
doomed the American effort despite the mobilization of
infinitely superior resources,   despite the defeat of
the 1968 Tet offensive and despite the virtual destruction
of the Vietcong in the intensive fighting that accompanied
Tet.

Full-scale nuclear warfare has a different logic.

Since the development of parity between the United States
and the U.S.S.R., it could be fought only with forces in
being. In a massive apocalyptic stroke, executed in a
limited period of time, the temporal imperative would
cease to function. In the full SIOP option for all out
war, the dial of time now lies upon the face of terror.
Twenty minutes, thirty minutes, twenty days, thirty
days? How long could any democratic government continue
to count on the support of its public as annihilation
rained down upon America? Spasm war would obliterate
the significance of time in the management of operations,
the production and deployment of resources, and the
maintenance of public support.

Reflections on a future nuclear war bring us back
inevitably to the dawn of the atomic age and the decision
to drop the bomb on Hiroshima and Nagasaki, a decision
powerfully spurred by the pressures of the temporal
imperative: the need to bring the war to as rapid an
end as possible. As citizens of the one nation so far
to use atomic weapons, Americans remain profoundly
uneasy over the ultimate decision of World War II.
Was it necessary? Would more skillful diplomacy have
avoided this terrible choice? No matter what explanations
and justifications are given, the feeling of guilt
remains.

Those who justify it easily as a necessary measure
of war and those who disassociate themselves by denouncing
it as the needlessly barbaric slaughter of the innocent

citizens of an already defeated nation can perhaps
escape moral discomfort within themselves. Others,
however, who understand how the pressures of time in
war mold decisions and foreclose options can never find
an easy escape. Since there are no certain answers to
the questions raised by this momentous decision, it
can never be accepted easily or totally.

Revisionist historians place their case upon the
indisputable fact that Japan was defeated by the summer
of 1945 and that Japanese officials were frantically
seeking a way out of the war. They ignore the distinction
between defeat and the admission of defeat. Although
certain officials were seeking an end to the conflict
through diplomacy, the formidable Japanese Army Command,
which had an influence over policy unmatched in any
Western nation, was still adamantly opposed to the
acceptance of unconditional surrender. It was still
confident that its Army would inflict devastating
casualties on the American invaders in the battles for
the sacred homeland, casualties which would force the
Allies towards a compromise peace. Spirit would overcome
steel. In July 1945, there was no guarantee that the
peace faction within the government could overcome
the hardliners. Revisionist historians fail to consider
carefully the Japanese role in the American decision
to drop the bomb.

Another revisionist criticism, far sounder in my
opinion, is that the United States was too rigid in its

continued insistence on unconditional surrender. After
all, it accepted the terms of a conditional surrender
after the dropping of the bomb. These terms, which
gave explicit assurances about the retention of the
Emperor, were advocated by Secretary of War Henry L.
Stimson and Undersecretary of State Joseph Grew. They
were rejected by Secretary of State James F. Byrnes,
largely on the advice of one of his predecessors,
Cordell Hull. Because of fears that an explicit assurance
would be branded as appeasement, the authors of the
Potsdam Declaration confined themselves to general
assurances to the Japanese people concerning their
future right to self-determination. After the bomb
was dropped, the assurances regarding the Emperor's
status requested by the Japanese government were granted
by the Allies. Naturally, it was easier to accept
conditional surrender terms offered by an enemy than
to propose the same terms oneself. The chance that the
United States was unwilling to take foreclosed a more
flexible diplomacy that might have ended the war without
the use of nuclear weapons.

Might have. Diplomacy was not tried because there
was little hope that it would work speedily enough.
If it had been tried, if assurances had been given
regarding the post-war status of the Emperor, would
the Japanese have yielded immediately. Or, like
traditional bargainers, would they have raised the
ante by demanding that the Allies abandon their occupation

and war trials plans? Moreover, shocking as it now
seems, the atomic bomb was regarded as a weapon of hope,
a weapon that could end the war by administering a
frightful shock to the Japanese government forcing it
into unconditional surrender. Despite revisionist
carping at the exaggerated and popularly accepted estimate
that the invasion of Japan would cost more than half a
million casualties, there is no question that the execution
of Operation OLYMPIC-CORONET would have been immensely
costly. Some American officials, still shocked by the
heavy casualties on Iwo Jima and Okinawa, were not certain
that invasion casualties would be tolerable to the
American public. Moreover, American planning papers
show that U.S. strategists were not sure that the Pacific
War would end with the conquest of Japan. Recently
declassified documents conjure the image of an endless
war stretching across the still unconquered reaches
of the Japanese Empire. Even the use of atomic weapons
represented only a qualified hope. The shock might not
be sufficient to force the Japanese into unconditional
surrender. Many of the revisionist historians conveniently
ignore the impact of the cost in American lives in the
Pacific campaigns. The sounds of battle are muted in
the works of Arperowitz and Sherwin.

The American way of war, to use Russell Weigley's
apt phrase, stresses firepower over manpower. To cut
down on the casualties inflicted by the tenacious
Japanese soldiers, holed up in formidable bunkers and

caves throughout a multitude of Pacific islands, American
soldiers and marines maximized the tactical use of firepower:
heavy naval and air bombardment preliminary to landing,
the use of flamethrowers and grenades to reduce Japanese
strongholds. In the strategic air offensive against Japan,
incendiary urban attacks were used to reduce Japan's will
and her industrial capacity to wage war. Few of the leaders
who knew about the MANHATTAN project suspected at the
time that the atomic bomb was anything except superior
firepower. As commander-in-chief, responsible for the
lives of those who served under him, Truman could not
forego using a weapon which, in his opinion, would
prevent needless American and Allied casualties.
Moreover, he would have had considerable difficulty
in explaining such a self-denying decision to the American
public and the United States Congress.

Of course, the atomic bomb was not merely another
form of firepower. Its radiational effects, imperfectly
recognized at the time, brought a new dimension to
warfare. Use of nuclear weapons, therefore, preceded
any clear realization that a new age was dawning which
would call for constraint, rather than for exploitation
of force.

What gave this weapon its special horror (and this
effect should have been foreseen) was its concentrated
force. It epitomized the horrors of war by annihilating
the barriers of time and space. A single bomb bore
within itself the image of Absolute War. Assuming

xliv.

theological dimensions, it has become the Bomb.

A tragic, perhaps inevitable, decision. As Secretary
of War Stimson summarized so graphically: "The face of
war is the face of death; death is an inevitable part
of every order that a wartime leader gives." But, if
the choice was inescapable, the doubts will always
remain, the regrets will never be stilled.

Deterrence, Limited War, Total War, Absolute War:

In 1945, in the wake of the bombing of Hiroshima
and Nagasaki, Bernard Brodie defined the revolutionary
impact of nuclear weapons upon the concept of security:
"Thus far the chief purpose of our military establishment
has been to win wars. From now on its chief purpose
must be to avert them. It can have almost no other
useful purpose." In the new world of nuclear weapons,
security could no longer be assured through the single
efforts of a nation. International security replaced
national security.

Brodie's prophetic statement, later incorporated
in a book with the significant title The Absolute Weapon,
prefigured the doctrine of nuclear deterrence which
gradually emerged in the post-war world after the United
States monopoly on atomic weapons was broken. The goal
of deterrence flatly contradicts the traditional goal
of military planning. Instead of victory, the objective
is stability. Instead of seeking to get the jump on
the other fellow, the objective is to prevent either

side from securing a decisive advantage over the other.
Instead of seeking to knock out the enemy's command and
control system, thereby crippling his operations, an
opponent must now seek to insure that the hold of the
antagonist's national command over the operations of
his forces is not ruptured, thereby unleashing a spasm
nuclear attack. The traditional military approach,
successful war-waging, must be discarded since it
automatically destabilizes the balance of terror.
Paradoxically, therefore, as Schelling pointed out
in The Strategy of Conflict, weapons aimed at counter-value
objectives (cities) are more stabilizing than weapons
directed against counter-force objectives (the enemy's
military strength).

To talk, however, of maintaining stability by confining
oneself to counter-value objectives is to ignore credibility.
The strength of deterrence after all lies on a hazardous
premise: the ability and the resolution to do what
one doesn't want to do in order not to have to do it.
Counter-value strategy also ignores the Soviet emphasis
upon war-fighting. Inevitably, concern with maintaining
the stability of deterrence led away from Brodie's
warning. It was now claimed that deterrence could be
maintained only by developing the capacity to wage a
protracted nuclear war. In the words of Colin Gray:
"...the best way to prevent war is to be able to fight
it effectively." Unfortunately, this logic could lead
to an instability implicit in the dilemma of nuclear

strategic war planning. Inevitably, scenarios for
protracted nuclear war, the more recent SIOP plans
with their sophisticated divisions into target systems
and attack options, seek to make rational what is
essentially irrational. As Robert Jervis cautions:
"A rational strategy for the employment of nuclear
weapons is a contradiction in terms." The danger
is that such planning will mask this irrationality
or be seen by an opponent as a threatening attempt
to secure first strike capability. Thus the logic
of deterrence, which seeks to preserve stability, can
come full circle. War-fighting represents a rebirth
of traditional military concepts within an alien host.

If nuclear deterrence has succeeded in averting
armed conflict between the super powers, if extended
deterrence has provided stability on the NATO front,
neither has brought peace to the world. Without difficulty,
the historian can count at least seventy colonial,
interstate and civil wars between 1945 and 1985. Some
of these conflicts involve over a million casualties:
the Chinese Civil War (1945-1949), the Korean War
(1950-1954), the two Indo-Chinese Wars (1946-1954,
1959-1975), the Nigerian-Biafran War (1967-1969).
And who knows what the final casualties of the Gulf
War between Iran and Iraq (1980-   ) will amount to.
Only some of the post-1945 conflicts can be classified
as limited in time, space and scale of violence: the
earlier Arab-Israeli Wars (1948-1949, 1956, 1973),

the Falklands Islands War (1982). Other conflicts,
especially the open-ended wars in southeast Asia, Africa
and Latin America and the border clashes between China
and India, Russia and China fall into an intermediate
category.

The more extensive conflicts with their casualties
running above one million can more accurately be described
as local total wars than as limited wars. The two American
wars, Korea and Vietnam, were kept localized largely by
the mutual fear of escalation. Deterrence worked in
preventing a wider conflict. It did not work in controlling
the level of violence used within the defined theater
of operations. The Korean War in which the Chinese
hurled their soldiers in waves against the firepower
of the American line recalled the World War I attritional
battles along the Western Front. In Vietnam, as operations
mounted, restraints were progressively abandoned. As
Russell Weigely notes in The American Way of War,
General Westmoreland soon abandoned the concept of a
counter-insurgency conflict and shifted to a re-enactment
of World War II offensive strategy. Precision bombardment
and area bombardment were adapted to a rural rather
than an urban enemy. The use of herbicides in Operation
RANCH HAND and the anti-crop program represented a new
form of area devastation whose origins, however, lay in
strategies proposed towards the close of World War II
in the Pacific. In ground-air operations, the creation
of "free fire zones" and the emphasis on body count as

a criterion of success turned vast sections of South Vietnam into indiscriminate killing fields. Towards the close of the American involvement in the war, the United States mining operations closed off North Vietnam's coast to foreign shipping, thereby re-enacting the blockades of the two world wars. But the conditions for a successful application of World War II offensive strategy, defined lines separating friend and foe, visible operational progress within an acceptable period of time, were totally lacking. In Vietnam, strategy turned upon itself.

Korea and Vietnam are cautions against a loose use of the term "limited war."

There are also hypothetical models of future conflicts which point in the same direction, revealing that the customary distinction between total and limited war is hardly absolute. It is inconceivable, for example, that a European war waged with tactical nuclear weapons could be classified as limited. Even a conventional European war, if protracted, would utilize such tremendous firepower that it could not be classified as "limited." For modern conventional weapons are approaching a level of potential devastation that, except for radioactive effects, approximate tactical nuclear weapons.

In considering nuclear war, one moves from experience to abstraction, from the concrete to a world of assumptions and convictions. Not surprisingly, therefore, the images of World War III vary from models of partial and controlled action, especially operations waged with precision guided

munitions and in the future third generation nuclear
bombs, to the model of an apocalyptic spasm war graphically
depicted in Jonathan Schell's The Fate of the Earth and
popularized by doomsday pictures such as Dr. Strangelove.
Over all these scenarios hovers the factor of uncertainty.
The partial models of nuclear war are challenged by
the critics who remind us of the invisibility of intentions
and the conflict of perceptions. For example, how
could either the Soviet Union or the United States be
certain that a limited counter-force attack was that
and nothing else? The effects of the attacks which
might involve considerable civilian casualties ("collateral
damage") could be more persuasive in shaping a response
than the intentions of the attacker. In the midst of
unprecedented pressures, could anyone recognize proportionality?
Or, after a certain level of destruction and pain, would
anyone want to recognize it? Moreover, one of the
SIOP options calls for targeting the leadership, the
command and control centers of the enemy. If such a
strike were successful, the chances of accidental spasm war
would be automatically magnified. The indiscriminate
nature of nuclear operations would overthrow the discrete
intentions of man. Each partial model, therefore, prefigures
the absolute model. The spector of spasm war hovers
over each rung of the escalation ladder.

Finally, the apocalyptic image of nuclear war is
easy to envision. In a world dominated by uncertainties,
that image remains more persuasive than the sophisticated

models advanced by strategic planners and thinkers.
The apocalypse is an image of nuclear war that we can
see vividly in our imaginations. The other scenarios
lack this compelling power. Perhaps this conviction
that any nuclear war between the United States and the
U.S.S.R. would be total is reinforced by the desire
to believe that it will be total. Paradoxically,
therefore, it becomes unacceptable and unthinkable.

And so we come to Absolute War, the war that has
never been. For total nuclear war would be the closest
approximation yet seen to Absolute War. In Clausewitz's
terms, it could turn into "an act of force" to which
there would be "no logical limit." Due to the reciprocal
act of the enemy, it would end in mutual devastation.
During the Civil War, Henry Adams predicted such an
outcome to Charles Francis Adams: "I firmly believe
that before many centuries more, science will be the
master of man. The engines he will have invented will
be beyond his strength to control. Some day science
shall have the existence of mankind in its power, and
the human race commit suicide by blowing up the world."

Absolute War would be the perfection of the battle
of annhilation fought by a direct strike at the heartland
of the enemy. If the United States struck after being
struck, it would comply with the traditional ritual
of the "first shot" although the extreme violence of
retaliation would render justification meaningless.
The American emphasis upon the expenditure of firepower

over manpower would be turned into self-inflicted mockery.
And political purpose would die in the holocaust.

In Absolute War, the offensive would overwhelm the
friction that Clausewitz saw as turning the theoretically
simple into the practically complex. Primary friction
comes from the opposition of the enemy. If "war is...<u>an
act to compel our enemy to do our will</u>," it is an act in
which he simultaneously seeks to overcome us. It leads
to extremes as Clausewitz noted. In Absolute War, the
offensive power of the weapons would overwhelm the
mutual resistance generated by the collision of two
forces.

It would overcome other frictions, the frictions of
space and time which have limited the destructive impact
of weapons. Arriving almost instantaneously, nuclear
missiles would carry war to the far regions of the globe.
Even if the theories of the nuclear winter are exaggerated,
the ecological consequences of such an exchange would be
catastrophic.

It would overcome the controls imposed by policy: a
friction which limits the use of force to prevent its
escape from political purpose. It would obviously escape
the limits of morality, an escape made easier, in the
missile age, by the vast distances between the order to
kill and the act of killing, between those who kill and
those who are killed. That escape is prefigured in the
glacially conceptual language which veils nuclear war
planning and in the reduction of human lives to acceptable

and non-acceptable casualty levels. In modern war planning, Manichaean imagery yields pride of place to Orwellian pseudo-scientific language and to statistics.

Strategy, as I stress in my work, is a form of compromise reflecting the balances between different personalities, organizations and concepts. It is molded by an accomodation of pressures. These delicate balances would be ruptured in the waging of Absolute War. All wars simplify because they destroy the normal procedure of accomodation which is the essence of diplomacy. In Absolute War, force would eliminate accomodation.

Absolute War would be the rebirth of the battle of annihilation freed from the bonds of deterrence set by policy. It is the ideal, the impossible, towards which the five strategic beliefs studied in this work strive: the release of maximum force within the shortest amount of time. Blinded by seeing from within, the warriors of direct offensive action born of defensive purpose would obliterate the world without. Absolute War, potentiality converted into instant actuality, would mean the death of policy within strategy.

If all wars simplify, Absolute War would simplify absolutely.

Hastings-on-Hudson, New York
Brookline, Massachusetts
1987

NOTE AND ACKNOWLEGEMENTS:

I have editorially revised the text of this work.
Part I was completely redone. Sections of Part II and
Part III were also revised and retyped. Minor errors
are listed in an appended list of errata (pp. 1121-1148).
Moreover, I have added a list of abbreviations and code
names at the end of the work to facilitate reference
(pp. 1149-1152).

All revisions are editorial. I have not changed
conclusions, added or deleted material or taken
advantage of newly released documents and newly
published books. However, I have taken the opportunity
to trim the extravagances of my earlier style.

My thanks to Professor Ernest May, Harvard University,
and to Professor Frank Freidel, University of Washington,
for selecting my thesis for publication. I have also
profited immensely throughout this revision from the
encouragement and advice of Professor May who read
the new introduction. I thank, once again, Palma A. Roberge
who typed the original manuscript of the thesis.
My special thanks to my wife, Joan Mary van Courtland Moon,
who read the manuscript and the new introduction and
helped me in the search for elusive errors. As an
Assistant Professor of Analysis and Communications,
University of Massachusetts/Boston and as a former
Assistant Professor of English at Boston State College,

she is exceptionally adept at this task. My thanks also
to Professor Ann Howe, English Department, Southeastern
Massachusetts University, who read the new introduction.
As always, I am indebted to her for her practiced ability
in the detection of errors. The author deserves exclusive
credit for the remaining undetected errors.

Finally, my thanks to Boston State College, discontinued
since 1982 by an act of the Massachusetts General Court.
Since I completed my dissertation while teaching at
Boston State, it is forever associated with this work.
It was an institution that did not deserve to die.

CONTENTS

Preface   lxxi.

Part I: Strategy, Concepts and Preconceptions

   Chapter I: Towards a Definition of Strategy   1.

     1. The Dialectical Nature of War   1.

     2. Causes of Escalation: Towards Total War   4.

       a. The Prolonged Conflict   4.

       b. The Ideological Conflict   5.

       c. The Struggle for Survival   7.

     3. Limited War   8.

     4. The Controlling Factor: Strategy   9.

       a. The Myth of the Master Strategist   11.

       b. The Myth of the Objective Approach   15.

         1) The "Eternal" Principles of War   15.

           a) The Principle of the Objective   17.

           b) The Principle of the Offensive   19.

         2) The Narrow Alternatives   21.

           a) Alternatives that Clash with
              Current Reality: The Impracticable   22.

           b) Alternatives that Clash with
              Preference: the Radical   24.

           c) Alternatives that Clash with Moral
              and Psychological Commitment:
              the Unthinkable   24.

     5. Conclusion: A Definition of Strategy   25.

Chapter II: Compromise and Decision: Broad Front
              versus Narrow Thrust   28.

Chapter III: Concepts and Preconceptions: The Defensive-
              Offensive Complex and the Direct Approach   41.

   1.   Strategic Beliefs: Concepts and Preconceptions   41.

   2.   The Defensive-Offensive Complex: Definition and
        Preliminary Exposition   42.

        a.   Ambiguity of Motive: The Russo-Finnish War   43.

        b.   Ambiguity of Means   44.

             1) A Defensive versus an Offensive Position   45.

             2) Defensive versus Offensive Weapons   46.

        c.   The Consistent Core   47.

   3.   The Direct versus the Indirect Approach   48.

        a.   The Battle of France: the Direct and the
             Indirect Approach to Land Warfare   50.

        b.   The Oil Offensive: the Assault against
             German Industry   52.

        c.   The Area Offensive: Assault against
             German Morale   54.

        d.   Victory through Air Power: Direct or
             Indirect Strategy   56.

Chapter IV: Concepts and Preconceptions:
             the Autonomy of War   59.

   1.   The Indictment and the Problem of American
        Military-Civil Relations   59.

   2.   Case Histories: the Pursuit of False Objectives   64.

3. The President as Commander-in-Chief:
   Franklin Delano Roosevelt   68.

Chapter V: Concepts and Preconceptions: the
            Righteous War   73.

1. The Indictment   73.

2. The Righteous War: Definition   74.

   a. Its Dual Nature   74.

   b. Its Dual Function: Instrument and Mirror   74.

3. Process of Justification: Totalitarian Nations   76.

   a. Nazi Germany: The Perverted Crusade   76.

   b. Soviet Russia: The Suppressed Crusade   81.

4. Process of Justification: Democratic Nations   87.

   a. Great Britain: the Churchillean Crusade   88.

   b. The United States: the Rooseveltian Crusade   93.

5. The Crusade: Phenomenon of Total War   101.

6. Summation   102.

Chapter VI: The Temporal Imperative   103.

1. The Temporal Imperative: Definition and
   Exposition   103.

2. Germany: the Dangers of a Long War   106.

   a. The Wehrmacht: Flawed Sword   108.

   b. The German Economy: "Guns and Butter."   109.

   c. Germany's Psychological Mobilization:
      without Enthusiasm   110.

   d. The Strategy of the Swift War   110.

3. The Soviet Union: the Dangers of a Short War 111.

    a. The Soviet Army: Only in a Long War 112.

    b. The Soviet Economy: The Time Lag 113.

    c. Psychological Mobilization and the Need for

      a Long War 114.

4. The United Kingdom: A Matter of Time 116.

    a. British Military Mobilization: Present Weakness,

      Future Promise 118.

    b. British Economic Mobilization: Re-armament

      in Depth 121.

    c. British Psychological Mobilization: the

      Awakening 123.

    d. Play for Time: the Strategy of Attrition 124.

5. The United States: the Sluggish Giant 125.

    a. American Military Mobilization:

      a Lethargic Awakening 126.

    b. American Economic Mobilization:

      the Ultimate Solution 132.

    c. American Psychological Mobilization:

      from Apathy to Commitment 135.

6. Conclusion: Time is of the Essence 138.

Part II: Time of Uncertainty

Introduction 140.

Chapter VII: the Evolution of Global Defense 142.

    1. From Stonewall to Hemisphere Defense 142.

    2. The Nature of the Threat 147.

a. Indirect Aggression   147.

b. The Ultimate Threat   150.

3. The Path of the Enemy's Approach   154.

    a. Combined Attack: Pacific and Atlantic   154.

    b. The Threat from the Atlantic Approaches   155.

       1) The North Atlantic Highway   158.

       2) The South Atlantic Highway   161.

    c. The Threat from the Pacific   163.

4. The Problem of Defensive Priority   163.

    a. Geographical Priority: the Problem of

       Drawing a Defensive Line   164.

       1) The Extension of America's Defensive

         Line into the Central Atlantic   168.

       2) The Extension of America's Defensive

         Line into the Western Pacific   171.

    b. Political Priority: Rearmament

       versus Foreign Aid   177.

5. Conclusions   185.

    a. From Hemisphere Defense to Global Defense   185.

    b. The Consistent Core: The Interdependence

       of America and Defense with Global Security   185.

Chapter VIII: The Evolution of Strategic Priority   189.

1. Production versus Participation   189.

2. Avenues for the Strategic Offensive   199.

    a. The North Atlantic Approach   199.

    b. The South Atlantic Approach   200.

    c. Pacific Approaches   201.

3. "Germany First": the Evolution of the Direct
   Approach   201.

   a. ORANGE Strategy: Single War in a
      Single Theater   203.

   b. RED-ORANGE: Early Concept of a
      Two-Front War   208.

   c. RAINBOW 2 and 3: Reversed Priority   208.

   d. From Plan Dog to the Victory Program   210.

      1) Plan Dog   210.

      2) The ABC Agreement   212.

      3) RAINBOW 5   213.

      4) The Victory Program   214.

   e. Transition: Defense to Offense: the
      Foundations of the Direct Approach   214.

4. The Evolution of the Indirect Approach   215.

   a. The Impact of British Strategic Thinking   216.

   b. The Indirect Approach in American
      Strategic Thought   219.

      1) American Naval Strategy: ORANGE   219.

      2) American Air Strategy: AWPD/1   223.

5. A Core of Agreement Beneath Strategic Dissension   224.

6. Conclusion: The Indeterminate Condition of
   American Planning in the Prewar Period   226.

Chapter IX: From Isolationism to Interventionism:
            the Genesis of American National-Military
            Policy   230.

   1. Introduction   230.

2. Study in Incompatability: The Debate over the
   Philippines   230.

3. The Isolation of the Military Planners   234

4. The Consequences of Isolation   239.

   a. The Military's Opposition to any Final
      Definition of National Policy   239.

   b. National Policy: the Planners' Version   241.

   c. The Attempt to Balance Ends and Means   244.

5. Prewar Civil-Military Conflicts   244.

   a. Conflict over the Occupation of the
      Atlantic Islands   245.

   b. The Debate over Pacific Strategy   248.

      1) The Decision to Base the Fleet at Pearl
         Harbor   248.

      2) The Decision to Impose an Oil
         Embargo on Japan   249.

6. Panacea Solution versus Calculated Cost   254.

   a. The Cost of Full-Scale Involvement   254.

   b. Panacea Weapons versus Balanced Forces   255.

7. The Nexus of Civil-Military Relations   259.

8. Conclusion   263.

Chapter X: The Foundations of the Just War   266.

1. The Problem of Justification   266.

2. The Nexus of Justification   268.

3. The Battle over Conscription   268.

   a. The Debate over the Burke-Wadsworth Bill   269.

b. The Debate over the Extension of Selective
Service   275.

4. The Debate over Foreign Aid   279.

a. The Destroyer Deal   282.

b. Lend-Lease   292.

1) Significance   292.

2) The Churchill Messages   294.

3) The Obstacles to Justification   297.

4) The Process of Justification   300.

a) The British Case   300.

b) The President's Case   302.

c) The Administration's Case   307.

d) Congressional Debate   312.

5. The Implications of Lend-Lease   318.

Chapter XI: The Seeds of the Crusade   320.

1. The Automatic Transition   320.

a. The Genesis of Total Victory   320.

1) "You Can't Do Business with Hitler"   320.

a) The Fear of Another Munich   323.

b) The Welles Mission   324.

2) The Hopelessness of Hope   331.

b. Japan: the Uncertain Image   335.

1) The Total Solution: Conversion   336.

2) The Alternatives of the Alternative   338.

a) The Divided Foe   339.

b) The Timid Foe   339.

3) The Image Hardens: the Alternatives
Vanish, but the Need for Negotiations
Remains   340.

   a) The First Embargo Proposal   342.

   b) The Impact of the Tripartite Act:
National Association by Guilt   342.

4) Conclusion   345.

2. Attack against Civilian Targets: the Basis
for Democratic Rationalization   346.

  a. Original Vision: Justification of
Apocalyptic Strategy   347.

  b. From Morale Bombardment to Precision
Bombardment   352.

   1) The Gorrell Plan   353.

   2) Development of Doctrine at the Air
Corps Tactical School   354.

   3) The Impact of Combat   357.

3. "The First Shot"   359.

  a. The Undeclared War in the Atlantic   360.

   1) The "Attack" on the Niblack   361.

   2) The Sinking of the Robin Moor   362.

   3) The Attack on the U.S.S. Greer   363.

   4) The Torpedoing of the U.S.S. Kearney   366.

   5) Presidential Caution   368.

  b. The Pacific Dilemma   372.

4. Conclusion   374.

Chapter XII: A Time to Prepare for Time   375.

1. Crisis and the Limits of Time   377.

    a. From the Sudetan Crisis to the Beginning of the War   378.

       1) The Public: Apathy   378.

       2) The Administration: Alarm   379.

       3) The Military: Mounting Fears   381.

    b. At the Opening of the War   383.

       1) The Public: Sympathy and Complacency   383.

       2) The Administration: Doubts and Fears   384.

       3) The Military: Public Silence   385.

    c. The Phony War   385.

       1) The Public: Continued Lethargy   385.

       2) The Administration: Private Fears and Public Silence   386.

       3) The Military: the Slow Pace of Mobilization   388.

    d. The Impact of the May-June 1940 Crisis   390.

       1) The Public: the Disintegration of Complacency   390.

       2) The Administration: Initiative and Action   391.

       3) The Military: Single Solution   395.

    e. From the Battle of Britain to the Election of 1940   397.

       1) The Public: A Lapse into Lethargy   397.

       2) The Administration: Unceasing Urgency   398.

3) The Military: Optimism and

Continued Caution   401.

f. From Lend-Lease to the German Invasion

of the Soviet Union   405.

1) The Public: Comparative Enlightenment   405.

2) The Administration: the Uncertain

Pattern   406.

3) The Military: Continued Optimism,

Continued Apprehension   416.

2. To the Final Limit: From the Invasion of the

Soviet Union to the German Declaration of War   419.

a. The Public: the Ebb and Flow of Opinion   421.

b. The Administration: Increasing Commitment   425.

c. The Military: the Dangers of Time   432.

Chapter XIII: The Temporal Imperative: the Race

against Time in the Pacific   443.

1. The First Stage: Prelude   448.

a. Public Antipathy towards Japanese Aggression   448.

b. The Administration's Caution   452.

c. The Military: A Profound Sense of Urgency   456.

2. The Second Stage: Decision   456.

a. Public Pressure for the Imposition of

Economic Sanctions   457.

b. The Great Debate   464.

1) The Logic of the Hard Line   464.

2) The Logic of the Moderates   465.

3) The Evolution of Tactical Time   469.

4) The President's Muted Role   477.

   c. Military Caution   479.

3. The Third Stage: Confrontation   481.

   a. The Ambiguities of Public Opinion   482.

   b. The Administration: Perspective before

     Disaster   485.

   c. The Military's Continued Demand for Time   494.

Chapter XIV: The Temporal Imperative: the Ultimate Threat 502.

1. The First Impulse: the Vision of the

   Exiled Scientists   503.

2. The Second Impulse: the Vision of Vannevar Bush   509.

3. Commitment   515.

4. Conclusion   521.

Part II: Conclusion: Time of Uncertainty   524.

Defensive-Offensive Complex   524.

The Direct Approach   525.

The Autonomous War   526.

The Righteous War   527.

The Temporal Imperative   527.

Part III: Culmination and Conclusion

Introduction   528.

   The Defensive-Offensive Complex   528.

   The Direct Approach   529.

   The Autonomous War   529.

   The Righteous War   530.

   The Temporal Imperative   530.

Chapter XV: Aftermath — 532.

1. Prelude: the Impact of the Pearl Harbor Attack — 532.

2. The Defensive-Offensive Complex: from Global
   Defense to Global Offense — 532.

   a. The Multiplying Menaces of Global War — 533.

   b. Allied Siege Strategy — 535.

   c. Conversion to Global Offense — 539.

   d. Recorso — 545.

3. The Direct Approach: the Problem of Strategic
   Priority and Choice in Global War — 558.

   a. Solutions to the Problem of Global Dispersion — 560.

   b. Pacific Alternative — 562.

   c. OVERLORD versus the Mediterranean — 566.

   d. The Challenge of the Strategic Air Offensive — 583.

   e. The Pacific — 594.

      1) The Strategy of Attrition versus the
         Strategy of Annihilation — 595.

      2) The Interrelationship of the Multiple
         Theaters — 601.

      3) The Strategic Air Offensive against
         Germany — 610.

4. The Autonomous War: the Controlling Force
   and the Guiding Hand — 613.

   a. F.D.R. as Commander-in-Chief — 613.

   b. Charge and Refutation — 618.

      1) The Decision for TORCH: the President
         Overrules the JCS — 620.

2) The British Import Crisis   622.

3) Decisions by Default   624.

    a) The Decision not to Conquer Berlin   624.

    b) The Decision not to Liberate Prague:

       the Czechoslovakian Epilogue   631.

Chapter XVI: Aftermath: The Righteous War and the

    Temporal Imperative   635.

1. The Righteous War   635.

    a. Premises   635.

    b. Carthaginian or Conditional Peace   638.

       1) Unconditional Surrender   638.

       2) The Morgenthau Plan   640.

       3) Unconditional Surrender, the Retention

          of the Emperor and the Believable

          Alternative   650.

    c. The Erosion of National Inhibitions: the

       Reversion to Area Bombardment   658.

2. The Temporal Imperative   668.

    a. The Interrelationship between Military,

       Economic and Psychological Mobilization   669.

    b. The Driving Force of the Temporal

       Imperative in American Military Strategy   671.

       1) The Frantic Search for Tactical Time:

          Over-all   671.

       2) The Transition to Strategic Time:

          European Theater   674.

3) The Transition to Strategic Time:

Pacific Theater 677.

c. The Decision to Use the Atomic Bomb: the

Closed Circle of the Temporal Imperative 683.

Conclusion: Confines of Concept 694.

1. The Critics' Illusions 694.

2. Idea and Circumstance 695.

3. American Strategy: Form and Substance 711.

4. Strategy as Compromise and Strategic Beliefs 712.

5. The Essence of the Problem: Nationalism and

Total War 714.

Part IV: Appendixes

Appendix I 717.

Appendix II 726.

Appendix III 729.

Appendix IV 731.

Appendix V 734.

Appendix VI 741.

Appendix VII 747.

Appendix VIII 752.

Appendix IX 754.

Part V: Footnotes

Preface 757.

Chapter I 758.

Chapter II 766.

Chapter III 775.

Chapter IV 784.

Chapter V   791.

Chapter VI   806.

Chapter VII   829.

Chapter VIII   859.

Chapter IX   875.

Chapter X   891.

Chapter XI   923.

Chapter XII   942.

Chapter XIII   971.

Chapter XIV   991.

Chapter XV   999.

Chapter XVI   1048.

Appendix I   1068.

Appendix II   1073.

Appendix III   1075.

Appendix IV   1076.

Appendix V   1077.

Appendix VI   1079.

Part VI: Bibliography   1082.

Preface

At the end of the Second World War, the American market was glutted with a flood of memoirs, studies, official and partisan histories. Despite the excellent quality of many of these works, a stereotype image of American strategy emerged. It is an image vociferously exploited by hostile critics, often parroted in popular histories. The damning charges run an unevern course, depending upon the intensity of the critic's passion; but the indictment of America's conduct in the war might read as follows:

1. The United States was guilty of waiting too long before intervening in a war which it could not escape. Initially, it was too defensive minded, too hide-bound by isolationism, to take offensive action. Then, rather than intervene when intervention might have counted to turn the strategic balance, it waited until attacked. And when attacked it went on the rampage. Like the typical western hero, America was slow to anger and quick on the draw.[1]

2. Americans were "militarily unsophisticated and blunt."[2] Rather than seeking victory by maneuvering agilely around the enemy's flanks, wearing him down before polishing him off, they sought an immediate confrontation: a western showdown on the grand scale.[3]

3. Americans were guilty of directing their military operations towards a single goal: victory. Thereby, they broke the Clausewitzean command that "war is a continuation of policy by other means."[4] They shot up the town, destroyed the wicked sheriff, and left without caring about the havoc

or the dangerous new characters who moved in and took control. [5]

4. They waged war as a crusade, utterly and ruthlessly
beating down their enemies, allowing strategy to become the
tool of vindictiveness. They didn't give the varmits any
quarter; and in the heat of the encounter, polished off innocent
by-standers. [6]

5. They were too impatient, too anxious to end the war,
to clean up the town and return home to the ranch. [7]

If we accept the critics' presentation, we come up with
an appalling picture. And their depiction of history is not
too comforting. History becomes a Proustian or Jamesian novel
in which nations, like individuals, impose their illusions
upon the patterns of time. The mild-mannered but tough,
blunt but innocent, fervent and impatient American, untrained
to the arts of war and peace but proud with the strength of
the young, moves from his sheltered world into the Old World
of sophistication and sophistry. His innocence and his
illusions combine to blind him to the reality around him.
The outcome is disaster.

Of course, the above is caricature, not character. But
the charges are real and often convincing, supported by
a mass of incriminating evidence. More important than the
individual charges is the picture of American strategy that
emerges: ingenuous, subjective, unrelated to the realities
of foreign policy, a preconceived pattern imposed upon the
world of war. This portrayal presents strategy as molded
and governed by inborn or innate ideas, strategic beliefs
projected or imposed upon circumstances.

No one will deny either the existence or the importance

of these beliefs, nor will anyone deny that the critics have
delineated accurately and often brillantly some of the
characteristics of the American approach to strategy. But
is it the whole picture? Is it a balanced picture? And what
of the general theory that emerges from it?

Four general criticisms arise. First, the critics have
oversimplified, often assuming that strategy is the product
of innate ideas (i.e. American) that clash against other ideas
(i.e. British). Second, they have equated American strategic
thought with strategic beliefs, linked together in a single
closed system: rigid, unimaginative and naive. Third, they
have oversimplified the ideas themselves. A more detailed
analysis will reveal that no strategic belief is a simple
entity. Rather it is a complex mirroring the reality
around it, a complex subject to multiple interpretations,
a complex often assuming contradictory and paradoxical
forms. Fourth, they have not studied the origins of these
beliefs, origins which lay deep in the history of the prewar
period. For the years preceding the Pearl Harbor attack
set the mold and the pattern of American strategic thought.
By studying their roots, we can comprehend the course of
American strategic thought and practice in the Second
World War.

PART I

<u>Strategy, Concepts and Preconceptions</u>

Chapter I

Towards a Definition of Strategy

1. The Dialectical Nature of War

Too often the student of civilization dismisses war
as the antithesis of progress. He condemns it as a chaotic,
irrational explosion of force setting off a chain reaction of
violence, challenging the rational aspirations of civilized
man. Under its blows, empires fall; and the achievements and
triumphs of slow time crumble into dust. War, therefore,
is purposeless and directionless: man's capacity for
destruction overwhelming his capacity for construction,
Thanatos triumphant over Eros.

And yet a more profound analysis would reveal that
man ceaselessly seeks to master and to control this chaos,
to give it direction and purpose. And so war actually
becomes a constant struggle between the accelerated forces
of disruption and the will of man, seeking to utilize an
irrational force for a rational purpose.

Clausewitz caught the dialectical nature of armed
conflict in his famous definition. First, he defined its
theoretical nature: "War is an act of force, and to the
application of that force there is no limit."[1] Here
Clausewitz characterized absolute war: a limitless act of
force, magnified and extended by reciprocal action as the
participants throw more and more strength into battle.[2]

But absolute force is an abstraction. In reality,
it is modified by the circumstances and pressures which
form it. Real war, in contrast to absolute war, operates
under limitations.[3] Some of these limitations are physical
and involuntary: the topography of the territory, the
material resources of the opposing forces, the state of
the nation's economy and technology.[4] But the most
significant modifications imposed upon the rage of violence
are imposed by the political objectives of the opponents.
These modifications reflect the institutions, traditions
and ideologies of the opponents. "We see that war is not

merely a political act but a real political instrument, a
continuation of political intercourse, a carrying out of the
same by other means."[5] It is "a continuation of policy by
other means."[6]

There are several types of real war: guerrilla wars,
wars of national liberation, struggles for survival,
revolutionary wars, limited and total wars. The more unrestricted
the conflict, the closer it veers towards the absolute; the
more limited, the farther it veers from the absolute. But
even total armed conflicts restrict and control the raw
forces of destruction. Only the nuclear age threatens to
abolish the difference between the real and the absolute.

Control operates in inverse proportion to force.
The greater the force, the lesser the control. The weaker
the force, the stonger the control. This proportion
determines whether a conflict remains limited or becomes
total. Some limited wars, like the dynastic conflicts of
the 17th and 18th centuries, were circumscribed by physical,
political and social conditions. Others, like the Korean
War, were controlled by official policy.

The nature of total conflict is molded by the nature
of the modern state. A modern nation is an immense
organism in which several systems sustain and reinforce
one another. Its economy, its manpower and its military
forces are inescapably interlinked. Ever since the French
Revolution, military forces have become another incarnation
of the Nation in Arms, and national manpower has become
available for military and industrial service.[7] Moreover,
the complexity of modern war and of 20th century weapons
systems entails a dependence on industrial technology.
Issued in great numbers from factory and city, from
supply depot and maintenance center, supplies of infinite
variety answer the complex needs of the separate services
over the vast distances of global war. Twentieth century
industrialized nations have to learn to command and to
control unprecedented force.

The communications and transportation systems--which balance the demands of the front with the supplies of the rear-- extend like multitudinous channels, linking all parts into an entity. This integration of the military, economic and manpower elements of national power is accompanied by the mobilization of psychological forces which, in total conflicts, may play the key role. The longer and more costly the war, the greater the problem of public support. Unless the people are convinced that their government is waging a righteous war, deterioration of public morale will undermine the policy of the administration.

This integration of national resources increases the nation's war potential. But it also increases its vulnerability and complicates the problem of discriminating between competing strategies. The destruction of the enemy's armed forces becomes merely one means to achieve victory. A nation's powers of resistance can theoretically be undermined and overthrown by the total annihilation of his industrial capacity, by the destruction of his morale. As Cyril Falls remarks:

> A major war has now come to involve in principle one 'waged by means of all the man-power, all the energies, and all the material and moral resources of the state, and directed in "totality" against the hostile state. It is all-out warfare, nothing being held back by the state which practices it.... Since, wholly in theory and in the Second World War nearly in practice, war is directed against nations as such, against their industries which provide the means of war as much as the men in uniform who use these means, it follows that the conception of illegitimate objectives or targets ceases to have any significance.[7]

In total war there are no lasting sanctuaries.

The boundary between limited and total confict is undefinable. A single miscalculation and one escalates into the other. Although men may evoke total war, they cannot easily end it. It has an explosive dynamism, a revolutionary force all its own. Its violence mounts like a tidal wave, sweeping away the restraints of placid times and patient men, shattering the habits of the past, leaving in its wake

a strange landscape transfigured by devastation. It transforms
the aims of policy far beyond man's imagination and design.
Evoked to preserve the present, it summons a new world out
of the darkness of the future.

2. Causes of Escalation: Towards Total War

Several developments in modern war unleash escalation:
prolongation, conversion into an ideological conflict,
degeneration into a struggle for survival.

a. The Prolonged Conflict

Unless Fritz Fischer is right in his contention that
the Germans entered World War I with extensive annexiationist
aims, the major belligerents sought limited gains at the
beginning of the war. In August 1914, the Central Powers
and the Triple Entente probably did not anticipate a long
conflict. They expected a swift war fought by mobile armies,
a series of violent but decisive offensives. Elan, spirit,
sheer aggressive drive would decide the issue.[10]

The main French plan, Plan 17, was vague, a design
dominated by exhortations to the offensive. It envisioned
a war of broad strokes with the French Army accomplishing
two mission: the isolation and destruction of the German
enveloping wing descending east of the Meuse; and a
massive drive by the French armies, smashing into Lorraine,
pushing over the Rhine near Mainz and driving onward to
Berlin.

The Schlieffen Plan was Germany's attempt to escape
the strategic dilemma posed by political encirclement.
To win a two front war against the Triple Entente,
Schlieffen, Chief of the German General Staff (1891-1905),
envisioned a vast envelopment movement sweeping through
the plains of Belgium and northern France, circling
west and south of Paris, pushing the French Army eastward
to hammer it apart on the anvil of the German defenses in
Lorraine. If the French launched an offensive into
Lorraine at the onset of the war, so much the better.
They would push into a trap which would close behind
them like a revolving door.[11]

Both plans failed. After the preliminary battles,
the opposing armies entrenched themselves from the Channel
to the Swiss border. For almost four years, the Western
Front remained relatively static, the two opponents locked
in a stalemate. Instead of a fluid, flowing conflict dominated
by gallant cavalry charges, the war degenerated into
massive "siege operations in the field,"[12]into spectacular
displays of human wastemanship. The opposing forces lay
like two paralyzed giants, prostrate on the ground with
only enough strength to claw and maul one another. No one
had anticipated either the course of the war or the decimating
effect of modern fire power. Moreover, no one had measured
the capacity that modern nations have for war. Instead of
being quickly exhausted, the antagonists mobilized more
and more resources to feed the gluttony of the battlefield.
Nations revealed unsuspected depths of strength. The failure
to anticipate meant the failure to plan adequately, and
consequently the failure to adjust rapidly to the new
battlefield. So the six week war escalated into a merciless
conflict of attrition in which each side sought to outlast
the other.[13]As novelist Jules Romains graphically described
it: "...men began to fall back on the thought of 'hanging on'
much as a sick man will turn his mind to old country
remedies when the drugs of the medical faculty have been
proved useless. 'The war will be won by the side that can
last fifteen minutes longer than the other.'"[14]

b. The Ideological Conflict

A just war fought to destroy the infidel or the
heretic also unleashes tremendous passions and pressures.
In the Albigensian crusade of the 13th century and the
religious wars of the 15th century, Christians
massacred one another with an ideological relish unmatched
until the 20th century and limited only by the

circumscribed range of their weapons. Furthermore, violence
satisfied the warrior's most elevated convictions while it
fed his most primitive passions. Personal and political
greed aptly reinforced the crusader's religious rage.
Since extirpation of a particular creed was the aim of
these just wars, their leaders scorned conciliation or
compromise and demanded the final solution of sanctified
genocide. Only success or mutual exhaustion brought these
conficts to an end. Fortunately, ideological passion was not
matched by technological capacity. These holy warriors did
not have the means equal to their emotional intensity.

In the 20th century, the gap between technology and
conviction narrowed. The unexpected savagery of World War I,
the havoc wrought by defensive lines of barbed wire entrenchments
and machine guns, the prolongation and extension of the conflict,
made a compromise peace increasingly difficult. Nationalistic
fervor was succeeded by grim determination. To sustain the
will of vast populations, utopian aims replaced limited war aims.
World War I became a war to end all wars, to extend the
principles of self-determination and the institutions of
democracy; or, on the other side, to establish German hegemony
over Europe. Attempts to bring the war to an end by proposing
a return to the status quo ante bellum were ignored or rejected.
As Charles Seymour reflected, "For each Government, in order to
evoke the belligerent enthusiasm necessary to a prosecution
of the war, had created a Frankenstein monster which emphatically
vetoed any whisper of peace."[15] The dynamism of total war
had altered the aims for which the Entente and the Central
powers fought one another. According to Raymond Aron, "The
demand for total victory was not so much the expression of a
political philosophy as a reflex reaction to total war."[16]

But World War I was also fought with the desperation of a
struggle for survival, born from the conviction that the
victory of the enemy would be intolerable. The Germans insisted
on the retention of Alsace Lorraine, the expansion of their
colonial empire, adjustments in their western frontier to the

detriment of France, the establishment of German influence
over Belgium and a free hand in the east. These conditions
were intolerable to the Allies. They negated the sacrifices
of the war. And to the Germans the idea of returning to
the status quo ante bellum was inconceivable while their
armies occupied large stretches of France. Popular passion,
the fear of revolution, the dominance of militarism demanded
a peace based on victory, a peace which would leave Germany
infinitely stronger than before 1914.[17] The prolongation and
cost of the war made it a "do or die" conflict.

In World War II, the unequalled viciousness of the Hitler
regime, committed to its degenerate Darwinism, and the
determination of the Allies to destroy Naziism, converted a
a limited war over Danzig, the Corridor and Poland into a
struggle for survival. Particularly for England, Russia and
Germany, there was no alternative to victory.

c. The Struggle for Survival

A cornered nation, fighting for survival, will probably
use every weapon at its disposal. Its release of violence
will be checked only by the limits of its arsenal or the fear
of retaliation. England, in the summer and autumn of 1940, and
Germany at the close of the European war, waged bitter
battles of survival. If the Germans successfully landed in
England, the British were prepared to use radical measures
to eliminate their bridgeheads.[18] One writer alleges that they
were ready to release mustard gas upon the invaders.[19] After
the battle of Normandy, Hitler dredged German manpower
resources, drafting old men and untrained youths in his attempt
to halt the Allied onslaught. He planned to destroy systematically
Germany's economy. His conquerors would gain only the ashes
and rubble of a burnt-out land, a barren token of triumph.
Desperately, he sought to reverse the inevitable--unleashing
his long expected, long dreaded secret weapons: rocket bombs,
Snorkel submarines and jet planes. The desperateness
of the situation was matched by the nihilistic fury
of a leader committed to triumph or annihilation.[20]

3. Limited War

If some conflicts escalate from limited to total war, others remain limited by nature and by design. In the 18th century, monarchy, artifical class sytems, economic rivalries and the Enlightenment united to limit the explosive force of war. This limitation was strengthened by the weapon systems, tactics and military organization of the time. Nations had neither the physical means nor the moral desire to escalate violence. War became a game governed by a set of elaborate rules, bound by protocol and fought for limited objectives.

In the Korean War the means to unequalled violence were available, but the United States decided not to use them. Political decisions circumscribed the use of power. The area of operations was contained. The United Nations Air Forces were ordered not to attack the "sanctuary" beyond the Yalu, and Chinese Nationalist troops were confined to Formosa and the off shore islands. Restrictions were also clearly drawn, defining allowable tactics. The use of tactical air power to support ground operations, according to airmen a secondary mission, was emphasized; the use of strategic air power against the industrial and military centers of enemy strength, the primary air mission, was forbidden. Finally, the means and degrees of allowable force were strictly limited. Believing that nuclear weapons were ineffective against such tactical targets as bridges, feeling that the limited U.S. nuclear stockpile should be conserved for possible use against a Soviet attack in Europe, sensitive to the opinion of allies on their use, the United States fought the Korean War with conventional means.[22]

The contrast between the limited wars of the 18th century and the Korean War is considerable. The earlier conflicts were limited primarily by external conditions of the time. Although inhibitions and concern about previous wartime excesses were strong, these feelings played a secondary role. Even if the will for total war had existed, the means were inadequate. In Korea, however, the means were ample. Restraint was not the result of technological or military limitation; it was the

result of the decisions of the Truman Administration.
Self-denial was ordered, not preordained.

4. The Controlling Factor: Strategy

Absolute war stands at one extreme, limited war at another.
Between them stand the World Wars which, in our century,
have moved closer towards the absolute, towards the
complete release of force. In every war there is some
degree of control and purpose deliberately releasing or
checking violence. This control is strategy.

Most definitions of strategy are narrowly circumscribed.
They define it as exculsively military, excluding the political
element which gives it a direction and an aim. They describe
strategy as the conduct of military operations on the large
scale, contrasting it to tactics which is the conduct of
military operations on the battlefield. According to Cyril
Falls' definition, "Strategy is the art of conducting a
campaign. Tactics is the art of conducting a battle or a
section of a battle."[23]A similar definition reads: "The art
of moving troops and supplies to made contact with the enemy
on the most favorable terms is strategy; and the manipulation
of troops in contact with the enemy during a battle or a
skirmish is called tactics."[24]

Soldiers, even sophisticated generals like Lord Wavell,
have tended to deprecate strategy while exalting tactics.
They assume that the latter is far more difficult than the
former. This judgment follows from the traditional definition. [25]
But what is 20th century strategy? The first definition is
so general as to be universally applicable; but its generality
diminishes its usefulness. It teaches us nothing of the
purpose of strategy. The second definition is more applicable
to ground operations than to naval or aerial campaigns. Both
are adequate 18th century definitions; neither even begin
to define modern strategy.

If we consider the strategic decisions of World War II
and the Korean War, we realize that they do not conform to
the classic formula. The atomic bombs dropped on Hiroshima and

Nagasaki were not directed exclusively against the military forces of the enemy. They were directed against the morale of the Japanese government. Both cities were partly military, but primarily civilian targets. Similarily, the incendiary B-29 campaigns against Japanese cities, the British Bomber Command's offensives against German cities, were primarily directed against the enemy's morale, only incidentally against military installations and industries The decisions not to use atomic weapons in Korea, not to unleash Chiang, not to blockade China, were strategic. Yet deliberate abstention from the use of force does not fit the conventional formula.

We can now define the function of strategy: to release and control the forces of violence, thereby achieving a victory which will advance the interests of the nation. The idea of control, direction and purpose is integral.

Our definition explains the objectives of strategy; it also suggests how these objectives are achieved. Apparently, strategy is the forceful application of will to brute matter. The strategist creates order; he imposes design. This definition implies a dynamic relation between man's will and the disruptive forces he seeks to control. But something escapes our definition. It tells us what strategy strives to do, not what it does. It gives us the function, not the form; the conception, not the implementation. It does not allow for the accidents and failures that play a large role in the execution of strategic plans. It implies that the explanation for success or failure lies in the correct or faulty application of will and intelligence.

There are two variants to this explanation, alleged keys to the secret of victory, keys to unlock the strategic secrets of the past, to expose the causes of success and defeat, to teach future generals how to control the uncontrollable. These variants are simplistic explanations, popular myths which infect military history. They are the myths of the master strategist and of the objective approach.

a. The Myth of the Master Strategist

The myth of the master strategist is a holdover from
the 18th century, a reincarnation of the theory of the
natural genius which assumed that the art of generalship
could not be taught. It was an intrinsic talent, an inborn
gift of the chosen few.[26] Since the 18th century, the art
of war has been immeasurably complicated by a series of
19th and 20th century revolutions. As Louis Morton summarizes
them:

> This revolution may be said to consist of four
> revolutions or, more accurately, of four overlapping
> and interrelated movements--one in manpower, one in
> economics, one in science and technology, and the last
> in management and organization. The first produced
> the mass armies of the 19th and 20th centuries; the
> second the means to supply, feed and move these armies
> while at the same time releasing more men for military
> duty. Developments in science and technology led to
> a revolution in weaponry and a steady increase in
> firepower that has enormously increased the capacity
> for destruction. And the revolution in the technique
> of management has made it possible, through military
> staffs and civilian agencies, to mobilize other
> resources in men, weapons, and production for the
> purpose of making war.[27]

The Franco-Prussian War demonstrated the military effectiveness
of staff planning and organization. The Prussian system was
studied and imitated throughout the world, with the United
States (1903) and Great Britain (1904) proving the laggards.[28]
This system transformed the art of war. The Napoleonic
generals--whose depth of experience and tactical ability
determined the difference between victory and defeat--were
replaced by the staff officers who brought careful method
and organized efficiency to the art of war. Genius was no
longer at a premium.[29]

This managerial revolution has not disturbed military
narratives which still unrepentantly mythologize the individual
hero. Obviously it would be difficult to pivot an historical
narrative around "a heroic committee" or a "persistent,
methodical staff." Although the committees and the staffs
sometimes receive generous praise for the work, they do not
dominate the foreground. The reader's attention lightly
skims over them, reducing them to the status of an extended
footnote. It fastens upon the select few, not the essential
many.

Sometimes, moreover, these titanic figures increase
their stature by becoming symbols. The reader identifies
Churchill with England, Montgomery with the Eighth Army,
Eisenhower with SHAEF. Memoirs reinforce this popular
appraisal by presenting history through an intensely
personal perspective. The writer dominates the action
while the other leading characters provide the background
for his drama. The more formidable the personality of
the hero, the more impressive his remembered role.

If Sir Winston Churchill looms in the memoirs of
other men, he bestrides his own world   like a colossus.
This personal dominance is reinforced by his approach to
history, an approach which places major emphasis upon
the accomplishments of great men.

In the first volume of his memoirs, <u>The Gathering Storm</u>,
Winston Churchill plays Cassandra, warning the appeasement-
ridden Conservative Party of the Nazi menace. He foretells
disaster while others, well meaning but blind, follow the
wishful delusions of their own benevolence. At the close
of his first chapter, "The Follies of the Victors",
Churchill announces the themes that dominate this volume:

> It is my purpose, as one who lived and acted in
> these days, first to show how easily the tragedy
> of the Second World War could have been prevented;
> how the malice of the wicked was reinforced by
> the weakness of the virtuous; how the structure
> and habits of democratic states...lack those
> elements of persistence and conviction which alone
> can give security to humble masses; how, even in
> matters of self-preservation, no policy is pursued
> for even ten or fifteen years at a time....We shall
> see how absolute is the need of a broad path of
> international action pursued by many states in
> common across the years, irrespective of the ebb
> and flow of national politics.
> It was a simple policy to keep Germany disarmed
> and the victors adequately armed for thirty
> years, and in the meanwhile, even if a reconciliation
> could not be made with Germany, to build even more
> strongly a true League of Nations capable of making
> sure that treaties were kept or changed only by
> discussion or agreement....But this modest
> requirement the might, civilisation, learning,
> knowledge, science, the victors were unable
> to supply.[30]

In the House of Commons, Churchill repeatedly denounces the
policy of appeasement and disarmament, rising again and again
to prophesy the oncoming catastrophe.[31] But, according to
Churchill, this foreseen diaster is not inevitable. Only
man's persistent pursuit of illusion subverts freedom
into fate.

The dramatic duel between the archfiend Hitler and
crusader Churchill begins long before the opening of the
Second World War. As C. P. Snow remarks, Churchill's insight
was unerringly accurate: "When Hitler came to power in 1933,
Churchill did not use judgment, but one of his profound
insights. This was absolute evil, and there was no way
round. That was what we needed. It was a unique occasion
in our history. We needed that insight, and that absolute
strength."[32] To Churchill the war is a metaphysical struggle
between good and evil.

After the failure to relieve Poland, after the abortive
Norwegian campaign, the supreme hour arrives. Churchill is
called to power. The prophet becomes the leader.

> I felt as if I were walking with Destiny, and that
> all my past life had been but a preparation for
> this hour and for this trial. Eleven years in the
> political wilderness had freed me from ordinary
> party antagonisms. My warnings over the last
> six years had been so numerous, so detailed, and
> were now so terribly vindicated, that no one could
> gainsay me. I could not be reproached either for
> making the war or with want of preparation for it.
> I thought I knew a good deal about it all, and I
> was sure I should not fail. Therefore, although
> impatient for the morning, I slept soundly and
> had no need for cheering dreams. Facts are better
> than dreams.[33]

This magnificent passage is unmarred by a whisper of modesty.

But success does not come easily. The hero now undergoes
a series of trials and tribulations. The disaster in France,
the siege of England, the failure in the Balkans, the
frustration in North Africa, the fall of Singapore and
Tobruk, the prolonged agony over the Battle of the Atlantic:
These crises test the spirit of the hero. Throughout the
narrative, he moves from theater to theater, from London to
Washington, Marrackech to Tunis and Ankara, corresponding
and conversing with other great men, interesting himself

in everything from strategy to the engineering of artificial harbors. He is omnipresent and omniscient.

But he is not omnipotent. Although he is one of the chief architects of victory, securing the abandonment of SLEDGEHAMMER and the adoption of TORCH over the opposition of the American military staff, although he helps to forge and to maintain the Allied coalition, his control over grand strategy gradually weakens. And this shift is the direct result of the coalition he labored to create. The eventual cost of American participation is the inevitable end of British predominance.

The Churchill memoirs move from tragedy through trial and triumph to return to tragedy. The theme of the final volume is indicative: "How the Great Democracies triumphed, and so were able to resume the follies which had so nearly cost them their life."[34] We come full circle. At the close of the war, Churchill returns to his former role. Once again he becomes the prophet who clearly recognizes the dangers of Soviet expansion, who proposes a series of military operations to forestall or limit the Soviet advance into Europe, to "'shake hands with the Russians as far to the east as possible.'"[35] A terrible sense of foreboding haunts the pages of Triumph and Tragedy: "'...the end of this war may well prove to be more disappointing than was the last.'"[36] As his advice is repeatedly ignored and as the chasm between the Soviets and their western Allies widens, Churchill's pessimism deepens. Farseeing, he can no longer implement his military or political views largely because the United States insists on being impartial and thereby fails to align herself with Great Britain. Finally, Churchill's defeat in the British elections of July 5, 1945, is a personal tragedy which mirrors the international tragedy of an unparalleled world conflict immediately followed by an unresolvable world crisis, of triumph consummated by tragedy. From first to last, the myth provides the thread weaving events into a unified whole.[37]

b. The Myth of the Objective Approach

1). The "Eternal" Principles of War

The second myth, the objective approach, begins with the
assumption that the laws of strategy are immutable and eternal.
Strategic success depends upon the ability to grasp and to apply
them systematically. Failure results when these eternal
precepts are violated. The laws themselves are easily
comprehensible; but their application is intrinsically
difficult. Therefore, the art of strategy depends upon a
soldier's ability to elicit clear eternal laws of war within an
ambiguous context. These laws are the revered "principles
of war." Bernard Brodie defines them as follows:

> The propositions usually stress the desirability of
> avoiding undue dispersion of strength in order to
> maximize the chances for superiority at the decisive
> point (principle of mass or concentration); choosing
> firmly one's course of action and adhering to it
> despite distracting pressures (principle of the
> objective); pressing vigorously any advantage gained,
> especially after a victory in battle (principle of
> pursuit); seizing the initiative at the appropriate
> time and exploiting it to force a favorable decision
> (principle of the offensive); guarding one's forces
> and communications against surprise attack, even when
> on the offensive (principle of security); making
> good use of stealth and deception (principle of
> surprise); putting to the fullest effective use all
> the forces available (principle of economy of
> force); and so on.[38]

According to their proponents, even revolutionary changes in
weapon systems do not affect the infallibility of these laws.[39]
The ability with which they are applied and combined determines
the effectiveness of one's strategy. Therefore, they form
useful pedagogical tools whereby military campaigns can be
studied and taught. Military history unfolds like a
morality play, sounding variations on the theme of obedience
and disobedience to eternal law.

Colonels R. Ernest Dupuy and Trevor N. Dupuy, in
Military Heritage of America, use the principles of war
to explain military history. This book is a marvel of clear
exposition, describing the tactics and strategy of campaigns
intelligibly and comprehensively. However, it is also a guide
book to the game of war. In the first chapter, the rules,

the principles of war, are expounded. The rest of the text is
an exposition of performances by celebrated players from
Alexander the Great to Douglas MacArthur. The result is a
study guide from which the soldier, by constant application,
can learn to become a qualified player.

As Bernard Brodie admits, these principles have a certain
"utility".[40] There are many cases where "violations of these
laws have brought military disaster."[41] There are, however, cases
when the principles of war have been violated successfully
(Chancellorsville),[42] and still others where they should have
been violated (Leyte Gulf).[43] When the Japanese opened their
offensive to seize the Southern Resources Area, they consistently
ignored the principle of concentration. Cecil Brown, noted
CBS correspondent, reported the incredulity of British
officers abroad the Repulse:

> "Those Japs are bloody fools," one of them said.
> "All these pinpricks at widely separated points
> is stupid strategy. The Japs should have sent over
> three hundred planes over Singapore, not eleven."
> "Bloody fools!" another snorted. "Those Japs can't
> fly," one of the officers said. "They can't see at
> night and they're not well trained." "They have
> rather good ships," one of the officers remarked,
> "but they can't shoot." I listened to these remarks
> about the enemy for some time and then remarked to
> the fifteen officers in the wardroom: "You English
> are extraordinary people. You always underestimate
> the enemy. You did it time and again, in Norway and
> France, in Greece, in Crete...." There was a moment
> of shocked silence in the wardroom at this criticism....
> A number of them chimed in, each in his own way:
> "We are not overconfident; we just don't think the
> enemy is much good. They could not beat China for
> five years and now look what they are doing out
> here, jumping all over the map instead of meeting
> at one or two places. They cannot be very smart
> to be doing that."[44]

By following this "inferior" strategy, the Japanese
paralyzed the United States fleet at Pearl Harbor, seized
Hong Kong and Singapore, conquered Malaya, Thailand, Burma,
the Philippines and the Netherlands East Indies and almost
severed the Allied lifeline to Australia. The success of
Japanese strategy depended on exploiting the momentum
of surprise. Because the attack against Pearl Harbor

neutralized American seapower in the Pacific, Japan could
conquer and consolidate its hold over the Southern Resources
Area. The Japanese needed time to fortify their conquests
into an impregnable bastion, strong enough to repel the
inevitable American counteroffensive. Therefore, everything
depended upon speed. A strategy which concentrated on the
reduction of one strong point after another would allow the
Allies to take active counter-measures. Given the general
weakness of Allied forces in the Far East, Japanese strategy,
in the short run, was flexible and sound.[45] The principle of
surprise annihilated the principle of concentration. One
eternal law abolished another.

The difficulties and dangers of using these generalizations
as guides to action is evident if we utilize the principles
of the objective and the offensive as analytical tools.
Do they provide a useful guide to action and decision? An
analysis of Spruance's conduct of the Battle of the Philippine
Sea and Halsey's conduct at the Battle of Leyte Gulf will
reveal the impossibility of applying the principle of the
objective with certainty. The conduct of field operations in
World War I and the over-emphasis on the Bomber Offensive in
the interwar period reveal the pitfalls of the principle
of the offensive.

a). The Principle of the Objective

Admiral Raymond A. Spruance, Commander of the Fifth
Fleet, was severly criticized by naval aviators for his conduct
of the Battle of the Philippine Sea (June 19-20, 1944), for his
"failure" to destroy the Japanese fleet, the true objective of
naval action.[46] This criticism arose after his forces destroyed
476 to 480 enemy planes, 445 aviators, and 3 aircraft carriers.[47]

According to the critics, Spruance missed his chance on
the night of June 18-19, 1944. That evening Admiral Nimitz
at Pearl Harbor informed Spruance that a high-frequency
direction-finder (HF DF) station had located the enemy carrier
fleet, commanded by Admiral Ozawa, approximately 300° WSW of
Spruance's force.[48] The Commander of the Fifth Fleet had
already turned his fleet eastward towards the Marianas.
Admiral Marc A. Mitscher, Commander of TF 58, recommended

that the fleet reverse course westward. This move would have placed TF 58 in striking position by the morning of June 20. After discussing Mitscher's proposal with his staff, Spruance turned it down. The fleet continued towards the Marianas.[49] According to Mitscher and others, this decision was the turning point of the battle. By trading victory for security, Spruance lost his chance to launch a direct attack on the Japanese fleet.[50]

Spruance's decision was based on his intelligence reports, his estimate of enemy intentions and his instructions. Although the HF DF fix was accurate, Spruance received other intelligence which challenged its reliability, suggesting that the Japanese fleet was advancing along two approaches towards the Marianas.[51] Based on these reports and on his knowledge of Japanese naval doctrine and practice, Spruance decided that Ozawa was trying an end run against U.S. shipping off the beachhead on Saipan.[52] Ozawa would feint with one arm of his fleet while he struck with the other.[53] And finally, although naval tradition taught that the proper objective was the enemy fleet, Spruance's instructions defined his mission as defensive: the protection of the beachhead. Spruance was as eager as Mitscher to engage the enemy fleet, but his primary duty foreclosed any emphasis on the destruction of the enemy carriers.[54]

In the Battle of the Philippine Sea, Spruance had to choose between a force and a mission objective. He chose the latter. Believers in the principles of war might resolve their quandry by judging that he chose the real and discarded the false objective. But what if he had decided to throw everything into an attack against Ozawa's carriers? Since the Japanese admiral had no intention of trying an end run,[55] Mitscher's carrier pilots probably would have inflicted serious losses on the enemy fleet.[56] Undoubtedly, these same analysts would still claim that Spruance chose the right objective.

In the Battle of Leyte Gulf, Admiral William Halsey was presented with the same choice as Spruance. He chose the opposite objective, thereby falling into a trap. The

enemy's plan, initiated immediately after MacArthur's landings
on Letye, involved a coordinated attack by three Japanese
fleets: Kurita's Center Force, Nishimura's Southern Force and
Ozawa's Northern Force. The first and second fleets, pushing
respectively through San Bernardino Straits and Surigao Straits,
were to envelop Leyte Gulf, smashing the American landing
force and its transports while Ozawa's Northern Force lured
Halsey's Third Fleet away from San Bernardino Straits. However,
Kurita's Center Force was discovered first. Halsey's air
arm dealt it such a stiff blow that it turned tail and fled.
Meanwhile, Admiral Ozawa, frantically seeking to reveal his
position, was finally spotted. Now Halsey had his choice of
objectives. Should he pursue Ozawa's Force, or should he
remain off San Bernardino Straits on the chance that Kurita
would turn back and break through? Halsey, more impulsive
than Spruance, never hesitated. He charged towards Ozawa's
carriers. Consequently, when Admiral Kurita's force passed
through San Bernardino Straits, the American landing forces
on Leyte were mortally exposed. Only the courageous, almost
suicidal, delaying actions of Admiral Sprague's escort carriers
and the Japanese commander's loss of nerve prevented a disaster.[57]

The principles of war are not helpful to a commander
forced to choose between alternatives masked by the "fog of
war." As shown above, certain principles are subject to
multiple interpretation. Moreover, these generalizations
often conflict with one another. In the Japanese strategy
after Pearl Harbor, the principle of surprise overrode that
of concentration; in Spruance's and Halsey's decisions, the
principles of security and the offensive alternated in
excluding one another.

b). The Principle of the Offensive

Sometimes the principles of war are not only inadequate,
they are dangerous. For example, one of the most exalted
principles is the offensive. In the decade preceding
World War I, Foch and Grandmaison elevated the doctrine of
the offensive into the ultimate law of military art:

> "To make war was always to attack." (Frederick)
> We must always seek to create events, not merely to
> suffer them, we must first of all organize the
> attack, considering everything else of secondary
> importance and to be planned only in respect to
> the advantages which may result from it for the
> attack.[58]

Since this doctrine stressed the superiority of the moral over
the material, it ignored the impact of modern firepower on
the battlefield, a development which temporarily paralyzed
the power of the offensive. What was strategically desirable
was operationally unfeasible.[59]

Similarily, British Bomber Command believed fervently
that the only proper use of air power was a strategic air
offensive against the enemy's industrial and urban centers.[60]
In the interwar period, airmen were doctrinally obsessed with
images of the "knock out blow", of vast fleets of unescorted
bombers sweeping the enemy's air force from the skies and
pounding the enemy's homeland with a deluge of bombs.
Under such an assault, the enemy's morale would crack. As
industries and towns collapsed in a holocaust of fire, civilians
would panic and the government would sue for peace.[61] Again the
moral effect would outweigh the material. As Major General
Trenchard asserted in 1919: "'At present...the moral effect of
bombing stands outdoubtedly to the material effect in a
proportion of 20 to 1.'"[62]

World War I ended before Bomber Command could try out its
theories. In the interwar period, England had neither the
the financial resources not the training facilities to check
assumptions. Therefore, belief in the efficacy of the strategic
air offensive remained unchallenged during the twenties and
early thirties.[63] Only the rising threat of Hitler's air power
provided the stimulus for a re-examination of doctrine. Only
in the last years of peace and the early years of war did
Bomber Command discover that it lacked the means and the capability
to effect its main purpose. It was quantitatively and
qualitatively deficient. Its bombers were insufficient in
numbers and inefficient in range, defendability and reliability.[64]
Moreover, because of its fascination with the offensive, because
of its belief that no defensive measures could prevent

bombers from reaching their objectives, the air planners
underestimated the potentialities of defense.[65]Fortunately,
a series of technological breakthroughs in radar and fighter
design, and a Cabinet decision assigning priority to the
strengthening of Fighter Command,[66]partly reversed this
obsession with the offensive. Otherwise, the RAF would
have lost the Battle of Britain.

The principles of war are, therefore, misleading and
dangerous. They are also too generalized to serve any
military purpose. As Bernard Brodie observes, these exaltations
of common sense are applicable to fields far removed from war,
such as business promotion or sexual seduction. Perhaps
Trotsky should have the final say:

> "If we check the inventory of the 'eternal truths'
> of military science, we obtain not much more than a
> few logical axioms and Euclidean postulates. Defend
> your flank; secure your lines of communications and
> retreat; strike at the enemy's least defended point,
> and so on. Such principles...may well be applied
> even to matters very remote from the art of warfare.
> The donkey that steals oats from a hole in a torn
> sack ('the enemy's least defended point') and
> vigilantly turns its croup in the direction opposite
> to that from which danger threatens, certainly
> behaves according to the eternal principles of
> military science.[68]

The principles of war are also poor pedagogical tools.
Military schools would be wise to emphasize that every battle
or war poses   entirely new and different problems. Ignoring
the context of decision making, the champions of the principles
of war narrow, often close, the existing alternatives.

2) The Narrow Alternatives

The myth of the objective approach to strategy suffers
from another basic flaw: the assumption that reality is
comprehensible and coherent, that alternatives are open and
understandable. But this assumption is negated by the
ambiguous nature of experience. Theoretically, the choice
of alternatives is broad; realistically, it is restricted.
Often the existing alternatives are overlooked or bypassed
by the strategist.

There are four explanations for this restricted
exploration of alternatives. Proposals are rejected

because 1) they clash markedly with current reality; 2) they
contradict the major plans and commitments of the leadership;
3). they are repulsive and unnatural; 4) they are cloaked
by the fog of war.

      a). Alternatives that Clash with Current Rality:
The Impracticable

Throughout the course of military planning, some proposals
are quietly buried. The staff sytem acts as a filter, sifting
out strategic plans, condemning some as impracticable while
passing others to higher authority for a decision. The files
of the National Archives are filled with this driftwood,
discarded proposals tossed aside as useless or irrelevant.
Some of these schemes contain strategic ideas which are later
developed in other forms. One of these abandoned projects was
an early version of OVERLORD in which all strategic problems
were solved by a rigorous application of the equilateral
triangle.

After pointing out that the situation on the Russian
front demands the creation of a diversionary front in the
west, the author sallies forth:

> The successful creation of a diversion front in the
> near future offers the only possible method of approach
> to an ultimate victory of the Democracies. While the
> immediate objective of this front would be to
> reduce pressure on the Russians, it would also serve
> as a base for possible future operations provided
> its location is in a theater containing a vital
> strategic objective. Granted, then, that the
> question of a second land operations front is imperative,
> three questions arise....
> 1. Where?
> 2. How?
> 3. With what means?
> ....In order to accomplish such a landing, an area
> must be selected which is in close proximity to
> possible bases of operations. The 18th Century
> von Bulow triangular strategic theory of land
> operations is unquestionably applicable to landings
> on hostile shores inasmuch as it prescribes the
> necessity of a line of operations bases opposite
> the objective so that the line of bases and the
> objective form an equilateral triangle.[69]

After discarding several potential landing areas because
none of them fit into the equilateral triangle, the author
blithely and painlessly alights on the French coast:

> If we admit the validity of our theory of the
> strategic triangular relationship of bases to the
> objective, only that part of the French coast which
> lies directly opposite the southern and southeastern
> coast of England can be chosen as a suitable object-
> ive. Furthermore, the apex of the triangle, or the
> objective, must extend sufficiently far inland so
> that debarkation points on the hostile coast cannot
> be brought under effective ground fires. The penin-
> sular geographic formation extending from DUNKERQUE
> to LE TOUQUET is the only part of the French coast
> which, in its juxtaposition to English bases, complies
> with our triangular theory of bases.[70]

After exploring the geometric superiorities of the region,
the author turns to the enemy who "MUST BE MADE TO CONFORM
TO OUR PLANS." The foe is easily disposed of despite an
admitted ignorance of the enemy situation. "We shall...disregard,
more or less possible enemy reactions within the theater in
planning our maneuver and base our plans more on consideration
of terrain of the theater of operations."[71] After a long section
in which the author details the precise operations involved,
he offers his conclusions:

> However, sketchily drawn it is the belief of the
> author that such an operation is entirely feasible
> at this particular time, subject unfortunately to
> the following provisos:
> 1. That sufficient shipping is available to ferry
> troops from English bases.
> 2. That a sufficiently large number of trained troops
> and the necessary material are available in England
> to carry out the operation. It is estimated that the
> seizure, occupation and defense of this front would
> require the following effectives:
> a. Thirty-five infantry divisions.
> b. Ten engineer regiments.
> c. Sixteen corps artillery regiments, particularly
> for the subsequent defense phase after the theater
> has been taken.
> d. All available observation, pursuit and bombardment
> aviation.
> e. One armored division.
> f. Fifteen GHQ tank battalions.
> g. At least one anti-tank battalion for each
> infantry division.
> h. Corps troops and staff for eight corps.
> i. Two army staffs.
> j. Eight regiments anti-aircraft artillery.[72]

After listing the advantages of the enterprise, the author
concludes sententiously: "The attempt is worth the price.
Nothing ventured, nothing gained."[73] Not suprisingly, this

strategic plan, dated August 1941, bears the following
notation: "This paper to be returned to files of War Plans
Division, War Department."[74]Since the British would have had
to provide all the troops and the United States was still
neutral, this scheme was completely out of touch with reality.

b). Alternatives that Clash with Preference:
The Radical

Some projects have no chance of adoption even though they
reach the Joint Chiefs of Staff (JCS) level. Top planners
are too strongly opposed for the proposals to receive prolonged
discussion. In the summer of 1943, four planners urged a
Mediterranean strategy even at the expense of a cross-channel
attack. Since the Allies were already heavily engaged in the
Mediterranean, their forces and resources should remain
there. Opportunities should be exploited and the offensive
against Germany should be maintained from the south.[75]

Since the American army chiefs had been consistently
loyal to the cross-channel attack, this proposal was heretical.
One of the advocates of the Mediterranean alternative, General
Hull, Chief of the Operations Division (OPD) Theater Group,
had been a persistent supporter of OVERLORD. He proposed
the Mediterranean alternative partly out of desperation: there
was no immediate prospect for a cross-channel attack. Under
these circumstances, concentration in a secondary theater was
preferable to strategic dispersion.[76]The proposal, however,
had no chance at the JCS level. American strategic planning,
previous commitments and assumptions, the beliefs of the Chiefs,
militated against its adoption.[77]

They also militated against another proposal, the invasion
of Europe through the Iberian peninsula. This proposal had
support from a member of the JCS, Admiral Leahy, who thought
that this "route might be less expensive in casualty lists
as well as in material."[78]Although this proposal was discussed
by the JCS and Roosevelt, General Marshall was adamntly
opposed. Rejection was inevitable.

c). Alternatives that Clash with Moral and
Psychological Commitment: The Unthinkable

Some alternatives are never seriously presented. They are
morally or psychologically unthinkable. Now these

alternatives may or may not be practicable. However, they
are not debated or analyzed. If they are suggested, they
are quickly repressed. When the Japanese government debated
the issue of war and peace with the United States, its
choice was circumscribed. The decisions it could take
were restricted by the decisions it could not take. Because
of the virtually undisputed position of the military, a
position which allowed generals and admirals to topple
cabinets at will, the services could impose their programs
over the opposition of civilian ministers.[79]The military,
especially the Army, were obstinately opposed to any policy
of retreat in China, a move which the U.S. government
considered essential to any permanent Far East settlement.[80]

Similarily, in World War II, certain courses of action
were inadmissable for the United States: leaving the Soviet
Union to its fate at the hands of the German Wehrmacht,
prolonging the war for political advantage, or using force
in 1945 to liberate Poland from Russian domination.

d). The Unseen Alternatives

Experience also distorts alternatives so that the
impossible sometimes seems attainable; and the attainable,
impossible. In war, no general staff or military commander
has enough information to make an objective judgment. Since
they move in a medium of uncertainty, in the fog of war, their
decisions are calculated gambles or informed guesses. They
must make their choices and commit their forces without
knowing precisely the enemy's capabilities, dispositions
and intentions. When Spruance at the Battle of the Philippine
Sea and Halsey at the Battle of Leyte Gulf chose their
objectives, they acted on incomplete information. If they
had known the enemy's intentions, they probably would have
reversed their decisions.

5. Conclusion: A Definition of Strategy

The theories of the omniscient strategist and of the
objective approach share a common assumption. Strategy is
an act of the will or a predetermined design, imposed upon
the circumstances of the moment. The successful commander
perseveres with his plan, relentlessly sweeping aside all
obstacles while he systematically applies the principles of

of war. The will of the commander is the active agent; the
forces of circumstance, the malleable material from which
the strategy is woven. But the command decisions analyzed
above show that the circumstances which surround decision
play as active, as dynamic a role as the will and intelligence
of the commander. Strategy is molded by the interplay
between will and circumstance, intelligence and chaos,
direction and chance. Ultimately, therefore, the aims of
the commander and the forces of the moment must be fused
together by a series of voluntary and involuntary adjustments.

We can now formulate a definition of strategy, a
definition which encompasses purpose and form, the why and
the how, what is as well as what is intended to be.

Strategy is a form of compromise designed to achieve
maximum control over conflicting, sometimes mutually
exclusive, designs and forces. Every strategic compromise
is both instrument and mirror, reflecting the forces that
produce it while seeking to control them. A complex world
formed of interwoven relationships, its adjustments are
either internal or external, reflective or instrumental.
Its internal relationships evolve within a specific organization: a military service, a nation or a coalition. Its
external relationships evolve in the interplay between the
designs of strategic planners and the forces of outward
circumstances, between human intelligence and fate's decrees.

These relationships are neither separable nor static.
They are interrelated and dynamic. They are merely the
expanding ripples of the same pool, spreading and revolving
around a single center. Essentially interdependent, these
relationships are often distinguishable from one another
only according to the perspective through which they are
viewed. A compromise between the army and the navy is an
external adjustment to either service; it is an internal
adjustment within the context of national military policy.

Internal and external compromises are interrelated
in another manner. Originally, strategic views emerge
from the challenge and response of experience. Those
views and beliefs which prove most lasting and useful

are eventually adopted as articles of faith.   External
response become internal belief.

Neither the internal nor the external relationships
are final.   Internal adjustments express the transitional
or recurrent tensions within an organization, the reconciliation
of diversity within an institutional framework.   They
reconcile conflicting needs and pressures, wedding
incompatible demands while maintaining them.   Never final,
they harmonize these incompatible demands by expressing them;
they control, by releasing them.   Accomodation is the heir
to dissent.   Since it mirrors incompatibles, it is
constantly threatened with disruption from within.   But
every adjustment is transitional.   It must constantly be
readjusted to meet challenge and change.   So strategy is
a process, not a product.   Its internal and external
relationships form bridges which must constantly be
rebuilt.[81]

Chapter II

Compromise and Decision: Broad Front vs. Narrow Thrust

Compromise and decision are antithetical: this assertion
is a common assumption. If compromises are inclusive, seeking
to satisfy all parties, decisions are exclusive, choosing
one alternative over another. Therefore, military writers
often condemn a command decision by denouncing it as a
"compromise." Their premise is that such a decision is
marred; it is a choice foregone. It is no decision at all.

Bernard Montgomery explicity condemns Eisenhower's
Broad Front strategy in these terms:

> The dismal and tragic story of events after the
> successful battle in Normandy may be boiled down to
> one fundamental criticism. It is this--whatever the
> decision, it wasn't implemented. In Normandy our
> strategy for the land battle, and the plan to achieve
> it, was simple and clear-cut. The pieces were
> closely "stitched" together. It was never allowed
> to become unstitched; and it succeeded. After
> Normandy our strategy became unstitched. There was
> no plan; and we moved by disconnected jerks.[1]

The Australian correspondent, Chester Wilmot, also
strongly condemns Eisenhower's Broad Front strategy. According
to Wilmot, its defects clearly reflected Eisenhower' character
and approach to military operations:

> Because he had no philosophy of battle which he
> himself had tested in action, Eisenhower was reluctant
> to impose his own ideas, unless the decision was
> one which he, as Supreme Commander had to make. As
> a general rule, he tended to seek the opinion of
> all concerned and to work out the best compromise....
> It seems fair to say that the very qualities which
> made Eisenhower a successful Supreme Commander
> prevented him at this time from becoming a successful
> commander in the field. His great talent lay in
> holding the Allied team together, and in reconciling
> the interests of different nations and services.
> In a situation which had now developed, however,
> Eisenhower's conscientious tolerance and inclination
> to compromise were liabilities. The occasion called
> for a man with a bold plan, a Commander-in-Chief who
> knew what was essential and had the will to impose
> his strategic ideas without regard for personalities
> or public opinion.[2]

This famous controversy reflects the conflicing approaches
of Montgomery and Eisenhower towards strategy. The former's
Narrow Thrust was a careful master plan, committing the Allies
to a single objective; the latter's Broad Front was a flexible
scheme of operations, allowing for maximum freedom in the
use of military forces.[3]

Believing that the end of the war was in sight,[4] Montgomery
planned to destroy the routed German forces, stunned by their
defeat in Normandy. His ultimate objective was Berlin, but
his immediate objective was the rapid crossing of the Rhine
and the seizure of the Ruhr before the Germans could recover
their balance.[5]

Montgomery's plan advocated a single "powerful full-blooded
thrust across the Rhine and into the heart of Germany, backed by
the whole of the resources of the Allied Armies."[6] Montgomery
recognized that there were two "favorable axes" of advance
towards the Ruhr: the first through Belgium and over the
Rhine into the plains of northern Germany, leading
towards Berlin; the second, through Metz and the Saar into
central Germany, pointing ultimately towards Leipzig and
Dresden. For personal, military and political reasons, he
favored the former route.[7]

This northern drive would be executed by a concentration
of the Twelfth and Twenty-First Army Groups. The Twenty-First
would clear the Channel coast and western Flanders, seizing
Antwerp and South Holland. The Twelfth would drive towards
Aachen and Cologne, keeping its right flank on the Ardennes.
Meanwhile American forces would secure the Allied right
flank stretching from Nantes along the Loire towards Reims
and Laon. The task of these forces would be primarily passive.[8]
While these forces guarded his flank, Montgomery would encircle
the Ruhr, the Twenty-First Army Group descending from the north
and the Twelfth Army Group sweeping up from the south.[9]

Montomgery justly decries the popular designation of
his plan as "'a narrow front,'" "'a pencil-like thrust,'"
and "'a knife-like drive.'" Since his plan envisioned a
a major blow by forty divisions, his strategy obviously called
for a massive concentration of force in time and place.[10] As
Montgomery later explained: "I was expounding the doctrine

of the single push against an enemy who was now weak on his
pins. It was on the lines of the 'left hook' of the desert
battles, leading to the knock-out blow; after all I knew
something about that sort of thing."[11]

Besides honoring the principle of concentration,
Montgomery's plan had logical military advantages. It meant
a relentless pursuit of a defeated enemy, a pursuit directed
towards the economic and political centers of enemy power:
the Ruhr and Berlin. The Allied threat to these vital areas
would force the Germans to expend their last military reserves
in a frantic effort to halt the complete disintegration of
the Reich.[12]

Geographic, logistic, command, economic and political
factors reinforced military considerations. The northern
route with its stretches of flat plains would allow the
Allies "to exploit our greatly superior mobility and strength
of armoured forces in the plains of northern Germany, with
greater effect than would be possible in the more difficult
southern country."[13]To Montgomery the geography of the
northern approach reinforced its military advantages.

Moreover, logistic limitations excluded the possibility
of multiple drives. As Montgomery argued forcibly in his
September 4, 1944 message to Eisenhower:

> "I consider we have now reached a stage where one
> really powerful and full-blooded thrust towards
> Berlin is likely to get there and thus end the
> German war.
> We have not enough maintenance resources for two
> full-blooded thrusts."[14]

As he told Eisenhower on August 23, 1944: "'If we split
the maintenance and advance on a broad front, we shall be
so weak everywhere that we will have no chance of success.'"[15]
Therefore, Montgomery persistently pressed Eisenhower to
consolidate his maintenance behind the drive of his
Twenty-First Army Group, despite the cost: the immobilization
of Patton's Third Army.[16]

Principles of command strengthened Montgomery's
logistical reasoning. An effective master plan calls for
a single commander; "'Single control and direction of

the land operations is vital for success. This is a WHOLE
TIME job for one man.'"[17]Since he had directed the field
operations of the Battle of Normandy, Montgomery argued that
Eisenhower should retain him as the ground commander. Instead
of assuming control of operations as scheduled on September 1,
1944, Eisenhower should remain the distant, unobtrusive,
Supreme Commander. Montgomery would manage the show for
him: "The Supreme Commander must sit on a very lofty perch
in order to be able to take a detatched view of the whole
intricate problem--which involves land, sea, air, civil control,
political problems, etc. Someone must run the land battle
for him."[18]This proposal, if accepted, would have maintained
unity of command under the Supreme Commander. It would have
left Montgomery in command not only of British and Canadian
troops, but also of at least twelve American divisions.[19]
Finally, Montgomery's command plan was probably partially
motivated by his distrust of Gernal Patton. The British
Field Marshal feared that Patton would run away with the
ballgame unless he was forcibly restrained by a master plan.[20]

Finally, certain broader considerations influenced
Montgomery. As he knew keenly, Britain's economic and
manpower resources were strained to the ultimate. Totally
mobilized, the British had reached the end of their tether.
If the war lasted much longer, Britain's contribution would
decrease while her hardships increased. Unless the war
ended quickly, her role in the post-war world would be
seriously weakened.[21]In later life, Montgomery pontificated
further: the approval of his plan would have left Europe
with a stronger balance of power versus the Soviet Union.[22]
Although there is no available evidence that he foresaw the
Soviet menace at the time, his superiors, the British Chiefs
of Staff and Churchill, certainly did. Possibly their support
of his plan was partly based on this political awareness.[23]

Although Eisenhower's approach differed considerably
from Montgomery's, his main objective was essentially
identical. The "purpose of destroying enemy forces was
always our guiding principle; geographical points were
considered only in relation to their importance

to the enemy in the conduct of his operations or to us as
centers of supply and communications in proceeding to the
destruction of enemy armies and air forces."[24]

Like Montgomery, Eisenhower felt that Germany was close
to disaster: "'The German Army in the West has suffered a
signal defeat in the campaign of the Seine and the Loire....
The enemy is being defeated in the East, in the South and in
the North; he has experienced internal dissension and signs
are not wanting that he is nearing collapse.'"[25]Like Montgomery,
he saw a great opportunity: "'It is my intention to complete
the destruction of the enemy forces in the West, and then--to
strike directly into the heart of the enemy homeland.'"[26]
Unlike Montgomery, however, Eisenhower remained cautious. If
the Germans did recover their balance, the Allies could be
caught in an overextended position. Consolidation should
precede further advances.[27]

If Montgomery saw the future strategy of the war as a
single concentrated blow, Eisenhower saw it as two consecutive
blows: "'...one for getting the Ruhr, one for getting Berlin....
He asked his commanders to make a clear distinction between
the final drive on Berlin and present operations which aimed
at breaking the West Wall and seizing the Ruhr.'"[28]The two
drives corresponded to his dual objectives: one economic,
one political. Naturally, after the occupation of the Ruhr,
the capture of Berlin would be merely symbolic. Eisenhower's
military analysis centered on his estimate of Germany's
economic strength. As he pointed out, the basis of her
industrial war power lay predominantly in the Ruhr, secondarily
in the Saar.[29]Because of their crucial importance, these
areas and their approaches would be tenaciously defended by
the German army. This inevitable enemy reaction would give
the Allies the opportunity to destroy the German armed forces
in the field.[30]Pre-D-day planning had geared the future Allied
advance towards this objective. One month before the invasion
of France, SHAEF had reviewed the approaches to the Ruhr and the
Saar. There were four: 1) the Metz, Saarbruecke, Frankfurt route

south of the Ardennes; 2) the Ardennes; 3). the Maubeuge-Liege
route north of the Ardennes; and 4) the Flanders plain. The
second and fourth routes were rejected because of terrain.[31]
According to the original plan, therefore, the Allies would
converge on the Ruhr from north and south, effecting a wide
strategic encirclement.[32]Although the northern drive would
dominate, the southern drive would provide a strong subsidiary
push.

Eisenhower either initiated or accepted this dual approach.[33]
Rather than concentrate on a single thrust, he intended "to
push forward on a broad front, with priority on the left."[34]
Although Montgomery's northern advance would retain its
predominance, the southern thrust towards Lorraine and the
Saar would be continued. Patton would not be stopped to
benefit Montgomery. The Allied armies would converge towards
the German frontier and the Rhine along the length of the
western front.

Eisenhower's plan tallied with his emphasis on strategic
mobility and the maximum utilization of available force: "We
wanted to bring all our strength against him, all of it mobile
and all of it contributing directly to the complete annihilation
of his field forces."[35]Whereas the single thrust would utilize
only thirty-five out of the Allies' sixty-eight divisions, the
Broad Front strategy would utilize every division. By
adopting this approach, the Allies would avoid a possible
stalemate. The Single Thrust strategy would allow the
enemy to concentrate his forces against the Allied advance;
the Broad Front strategy would leave the enemy in doubt,
forcing him to divide his forces.[36]Wrote General Omar Bradley:

> No longer was Eisenhower to be committed to a single
> axis of advance against which the enemy could mass his
> defenses. Now having spread his offensive across a
> broad Allied front, Eisenhower could feint and dodge
> with his double thrust and confuse the enemy on his
> intentions....As long as we held the initiative on
> so broad a front, the enemy would find his defenses
> stretched beyond the breaking point.[37]

Eisenhower saw his plan as completely compatible with the
principles of war. It would give the Allies "'capability of

concentration....It is going to be very important to us later
on to have two strings to our bow.'"[38]

Two additional military reasons favored this strategy:
it would allow the Allies to destroy German forces west of the
Rhine, and it would protect the flanks of the Allied armies
when they undertook their final concentrated drive into Germany.[39]
As Eisenhower explained to the Combined Chiefs of Staff on
January 20, 1945: "'Only when we too have closed the Rhine shall
we share with the enemy a strong defensive barrier giving us the
ability to hold defense sectors with security and economy
of effort.'"[40]

Basically Eisenhower's strategy balanced advance and
consolidation, a drive to the Rhine along several axes followed by
a consolidation of forces, followed by a renewed drive to Berlin
or to Leipzig.[41] Although geography favored Montgomery's plan, it
did not preclude an advance to the south. The Metz Gap, leading
from the plains of Lorraine to the Saar, would channel the
sweep of invading forces towards Frankfurt am Main. The terrain
presented no insuperable difficulties to military advance.[42]

If military reasoning favored a dual approach and geographical reasoning did not forbid it, logistics decreed it. The
OVERLORD plan prefigured the Allied offensive as a series of
movements: advance followed by consolidation. According to the
plan, the breakthrough from Normandy would be followed by an
advance towards the Seine. There the regrouping of German
forces would allow a corresponding regrouping of Allied forces.
Maintenance would remain geared to operational necessity.[43] But
this anticipated balance, with its non-existent "margin of
safety,"[44] was shattered when the Allies swept across France.
Since the French railway system had been severly disrupted by
Allied air operations, the advancing armies were largely limited
to motor and air transport. Dependent on inadequate and
increasingly distant port facilities, extended and damaged lines
of communication, and an inadequate and obsolete supply schedule,
the momenetum of the Allied drive slowed as it neared the
German frontier. Even the OVERLORD plan had predicted that
consolidation would follow the advance from the Seine. The
unanticipated pursuit across northern France naturally
aggravated the inherent limitations of the original logistic

plan.   Therefore, slow-down and consolidation became inevitable.
The strategically desirable full-scale drive into Germany
became operationally unfeasible.[45]The Allies were the victims
of their own success.

Eisenhower felt that the solution to the logistic crisis
lay in the acquisition of additional port facilities :   Antwerp
and the Channel ports in the north, Marseilles and Toulon in
the south.   Although Eisenhower allowed Montgomery to attempt the
crossing of the lower Rhine, Operation MARKET GARDEN, before
clearing the approaches to Antwerp, he repeatedly emphasized
the priority of the latter task.   To the Supreme Commander,
the possession of a northern deep water port was a logistical
prerequisite to the drive into northern Germany.[46]

Even if there had been no logistical problem, command and
politics would have prevented permament subordination of
Bradley's forces to Montgomery's command or the relegation
of Patton's Third Army to a passive role.[47]

To Eisenhower, Montgomery's command proposals were inappropri-
ate and inapplicable.   They were defensible when the Allied
armies were confined to the narrow Normandy bridgehead, when
"'a single battlefield commander' was needed who could devote
his whole attention to a particular operation."   But now that
the battle lines stretched from the Channel to the Swiss border,
only the Supreme Commander could oversee the front:

> ...the campaign over such an extended front was
> broken up into more or less clearly outlined areas of
> operations....The over-all commander...then had the
> task of adjusting the larger boundaries, assigning
> support by air or by ground and airborne troops, and
> shifting the emphasis in supply arrangements.[48]

But these purely military aspects of command were overshadowed
by political considerations.

To be successful a Supreme Commander must combine tact,
patience and understanding.   He must refrain from controversy
bearing a national taint.   An Eisenhower would fit the bill,
not a Montgomery.   From the battle of Normandy to the end of
the war in Europe, Montgomery was controversial.   American
commanders had a long list of recriminations against him.[49]
His conduct of the Battle of Normandy had provoked disgust
and sharp criticism from SHAEF.[50]Montgomery could not understand

why American commanders should resent his tactlessness or why
democratic politics should modify military strategy. The Field
Marshall felt that the subordination of either the Twelfth Army
Group to the Twenty-First or the subordination of the Twenty-
First to the Twelfth was natural. It made military sense.
But it didn't make political sense. Although the initial British
troop commitment to OVERLORD equalled the American, Bradley's
subordination to Montgomery after the Battle of Normandy[51] was
deeply resented in the States. Now that American forces
outnumbered the British,[52] continued subordination would be
politically indefensible.[53] Montgomery stubbornly refused to
appreciate this point.

Since Montgomery's plan would strip the Twelfth Army Group
to one army, Eisenhower accruately foresaw that "public opinion
in the States would object." Montgomery brusquely rejected
this judgment: "I asked him why public opinion should make us
want to take military decisions which were definitely unsound."[54]
When the Field Marshal urged the concentration of resources in
Bradley's Twelfth Army Group, Eisenhower tactfully reminded
him that the British public would not tolerate his consequent
immobilization.[55]

Obviously, the American public would have strongly objected
to the subordination of Bradley to Montgomery. It would also
have balked at the halting of Patton. General George Patton's
drive through France had been a spectacular headliner. It had
contrasted sharply with Montgomery's cautious handling of the
Battle of Normandy. Inevitably, the invidious comparisons
were made. And, if the Third Army were confined to a defensive
role, the American press would howl. Nor would Patton passively
accept such a decision.[56] If the Allies won another major
victory bringing the German to their knees in 1944, the protests
would be forgotten. But, if Montgomery's reinforced divisions
failed to score, the political repercussions would be serious.
Since Eisenhower doubted that the Single Thrust was militarily
feasible, since he foresaw another hard campaign before the
capitulation of Germany, his political caution reinforced his
military skepticism.[57]

Eisenhower's plan was a perfect compromise, neatly balancing

military, geographical and political factors. It perfectly
utilized the full organization of the Supreme Command, assigning Montgomery's Twenty-First Army Group an important role
but not neglecting the Twelfth or the Sixth Army Groups.
Its perfection as an organizational tool overshadowed its
military advantages. Like all "perfect compromises," it
satisfied no one. Bradley and Patton felt that Eisenhower
was too partial to Montgomery's schemes.[58]Montgomery felt that
the Broad Front totally vitiated his plan of campaign.[59]The
American commanders agreed with Montgomery in one respect.
They also felt that too many changes were made in the
campaign plan.[60]But Eisenhower and Bedell Smith maintained
that the OVERLORD plan anticipated the Broad Front strategy.
Execution followed planning. How are we to reconcile these
quarreling witnesses?

The Broad Front was a generalized scheme of maneuver
which projected the overall pattern of the Allied advance
without detailing the specifics. It outlined the trends;
it did not diagram their course into static design. Adjustments
were consequently possible without violating the overall plan.
And Eisenhower took advantage of this built-in flexibility.

The general plan anticipated the envelopment of the
Ruhr as a broad movement, with one army descending from
north of the Ardennes while another thrust upward from the
Saar. These forces would join hands in the vicinity of
Kassell.[61]This projection was substantially effected.

However, there were several tactical developments.
First, in the original plan, the Twenty-First Army Group
was to advance towards Germany through the Maubeuge-Liege
route north of the Ardennes, avoiding the Flanders plain.[62]
However, with the breakdown of German resistance in France
and Belgium, the British and Canadian armies swept with ease
over the Flanders plain. The opportunity to seize the Channel
ports, Antwerp and the rocket launch sites was too great
to be foregone.

Secondly, Eisenhower repeatedly shifted priorities.
His pre-D-day plan had predicted a slower, more systematic
advance, alternating between offense and consolidation.

If the Allied advance had conformed to this pattern, the dual
approach would have developed as planned, neatly balanced
between the predominant drive in the North and the subsidiary
one in the South.[63] But the drive from Normandy to the German
border disrupted this strategy, with its balanced priorities.
Eisenhower now had to adjust and readjust the relationship
between the two drives to the Rhine. He had to accomplish
this task while seeking to restore his original plan, which
was sufficiently flexible to allow for modification and
temporary suspension. The continued alterations, however,
confused his subordinate commanders. Bradley and Patton
complained that Eisenhower was outrageously partial to
the British.[64]

Actually, the "frequent changes" narrow down to five
specific shifts. On August 23, 1944, Eisenhower agreed to
reinforce Montgomery's drive with the First U.S. Army.
Strategic emphasis thus fastened on the northern drive.
Eisenhower effectively grounded Patton.[65] On September 2,
1944, at the Chartres Conference, Eisenhower gave qualified
approval to the secondary drive through the Metz Gap. Patton
was unleashed.[66] This shift was confirmed on September 10, at
the Brussels Conference, when the Supreme Commander turned
down Montgomery's Single Thrust concept while accepting his
plan for operation MARKET GARDEN.[67] He followed this decision
by urging Patton, on September 15, to keep going.[68] On September
22, the third clear shift occured. At the Versailles
Conference, Eisenhower placed priority on the northern
approach: "'The envelopment of the Ruhr from the north by
21st Army Group supported by 1st Army, is the main effort
of the present phase of operations.'"[69] General Bradley's
northern force would give full support to Montgomery. Supplies
to Patton's Third Army would be strictly limited to the
leftovers.[70] It is not surprising the De Guingand exalted that
Montgomery's "'plan had been given 100 per cent support.'"[71]

But the failure of MARKET GARDEN and Montgomery's slowness
in clearing the approaches to Antwerp prompted Eisenhower
to shift priorities for the fourth time. Since the
Twenty-First Army Group was immediately engaged in
clearing the Schelde Estuary's approaches to Antwerp,

it could not mount the primary drive against the Ruhr. Therefore, the Twelfth Army Group would do the job while the Twenty-First played the supporting role.[72]This shift was confirmed at the Brussels Conference on October 18 and in General Eisenhower's October 28 directive.[73]Since the Sixth Army Group would also attempt to cross the Rhine in the south, Eishenhower's decision fundamentally altered the accepted plan. As Forrest Pogue summarizes:

> For the first time since late August, the main
> thrust was given to the U.S. forces, and the Allied
> forces were oriented directly at and south of
> the Ruhr, instead of north of that area. If these
> various drives proved successful in establishing
> bridgeheads across the Rhine before the 21st Army
> Group was free to return to its missions, it would
> be impossible to return to the strategy which Field
> Marshal Montgomery had favored since late August.[74]

But the frustrations of the Siegfried Line Campaign and the battles of attrition in Huertgen Forest eliminated every prospect of early success and led to the fifth shift. At the Maastricht Conference on December 7, 1944, nine days before the German counteroffensive in the Ardennes, the priority of the northern route was restored. Although Eisenhower refused to immobilize Patton's forces, he did agree "that the main attack would be made north of the Ruhr by the 21st Army Group with the support of a U.S. Army (the Ninth) of ten divisions."[75] Since Montgomery's forces had cleared the Schelde estuary, they were free to concentrate on the Rhine. Essentially the Maastricht Conference confirmed Eisenhower's dual-drive policy. Although his decision was challenged by the British Chiefs of Staff in January 1945, he never wavered.[76]Actually, Eisenhower's shifts had been changes in emphasis, not in plan. He remained faithful to the dual approach, changing priorities and shifting emphasis only in response to the challenges of the hour.

Eisenhower's plan was adopted to the realities of coalition warfare. It was a tapestry woven of multiple patterns of contesting participants, blended together in a single texture dominated by no single theme. Montgomery's plan overthrew the previous campaign plan; Eisenhower's temporarily modified it, maintaining its essential

structure while altering its details. Montgomery favored
a revolutionary design rigidly applied; Eisenhower, a
predetermined design flexibly applied. Moreover, Montgomery's
plan was exclusive; Eisenhower's, inclusive. Montgomery
emphasized a strictly objective, exclusively military
approach; Eisenhower reconciled objective needs and
subjective pressures, the demands of the situation with the
demands of the organization. Dispersion was the cost for
coordination, the price paid for maintaining flexibility.

Chapter III

Concepts and Preconceptions:

The Defensive-Offensive Complex and the Direct Approach

1.   Strategic Beliefs: Concepts and Preconceptions

Strategy is a form of compromise. And yet certain ideas
recur in American strategic thought, ideas which seem to have
an immortality far beyond any present situation. If strategy
is a form of compromise woven from the texture of time and
circumstance, then these ideas, these strategic beliefs,
seem to provide the major threads.

They vary, however, in strength. Some bend to the force
of circumstance, altering when necessary. These beliefs
are concepts. Some are so powerful, so insistent, that they
seem to challenge all compromise; they seem to stand unbending
before every assault of force and circumstance. These latter
beliefs are preconceptions.

These concepts and preconceptions are produced by long-
term historical forces, reinforced by national experience
and tradition. They are a blend of feeling and thought,
experience and passion, the conscious and the unconscious.
Like an iceberg, any concept or preconception merely reveals
a glimpse of itself.

What are the differences between these two forms of
strategic beliefs? Concepts are often challenged. Preconceptions
are accepted without question. Concepts are more variable
and abound with alternatives which contradict them. Preconceptions, however, seem incontestable, inviolable,
unchallengeable. Since their alternatives seem "monstrous"
and "unthinkable", they are excluded by automatic repression
rather than by systematic debate. Their strength depends on
unspoken depths of historical experience. National traditions,
ideological commitments, historical inheritances and
contemporary situations: this substratum of thought and
feeling defines and limits responses, molding or rejecting
alternatives.

Five predominant strategic beliefs emerge from most analyses of World War II strategy: the defensive-offensive complex, the direct approach, the autonomy of war, the righteous war and the temporal imperative. These concepts and preconceptions delineate and determine the functions of strategy: its aims and its means. The distinction between them is never absolute. Specific ideas are not consigned to one category and excluded from another. The distinction is based on the nature and role of concepts as opposed to preconceptions. A specific strategic belief, therefore, will often play a dual role. As we will discover, each one of our five strategic beliefs is both concept and preconception.

The first strategic belief defines strategy as a function of security identified in terms of geography. The direct approach defines it in relation to the conflicting objectives of the armed forces. The autonomy of war formulates it as the outcome of civil-military relations. The righteous war uses it as a tool in a moral struggle between the forces of good and evil. The temporal imperative defines it as a function of the mobilization of national strength.

In delineating the functions of strategy, however, these concepts and preconceptions serve a second purpose. They are not merely instruments, but are mirrors, reflecting the world that produces them. They symbolize the psychological, social, economic and ideological forces that create them, while they simultaneously seek to transform these forces, to utilize them for a chosen end. By studying these strategic beliefs and explaining their dependence on and relationship to circumstance and change, we can discover their complexity in structure and function.

2. The Defensive-Offensive Complex: Definition and Preliminary Exposition

The defensive-offensive complex defines strategy as a function of security, but it assumes a paradoxical form. It seeks to unite opposites. In World War II, it sought to reconcile the irreconcilables: the advantages of isolation in peacetime with the advantages of rapid

intervention in wartime; the supposed security of non-involvement,
with an implicit determination to wage war far from American
shores. Before the declaration of war, the U.S. maintained
its defensive stance, allowing the enemy to deliver the "first
strike." Once attacked, however, it switched to the offensive
as rapidly as possible. Even today American policy revolves
around this paradox. The U.S. vows that it will never wage
preventive war against its Communist foes. Yet the Strategic
Air Command is an offensive weapon system. In the thermonuclear
age, the necessity for immediate conversion to a full-scale
offensive is ineluctable. The inhibition against striking
the first blow must be matched by a capacity to strike an
immediate, devastating retaliatory blow. So the U.S. maintains
a defensive policy while arming itself with weapons for
ultimate offense.

But this basic paradox is reinforced by ambiguity. What
constitutes offense? What constitutes defense? Obviously,
definition depends on perspective.[1] The words "offense" and
"defense" are ambiguous. Where does one end and the other
begin? When a nation invades its neighbor's territory, it
may justify its action by claiming that it is securing itself
against attack. To the victim, however, this justification
is hypocrisy. Perhaps the best expression of this paradox is
the old cliche: "the best defense is offense." If a nation
seeks total security, it can achieve it most effectively by
attacking and defeating, if not annhilating, its potential
opponents.

The two most persistent sources of this ambiguity lie
in human psychology and physical geography.

a. Ambiguity of Motive: The Russo-Finnish War

When the U.S.S.R. attacked Finland in the winter of
1939-1940, she was almost universally condemned as an aggressor.
She was doubly condemned because she struck without warning.
And yet this action was probably motivated by Russia's
inescapable sense of insecurity. Occupying a long-exposed
frontier, vulnerable to attack, invaded three times before
the outbreak of World War II, isolated on the fringes of
outer Europe in the twenties and thirties by a <u>cordon sanitaire</u>

of hostile states stretching from the Baltic to the Black Sea, Russia lived in fear of encirclement and annihilation. The rise of a Nazi ideology committed to the destruction of communism reinforced this traditional insecurity. Russia was now confronted with two enemies: fascism and capitalism.

To prepare itself for the apparently inevitable assault, the U.S.S.R. sought to cover its western approaches by the conquest of the formerly Russian lands lost at the close of World War I. The Molotov-Ribbentrop non-aggression pact of August 23, 1939, with its definition of eastern spheres of interest, give Russia the opportunity to improve her defensive position. The Finnish frontier on the Karelian Isthmus, uncomfortably close to Leningrad, was one of Russia's most vulnerable borders. A powerful Finnish offensive driving through the Isthmus could quickly invest, if not seize, the old capital of the Russian empire. Understandably, therefore, Russia's attack on Finland was largely motivated by her defensive fears. The Russians allayed their insecurity by waging preventive war, not against their major foe but against his potential accomplice.[2]

But Soviet motives were mixed. If Russia sought expansion mainly for defense, she also saw an opportunity for the spread of Communism. Originally, Russian planners expected that their initial air attack on Helsinki and the simultaneous advance of their armies on five fronts, accompanied by amphibious assaults, would precipitate a workers' revolt. Communism would catapault into power, and Russia's influence over Finland would be restored.[3] Defense would be secured by offensive strategy.

Defining war as a continuing ideological struggle between hostile systems, the Soviets saw peace as achievable only through the triumph of communism. As long as capitalism exists, it is a threat to the Soviet Union. In this sense, every offense is a function of defense.

b. Ambiguity of Means

The ambiguity of offense and defense lies not only in the variability and uncertainty of human motives, but also in the dual nature of a single means. Geography and weaponry are

prime examples. What is the difference between a defensive and
an offensive position? Between a defensive and an offensive
weapon? The Norwegian campaign of 1940 dramatized the
inseperability of defensive-offensive factors in geography.[4]

      1) A Defensive versus an Offensive Position

      Geographically, Germany was almost land-locked. Her
sea frontier on the North and Baltic Seas was limited and
vulnerable to blockade. As Vizeadmiral Wofgang Wegener had
explained in his Die Strategie des Weltkrieg, England could
maintain a blockade from the Shetlands to Norway. But the
German possession of bases on the Norwegian coast would push the
British back to the Shortlands-Faeroes-Iceland line. This new
position would free Germany from her confinement and complicate
the blockade problems of the British.[5]

      The possession of the Norwegian coast would answer another
defensive need by insuring the delivery of Swedish iron ore to
Germany. This ore, produced mainly in the mines of Kiruna and
Gallivare, was shipped to Germany through the Swedish port of
Lulea in the Baltic and the Norwegian port of Narvik on the
North Sea. From December to April, when Lulea was ice-bound,
the German were almost totally dependent upon Narvik. Here
geography and neutrality protected them. From Narvik to the
southern tip of Norway, German commerce was shielded by the
Leads, a natural channel running between the coast and its
countless offshore islands.[6]

      But this protection depended upon Allied respect for
Norwegian neutrality. Since the Leads represented a serious
leak in their blockade, the British might decide to disrupt
the iron ore traffic by mining or patrol.

      Furthermore, the British and the French could decide
to extend the war to the Scandinavian Peninsula. They could,
with the mobility of their superior sea power, secure bases
on the Norwegian coast and then advance towards the Swedish
iron fields.[7] If the Allies limited themselves to cutting
off the ore traffic from Narvik, the German economy would
probably absorb the shock. But, if the Allies seized the
Swedish fields, the effect would be profound. It

might be lethal.[8] If the Allies seized the initiative in
Scandinavia, the Germans would inevitably respond. They could
not watch the seizure of their iron ore supply with equanimity.
An originally limited campaign might escalate into a full-scale
campaign. Therefore, even the unprovoked seizure of the Norwegian
coast could be rationalized on defensive grounds.

But a German occupation had other advantages. Besides
shielding Germany for a new "hunger blockade," it would provide
the Luftwaffe and the Kriegsmarine with bases from which to
launch a siege of Britain, a direct shift to the offensive.[9]

2) Defensive versus Offensive Weapons

Weapon systems are as ambiguous as geographical positions.
Today modern military technology re-emphasizes the paradoxical
character of the defensive-offensive complex. As modern
weapons overcome the barriers of distance and geography, the
invulnerability of isolated regions shrinks. Previously, a
space gap entailed a time gap. The greater the distance
between potential enemies, the greater their mutual security.
An isolated nation had time to read its enemy's intentions,
time to prepare itself against an anticipated onslaught.
Now this safety factor has vanished.

Ultimately man's technological capacity for destruction
may free him completely from geography. The Doomsday Machine,
as sardonically depicted by Hermann Kahn, is terrifyingly
self-sufficient, independent of the frontiers of time and
space. The ultimate expression of the defensive-offensive
complex, it is:

> ...a device whose only function is to destroy all
> human life. The device is protected from enemy
> action (perhaps by being put thousands of feet
> underground) and then connected by a reliable
> communication system, to hundreds of sensory
> devices all over the United States. The computer
> would then be programmed so that if, say, five
> nuclear bombs exploded over the United States, the
> device would be triggered and the earth destroyed.[10]

We are dealing here with a dynamic paradox whose two
opposing terms are inherent in one another. Since defense and
offense complement one another, since the motives of military
and diplomatic action are usually mixed, the transition from one

to the other moves through ambiguity and uncertainty.

      c. The Consistent Core

      Is tnere any consistent core within this complex free from the touch of ambiguity? Certainly some consistency exists within any national context. In United States military thought, there is an "immovable" point of departure: a central defensive purpose. Offense, no matter how extended, no matter how aggressive, remains a form of defense. In practice, however, this adherence to a single aim is confirmed and reinforced by another strategic belief: the righteous war, the moral correlative to the defensive-offensive complex.

      In a sense, therefore, defensive and offensive measures and policies are means to a single end: the security of the nation. But here the question arises: to what extent is the defensive-offensive complex a concept; to what extent is it a preconception? The alternative which this strategic belief chooses--stonewall defense vs. hemispheric defense, occupying advanced 'positions vs. fortifying the homeland-- is the means whereby a country seeks to implement its security. Before an alternative is chosen, there is endless debate. One set of advocates, for example, might argue for the occupation of advanced positions, even on neutral and neighboring territories. Another mignt argue for a policy of fortifying the homland against attack; another, for preventive war; and yet another, for the total annihilation of the enemy. These arguments or forms are concepts.

      But the persistent, unchanging element (the fear of encirclement and invasion) is a preconception. Unlike the concepts, debated and then chosen or rejected, the pre- conception is inescapable, unchallengeable, unconditional. It is a dogma whose strength depends largely upon its emotional intensity, an intensity of fear or moral fervor which it never loses. One concept can replace another. A preconception, more deeply rooted, draws its strength, its persistence and its force from deeper sources.

3. The Direct versus the Indirect Approach

The defensive-offensive complex leads logically into the direct approach. Once the threshold of war is passed, the United States passes rapidly from the defensive to the offensive. It now seeks the most direct implementation of the offensive, moving to strike at the heart and guts of enemy strength, to annihilate the enemy's resistance by an advance into his heartland. This direct approach is a strategical extension of an old tactical rule: a global application of the principle of concentration. It seeks the rapid implementation of the end play through direct confrontation.[11]

Since this approach fastens on the ultimate objectives of war, it tends to neglect the preparatory preliminaries, to underestimate the opening gambit. In contrast, the indirect approach postpones the ultimate test, avoids the enemy's strength and exploits his weaknesses. It follows a strategy of attrition, seeking to erode rather than to overthrow. The ultimate objective is merely the final act of a play whose outcome is assured by the design of the preceding scenes. The preliminaries declare the outcome, the approach dictates the climax. Since it seeks to weaken first and to confront later, the indirect approach teaches that the enemy must be isolated and interdicted before he is immolated. "Closing the ring" must precede the assault on the citadel. If enemy power is sapped in the preliminary stages, ultimate confrontation may become mere formality.

For the direct approach, the preliminaries are secondary; for the indirect approach, they are primary. Basil Liddell Hart defines the indirect approach as follows:

> To move along the lines of natural expectation
> consolidates the opponent's balance and thus increases
> his resisting power. In war, as in wrestling, the
> attempt to throw the opponent without loosening his
> foothold and upsetting his balance results in
> self-exhaustion, increasing in disproportionate
> ratio to the effective strain put upon him.
> Success by such a method only becomes possible
> through an immense margin of superior strength in
> some form--and, even so, tends to lose
> decisiveness. In most campaigns the dislocation
> of the enemy's psychological and physical balance

has been the vital prelude to a successful attempt
at his overthrow.
This dislocation has been produced by a strategic
indirect approach, intentional or fortuitous. It
may take varied forms, as analysis reveals. For
the strategy of indirect approach is inclusive of,
but wider than, the manoeuvre sur les derrieres
which General Camon...showed as being the constant
aim and keymethod of Napoleon....Camon was concerned
primarily with the logistical moves....But analysis
of the psychological factors has make it clear that
there is an underlying relationship between many
strategical operations which have no outward resemblance
to a manoeuvre against the enemy's rear--yet are,
none the less definitely, vital examples of the
'strategy of indirect approach.'[12]

If dislocation is sufficiently devastating in its effects,
confrontation can be avoided.[13]

Temporarily ignoring any identification with national
strategies, we can easily associate the direct and indirect
approaches with service viewpoints. The direct approach is
primarily an Army strategic concept. Army orthodoxy dictates
that only land forces can strike "directly and decisively at
the heart of the enemy's power."[14] During World War II, American
planners "believed and consistently maintained that Germany's
defeat 'could only be effected by direct military action' and
that that action must be directed against the main body of
the German army in the west."[15]

The indirect approach, which seeks to exploit the chinks
in the enemy's armor, is predominantly a naval or air force
concept.[16] Until the nuclear age, army planners automatically
downplayed the role of the navy and the air force. Sea power
and air power, they emphasized, could weaken the enemy; they
could never overthrow him. The navy could destroy the enemy's
sea power, interdict his trade and blockade his ports; but it
could not defeat his army, occupy his country or impose surrender.
The air force could harass the enemy's communications, whittle
his sources of supply and damage his industry; but, and on
this assumption the direct approach rested, total victory
could not be won by air power alone. The defeat of the enemy's
army was the imperative path to victory.

Although the direct approach is exclusively an Army concept,
the indirect approach, predominantly naval and aerial, is

applicable to all three forms of warfare. Like the direct
approach, it can overthrow the enemy's armed forces; unlike
the direct approach, it can attack and possibly destroy the
enemy's industry or his morale without touching his army.
Three examples (one from land warfare, two from aerial
warfare) will show the contrast between the two approaches
and their possible interrelationships. It will also suggest
that any absolute distinction between them is arbitrary.

    a. The Battle of France, 1940: the Direct and the
                Indirect Approach to Land Warfare

    The opposing plans for the 1940 Battle of France dramatize
the contrast between the two approaches in land warfare.[17]
General Maurice Gamelin, Allied commander-in-chief, planned
a direct counter move to the expected direct attack. Certain
that the Maginot Line would discourage any German attack on
the German-French frontier from Switzerland to Luxembourg,
General Gamelin expected the enemy blow to fall on the plains
of Belgium. The aim of Allied strategy, therefore, was to
halt the German offensive as rapidly as possible. Once the
opposing lines were stabilized, the battles of attrition
would begin. While steadily grinding down German strength,
the Allies could build up their own. Time was on their side.
A prolonged campaign would allow the potentially stronger
industrial systems of the Allies to mobilize. Finally, when
their preparations reached peak strength, they could launch
a massive counteroffensive which would roll over their
weakened foe, purchasing victory without exorbitant casualties.

    Where would the Allies seek to stall and stop the German
onslaught? The Allied choice, the Dyle-Meuse line, provided
the best defense against direct attack; it was also the best
springboard for an eventual counterattack. Placing the Allies
behind a resilient wall, capable of swinging back without
snapping apart, it gave them the advantage of flexibility.
If the Allies could not hold this position, they could retire
in good order to the French border or to the Somne. In
every respect, the Dyle-Meuse line seemed to counter the
dangers posed by a direct German attack. Unfortunately
the enemy did not cooperate.[18]

The original German plan (Fall Gelb) envisioned a direct
assault on the Allied armies. Seeking a limited objective,
the seizure of "as much territory as possible in Holland,
Belgium, and Northern France, to serve as a base for the
successful prosecution of the air and sea war against England
and as a wide protective area for the economically vital
Ruhr...",[19] it placed the main blow, delivered by Bock's Army
Group B, in the north. Rundstedt's Group A, swinging through
the "impassible" Ardennes, would cover the flank of the main
advance. No reincarnation of the Schlieffen plan,[20] O.K.H.'s
scheme was a direct attack with a limited aim.[21]

Generalleutenant Manstein, Rundstedt's chief of staff,
noted the plan's inadequacies. It would merely shove the Allies
back to the Somne, probably allowing them successfully to
stabilize their front. Pushing the Allies back, this frontal
assault would shorten their lines of communication while extending those of the Germans. It would, therefore, concentrate
Allied strength while dissipating German power.[22]

Manstein advocated a new plan, based on an indirect
approach, which would dislocate Allied resistance, ultimately
strangling their forces in a noose. His plan had two elements:
the bait and the trap. The bait was a secondary attack by
Bock's Group B through the Low Countries. Since the Allies
would probably respond by swinging their forces into Holland
and Belgium, their advance would provide the Germans with
their opportunity. North-west of the Maginot Line lay the
weak hinge on which the Allied advance would pivot. Therefore,
Manstein proposed to spring his trap by dislocating this hinge.
The main blow would be delivered by Rundstedt's armored
divisions striking through the Ardennes, vaulting over the
Meuse and then racing towards the Channel. This lightening
drive, whose success depended on audacity, surprise and speed,
would encircle the retreating Allied armies which would be
crushed between the jaws of a gigantic nutcracker. By an
indirect approach, Manstein planned to achieve a major victory
over the Allies, leaving their forces so weakened that a
final drive to the south would rapidly eliminate all remaining
resistance.[23] Since the Allies cooperated splendidly, his

anticipations were almost infallible.

In this campaign, the indirect approach played the major role. The Germans' approach through the Ardennes unhinged the Allied army so thoroughly that resistance crumbled. The physical dislocation created by an unexpected assault produced a psychological dislocation. The shock of surprise threw the French off balance, thereby facilitating German success.

b. The Oil Offensive: the Assault against German Industry

In the Battle of France, the indirect approach sought the same aim as the direct approach: the overthrow of the enemy's military forces. The difference lay in technique, not in objective. However, the indirect approach can also attack the underpinnings of the enemy's military power: his industrial strength and his morale. Total war has created new approaches to the enemy's strength, new means to subvert his resistance. His armed forces can be weakened, perhaps overthrown, by an offensive against his industrial economy or his civilian morale. Since the military health of a nation depends upon these elements of national strength, this assault can theoretically corrode all resistance.

The industry of a modern nation was too extensive to be totally destroyed with the weapons available in 1939. Initially, therefore, British and American air force enthusiasts advocated a selective campaign, a precision bombardment offensive, which would destroy the links binding this system together. Once selected, theory taught and faith confirmed, they could be obliterated with mathematical precision and calculated intensity.[24]

In World War II, British economic experts and strategic advisers were initially convinced that the German economy was stretched to the limit, vulnerable to rapid disruption. Even a limited air offensive would crack apart the German industrial system.[25] Actually, the German economy was only partially mobilized; it contained unexploited resources, cushions of strength which could absorb the shock of attack.[26]

In one respect, British assumptions were realistic. Germany's oil situation was precarious; her oil industry,

exceptionally vulnerable.[27] As an early British directive reported:
"...oil is the weakest link in Germany's war economy...."[28]
This vulnerability opened the opportunity for an indirect
attack with incalculable results. Obviously, Germany's
oil supplies were the lifeblood of her military mobility. Her
oil industry was also vitally interrelated with the production
of explosives and rubber.[29] Therefore, an aerial strategy which
concentrated upon Germany's oil complex would have a fantastic
effect upon her military strength. A rapier stroke[30] straight
into the solar plexus of German power, this indirect blow
could ultimately paralyze the Wehrmacht.

Although this essential connection between the oil and
the chemical industries was largely ignored, the Hankey and
Lloyd committees were convinced that a concentrated attack
on oil production would be decisive. In their January 13,
1941 report, the military chiefs recommended the initiation
of an offensive against seventeen synthetic oil plants.[31]
The subsequent campaign was ineffective, defeated by operational
difficulties and strategic diversions.[32] The British shifted
from precision bombardment to area attacks; and the oil
offensive lost its priority.

Unlike the British, the Americans never lost faith in
selective bombardment. Not surprisingly, therefore, it was
General Carl "Tooey" Spaatz, Commander of the United States
Strategic Air Forces in Europe (USSTAF), who broke the
stalemate. In his "Plan for the Completion of the Combined
Bomber Offensive,"[33] he advocated a concentrated offensive
against the oil resources of the Reich, a campaign designed to
effect "about a 50 per cent reduction in German gasoline supplies
within six months."[34] Despite the opposition of Sir Arthur Harris,[35]
Spaatz, aided by the British Air Staff,[36] finally won his point.

Initially, the agreement throwing Bomber Command and the
American Air Forces into a common offensive was informal;
no directive was issued.[37] Competing with the transportation
plan[38] and with the area bombing campaign, the new oil offensive
waged by UUSTAF was intermittent and spasmodic. But it
brought surprising results:[39] "For the first time in the war
a vital target system had been chosen when the force and

skill necessary to destroy it was available."[40]

On September 23, 1944, oil finally received first priority.[41] This prolonged offensive was successful, devastating the oil resources of the Reich,[42] reducing the supply of explosives,[43] effectively eliminating any counterattack by the Luftwaffe[44] and impairing the mobility of the German ground forces.[45] Some experts argue that persistent concentration on this target system would have produced an earlier victory.[46] Since the German oil situation reached crisis proportions in September 1944,[47] this judgment is credible.

    c. The Area Offensive: Assault against German Morale.

The industrial system of a nation may be too complex or too dispersed to be destroyed by selective bombardment. But, according to air power enthusiasts, there is one more alternative, one more objective, whose destruction would defeat the enemy's force totally: civilian morale. And the way to destroy morale is to devastate the enemy's urban centers, terrorizing the population into panic or revolt.[48]

At the beginning of the Second World War, strategic air planners were convinced that civilian morale was exceptionally vulnerable to aerial attack.[49] This optimistic forecast, partly based on the teachings of Giulio Douhet,[50] was rapidly modified by experience. During the Battle of Britain, British morale stiffened under the ordeal of the Blitz. But this first illusion was replaced by another: the belief that although British morale was resilient, German morale was brittle.[51]

Lord Trenchard, in a May 19, 1941 memorandum, explained this vulnerability. As he asserted, it was inextricably linked to the totalitarian system:

> Where then is Germany's weak point? It is to be
> found in precisely the sphere in which I began
> this paper by stating that we had a great strength.
> All the evidence of the last war and of this shows
> that the German nation is peculiarly susceptible to
> air bombing. While the A.R.P. services are probably
> organized with typical German efficiency, their
> total disregard to the well-being of the population
> leads to a dislocation of ordinary life which has
> its inevitable reaction on civilian morale. The
> ordinary people are neither allowed, nor offer to
> play their part in rescue or restoration work;

> virtually imprisoned in their shelters or within
> the bombed area, they remain passive and easy prey
> to hysteria and panic without anything to mitigate
> the inevitable confusion and chaos....This, then
> is their weak point compared with ourselves, and
> it is at this weak point that we should strike and
> strike again.[52]

Lord Tenchard argued forcibly for a concentrated and unremitting
attack, by day and by night, on "'military targets in Germany.'"[53]
Although designed to strike at precision objectives, the assault
would fall on the enemy civilian. "'If...our bombs are dropped
in Germany, the 99 per cent [sic] which miss the military
target all help to kill, damage, frighten or interfere with
Germans in Germany and the whole 100 per cent of the bomber
organization is doing useful work, and not merely 1 per cent
of it.'"[54] Aiming at precision targets, Bomber Command, because
of its notorious inaccuracy, would incinerate the surrounding
urban area, thereby directly assaulting the morale of the
civilian population. In effect, if not in intent, Bomber
Command would practice area bombardment. Trenchard's scheme
would utilize design and accident to achieve its end.[55]

The directive of February 14, 1942, committing Bomber
Command to a policy of wholesale attack on German morale,
was the turning point in British aerial strategy.[56] Though
Bomber Command did not have the minimum force of 4,000
heavy bombers required for the new apocalyptic strategy,[57]
the pressure for the shift to area objectives was immense.[58]

This new strategy found its uncompromising champion in
Sir Arthur Harris, Commander in Chief of Bomber Command.
According to Harris, victory lay on a single road. Only
the destruction of Germany's urban centers would topple
the Reich.[59] Harris scornfully damned advocates of precision
bombing as "'panacea mongers and parochial experts.'"[60]
Since the Germans could disperse and divert their industries,
since substitutes could always be found for scarce components,
since the German economy had unsuspected cushions and reserves,
the adoption of any selective objective was a delusion
and a snare.[61] The only strategic solution was to devastate
the major German urban centers, flattening out war industries

and eroding the moral strength and stamina of the German
population. Harris believed "'in piling the maximum on to
the structure as a whole.'"[62] As the official British historians
later summarized: "General area bombing worked almost on
the principle that in order to destroy anything it is
necessary to destroy everything."[63]

      d. Victory through Air Power: Direct or Indirect Strategy

      What then is the direct path to military success, the
straight road to triumph? Will the enemy's strength collapse
most rapidly if his shield is torn from him, if his military
forces are smashed on the battlefield, or if his industries
are bombed and disrupted, attacked relentlessly where most
vulnerable, until his military forces are left, immobile,
unequipped, stranded by defeat while yet undefeated in the
field? Or will it shatter if his cities are blasted into
rubble until his people, slaughtered or dispersed, despair
and demand an end to the war?

      To the army planner, air power during World War II was
an unproven quantity. The only certain way, therefore, to
defeat the enemy was to confront his military forces, to
strike and destroy his army. Air power, even strategic
bombardment, would merely weaken the foe. It could erode
his powers of resistance; it could not destroy his will or
his capacity. A strategy based totally on the use of
strategic air power would be indirect in its attack,
ineffective in its impact. It would merely sideswipe the
enemy's strength; the foe's power of resitance would
remain unaffected.

      To the air strategist, the opposite was true. The
advocates of precision bombardment and the champions of
area attack believed in victory through air power. The
devotees of this new military faith were more outspoken
among the British than among the Americans. (Perhaps the
more guarded advocacy by the latter reflected the
subordination of the AAF as opposed to the independence
of the RAF.)[64] Innately, however, many American advocates
of precision bombardment were motivated by faith: air

action alone could destroy German resistance. General Carl
"Tooey" Spaatz, reviewing the course of the war in 1948,
was emphatic:

> Because the last war saw the weapons of all services
> employed in profusion, one may argue the exact degree
> of contribution made by strategic bombing to the
> final decision. I believe, however, that the fund-
> amental lesson of the war in terms of airpower was
> expressed in two sentences by the United States
> Strategic Bombing Survey after an exhaustive study
> of the first major victims, Germany and Japan: "Even
> a first class military power...cannot live long under
> full-scale and free exploitation of air weapons over
> the heart of its territory...For the future it is
> important to grasp the fact that enemy planes
> enjoying control over one's head can be as disastrous
> to one's country as its occupation by physical
> invasion.[65]

This faith was not a post-war judgment. It was embodied in
the early strategic air plan AWPD/1 which asserted: "'...if the
air offensive is successful, a land offensive may not be
necessary.'"[66]

Sir Arthur Harris was also totally convinced that the
strategic air campaign could defeat Germany without invasion of
the continent.[67] On November 3, 1943, in a minute to Churchill,
he urged the continuation of area attacks, grandiloquently
prophecying: "'...Germany must collapse before this programme
which is more than half completed already, has proceeded much
farther....We can wreck Berlin from end to end...if the U.S.A.F.
will come in on it. It will cost between 400-500 aircraft.
It will cost Germany the war.'"[68]

Area and precision bombardment seek to defeat the enemy
while avoiding confrontation with his land forces. They
bear, therefore, the characteristics of the indirect approach.
But the strategic air offensive is indirect only by definition
--only when the military forces of the enemy are defined as
the objective. Air force strategists, however, do not
believe that the defeat of the latter is essential to
victory. They assert that the object of all military action
is the enemy's will to war.

To the airman, no form of attack is more direct than
air attack. J.M. Spraight defines it as follows:

> Now, for the first time in history, it has become
> possible to dispense with the preliminary

> stage. Air power can strike straight at the heart
> of the enemy....It can ignore armies and fleet...
> it can plunge in medias res and begin where the
> old warfare all but left off....It will cut out
> certain stages in the older method of approach
> to the real end of war--the imposing of one
> nation's will upon another.[69]

To the air strategist, military forces are intermediate
objectives, protective armor covering vital centers, shields
deflecting attack from the target. Other forms of military
attack strike at the shell of the enemy's strength; air
power strikes directly at the heart.[70]

Before the development of the bomber, it was necessary
to eliminate the enemy's army and navy. Decisive defeat in
battle would then expose the enemy's guts. Usually, therefore,
the issue was decided in the field. Once the armed forces
were destroyed, the foe would yield. But the development
of air power opened revolutionary possibilities. One could
now kill the enemy without striking down his shield.

The term "direct approach" is a variable; it is not
an absolute. It expresses the contradictory interpretations
and conflicting perspectives of rival organizations. It is
a relationship between means and end, technique and
objective. Indeed, the term is undefinable without its
objective. For only then does it conceptualize a means,
unintelligible without an end.

Does the direct approach have any preconceptual
center beneath the flow of interpretation? Unlike the
defensive-offensive complex, there is no invariable at
the heart of this strategic belief. Whatever consistency
it has lies in its compulsive drive. American strategic
planners felt compelled to seek and apply the direct
approach to strategy. Yet there seems to be nothing
inherently compelling about it. The direct approach
remains basically a concept, occasionally endowed with
preconceptual force. As we shall see, its compulsive
power comes from another strategic belief.

Chapter IV

Concepts and Preconceptions: The Autonomy of War

1. The Indictment and the Problem of American Military-Civil
    Relations

The ultimate aim of military action, direct or indirect,
is the imposition of one's will upon the foe. But military
objectives are merely means to an ultimate, political end.
War is, by Clausewitz's definition, "a continuation of policy
by other means."[1]

According to many critics, American policy makers failed
to remember this dictum. The United States was politically
blind; it failed to use military force for the achievement of
its policy objectives. The United States, they assert, treated
war an autonomous, unrelated to political pursuits. According
to Hanson Baldwin:

> The United States has fought wars differently from
> other people. We have fought for the immediate
> victory, not for the ultimate peace. Unlike the
> British or the Russians, we have had no grand design,
> no over-all concept. This lack of a well-defined
> political objective to chart our military action
> has distinguished...much of our past....The British
> and the Russians [in World War II] thought and
> fought in terms of the big picture, the world after
> the war; we thought and fought in terms of what we
> could do to lick Germany and Japan now.[2]

This failure reflected America's political immaturity: "We
fought to win--period. We did not remember that wars are merely
an extension of politics by other means; that wars have
objectives...."[3]

Chester Wilmot characterizes the American belief in the
autonomy of war more closely:

> The United States...should seek no national advantage
> or aggrandisement. Her sole purpose should be to bring
> about the defeat and punishment of the aggressor. Her
> aim should be Victory, nothing else. Since America
> fights for no political objective, except peace, no
> political directions should be given to American
> commanders in the field. They should be completely
> free to determine their strategy on military grounds
> alone, and the supreme military consideration is to
> bring hostilities to an end. To pursue a political
> aim is to practice imperialism.[4]

General Albert C. Wedemeyer, a politically sophisticated
wartime planner, is impartially damning: he blasts both the
British and the American conduct of the war:

> Stalin who had his own blueprint for Europe...knew
> exactly what he was fighting for....
> One looks in vain for any comparable projected
> thinking or preparing for war's end on the part of
> Churchill or Roosevelt....But sound and victorious
> strategy can never be devised unless a clearly
> defined aim or objective is laid down to provide
> purpose and direction. One can destroy an enemy
> or break his will to resist by military victories.
> But in Grand Strategy one must look beyond the
> military victory.[5]

The critics agree, therefore, that American strategy was
vitiated by the absence of any grand design relating military
means to political ends. War became the be-all and the end-all,
autonomous, self-sufficient. But the burden of proof rests
with the critics. To criticize the conduct of the war, one
must offer an alternative design relating strategy and policy.
Unhappily, sporadic criticims are more apparent than any
clear-cut blueprint. By organizing these fragments, however,
we can discern the goal and the means.

Baldwin, Wilmot and Wedemeyer agree that the main Allied
goal should have been to restore the "European balance of power"
by containing the Soviet Union. The Allies should have driven
as far east as possible, thereby protecting Central Europe,
possibly Eastern Europe, from the Russians.[6] Although the
critics agree on the aim, they disagree sharply on the means.
Wilmot and Baldwin feel that the Western Allies should have
invaded Europe from the south (in conjunction with, or in place
of, the invasion from the north).[7] Wedemeyer feels that the
Allies should have concentrated exclusively on the cross-channel
operation, thereby effecting OVERLORD in 1943, possibly 1942.
An earlier OVERLORD would have meant a speedier defeat of
Germany; presumably, it would have led to the liberation of
Central and Eastern Europe by the Allies rather than the
U.S.S.R.[8] Following this grand design, the Allies could have
occupied positions of strength against the Soviet Union.
By drawing a new cordon sanitaire around Russia, the Allies
could have restored the balance of power in Europe. The

military aim, the defeat of the German armed forces, would
have been subordinated to the political objective: containment
of the U.S.S.R.

The main animus of the critics is directed against the
belief in the autonomy of war. This belief can now be defined
in its positive and negative aspects. It teaches that the end
of war is the defeat of the enemy's armed forces and warns that
the pursuit of political objectives will divert and dissipate
military forces, complicating the accomplishment of legitimate
military aims. It illuminates the main but narrow road to
success while denouncing side roads as blind alleys leading
to disaster. A purely military strategy follows a single end,
avoiding the dispersion of multiple aims. It reflects the
principle of concentration while bypassing the dangers of
dispersion. Essentially, therefore, this concept segregates
war and peace, strategy and policy, into separate realms.
One begins where the other ends. Until the declaration of
war, policy prevails. Then strategy seizes control until
the enemy is thoroughly defeated. Strategy and policy
occupy different realms of thought and time.

The autonomy of war is a single concept produced within a
political-military context. To understand its impact on
American strategy in World War II, one must understand the
ways in which military and civilian thinking coalesced. One
must also understand the attitudes of soldiers and statesmen
towards the relation of military and civilian responsibilities.

The soldier's attitude was paradoxical, almost dualistic.
He acknowledged the preeminence of political considerations
while asserting the independence of the military. Therefore,
American generals easily accepted the Clausewitzean formula.
Eisenhower, discussing TORCH, admitted "that political
considerations can never be wholly separated from military ones
and that war is a mere continuation of political policy in the
field of force."[9] Yet, when discussing the final drive into
Germany, Eisenhower also asserted the independence of military
planning: "The future division of Germany did not influence
our military plans for the final conquest of the country.
Military plans, I believed, should be devised with the
single aim of speeding victory."[10]

As Supreme Commander, Eisenhower felt the impact of
policy upon strategy. Although he geared his plans to
military objectives, he could not always escape the political
implications of his planning. General Omar Bradley,
responsible only for field operations could take a purist view:
"As soldiers we looked naively on the British inclination
to complicate the war with political foresight and non-military
objectives."[11]

Bred in the tradition of civilian supremacy, no soldier
could dispute the axiom that war is a continuation of national
policy. The political leaders must establish the ultimate
goals for which the nation fights. However, once these goals
are set, the civilian's task ends and the soldier's begins.

> "Politics and strategy," said a Command and General
> Staff School publication in 1936, "are radically
> and fundamentally things apart....All that soldiers
> ask is that once the policy is settled, strategy and
> command shall be regarded as being in a sphere apart
> from politics....The line of demarcation must be
> drawn between politics and strategy, supply and
> operations. Having found this line, all sides must
> abstain from trespassing.[12]

Politics was for politicans; soldiering, for soldiers.
The soldier acknowledged the goals of national policy as his
objectives. But the planning of operations, the tactical deployment
of his forces in the field, were strictly military matters.
In the field of strategy, political considerations should be
eschewed. Moreover, the duty of the soldier was to defend
military plans against political complications. His job was
to defend the integrity of his sphere. The soldier strongly
resented and resisted frequent and detailed political control
over the movement and direction of his forces on the
battlefield.

The soldier would accept generalized directives, but balk,
though he knew he had to obey, detailed instructions from
his civilian superiors, setting specific objectives for his
forces. To the military leader, the main aim of any course
of action was to secure victory as rapidly and effectively
as possible. The true end was to check, defeat or destroy
the enemy's armed forces.

The soldier's attitude, as opposed to the politician's
preference, was epitomized by his aversion for prestige

prizes such as large cities. His real objective was the
enemy's centers of resistance. Prestige objectives were dangerous
temptations leading away from the main target. Armies
were vanquished, wars lost when military forces were diverted.
So the tactical deployment of armies should seek the
destruction of the enemy's army, not the occupation of his
land. Territorial objectives were significant only if they
brought the enemy into battle.

The soldier knew, however, that the politician was more
vulnerable to the temptations of prestige. Famous cities were
attractive prizes. Their seizure easily redounded to the credit
of the national leadership. Public opinion would naturally
identify success and failure in military operations with territorial advance and retreat. A territorial prize could be useful
to the politician while meaningless to the soldier.

Obviously, this difference is interwoven with ambiguity.
The problem of determining the limits of political intervention
remains. For example, a capital city may represent a dual
objective: political and military. Its political importance
may serve a military purpose, drawing the enemy's forces into
battle. Moscow is an obvious example. In World War II, the
Russian capital was the vital center of the country. As
Field Marshal von Kluge said:

> "Moscow is both the head and the heart of the Soviet
> system. Besides being the capital, it is also an
> important armaments center. It is in addition the focal
> junction of the Russian rail network, particularly
> for those that lead to Siberia. The Russians are
> bound to throw in strong forces to prevent our
> capture of the capital."[13]

Other important cities, however, are prestige prizes with no
military significance. To the soldier, therefore, they
represent mere dots on the map.

Nevertheless, their political importance remains, and the
problem of interference often arises. This type of intervention
requires meddling with military plans. Although interference
may be justified by the policy aims of the state, it threatens
the independence of the military sphere. It is a repeated
source of conflict between military and civilian authority.
In each case, the question must be resolved: Do political
considerations override military judgment? Obviously, no

set rule fits. Each case must be resolved independently.

History yields many cases where the pursuit of political objectives had hampered or defeated military planning. World War II provides three particularly illustrative cases: the Battle of Stalingrad and the liberations of Rome and Paris.

2. Case Histories: the Pursuit of False Objectives

In the winter of 1942, Stalingrad became a magnet, a prestige objective which lured and trapped the German Sixth Army into total destruction.[14]Believing that all military problems could be resolved, all obstacles overcome, by the forceful application of will power,[15]Hitler brushed aside the logic of his military advisers. His eyes fastened on a single prize. Blinded by one piece in the strategic puzzle, he ignored its context. After the Russians surrounded the Sixth Army, military reasoning demanded their immediate breakout and relief, and the abandonment of the offensive. But Hitler refused to retreat: "'I won't leave the Volga! I won't go back from the Volga!'" Only the "toadies" at headquarters, (Keitel, Jodl and fatuous Field Marshal Goering), thought the position tenable. Manstein and Zeitler, the Chief of Staff of the Army,[17]urged him, both before the encirclement and after, to withdraw. But all the arguments of military strategy, all the dangers of the emergency, could not free Hitler from the lure of Stalin's city.[18]

Even military commanders are not immune to these temptations. In Operation DIADEM, General Mark Clark, Commander of the United States Fifth Army, was drawn by one of the world's sumptuous prizes: Rome.[19]General Alexander, Clark's superior, had a master plan for the Battle of Cassino, a plan primed for the destruction of the German Tenth Army which was blocking the Allied advance along the west coast of Italy. A frontal assault by the two Allied armies (the British Eighth in the Liri Valley and the American Fifth on the west coast) would release the reinforced VI Corps, then confined to the Anzio Beachhead. The VI Corps would break out and flank the German position, a maneuver which could turn the Allied advance into a decisive battle of annihilation. The VI Corps breakout

would disorganize and possibly stampede the Tenth Army, already
retreating under the blows of the Fifth and the Eighth Armies.
Then, by driving from Valmontane on Highway 6, the Corps could
sever the German's main line of retreat. From Valmontane it
could drive to Tivoli, spread along the lateral highway
towards the Adriatic and thereby trap the German Tenth Army.[20]

But General Clark doubted the feasibility of this plan. He
was determined to maintain flexibility: "...I did not want
to have to follow any rigid, preconceived ideas on the
breakout...."[21] Clark also feared that Alexander's plan would
deprive the Fifth Army of its legitimate reward. The American
general was hell-bent for Rome:

> We had massed all our strength to take Rome; We
> were keyed up....We not only wanted the honor of
> capturing Rome, but we felt that we more than
> deserved it; that it would to a certain extent
> make up for the buffeting and frustration we had
> undergone in keeping up the winter pressure against
> the Germans....Not only did we intend to become the
> first army in fifteen centuries to seize Rome from
> the south, but we intended to see that the people
> back home knew that it was the Fifth Army that did
> the job and knew the price that had been paid for it.[22]

This motive was reinforced by Clark's knowledge that time was
running out. Eisenhower's invasion of Europe was imminent;
soon the Mediterranean would become a secondary theater:
"...we wanted Rome prior to the beginning of Eisenhower's
invasion of France."[23]

The Allied forces broke through the enemy lines around
Cassino; the VI Corps erupted from the Anzio Beachhead.
German resistance crumbled. Yet the trap never closed: the
Tenth Army escaped. For General Mark Clark was unable to
resist the drive of his dream.

Other American generals religiously eschewed capital
cities. Sometimes their profound scruples were unavailing.
They had to make a political decision. But then they rationalized
their actions in non-political terms. General Eisenhower
and General Bradley were as anxious to avoid seizing Paris[24]
as Clark was anxious to capture Rome. In his memoirs,
Bradley comments on the problems which the liberation of
Paris would pose to the Allied advance:

> To a generation raised on fanciful tales of their
> fathers in the AEF, Paris beckoned with greater
> allure than any other objective in Europe. Yet
> tactically the city had become meaningless. For
> all its past glories, Paris represented nothing
> more than an inkspot on our maps to be by-passed as
> we headed towards the Rhine. Logistically it would
> cause untold trouble, for behind its handsome facades
> there lived 4,000,000 hungry Frenchmen....Food for
> the people of Paris meant less gasoline for the front. [25]

Good soldiers, Eisenhower and Bradley, were determined to stick
to the professional ethic.

Tactically the city was dangerous. Assaulted frontally,
it would provide the Germans with an excellent base for a
counteroffensive. Street to street fighting would involve
high casualties and considerable delay. It would also mean the
almost certain destruction of the city.[26] Logistically, the cost
of supplying the French capital would be prohibitive: it would
require 4,000 tons per day, a diversion which would weaken the
drive on Germany. Since the Allied commanders felt victory
was imminent, Paris could wait for its liberation.[27]

Military reasoning was reinforced by political considerations.
The premature liberation of Paris might reinforce the claims
of that difficult ally, General de Gaulle. Since he had
proclaimed that his National Committee of Liberation was the
provisional government of France, his triumphant entry into
Paris would solidify his control. But President Roosevelt
was determined to oppose any French government which was not
freely supported by the French people. Under these circumstances,
the liberation of Paris by Allied forces, which included de
Gaulle's military units, could seriously complicate U.S. policy.[28]

But Paris was the chief objective of the French leaders.
It was the center of France: "...Paris was the only place
from which the country could be effectively governed."[29]
Control of the capital would mean control of the country.
De Gaulle and his adherents were, therefore, intent on its
early liberation by French units operating with the Allied
armies. Any other liberation would be dangerous. For a premature
but successful insurrection, incited and led by Communist
leaders, might propel de Gaulle's left-wing opponents
into power.[30]

Ultimately, Eisenhower's hand was forced by the French

underground. On August 19, 1944, the French Forces of the
Interior rose in insurrection, seizing important sectors of
Paris. De Gaulle and Leclerc, Commander of the French 2nd
Armored Division, immediately pressed Eisenhower to direct his
forces towards the French capital.[31] Until August 21, Eisenhower
stood firm, still determined to bypass Paris.[32] Leclerc's
pleas also failed to move his immediate superior General
Gerow, Commander of the Fifth Corps.[33]

Finally, on August 22, Eisenhower decided to divert Allied
forces towards the French capital. His military objections
were weakened when he realized that von Choltitz, the German
commander of the city, had decided against a street
by street, defense of the city.[34] The prestige of the prize,
the gratification of the French, the maintenance of public order
throughout the capital, the seizure of the Seine bridges might
seem sufficiently compelling.[35] But Eisenhower needed a clear
military reason. He found it. His forces would reinforce
the F.F.I. units already in action in Paris: "Reinforcement,
a legitimate military action, thus, in Eisenhower's mind,
transferred the liberation of Paris from the political to the
military realm and made it acceptable."[36]

Logistically, the consequences of liberating Paris were
unfortunate. As foreseen, it added another burden on the
already overstrained supply lines stretching from the Normandy
beachheads to the Allied front. It helped to slow the
momentum of the drive towards Germany[37] and may have prolonged
the war. However, it is hard to believe that the Allies could
have indefinitely postponed the liberation of the French capital.

The attitude of military men towards political objectives
is understandable. Political objectives complicate military
planning. They threaten the principle of concentration and
lead to diversion and dispersal. In our first case, political
authority overbore military judgment; in our second, a military
commander, under no political direction, was lured by a prestige
objective; in our third, a professional made an essentially
political decision while justifying it on military grounds.
In the battle of Stalingrad, an army was lost; in the liberation
of Rome, an army escaped; in the liberation of Paris, the

pursuit of a defeated army slackened and stalled.

Since the soldier subscribes to the supremacy of civilian authority, since he concedes that strategy is subordinate to policy, control ultimately belongs to the civilian. Theoretically, in the United States, there is no limit to this power. Constitutionally sustained, ideologically justifiable, the principle of civilian supremacy is entrenched in the structure of the American government. It is beyond debate. Therefore, civilian leadership has the unqualified right to use military force for political purposes. In peacetime, it can restrain, harass, frustrate, even obliterate the military establishment.[38] In wartime, it must forego these exercises. More than forego, it must abjure. Until the Korean War, this potentially unlimited control over the conduct of operations was seldom exerted after the outbreak of hostilities. Surprisingly, civilian leadership was extraordinarily permissive.[39]

3. The President as Commander in Chief: Franklin Delano
   Roosevelt

Civilian leadership centers around the President, Commander in Chief of the armed forces. Although he combines civilian and military leadership, the President almost invariably looks at military affairs from the civilian point of view.[40] Moreover, once war is declared, his powers as Commander in Chief are virtually unlimited. Although he depends largely on legislative support, Congress has seldom challenged, since the Civil War, either his authority or his demands. Necessity and patriotism confirm his power. The President, therefore, has unlimited opportunities to intervene in the conduct of military affairs. And he can defend his prerogative easily by citing the Constitution: "The President shall be Commander in Chief of the Army and the Navy of the United States, and of the Militia of the several states when called into the actual service of the United States...." There it is. Theoretically, the President can conduct field operations, draw up military plans and persistently overrule the advice of his soldiers.[41] No president was more conscious of the uses of power than F.D.R. Moreover, no president was more intent on defending his authority against either usurpation by Congress or

depletion by delegation to his own subordinates. Roosevelt
applied the principle of divide and conquer to the management
of administration. He delegated powers on a wide scale,
exposing himself to advice from multitudinous sources. His
control was exerted through five techniques which enabled him
to establish and maintain direction indirectly. His relationship with the War Department typified his approach.

First, he maintained liaison with subordinate officials,
often by-passing, and sometimes not even notifying, the chief of
the government bureau or department. For example, he undercut
his Secretary of War, Henry Woodring, an isolationist, to deal
with the Assistant Secretary, Louis Johnson, whose views on
military affairs and national policy were similar to his own.[42]
And, although Woodring's successor, Henry L. Stimson, was the
President's trusted adviser, Roosevelt largely by-passed him
on questions of strategic policy. He preferred to deal directly
with the Army Chief of Staff, General Marshall. He refused
to conform to hierarchical protocol. This attitude was
the despair of Secretary Stimson: "...the President is the
poorest administrator I have ever worked under in respect to
the orderly procedure and routine of his performance."[43]

In his Military Order of July 1939, F.D.R. legalized and
institutionalized his direct command over his chief military
and production advisers. This order "transferred the Joint
Army and Navy Board, the Joint Army-Navy Munitions Board, and
several other military procurement agencies from the service
departments into the newly-established Executive Office of
the President."[44] Through this order, F.D.R. by-passed the
heads of the War and Navy Departments.[45]

Second, he sometimes transferred authority over military
programs from the War Department, where it logically belonged,
to other departments. For the 1938-1939 negotiations over
French purchases of American planes and for the 1939 dealings
with the Anglo-French Purchasing Mission, Roosevelt utilized
the Treasury Department. Since the War Department was
headed by an avid isolationist, the President called on
Secretary Morgenthau, an Administration supporter of full-scale
aid to the Allies.[46]

Third, Roosevelt utilized informal advisers, particularly Harry Hopkins. He ran an unacknowledged, unorganized and seldom coordinated Kitchen Cabinet. Although Hopkins held a number of positions in the Federal Government, his role as presidential adviser on military and diplomatic affairs was paramount. Until his illness in 1944, he played a crucial role in most of the important military and diplomatic decisions of the Roosevelt administration. Moreover, he was an invaluable contact for clamorous claimants, anxious to present their schemes to the President.[47]

Fourth, in his dealings with foreign governments, Roosevelt took personal control. A fervent proponent of personal diplomacy, he dealt directly with Churchill, Stalin and Chiang Kai-shek, (sometimes making commitments and reaching agreements without consulting, or even informing, his political and military advisers).[48]

Finally, he maintained liaison with subordinate civil and military officials far down the hierarchical ladder. He maintained listening posts on several levels of the organization, never totally trusting a single source or channel of information.[49]

Roosevelt, therefore, seldom delegated power into single hands and seldom followed the established lines of hierarchical prerogative. He used multiple organizations to handle single questions, creating divided and often conflicting kingdoms within a single administrative province. This fragmentation of delegated authority was chaotic, but not without purpose. It was administrative anarchy deliberately nurtured. It obviously suited the President's temperament, his impatience with tidy methods sanctified by custom and tradition, his taste for experimentation and for starting multiple projects moving in the same direction to see which would work and which would not. But it also exposed him to numerous viewpoints. Although it created confusion and intensified factional and jurisdictional quarrels within his administration, it kept control strictly within his hands. It freed him from any exclusive reliance upon any departmental viewpoint, allowing him the final choice between alternatives.[50]

Franklin Roosevelt was keenly aware of his prerogatives
as Commander in Chief and anxious to assert them. His experience
as Assistant Secretary of the Navy convinced him of the
necessity for strong civilian control.[51] In World War II,
he exercised his powers repeatedly. Although some historians
and participants have contrasted President Roosevelt to
Prime Minister Churchill, describing the President as an
almost consistent supporter of the military's views and
plans, and Churchill as the constant meddler,[52] analysis
will not sustain their judgment.[53]

Analysis will show that throughout the Roosevelt Administration,
military leaders operated within the political guidelines set by
the national policy of the United States. From the pre-war
period, when the President kept a tight reign on military
planning, to the closing period of permissiveness, when
soldiers made command decisions normally reserved for political
leaders, military policy developed within the goals set by
American diplomacy. Moreover, the relations between the
President and his Chiefs were established in the years immediately
preceding the Pearl Harbor attack, and were confirmed and
strengthened in the first two years of the war when Roosevelt
educated them to the political objectives of his administration.
The conduct of military strategy became increasingly autonomous
in 1944-1945, but this autonomy harmonized with the Administration's
political objectives.

For the civilian and military leaders of the United
States, the autonomy of war was not an infallible dogma, a
preconception blindly and automatically followed. Despite
the critics, the dogmas of American civil-military relations
were apposite. They stressed the subordination of the military
to civilian authority, the use of military power to achieve
the foreign policy objectives of the nation. In World War II,
the autonomy of war was a strategic concept produced and
maintained by a fortuitous conjunction between political and
military thought. Both the political and military planners
accepted the Clausewitzean dictum on the relation between
strategy and policy; but after 1943 the policy envisioned by

the President could be most easily attained by allowing
the military to conduct their operations with maximum
freedom. The soldier was free to fasten his attention
exclusively on military objectives. After all, the relation
between strategy and policy was the province of the statesman,
not the soldier. Although war was never autonomous, never
separated from political considerations, the soldiers's job
was to plan and conduct it as though it were. Only his civilian
superior could, and should, overrule, contradict, or guide
him in another direction. Even for the military, the
autonomy of war was a concept limited by an overriding
context.

Chapter V

Concepts and Preconceptions: the Righteous War

1. The Indictment

Besides flaying the United States for its failure to correlate policy and strategy, the critics assail American leadership for waging war as a crusade. The two "errors" are complementary. To Americans, war was neither a continuation of policy by other means, nor the pursuit of realistic objectives. It was a crusade fought for a distant goal:

> One cannot achieve any purpose worth the terrible sacrifice of blood and treasure, as well as the demoralization experienced by victors and vanquished alike, if war is engaged in either as a game or a crusade against a mythical 'power of darkness' symbolized by the person of the enemy. War can only be justified as a last resort to attain concrete, clearly envisaged, legitimate or vital national aims which have been proved unrealizable by other means.[1]

According to General Wedemeyer, therefore, the failure to secure peace at the end of World War II was inevitable. Instead of pursuing an attainable political objective, the United States strove to achieve the impossible.

A more scholarly critic, Professor Samuel H. Huntington, relates this crusading fervor to American pacificism:

> The crusading approach to war has not been incompatible with pacificism. It is a common observation that American nationalism has been an idealistic nationalism, justified...by the assertion of the superiority of American ideals over other ideals....American idealism has tended to make every war a crusade, fought not for specific objectives of national security, but on behalf of universal principles such as democracy, freedom of the seas, and self-determination. Indeed for the American a war is not a war unless it is a crusade.... The tendency to swing from one extreme to another has a self-perpetuating quality. War aims phrased in sweeping ideological terms are seldom capable of achievement. Consequently, war is normally followed by a period of disillusionment....Emphasis [is] ...put upon eliminating war or finding a substitute

for war....Eventually, when these techniques fail
to safeguard the national interests, disillusionment
with liberal pacifism sets in, national interests
are rationalized in terms of new ideological goals
and enthusiasm mounts for a new crusade.[2]

2. The Righteous War: Definition

    a. Its Dual Nature

The critics' definition, however, is unsatisfactory. It
names a dogma without analyzing it. Treating it as an entity,
it ignores its components. Actually the doctrine of the
crusade is part of a greater whole. Its complement is the
doctrine of the just war. These two interact to form our
fourth strategic belief: the righteous war.

In essence, the righteous war is the moral correlative
of the defensive-offensive complex. A just war is primarily
defensive; a crusade, offensive. The nation waging a just war
renounces aggression and rejects the aggrandizement of power
through conquest,[3] fighting in self-defense against destruction.

But the doctrine of the just war is not static. In a
total conflict, it inevitably escalates into a crusade. For
then a nation fights not only to defend its existence, but
also to preserve its national ideals, ideals cast in universal
principles. So a war fought to preserve one nation becomes a
war to preserve all nations; a war in defense of self-interest
becomes a war to defend universal principles. Therefore, it
cannot remain defensive. A nation committed to a universalist
ideology passes naturally from the defensive to the offensive,
from a just war to a crusade. Final defense of universal
values lies in the destruction of the threatening foe and the
creation of a new world, purged of former danger. It lies in
the triumph, not the mere preservation, of ideology. A just
war, therefore, becomes a metaphysical struggle, a duel
between the forces of light and darkness.

    b. Its Dual Function: Instrument and Mirror

The righteous war is dual in function as well as in
nature, serving a pragmatic and an ideological end. It is
mirror and instrument, reflector and tool.

Instrumentally it plays a crucial role in the waging of
total war since all national resources must be mobilized.

Psychological commitment becomes as crucial as military, political
or economic mobilization. Ultimately, it depends on a government's ability to justify its declaration of war, to convince
the nation of the justice of its cause. The self-interest
of individuals must be identified with that of the nation.
Obviously, the intensity of this identification depends on
the extent to which individuals normally identify themselves
with their country and their government. If civil discord is
widespread, if the government is intensely unpopular, the
identification will be tenuous. If the government is popular
and civil harmony is widespread, it will be enduring. The
just war doctrine usually portrays the nation and its people
as victims of aggression, actual or potential, present or
future. War, therefore, is not fought merely for the interests
of the government or its power cliques; it is fought for
the interests of the entire nation. It is a war for the
people and of the people which must ultimately be fought
by the people. It is a just war.

But a nation waging total war does not restrict its
appeal to its own public. It also appeals to the opinions
of mankind. Of course, this appeal may be restricted. A
nation may merely justify its declaration of war as an act
of pure self-defense, proclaiming its "innocence" before the
bar of world opinion. But the crusade doctrine, making a
greater claim, has a wider appeal. Seeking actively to
mobilize world opinion, to bind together an allied coalition
and to attract the support of neutral powers, it exalts the
nation as the champion of universal principles. Whereas
the just war doctrine portrays the nation as the victim of
aggression, the crusade portrays it as the defender of
humanity.

Ultimately, these two appeals reinforce one another by
mobilizing two audiences. The just war courts world as well
as domestic public opinion; the crusade inflames the nation
while cementing the coalition.

But the belief in a righteous war is a mirror as well
as an instrument. A nation waging a just war does not merely
defend its existence, it defends its way of life, the values
of its society. These values, therefore, become indistinguishable

from the survival of the nation. Since its ideology holds two
basic premises, the equality of man and the universal desire
for freedom, this identification is natural for a democracy.
First, the belief that all men are created equal is axiomatically
applicable to all individuals, races and nations of mankind.
Second, all men desire, need and deserve freedom.

This ideology defines and defends the rights of man:
the freedom to choose and elect, the right of self-determination.
The ultimate justification of a democratic cause lies in
its universal claim.

Although totalitarian nations do not necessarily assume
that their aspirations are identical to those of other nations,
they also cast their ideology in universal terms. Only a national
leader can make this appeal, converting a just war into a
crusade. Every righteous war needs an Urban II to proclaim
it, mobilizing the passionate fury of the masses against the
immoral foe. Whether in a democracy or in a totalitarian
state, the process is basically the same.

3. Process of Justification: Totalitarian Nations

    a. Nazi Germany: The Perverted Crusade

The Nazis waged an ideological war. To the Nazi fanatic,
this crusade, waged against inferior races and cultures, provided
its own justification. For Nazi Germany could not use the
doctrine of the just war as a point of departure. Her vital
interests were neither threatened nor thwarted. Since justification couldn't be based on self-defense, it was founded on
the Nazi Weltanschauung or world view which taught that war
was part of the natural order of the universe.

To Hitler war was a synonym for life: "'...war is the
most natural, the most every-day matter. War is eternal, war
is universal. There is no beginning and there is no peace.
War is life. Any struggle is war. War is the origin of all
things.'"[4] To live is to struggle, for all nature and all
nations are governed by a Darwinian fight for survival:
"'...life is a cruel struggle, and has no other object but
the preservation of the species.'"[5] In this perpetual conflict,
the elite (the natural aristocracy of superior species, races,
nations and men) emerge: "'The law of selection justifies

this incessant struggle, by allowing the survival of the fittest.'"[6] War is natural; peace is artificial and destructive: "Mankind has grown strong in eternal struggle and it will only perish through eternal peace."[7]

If all nature forms a single battlefield, if peace is a delusion and war the only reality, then every nation is threatened with extermination. Agression is justified by the natural order. Since it is a form of self-defense, the right to attack is a natural right of the strong: "All passivity, all inertia...is senseless, inimical to life. From this proceeds the divine right of destroying all who are inert.'"[8]

Hitler saw this war as a Manichaean struggle between the forces of good and evil. To the Führer the only valid moral distinction was between strength and weakness, superiority and inferiority. His world view was dominated by two figures: one heroic, the other Satanic: the Aryan and the Jew. The Aryan is the "culture founder":[9]

> ...he alone was the founder of higher humanity as a whole, thus the prototype of what we understand by the word 'man'. He is the Promethus of mankind, out of whose bright forehead springs the divine spark of genius at all times, forever rekindling that fire which in the form of knowledge lightened up the night of silent secrets and thus made man climb the path towards the position of master of the other beings on this earth. Exclude him--and deep darkness will again fall upon the earth, perhaps even, after a few thousand years, human culture would perish and the world would turn into a desert.[10]

Because of his natural superiority, he subjugates and enslaves his inferiors.[11] And, because of his creative nature, he alone can build and maintain a State.[12]

If the Aryan is the savior, the creator, the hero, the Jew is his eternal opponent. The Jew is the "culture destroyer,"[13] the "very principle of evil."[14] If the Aryan is godlike, "The Jew is the anti-man, the creature of another god. He must have come from another root of the human race.... The two are as widely departed as man and beast....He (the Jew) is a creature outside nature and alien to nature."[15]

His wickedness inflames his insatiable ambition. For "...the implacable world Jew is struggling for domination over the nations. No nation can dislodge this fist from its throat except by the sword."[16] But though the Jew seeks domination, he can never maintain it. He can only destroy. The Jew is the "ferment of decomposition."[17] He is capable of revolution, not evolution; of disunion, not order. He can destroy a state, not create it.

Hitler always depicted his Jewish enemy in envenomed language, steeped in the imagery of disease, disintegration and destruction. The Jew is compared to wild predatory animals: "the hyena,"[18] the wolf,[19] the rat,[20] the vampire.[21] He is also depicted as a "pestilence, spiritual pestilence...worse than the Black Death."[22] The Jew is a disease carrier: a "germ carrier of the worst sort" who "poisons the minds of the world."[23] His race is the "eternal fission-fungus [sic] of mankind."[24] Jews are "poison mongers,"[25] parasites "in the body of other people."[26] Like a virus[27] or bacillus,[28] the Jew spreads infection through racial pollution infesting the racially pure.[29]

Like Captain Ahab who saw Moby Dick as the incarnation of all evil, Hitler envisioned the Jew as the Satanic master of the forces of darkness and decline. Since the Jew is the master conspirator constantly at war with the Aryan, seeking to subvert and destroy civilization, no peace is possible, no justification for war necessary. The Aryan is already under attack, and any action he now takes will be defensive.

Hitler's Manichaean vision inevitably led to the crusade. And Hitler saw this crusade on four complementary levels: as a national struggle, as a racial battle, as an ideological conflict and finally as a strife between civilizations: East against West.

On the first level, it is a struggle for _Lebensraum_, living space. This need is essentially linked to the struggle for survival among nations:

> Only nations living independently in their own
> space and capable of military defense can be world
> powers....This is why I must gain space for Germany,
> space big enough to enable us to defend ourselves
> against any military coalition. In peace-time we
> can manage. But in war the important thing is
> freedom of action, for in war one is mortally
> dependent on the outside world. Our dependence
> on foreign trade without even an ocean coastline
> would condemn us eternally to the position of a
> politically dependent nation.[30]

On the second level, Hitler's crusade is directed against the Jewish world conspiracy: "Jewish World Bolshevism."[31] It is a conflict between the Aryan and the Jew, between the Herrenvolk and the Untermensch: "'The struggle for world domination will be fought entirely between us, between Germans and Jews.... Even when we have driven the Jew out of Germany, he remains our world enemy.'"[32]

On the third level, it is an ideological struggle: Marxism versus National Socialism. To Hitler the great enemy on the world stage is Bolshevism, for behind Bolshevism stand the organized forces of Judaism. Therefore, "...the question of the future of the German nation is the question of the destruction of Marxism."[33] As he had saved Germany from a Communist revolution, Hitler would save Europe from Bolshevism.[34]

Finally, Hitler envisioned Germany as the defender of Europe against Asiatic Russia. Germany has, he declared on September 3, 1933, "a truly European mission."[35] The Drang nach Osten becomes a sacred mission which must be fulfilled if Europe is to be saved:

> "Asia, what a disquieting reservoir of men! The
> safety of Europe will not be assured until we have
> driven Asia back behind the Urals....They are brutes,
> and neither Bolshevism nor Tsarism makes any difference
> --they are brutes in a state of nature. The danger
> would be still greater if this space were to be
> mongolized....
> Since there is no natural protection against such
> a flood, we must meet it with a living wall. A
> permanent state of war on the Eastern front will help
> to form a sound race of men and will prevent us from
> relapsing into the softness of a Europe thrown back
> upon itself."[36]

The ideological struggle falls to second place. Only the battle between two alien civilizations remains paramount.

To corroborate his world view and to justify his course of action to his fellow citizens, Hitler could evoke the tragedy of recent German history: the defeat of World War I, the humiliation of Versailles, the savage reparation payments. Hitler's argument was simple: the "November criminals", who engineered the revolution of 1918 and the collapse of the Second Reich, and the Allies combined their force to impose a humiliating peace under the subterfuge of the Fourteen Points.[37]

Then, in the post-war period, they exploited Germany, undermining her from within, encircling her from without.[38]This
collaboration was predictable. For the domestic and the foreign
enemy were the agents of a master conspirator: the Jew, the
Great Destroyer. For this enemy moved every force, manipulated
every agent. Those who were not his conscious tools were his
dupes.[39]Mobilizing the grievances and agonies of contemporary
events, Hitler could exhort his public: Germany was under
attack, in danger of destruction. Posing as Germany's savior,
he could claim that his aggressive moves were merely measures
of self-defense.

Most revolutionary movements seek power as a means to an
end, as a necessary condition for the achievement of other aims
and dreams. A crusade seeks to revolutionize the relations
between nations, to remold international society. Superficially,
National Socialism seems to conform to this pattern: to aim
at the establishment of a new world.

But beneath the Nazi crusade lay a more powerful and
irrational drive. Unlike most revolutionary movements,
National Socialism sought power and mastery for their own sake,
exalting force and brutality as desirable in themselves. Its
Weltanschauung was merely a mask for an elemental lust for
supremacy.

National Socialism never lost its genetic traits. It
always remained a political philosophy expressing the aims
of a group struggling for power. It never converted itself
into a political philosophy suited to the long-range maintenance
of power. Its essence was the exaltation of struggle and
domination. As long as the National Socialist party was merely
one party struggling among many, as long as the Nazi state
was merely one nation contending with other nations, the
philosophy of the survival of the fittest fitted the circumstances of the moment. But if the master nation had triumphed,
if the perverted crusade had ended in victory, the problem of
maintaining this selective process under artificial conditions
would have arisen. For a crusade seeking merely the wholesale
destruction or enslavement of its opponents is suited to war,
not to peace. The National Socialist Weltanschauung bore the

seeds of its own dissolution. Basically, therefore, the Nazi crusade remained a nihilistic adventure, haunted by the alternatives of domination or annihilation. It remained an apocalypse without resurrection, a nightmare without awakening.[40] In the face of his enemy, Hitler saw a reflection of the anarchy of dissolution that dominated his own world.

  b. Soviet Russia: The Suppressed Crusade

For Nazi Germany the crusade was primary; the just war, secondary. For the U.S.S.R., the appeal to the just war was predominant; the crusade remained latent, unspoken. Justification arose naturally because the Nazi invasion made the question of justice academic. Now it was a struggle for survival. The U.S.S.R., especially the leadership of the Communist government, could not survive a successful German campaign. Although this mortal crisis seemed to call naturally and inevitably to a crusade, no such appeal was made. The propaganda battle was fought on patriotic, not ideological, grounds. The reasons for this restraint lie not in ideology, but in the external and internal complications of Soviet policy.

Essentially, the Soviet ideology begins with a premise similar to Hitler's Weltanschauung. The major theme of history is the theme of struggle: the struggle of classes pursuing their individual eoconomic interests. As long as social classes persist, as long as the exploiters dominate, as long as the capitalist system oppresses the proletariat, peace is impossible. War is the natural condition of man. There is no distinction between war and peace: "'If war is a continuation of politics by other means, so also peace is a continuation of conflict only by other means.'"[41]

Raymond Garthoff defines the communist theory of the just war as "...a war against an imperialist power; in fact, any war involving the Soviet power or its satellites."[42] This convenient definition is sufficiently broad to cover all types of war: offensive and defensive. It eliminates any distinction between the just war and the crusade. Therefore, all Soviet wars are just.

But war is not merely just. As long as capitalism survives, it is inevitable. Believing that the capitalist nations

sought to encircle and destroy them, the Soviets saw war as
the means for the destruction of their enemy. At the Sixth
World Congress of the Communist International, Lenin's views
on the inevitability of this conflict were sanctioned:
"'The overthrow of capitalism is impossible without violence,
i.e., without armed uprisings and war against the bourgeoisie.'"[43]

Like Lenin, Stalin believed that this war was inevitable.[44]
Djilas records that the dictator, in the midst of the Russo-
German conflict, foresaw the outbreak of a future war clearly,
almost rapturously:

> At one point he got up, hitched up his pants as
> though he was about to wrestle or to box, and cried
> out almost in a transport, "The war shall soon be
> over. We shall recover in fifteen or twenty years,
> and then we'll have another go at it." There was
> something terrible in his words: a horrible war was
> still going on. Yet there was something impressive,
> too, about the inevitability that faced the world in
> which he lived and the movement that he headed.[45]

How would this war begin? Obviously, it could be a response
to capitalist aggression, a purely defensive war which would
turn naturally and inevitably into an offensive war. But it
could also explode into a "war of liberation". In the interwar
period, Marshal Mikail N. Tukachevsky argued strongly for a
crusade which would carry Communist forces throughout the
world, promoting revolution in its path, the oppressed workers
forming the vanguard of the advancing Soviet armies.[46]For a
war to expand Soviet power is a war to liberate the world
proletariat. As Raymond Garthoff remarks, "a 'war of liberation',
...theoretically is the most 'just' war and a higly proper
Communist battle cry."[47]

There are echoes of this phrase in the Soviet propaganda
of World War II. In an impassioned speech delivered on
November 7, 1941, Stalin proclaimed his "war of liberation":

> 'Comrades, Red Army and Red Navy men, officers and
> political workers, men and women partisans! The whole
> world is looking upon you as the power capable of
> destroying the German robber hords! The enslaved
> peoples of Europe are looking upon you as their
> liberators....Be worthy of this great mission! The
> war you are waging is a war of liberation, a just war.'[48]

Only the night before, however, Stalin had defined his
"war of liberation" in disinterested and idealistic terms:

> ...Stalin said that the Soviet Union...had no
> territorial ambitions anywhere in either Europe or
> Asia....Nor did the Soviet Union intend to impose her
> will or her regime on the Slav or any other peoples
> waiting to be liberated from the Nazi yoke. There
> would be no Soviet interference in the internal
> affairs of these peoples.[49]

But this appeal to a "war of liberation" is not the
dominant theme of Soviet propaganda in World War II. Instead
of calling for a crusade, Stalin transformed the conflict into
a nationalistic endeavor, into the "Great Patriotic War" of
the Soviet Union,[50] the just war par excellence.

In Stalin's wartime speeches and in the official Soviet
propaganda, the emphasis was constant. Debasing the foe,
exalting the motherland (its history, traditions, heroes and
saints), Soviet propaganda transformed the German-Russian conflict
into a struggle for survival. The "Great Patriotic War" of
the Soviet Union was just because the Russian people were
defending their beloved country against a cruel invader.

On July 3, 1941, Joseph Stalin called for national unity,
exhorting the Soviet people to an unexcelled effort:

> "This war has been inflicted on us, and our country
> has entered into a life-and death struggle against
> its most wicked and pefidious enemy, German Fascism....
> Together with the Red Army, the whole of our people
> are rising to defend their country. The enemy is
> cruel and merciless. He aims at grabbing our land,
> our wheat and oil. He wants to restore the power of
> the landowners, re-establish Tsarism, and destroy
> the national culture of the peoples of the Soviet
> Union...and turn them into the slaves of German
> princes and barons."[51]

Even the Soviet-Nazi Non-Aggression Pact was grist for
the propaganda mill. Stalin and Molotov cited it as prime
evidence, as irrefutable proof of their innocence and
Hitler's guilt. As Molotov declared:

> "This unheard-of attack on our country is an
> unparalleled act of perfidy in the history of
> civilized nations. This attack had been made
> despite the fact that there was a non-aggression
> pact between the Soviet Union and Germany, a pact
> the terms of which were scrupulously observed by
> the Soviet Union.'[52]

This appeal to patriotism was orchestrated by the Soviet press,
which seized upon a number of primitive but effective slogans.
One lead came from Stalin's November 6, 1941 speech in which

the Soviet dictator violently exhorted his followers against
the enemy:

> 'The German invaders want a war of extermination
> against the peoples of the Soviet Union. Very well
> then! If they want a war of extermination they shall
> have it! (Prolonged stormy applause.) Our task now...
> will be to destroy every German, to the very last
> man, who had come to occupy our country. No mercy
> for the German invaders! Death to the German
> invaders!'[53]

Previously, Stalin had made a distinction between the Nazis and
the German people, exonerating the latter while condemning the
former.[54] The wholesale condemnation of the Germans did conform
to internationalist Marxian-Leninism.

Under the exigency of the German threat, this distinction
was forgotten. Soviet propaganda roared out a litany of hate
against the invader. Particularly effective were the articles
of the journalist Ilya Ehrenburg. His thesis was simple:
"'All Germans are evil.'"[55] With the vociferousness of a
prophet of hate, he advocated the extermination of the enemy:

> "We are remembering everything. Now we know. The
> Germans are not human. Now the word 'German' has
> become the most terrible swear-word....Let us kill.
> If you do not kill the German, the German will kill
> you. He will carry away your family, and torture
> them in his damned Germany....If you have killed one
> German, kill another. There is nothing jollier
> than German corpses."[56]

As Alexander Werth records: "'Kill the German' became like
Russia's Ten Commandments all in one."[57]

But Soviet propaganda had its positive as well as negative
side. If it stressed hatred of the foe, it also exalted the
motherland. In his November 7, 1941 speech, Stalin invoked
the Russian past, mobilizing the emotions associated with
the beloved rodina or motherland. At the conclusion of his
speech, he invoked the "blessing" and inspiration of the
Russian heroes and saints: "May you be inspired in this war
by the heroic figures of our ancestors, Alexander Nevsky,
Dimitri Donskoi, Minin and Pozharsky, Alexander Suvorov,
Michael Kutuzov!"[58] The invocation of the memory of Saint
Alexander Nevsky was particularly apt. In 1242, he had routed
the Teutonic Knights whom the Russians now regarded as the
"'foul hounds'", the evil progenitors of the Nazis.[59]

Soviet propaganda picked its cue from Stalin. The decadent
Tsarist past re-emerged as a source of inspiration. Invocations
to 1812, the memory of another invasion with its temporary
defeats and ultimate triumph,[60] and to the civil war in which
the Bolsheviks had fought their way to victory against
tremendous odds,[61] became common. Not only were the saints
restored to grace but even some of the outsanding Tsars
received the Communist blessing. Especially favored were Ivan
the Terrible and Peter the Great.[62] Caught in a merciless war
for survival, Stalin mobilized the memory of the Russian past
and threw it into battle.

Hatred of the invader, love of the motherland: these
were the major themes of Soviet propaganda in World War II.
Other themes were subsidiary and complementary, varying in
emphasis and tone according to Soviet military fortunes. In
the first year of the German-Russian war, the Russian people
were urged to "'...fight for every inch of Soviet soil, fight
to the very last drop for our towns and villages.'"[63] This
exhortation was the natural corollary to the "scorched earth"
policy ordered by Stalin in his July 3, 1941 speech.[64]

To summarize, except for the theme of liberation, the
major and subsidiary themes of Soviet propaganda revolved
around the just war. The nationalistic fervor poured into
the struggle by the Communist leadership and the Soviet press
gave this defensive war some of the emotional fervor of a
crusade. But the transition was never fully articulated.
Otherwise, the emphasis would have been totally different.
Stalin would then have proclaimed a revolutionary struggle,
a war to free the proletariat from its oppressors.

Given the messianic objectives of Communism, one might
wonder why no emphasis was placed on ideological objectives.
The reasons grew from the circumstances of the moment.
Essentially, the Soviets did not have to seek justification.
It was thrust upon them by the unprovoked German attack.
Since the Russian government had appeased the German government,
turning a blind eye to England's surreptitious wooing, it
could claim "innocence" in the most literal sense. It did
not need to appeal to any higher cause to strengthen its

call to arms. Moreover, any call to an ideological crusade
would have been dangerous as well as unnecessary. First, it
would have weakened Stalin's appeal to the peoples of the
disgruntled Soviet states; second, it would have embarassed
his relations with the Western Allies. Finally, although
the impact of the shattering German attack made any question
of Communist expansion temporarily academic,[65]the ultimate
course of the war made it unnecessary. The Soviet system
would inevitably follow the Soviet banner.

The first deterrent to any Soviet crusade was the attitude
of the Russian nationalities. Suppression had created a rich
mine of anti-Soviet dissent, a mine which could be exploited
by any invader who had the wisdom and the ability to utilize
it.[66]If the Nazis had waged a war of liberation, a war to
destroy the Soviet regime and to free the subject nationalities,
they could have mobilized the Ukraine and other nations of the
U.S.S.R. against the regime.[67]Mobilizing dissent against the
government, fostering national autonomy, restoring the
independence of the church,[68]and redistributing the land--
pursuing a policy of magnanimity and benevolence--the Germans
might have won their crusade. But the Nazis were racial
dogmatists, prisoners of their ideology. Hitler's failure
was Stalin's opportunity. While the Germans failed to
cultivate Russian particularism, Stalin evoked Russian
nationalism; for the feeling of patriotism survived even in
bitterly anti-Communist regions.[69]

If domestic considerations diminished the attraction of
any crusade, foreign considerations ruled it out completely.
A Communist crusade was impossible because of Soviet participation
in the Grand Alliance. Throughout the war, the Soviet
leadership took great care not to alarm or to alert the
western democracies. The dissolution of the Comintern, the
more liberal policy towards the Russian Orthodox Church,[70]
the adherence of the Soviet Union to the Atlantic Charter and
the United Nations Declaration. the cooperation of the U.S.S.R.
in the establishment of the United Nations, the apparent
loss of Soviet interest in world revolution: these measures
moderated western fears and suspicions. Across this pattern
of cooperation, other episodes and attitudes cut like darker

prophetic shadows. But, despite its truculence and suspicious-
ness, the Russian government studiously avoided any public
statement that revealed its ideological ambitions. Finally,
any crusade was unnecessary since the Soviet regime enjoyed
a supreme advantage. It could pursue its ideological goals
under the guise of the just war; it could secure Communist
domination of Eastern Europe and the Balkans while "liberating"
these areas from the fascists.

An opportunist, Stalin took advantages as they presented
themselves, and his attention never wavered from long-range
objectives. As he said to Djilas and Tito: "'This war is
not as in the past; whoever occupies a territory also imposes
on it his own social system. Everyone imposes his own
system as far as his army can reach. It cannot be otherwise.'"[71]
Obviously, Stalin thought that other powers were playing
the same game, carving up regions or spheres of influence
in the wake of their military forces.

The conflicting emphasis between the Soviet Union and
the Nazi movement (the former stressing the just war; the
latter, the crusade) reveals clearly the relation between
the doctrines of justification and the defensive-offensive
complex. The Soviet Union under attack waged a just war of
survival; Nazi Germany, waging offensive war, portrayed itself
as an ideological crusader embarked on the historic mission
of defending western civilization against its mortal enemy.

4. Process of Justification: Democratic Nations

For the United States and Great Britain, World War II
rapidly became a crusade. This transformation was a corollary
to the strategic situation. Since neither country was
invaded, forced to battle the foe on their homeland, both
nations engaged in an offensive war. They thought and fought
an ideological crusade.

In the process of transforming the war into a metaphysical
struggle, the democratic leaders, Churchill and Roosevelt,
developed four dominant themes that recur again and again
throughout their wartime speeches. First, they depicted
their main adversary as a master conspirator with insatiable
and unlimited ambitions: a plotter intriguing for world

conquest. Second, they described him and his partners-in-crime as epitomes of evil. Third, they portrayed the war as a metaphysical conflict between the champions of light and progress and the agents of darkness and dissolution. Fourth, they identified the national cause with universal goals. They reinforced these themes through the development of major patterns of imagery.

    a. Great Britain: the Churchillean Crusade

Churchill and Roosevelt followed similar procedures, developed identical themes, using at times almost identical language. Only the process of justification was different. While the United States struggled painfully over this problem until the declaration of war, the question was settled for Great Britain before the war: it was settled by the failure of appeasement. Munich was the unnamed price for the wartime unanimity of the British. This disaster proved conclusively that no other course except resistance was either feasible or conceivable. In his tribute to Neville Chamberlain on November 12, 1940, Winston Churchill acknowledged his debt:

> ...no future generation of English-speaking folks... will doubt that...we were guiltless of the bloodshed, terror and misery which have engulfed so many lands and peoples, and yet seek new victims still. Herr Hitler protests with frantic words and gestures that he has only desired peace. What do these ravings and outpourings count before the silence of Neville Chamberlain's tomb?[72]

Chamberlain's failure justified Churchill's policy, and the failure of appeasement committed the British to resistance: "Of all the wars that we have ever waged in the long continuity of our history, there has never been one which more truly united the entire British nation and British race throughout the world than this present fearful struggle for the freedom and progress of mankind."[73]

The conclusion was irrefutable. England was confronted by an unappeasable foe whose designs posed an ultimate danger to its existence. For Churchill was convinced that Germany's aggressive moves were part of a planned strategy: "Europe is confronted with a program of aggression nicely calculated and timed, unfolding stage by state...."[74] This plot moves "step by

step"[75]towards its "appointed climax":[76] "The subjugation of
the Western Hemisphere."[77]

This rational blueprint for aggression was paradoxially
the product of an irrational passion. Churchill envisioned
Naziism as a dynamism which could not control its own course:

> ...they must seek, from time to time, and always at
> shorter intervals, a new target, a new prize, a new
> victim. The Dictator, in all his pride, is held in
> the grip of his party machine. He can go forward;
> he cannot go back. He must blood his hounds and
> show them sport, or else, like Actaeon of old, be
> devoured by them.[78]

The Dictator: master of destiny without; slave of passion within.

In his wartime speeches, Churchill uses shocking images
and stunning insults to describe Hitler and his cohorts. The
Fuhrer is singled out for special honor: "Hitler is a master
of wickedness, insatiable in his lust for blood and plunder."[79]
More colloquially, he is a "bloodthirsty guttersnipe",[80] "a
haunted, morbid being",[81] a "wicked man, the repository and
embodiment of many forms of soul-destroying hatred, this monstrous
product of former wrongs and shame...."[82] This portrayal is
reinforced by images comparing the dictator to predatory forms
of life. Churchill compares him to wild and dangerous animals:
a boa constrictor,[83] tiger,[84] crocodile.[85] Sometimes, the image
turns into a succinct and apt epithet: "the beast is cornered."[86]
But the Prime Minister's metaphors discover new iniquitous
comparisons. The foe is a barbarian,[87] a criminal,[88] a fiend,[89]
a disease,[90] an incubus,[91] a monster,[92] an ogre.[93]

Against this infamous foe, the gangster prince of the
twentieth century, Churchill summoned the nation to arms.
He defined his crusade and identified the cause of England
with the future of mankind:

> You ask, What is our policy? I will say: "It is
> to wage war, by sea, land and air, with all our
> might and with all the strength that God can give
> us: to wage war against a monstrous tyranny, never
> surpassed in the dark, lamentable catalogue of
> human crime. That is our policy." You ask, What is
> our aim? I can answer in one word: Victory-victory
> at all costs, victory in spite of all terror, victory
> however long and hard the road may be; for without
> victory there is no survival. Let that be realized;
> no survival for the British Empire; no survival for
> all that the British Empire has stood for; no

> survival for the urge and impulse of the ages, that
> mankind will move forward towards its goal. But I
> take up my task with buoyancy and hope. I feel sure
> that our cause will not be suffered to fail among
> men. At this time I feel entitled to claim the aid
> of all, and I say, "Come, then, let us go forward
> together with our united strength."[94]

To Churchill, the Second World War was a mortal struggle
between righteousness and evil, between destructive darkness
and creative light. One of his primary aims was to marshal
"the good forces of the world against the evil forces which
are now so formidable and triumphant and which have cast their
cruel spell over the whole of Europe and a large part of
Asia."[95] The struggle revolved around a series of alternatives:
survival versus extinction, progress versus historical
regression, freedom versus tyranny.

Churchill noted the uniqueness of the Second World War:
"This is no war of chieftans or of princes, of dynasties or
national ambition; it is a war of peoples and of causes."[96]
Primarily, it was a frightful struggle for survival in which
the fate of the nation and its empire weighed in the balance,[97]
"a struggle for life."[98] But the British were not alone. The
United States, China and the U.S.S.R. were also threatened
with annihilation.[99]

The Allied cause was that of progress; the enemy's of
regression. Whereas the triumph of the former would accelerate
"the forward march of the common people in all the lands towards
their just and true inheritance, and towards the broader and
fuller age,"[100] victory for the latter would plunge mankind
back into "the dark ages,"[101] whose "atrocities...surpass
anything that has been known since the darkest and most bestial
ages of mankind."[102] To emphasize the difference between these
two courses, Churchill uses topographical imagery; the abyss is
set against the uplands, the pit of darkness against the heights
flooded with light. The alternatives were never so clear
as during the Battle of Britain:

> Hitler knows that he will have to break us in this
> Island or lose the war. If we can stand up to him,
> all Europe may be free and the life of the world may
> move forward into broad, sunlit uplands. But if we
> fail, then the whole world, including the United States,
> including all that we have known and cared for, will
> sink into the abyss of a new Dark Age....[103]

But the progress of mankind is inextricably bound to the maintenance and extension of freedom. Therefore, the crusade is directed against "the cruelest tyranny" in history:[104]

> We are fighting to save the whole world from the pestilence of Nazi tyranny and in defense of all that is most sacred to man....It is a war, viewed in its inherent quality, to establish, on impregnable rocks, the rights of the individual, and it is a war to establish and revive the stature of man.[105]

Churchill embodied his antinomies in a pattern of imagery which stretches throughout his wartime oratory, developing and expanding his major themes. Great Britain is portrayed as a "strong City of Refuge,"[106] an isolated fortress prepared for the assault of the barbarian, the protector of the defeated, still resisting governments of occupied Europe, refuge of civilization, freedom, progress.

If England is a fortress of righteousness, Hitler's Europe is a nightmare world filled with "miseries beyond the dreams of Hell,"[107] bound under a terrible enchantment: "the hideous spell of Nazi tyranny."[108] The Nazi kingdom is ultimately an empire of emptiness: "...Hitler has no theme, nought but mania, appetite and exploitation."[109] The New Order embodies the senseless combination of tyranny and anarchy.[110]

The central image which unites Churchill's themes, portraying the triumph and tragedy of his time, is the image of the journey. He sees contemporary history and England's destiny as a "movement,"[111] "path,"[112] "road,"[113] "pilgrimage."[114] This voyage has two rhythms: one downward towards the loss of national honor and safety; one upward towards redemption and victory. A descent into darkness followed by an ascent into light:

> There are upon our journey dark and dangerous valleys through which we have to make and fight our way. But it is sure and certain that if we persevere--and we shall persevere--we shall come through these dark and dangerous valleys into a sunlight broader and more genial and more lasting than mankind has ever known.[115]

In his prophetic speeches, reaching their climax in 1937 and 1938, Churchill charted the course of the impending catastrophe, approaching "inch by inch and day by day."[116] The emphasis of Churchill's language stresses the apparent inescapability of this descent.[117] Even the language seems to slide: "We seem to be moving, drifting, steadily against

the will of every race and every people and every class, towards
some hideous catastrophe. Everybody wishes to stop it, but
they do not know how."[118]The nation is caught "sagging and
sliding"[119]towards disaster. And as it apporaches the pit,
the ground gives way: "Already the ground is beginning to
crumble under our sliding feet."[120]This fall is not merely a
decline of power; it is a deterioration of national honor, a
loss of "moral health" and "martial vigor."[121]

And this plunge towards disaster can only reverse itself
if the English nation awakens. She slept in the thirties, while
Hitler armed and the Treaty of Versailles was violated. She
slept while Germany systematically undermined the security of
Europe. Worst of all, in her sleep, she forgot and abandoned
her traditions. So honor died; and without an awakening, so
too would England die:

> Now the victors are the vanquished, and those who
> threw down their arms in the field and sued for an
> armistice are striding on to world mastery....
> Now is the time at last to rouse the nation. Perhaps
> it is the last time it can be roused with a chance
> of preventing war, or with a chance of coming through
> to victory should our efforts to prevent war fail.
> We should lay aside every hindrance and endeavor by
> uniting the whole force and spirit of our people
> to raise again a great British nation standing up
> before all the world; for such a nation, rising in
> its ancient vigor, can even at this hour save
> civilization.[122]

England aroused sounds the glory of her past within the terror
of the present.[123]When the reawakening came, Churchill hailed
it as a resurrection of past greatness:

> I see the spirit of an unconquerable people. I see
> a spirit bred in freedom, nursed in a tradition which
> has come down to us through the centuries, and which
> will surely at this moment, this turning point in the
> history of the world, enable us to bear our part in
> such a way that none of our race who come after us
> will have any reason to cast reproach upon their sires.[124]

Reawakening came at the moment of disaster, "the darkest
days,"[125]when mankind lurched and plunged towards the abyss,
when Britain stood alone against Hitler; for the time of trial
was the "finest hour,"[126]the moment of redemption. England
recaptured her "health and martial vigor,"[127]taking her "stand
for freedom as in the olden times."[128]So the rhythm of history

altered its course. The descent was the prelude to the ascent
towards the uplands. The journey passed through "the dark
Valley"[129] towards the "dawn of liberation,"[130] the "mellow light
of victory."[131] But the dawn came only because the "light,"[132] the
"flame,"[133] the "torch"[134] of freedom was never quenched. The
terms are significant. For freedom is not merely a light
burning against the darkness of the night; it is also a flame,
consuming tyranny in its fury:

> What he [Hitler] has done is to kindle a fire in
> British hearts...which will glow long after all
> traces of the conflagration he has caused in London
> have been removed. He has lighted a fire which will
> burn with a steady and consuming flame until the last
> vestiges of Nazi tyranny have been burnt out of Europe,
> and until the Old World--and the New--can join hands
> to rebuild the temples of man's freedom and man's
> honor, upon foundations which will not soon or easily
> be overthrown.[135]

This image of light unites the terms of the righteous war. The
flame conserved freedom; it also destroyed tyranny.

It conserved freedom not only for the British nation, but
also for mankind. In victory, Churchill summed it up:

> The light is brighter because it comes not only from
> the fierce but fading glare of military achievement...
> but because there mingle with it in mellow splendor
> the hopes, joys, and blessings of almost all mankind.
> This is the true glory, and long will it gleam upon
> our forward path.[136]

The Battle of Britain was not merely a battle to save England.
It was a battle to save civilization: "the whole future of
mankind."[137]

The emphasis in Churchill's speeches was totally upon the
crusade. Circumstances obviated justification. Also, there
was no need to appeal to national unity. Finally, the extremity
of Britain's danger made a crusade imperative. Only by summoning
their offensive spirit could Churchill arouse the British to
their most spirited defense, bolstering their morale while
concealing their desperate predicament from the enemy.

b. The United States: The Rooseveltian Crusade

For the United States, isolated from the European con-
flagration, the problem of justification was dominant until the
moment of attack. Then the conversion to the crusade was as

spontaneous as that from a defensive to an offensive stance.
Justification was a problem because the threat to the United
States was ambiguous though keenly felt. High administration
officials foresaw that a German victory in Europe or a
Japanese victory in Asia would threaten the interests,
perhaps ultimately the existence of the United States.

But since this realization of peril was limited only
to a few, the administration had to convince the American
people and Congress that the danger was imminent or threatening enough to require involvement, possibly even intervention.
American foreign policy had to steer between two hazards:
neglecting a mounting threat by following the isolationists
or splintering national unity by following the interventionists. Justification was not easy for American policy makers.
It had to be developed; it had to be "sold" to the American
public.

No war is justifiable to Americans unless it is a
response to attack. As Robert W. Tucker defines it:

> The American doctrine is distinguished by the
> assumption that the use of force is clearly
> governed by universally valid moral and legal
> standards; it is distinguished further by the
> insistence with which these standards are
> interpreted as making the justice or injustice
> of war primarily dependent upon the circumstances
> immediately attending the initiation of force.
> In substance, the just war is the war fought
> either in self-defense or in collective defense
> against an armed attack. Conversely, the unjust
> --and, of course, the unlawful--war is the war
> initiated in circumstances other than those of
> self or collective defense against armed
> aggression.[138]

Since there is a set formula for justification, debate ends
once the formula is fulfilled. Moreover, America's prewar
restraint, her insistence on allowing the enemy to strike
the first blow, makes her reaction exceptionally violent.
As George Kennan acutely notes, a conviction of outraged
innocence releases vindicative forces:

> ...it does look as though the real source of the
> fervor which we Americans are able to put into a
> war lies less in any objective understanding of
> the wider issues involved than in a profound
> irritation over the fact that other people
> have finally provoked us to the point where
> we had no alternative but to

> take up arms. This lends to the democratic war
> effort a basically punitive note, rather than one
> of expediency.[139]

Because of her geographical immunity, the United States
was sheltered from direct and immediate attack, separated by
distance from the hostile systems of Europe and Asia. Yet,
when attacked, she was not content merely to defeat the enemy.
Launching a crusade, she set out completely to destroy the
hostile systems which challenged her. No longer believing
that separateness guaranteed safety, America sought immunity
through the creation of a stable world. For American security
was now threatened by the mere existence of the hostile systems
whose total elimination became a prerequisite to world-wide
security.

The American crusade was the inevitable product of the
debate over justification, In the neutrality period, the
Roosevelt administration actively aided the Allies against
Hitler. These moves were always justified as defensive acts.
In the process of justification, totalitarian nations were
represented as actively plotting to destroy the United States.
In themselves, these hostile systems represented a threat.

Once the actual attack occurred, the debate over justification
was resolved. Aggression was then automatically identified
with the totalitarian nations, immoral conduct with an evil
social system. The proof was irrefutable; the conclusion,
inevitable. If totalitarianism was an incentive to war,
democracy was a cure. If the belligerent systems were destroyed,
the problem of aggression would disappear. So America's
conversion to the crusade was a logical extension of the
prewar doctrines of justification.

President Roosevelt believed that the Axis, dominated by
Germany, had a long-range plan for world conquest. Because
democracy was incompatible with totalitarianism, dictatorship
sought the total destruction of freedom:

> The Nazi masters of Germany have made it clear that
> they intend not only to dominate all life and thought
> in their own country, but also to enslave the whole of
> Europe, and then to use the resources of Europe to
> dominate the rest of the world.

After citing Hitler's proclamation of the irreconcilable

conflict between democracy and fascism, the President concludes:

> In other words, the Axis not merely admits but
> proclaims that there can be no ultimate peace between
> their philosophy of government and our philosophy
> of government.[140]

The Nazi plot had three dominant characteristics. It was
systematic, unlimited and closely coordinated with the plans
of its partners: Italy and Japan.[141]

It was sytematic because it followed a time scheme and a
planned sequence of moves. Every future victim had a "place...
in the Nazi scheme for world domination...marked on the Nazi
timetable."[142] Moreover, Hitler deliberately sought to weaken
the prospective victim before moving in for the kill. As
Roosevelt realized, Hitler's method was consistent. After
lulling his victim, reassuring him with non-aggression pacts
and expressions of good will, and after weakening his resistance
by sabotage and conspiracy, Hitler would launch a well-prepared,
wholesale attack. The outcome was rapid and inevitable.[143]

This systematic plan advanced towards an unlimited end.
Step by step, country by country, Hitler would advance towards
the Western Hemisphere. The domination of the land masses of
Europe, Asia and Africa would play prelude to seizing command
of the oceans. For, as Roosevelt concluded after the attack on
the Greer: "It is the Nazi design to abolish the freedom of the
seas, and to acquire absolute control and domination of these
seas for themselves."[144]

But this triumph would merely prepare the ultimate act: the
conquest of the western hemisphere: "This Nazi attempt to
seize control of the oceans is but a counterpart of the Nazi
plots now being carried on throughout the Western Hemisphere....
For Hitler's advance guards...have sought to make ready for
him footholds and bridgeheads in the New World, to be used as
soon as he has gained control of the oceans."[145] Roosevelt ruled
out chance, accident and contingency. Incidents became the
plays of a well-prepared plot. Indeed the Nazi plot envisioned
not only the conquest but also the division of the New World
into "vassal" and "puppet states."[146]

Finally, according to Roosevelt, the Nazi conquerors had
allies. They were the masters of a coordinated conspiracy

directed against the Western Hemisphere. Japan sought to
dominate Asia and the Pacific Ocean, ultimately stretching out
to seize "the western coasts of North, Central, and South
America."[147]Italy moved inexorably towards her dream: a restored
Roman Empire. Her "goal was the domination of all North Africa,
Egypt, parts of France and the entire Mediterranean world."[148]
The dreams of the Nazis were more grandiose, providing "for
ultimate domination, not of one section of the world, but of the
whole earth and all the oceans on it."[149]With the signing of the
Tripartite Pact, these schemes fused into a grand design. The
actions of one partner were coordinated with those of the
others. Each had his part to play:

> ...Japan's role was obviously to cut off our supply
> of weapons of war to Britain, and Russia, and China--
> weapons which increasingly were speeding the day of
> Hitler's doom. The act of Japan at Pearl Harbor was
> intended to stun us--to terrify us to such an extent
> that we would divert our industrial and military
> strength to the Pacific area, or even to our own
> continental defense.[150]

To Roosevelt, these master conspirators were beings beyond
the touch of humanity: they were "the gods of force and hate,"[151]
enemies "of all law, all liberty, all morality, all religion."[152]
Although the enemy posed as the creator of a New Order, he was
the foe of all order.[153]This "inhuman foe"[154]neither understood
nor respected the morality of other men. Human rights had no
meaning for him: "His only method of dealing with his neighbor
is first to delude him with lies, then to attack him treacher-
ously, then beat him down and step on him, and then either
kill him or enslave him."[155]

But this enemy was also a pagan barbarian, determined to
destroy all religion: "Catholic, Protestant, Mohammedan, Hindu,
Buddhist, and Jewish alike."[156]Under Hitler's triumphant rule,
church property would be confiscated, religious orders would
be liquidated, the Bible would be replaced by Mein Kampf and
the cross, by the Nazi swastika and sword: "The god of Blood
and Iron will take the place of the God of Love and Mercy."[157]

Roosevelt uses animal, crime and disease imagery to describe
the enemy.[158]More significantly, totalitarianism and militarism
are for the President a disease, a plague: "an epidemic of
world lawlessness,"[159]a "deadly virus,"[160]a poison infecting

all it touches.[161]

Such a foe wages revolutionary war:

> It is not an ordinary war. It is a revolution imposed by force of arms, which threatens all men every-where. It is a revolution which proposes not to set men free but to reduce them to slavery--to reduce them to slavery in the interest of a dictatorship which has already shown the nature and the extent of the advantage which it hopes to obtain.[162]

Therefore, this war will be extraordinary: a metaphysical struggle, a "fight to destroy the forces of ignorance, and intolerance, and slavery, and war."[163] Victory for the United Nations will be "a world victory of the forces of justice and righteousness over the forces of savagery and of barbarism."[164]

Like Churchill, Roosevelt saw the war as a crusade, a conflict between mortally antagonistic forces: survival against extinction, salvation against a regression to barbarism, and human freedom against permanent enslavement and exploitation.

It was a war for survival in a pre-eminent sense. It was not merely a war to save the United States from conquest; more fundamentally, it was a war to preserve national values from extinction: "The Survival War. That is what it comes pretty close to being--the survival of our civilization, the survival of democracy, the survival of a hemisphere... which had developed in its own ways."[165] The physical danger, therefore, was merely emblematic of a more profound danger: spiritual extinction.

The war was also a struggle between civilization and barbarism, progress and regression. It would "determine whether the march of progress" would continue or whether it would be ended by the totality of conquest.[166] The possible triumph of the Axis forces would be "a relapse into ancient history,"[167] unmitigated by the slogans and trappings of efficiency:

> The ominipotent rulers of the greater part of modern Europe have guaranteed efficiency, and work, and a kind of security. But the slaves who build the pyramids for the glory of the dictator Pharaohs of Egypt had that kind of security, that kind of efficiency, that kind of corporative state. So did the inhabitants of that world which extended from Britain to Persia under the undisputed rule of the proconsuls sent out from Rome. So did the henchmen,

the tradesmen, the mercenaries and the slaves of
the feudal system which dominated Europe a thousand
years ago. So did the people of those nations of
Europe who received their kings and their government
at the whim of the conquering Napoleon. Whatever
its new trappings and new slogans, tyranny is the
oldest and most discredited rule known to history.[168]

Roosevelt, therefore, identified the progress of mankind
with the advance of democracy, and the regression of civilization
with the triumph of totalitarianism. The final alternative
lies between human freedom and inhuman tyranny. Essentially,
freedom is "Christian"[169] and slavery, "pagan."[170] The democratic
vision, seeing man as "created free, in the image of God,"[171]
promotes "a way of life" that lets "men hold up their heads
and admit of no master but God."[172] Only the free man is a
"whole man."[173] Only the free man can develop fully. Other men
must give allegiance to Gods of Force and Violence.

To Franklin Roosevelt, freedom was the only condition
which would allow men to develop. Only freedom could save
man from the forces that could warp his development. Freedom
was fourfold: "freedom of speech and expression," freedom of
worship, "freedom from want," and "freedom from fear."[174] These
rights, the core of the Atlantic Charter,[175] were for F.D.R.
"the ultimate stake."[176] Victory for the Axis would be followed
by their suppression; victory for the United Nations, by
their extension:

> ...if we fail--if democracy is superseded by slavery--
> then those four freedoms, or even the mention of
> them will become forbidden....By wining now, we
> strengthen the meaning of those freedoms, we increase
> the stature of mankind, we establish the dignity
> of human life.[177]

These four freedoms are essential to man's health and growth:
"...as much elements of man's needs as air and sunlight, bread
and salt. Deprive him of all these freedoms and he dies--
deprive him of a part of them and a part of him withers."[178]

They are interdependent; none can subsist without the
others. None can subsist isolated in a single country,
surrounded by a totalitarian sea. For the maintenance of
freedom in one country depends upon its extension to the entire
world. Only the triumph of the third and fourth freedoms,
freedom from want and fear, will eliminate the causes of war

and dictatorship in the post-war world, securing the full
enjoyment of every freedom.[179]

Roosevelt saw the war against the Axis as a crusade against
tyranny. It is obvious that the word "freedom" had an extended
meaning for him. It embodied his vision of the future: a City
of God on earth, a world consecrated to the progress of
humanity, a world in which man would have the opportunity to
develop his potentialities free from the curse of all tyranny:
political, economic, pyschological, spiritual.[180]

To develop his theme of war as a crusade, Roosevelt used
much of the same imagery as Churchill, He identified democracy
and progress with light; and evil and tyranny with darkness.
He spoke, for example, of "the dark forces of despotism"[181]
which had conquered Europe: imposing "a blackout of freedom...
from the tip of Norway to the shores of the Aegean."[182] In this
darkened world, "sturdy working men who once walked erect in
the sun now stumble and cower beneath the lash of the
slavemasters."[183] Against the power of darkness, he set the
force of light. His most persistent image is the flame or
torch of liberty, the fire that free men must preserve in a
darkening world:

> The light of democracy must be kept burning. To the
> perpetuation of this light, each of us must do his
> share. The single effort of one individual may seem
> very small. But there are over 130 million individuals
> over here. And there are many more millions in
> Britain and elsewhere bravely shielding the great
> flame of democracy from the blackout of barbarism.
> It is not enough for us merely to trim the wick or
> polish the glass. The time has come when we must
> provide the fuel in ever-increasing amounts to keep
> that flame alight.[184]

But the light remains a guide to be followed as well as a spirit
to be conserved. It becomes the goal towards which free men
strive in their quest for progress: "The brazen tyrannies
pass. Man marches forward toward the light."[185]

The Rooseveltian crusade is fought for mankind, not merely
for the United States. American ideals are those of common
humanity, and American victory is for all: "...the vast
majority of the members of the human race are on our side....
For in representing our cause, we represent theirs as well--
our hope and their hope for liberty under God."[186]

5. The Crusade: Phenomenon of Total War

Churchill and Roosevelt waged war as a crusade, identifying
their cause with mankind's. They represented World War II as
a struggle between the forces of enlightenment and the agents
of destruction. But they were not alone. Germany, too, waged
a crusade; and, although the Russians did not, their restraint
was due to circumstance. Communist ideology is as fervently
crusading as democratic ideology. Japan was the exception.
A semi-modern, semi-feudalistic government, its aims were not
as revolutionary as those of the democratic or totalitarian
powers. Japan sought in the twentieth century to emulate the
nineteenth century achievements of the imperial powers: to
create a Pacific empire which would make her self-subsistent.
She sought to wage a limited war with limited objectives.[187]
Unfortunately for the Japanese, they entered the war with an
act which aroused the massed fury and force of their opponents.
Since the Allies were potentially far stronger than the
Japanese, they could impose the yoke of total war upon their
assailants.

How effective was the totalitarian crusade of Nazi Germany
as compared to the democratic crusades of Great Britain and
the United States? Germany's crusade was based on an appeal
to the fanatical true believer. Since it was more likely to
promote opposition and resistance than to convert the uncommitted,
it was a poor tool, completely inadequate for the purpose of
psychological mobilization. In contrast, the democratic
crusades were based on an appeal to egalitarian ideology.
Revolving around the concept of self-determination, free from
annexationist designs, posited on the equal rights of equal
men, this ideology was a superb tool for the mobilization
of world public opinion. The impotence of one appeal and the
effectiveness of the other were predictable. For one was
exclusive, favoring a set of endowed beneficiaries against
the disinherited majority; the other was inclusive, favoring
and promoting the rights of all men at all times.

Germany, the U.S.S.R., Great Britain and the United States
had revolutionary aims, seeking to create a new world out of

the old. Although the Soviet Union waged a just war, not a
crusade, the other powers sought the ultimate ideological
objective: the destruction of the opposing system of values.
So a crusade is not an inherently American aberration;
rather it is a type of warfare suited to an age of total war.
Any war fought by any nation designed to achieve a total
victory, will ultimately turn into a crusade.

6. Summation

The righteous war played a dual role: pragmatic and
dogmatic. Embodying and reflecting a conviction of righteousness,
it played its useful role in the psychological mobilization of
national and world public opinion. Since the aims and objectives of the world cause were set and defined within a
national context, these aims and objectives posed no problem
for a domestic audience. For the average citizen, the
identification between self-interest, national interest and
the cause of humanity came almost automatically. For the
nations threatened or conquered by the Axis monster, the
western democracies represented the only escape from perpetual
enslavement.

Although pragmatically the two doctrines of the righteous
war played the role of a concept, cementing national unity
and building coalition concord, essentially, they remained
the preconceptions of rigid dogma: seldom challenged, rarely
debated. Waging a righteous war, a nation can seek,
sometimes achieve, the most revolutionary aims. Even the
most frightful ideological dreams are infused with self-
righteousness. In the dreams of national leaders, there
are no unjust wars.

Chapter VI

The Temporal Imperative

1. The Temporal Imperative: Definition and Exposition.
The United States sought to achieve its revolutionary
war aims as rapidly as possible. The fifth strategic belief,
the temporal imperative, is also singled out by the military
critics. The United States is chastized for its impatience,
its anxiety to bring the war to a rapid conclusion regardless
of cost or means. As Chester Wilmot phrased it: "The Americans
were eager to 'get the war over and get the boys back home,'
even if it meant that fewer would come back."[1] As he diagnosed,
"this was partly the result of a national inclination to
impatience, partly of the knowledge that the people of the
United States would pass open judgment on the conduct of the
war in the Presidential election of 1944."[2] This simple explanation conveniently fits the mythological analysis of the
American character. It can be supported by an impressive set
of contemporary witnesses. As Roosevelt succinctly summarized
it: "Time is of the essence."[3] Or as George Marshall phrased
it: "'a democracy cannot fight a Seven Years War.'"[4]
But this sense of urgency, this realization of the
pressures of time is not exclusively military. The time factor
is always crucial to success of failure. "Too little, too late"
is the infallible judgment of all Monday-morning quarterbacks.
On the tactical level, it provides an analytic key. The
Battle of Waterloo was lost by Napoleon because he did not
open fire until late morning. The Gallipoli campaign was lost
because the British moved too slowly with too few forces while
the initiative was still theirs. Lee lost the Battle of
Gettysburg because the Confederates failed to storm Cemetery
Ridge on the first day. Always the moral is the same: one
more company or division at the right place, at the right
time, marks the difference between victory and defeat.
Speed and quantity are linked together: how much, how fast.
Perhaps an old sergeant-major put it most effectively to

to future Field-Marshal Viscount Slim: "'There is only one
principle of war, and that's this. Hit the other fellow as
quick as you can and as hard as you can, where it hurts him
most, when he ain't looking!'"[5] Certain tactics, a suprise
attack and an effective pursuit, depend entirely upon timing.
Surprise depends upon striking the foe so rapidly that he does
not have the chance to react effectively. The success of any
pursuit turns upon not allowing the beaten foe sufficient
time to recover his equilibrium: speed is essential to
the maintenance of momentum.

But the expression, "time is of the essence," is not
merely applicable to battle tactics; it is also applicable to
entire campaigns, to the course of a war, to strategy. In war,
time is either on one side or another, for or against you.

When we say "time is on your side," what do we mean?
We are roughly expressing the differences in strength between
one power and another. But, more importantly, we are
weighing the shifting balance of force between two foes.
We are balancing the potential as opposed to the actual
strength of either side, and are measuring them not only in
relation to themselves (actual to actual, potential to potential)
but also in relation to their opposites (actual to potential).
In a hypothetical situation, this approach yields six measures
by which to gauge our strength versus our opponent's:

   a) Internal:
- 1) Our potential strength versus our actual strength
- 2) The enemy's potential strength versus his actual
strength

   b) External
- 1) Our actual strength versus the actual strength
of the enemy
- 2) Our potential strength versus the potential
strength of the enemy
- 3). Our actual strength versus the potential strength
of the enemy
- 4) Our potential strength versus the actual strength
of the enemy.

This approach, therefore, presents a series of unbalanced
equations, constantly fluctuating in time. It presents the

alignment, not the final disposition of forces. It reveals
the possibilities of the play, not the final act. For the
unknown element is always time. A short war, for example,
favors a mobilized power against a potentially stronger but
unprepared foe. A prolonged war, on the other hand, favors
the power with the greatest potential strength even when
his present force is weaker than his foe's.

Strength, moreover, is multi-level: it involves and
invokes all the "elements of national power": geography,
population, industrial plant, morale, national character,
command of natural resources, character of government.
Although some elements (for example, geography and national
character) are more stable than others (for example,
industrial production and morale), all elements of national
strength must be mobilized in total war. Therefore, by
weighing strength within the element of time, we can readily
measure the shift of power from one side to the other.

We must, however, always remember that power never
remains static. A source of strength can be neutralized
within a short period of time. In coalition warfare, the
hazards of this danger are multiplied. For example, the
shifts of the Soviet Union in World War II had a pre-eminent
effect upon the course of the war. Her first shift, marked
by the signing of the Molotov-Ribbentrop Non-Aggression Pact,
allowed Hitler to conquer most of western Europe. Her second
shift, forced upon her by Hitler's invasion, gave the United
States and Great Britain, a continental ally, indispensable
for the defeat of Germany.

To take another example: the question of the disposition
of the French fleet after the Armistice of 1940. Whether the
French fleet was voluntarily transferred or forcibly seized
by Hitler made no difference. The accretion to the Axis of
such strength would have tilted the naval balance of power
in its favor. As Churchill stressed: "The addition of the
French Navy to the German and Italian Fleets, with the menace
of Japan measureless upon the horizon, confronted Great
Britain with mortal dangers and gravely affected the safety
of the United States."[6] Fear of this potential threat led

to the tragedy at Oran.

The temporal imperative has two functions: pragmatic and ideological. It is a tool which allows the military planners of a nation to measure their strength against their opponent's. But it does not merely measure force. At times, the pressure of time on military operations assumes a compulsive cast. Then this pressure represents political and psychological pressures. These pressures may demand a rapid end to the war although military analysis may call for its prolongation. Here the temporal imperative overrides practical considerations. Then it reflects the ideological values and needs of the society most clearly, values and needs which must be fulfilled even when they contradict practical exigency.

An examination of the operation of this strategic belief upon the strategy of Germany, the Soviet Union, Great Britain and the United States will reveal its dual character and cast light upon its multiple functions.

2. Germany: the Dangers of a Long War

Germany sought a short war. Because the potential strength of her opponents (Britain, France, the U.S.S.R. and the U.S.) was far greater than her own, Germany's hope for victory depended upon two conditions: temporary superiority in military mobilization and a rapid war which would strike down her enemies before they could gather their combined strength. She needed the blitzkrieg victories of the age of Bismarck and Moltke: Sadowa and Sedan.

Germany's geographical position was exceptionally vulnerable: exposed to the continuous threat of two fronts, to the danger of a strategic envelopment by a Soviet-British-French coalition. Although the Rhine provided protection in the West, the East was an open, unbroken plain pushing into northern Central Europe, flowing forward without a major geographical obstacle more formidable than the Vistula and the Oder Rivers. For the Germans, therefore, the danger of a two-front war was a constant nightmare, a threat to be exorcised. In any European struggle, Germany would seek either to woo one side into acquiescence or complicity, or

to crush one opponent rapidly before the other could bring his
force to bear. In either case, Germany must seek a quick
victory; for even a one-front war, if protracted, could
develop into a two-front conflict.

But, in World War II, her impulsion to rapid victory
also came from the will and dreams of Adolph Hitler. Convinced
of his world historical role, the Führer was, nevertheless,
filled with foreboding about its ultimate accomplishment:

> Essentially it depends upon me, my existence, because
> of my political activities. Furthermore the fact
> that probably no one will ever again have the
> confidence of the whole German people as I do. There
> will probably never again be a man in the future
> with more authority than I have. My existence is
> therefore a factor of great value. But I can be
> eliminated at any time by a criminal or an idiot.[7]

This fear, this sense of the threat of time, haunted Hitler.
As he told his semi-confidant, Hermann Raushning: "'I have
so little time...too little time.'"[8]

Personal fear was reinforced by ideological considerations.
According to his Weltanschauung, which emphasized that a state
must either expand or die, Germany's opportunity was imminent
but momentary. If she did not act now, her hour would be
lost. If Germany did not resolve her main problem, Lebensraum,
she would decline as a national power:

> The German nation is composed of 85 million people,
> which because of the number of individuals and the
> compactness of habitation form a homogeneous European
> racial body which cannot be found in any other
> country. On the other hand, it justifies the demand
> for living space more than for any other nation.
> If no political body exists in space, corresponding
> to the German racial body, then that is the
> consequence of several centuries of historical
> development, and should this political condition
> continue to exist, it will represent the greatest
> danger to the preservation of the German nation...
> at its present high level....Instead of growth,
> sterility will be introduced....The German future
> is therefore dependent exclusively on the solution
> of the need for living space. Such a solution can
> be sought naturally only for a limited period,
> about 1-3 generations.[9]

As Hitler saw it, the choice was narrow. Germany must
solve her problem by 1943-1945 at the latest: "After this
we can only expect a change for the worse."[10] For then,
Germany would decline "in relative power."[11]

a. The Wehrmacht: Flawed Sword

By the late thirties, Hitler was well aware of the
deficiencies of German mobilization. He realized that
Germany had neither the military machine, the economy nor the
morale to sustain a long war. Although impressive, the German
military machine lacked depth and staying power. It suffered
from grave weaknesses, fatal in any protracted war.[12]

The Army was queen of the services with 106 divisions
in 1939 and 155 divisions in 1940.[13]But, at the outbreak of
the Second World War, the mobilization of military manpower
"fell nearly a million short of the number of the armed
forces at the outbreak of World War I."[14]If the Army was
large and well-equipped for continental warfare, the Navy and
the Air Force were not prepared for global operations. The
Navy had plans for the construction of a well-balanced high-sea
fleet capable of challenging the British.[15]But this program,
the Z plan, would not be completed until 1945. Therefore,
it was scrapped at the beginning of the war. The Führer could
not wait. He did not even wait to build a substantial submarine fleet, the weapon system which had brought England
close to defeat in World War I. At the opening of the war,
German production of U-boats was pitifully low: three per
month.[16]Finally, the German Navy had no air arm, a costly
deficiency in the future Battle of the Atlantic.[17]

The German Luftwaffe was immensely effective in the
first campaigns of the Second World War. But it lacked
balance. This weakness was doubly ironic since its chief,
Goering, was the second most powerful man in the Third Reich
and since the German Air Force was an independent establishment.[18]
Its personnel, however, were mostly Army men with Army
mentalities. Few professional aviators were available due to
the restrictions placed upon military aircraft by the Treaty
of Versailles.[19]And the absence of an elite professional
corps meant the absence of a service viewpoint. More seriously,
it meant that the Luftwaffe officers gave little thought to
the development of independent strategic theories.[20]The fighter,
the dive-bomber and other planes to support army operations
were produced in abundance. But not the long-range bomber.[21]
Unlike the British and the Americans, the Germans never

devised the tool necessary for an independent strategic air
offensive. To summarize, the Wehrmacht was basically suited
for a limited, rapid continental war; it was completely
inadequate for a protracted world war.

b. The German Economy: "Guns and Butter."

Economically, Germany was not prepared for a long war.
Her economic mobilization was neither total, efficient nor
effective. It was not total because it failed to weld the
economy together, wedding it to military needs. It sought
to provide the German people with both "butter" and "guns."[22]
Therefore, the German government failed to impose high taxes,
to scale down food imports, to insure its supply of raw
materials,[23] to pour sufficient funds into armament factories
and military facilities.[24] Public expenditures for rearmament
did not amount to more than forty per-cent of all public
spending.[25]

Germany's economic mobilization was not efficient because,
despite its totalitarian nature, the Nazi government was
poorly organized. It seethed with factions and vested
interests whose special wishes often clashed with those of
the state. These enclaves could hamper the development of
any government program which conflicted with their own
interests. The Party members, the steel cartels, the other
industrialists: these groups could fight, even defeat,
the commands of the state.[26]

Finally, Germany's economic mobilization was not effective
because it achieved neither the goal of Gleichschaltung nor
that of Autarky. Gleichschaltung (synchronization) involved
the coordination of all the activities of the Third Reich
under the Führer's absolute control. Although achieved
politically to a great extent, it was not accomplished within
the economy. Only the abandonment of the conservative
financial policies of Schacht and the adoption of bolder
policies of financing armaments could have yielded an economic
program commensurate with the rearmament program. But Hitler
and other members of the Nazi entourage shared Schacht's fears
of devaluation, inflation and the other dangerous effects
that a policy of extensive rearmament might have.[27]

The second goal, Autarky (economic self-sufficiency)

was an impossible objective. Although Hitler strove to make
Germany as self-sufficient as possible, [28] he undoubtedly
recognized its ultimate futility: "...the programs failed
to provide even a moderate degree of self-sufficiency
[in important materials], and if an all-out effort had been
immediately necessary, Germany would have had to gamble
on continued access to foreign sources."[29]

c. Germany's Psychological Mobilization: without Enthusiasm

Germany's psychological mobilization for war was even
less advanced than either her military or economic mobilization.
William L. Shirer, American correspondent in Berlin, noted
that the apathy of the Germans to the outbreak of the Second
World War formed a startling contrast to the enthusiasm with
which they had greeted the outbreak of World War I. The memory
of the trenches and the bloody losses of the First World War
was too strong for enthusiasm. Even the Nazis, superb masters
of mass propaganda, could not generate any martial fervor:

> In 1914...the excitement in Berlin on the first day
> of the World War was tremendous. Today, no excitement,
> no hurrahs, no cheering, no throwing of flowers,
> no war fever, no war hysteria. There is not even any
> hate for the French and the British--despite Hitler's
> various proclamations to the people, the party, the
> East Army, the West Army, accusing the "English
> warmongers and capitalist Jews" of starting this war.
> When I passed the French and British embassies this
> afternoon, the sidewalk in front of each of them was
> deserted. A lone Schupo paced up and down before each.[30]

d. The Strategy of the Swift War

Germany was not mobilized for total war because Hitler
did not plan one. Instead his strategy called for a series
of localized, limited conflicts: little wars in which the
enemy could be speedily crushed before the Western Allies could
intervene.[31] In each case, the foe would be isolated and devoured
piecemeal. Hitler's early successes in Austria and Czechoslovakia confirmed his predictions. Moreover, his "bloodless"
triumphs convinced him that since his foes were morally
gutless, he could settle his scores in Europe without worrying
about British and French reaction.[33] He initiated a continental
war without realizing that it would ultimately, almost
automatically, become a world war.[34]

3. The Soviet Union: the Dangers of a Short War

Even when planning his invasion of Russia, Hitler thought
in terms of a short war. Absolutely confident in the superiority of the German Army to the Russian, he blithely predicted
that the Wehrmacht would rapidly crush the Soviet Army and
overrun European Russia: "'You have only to kick in the door,'
he told Rundstedt, 'and the whole rotten structure will come
crashing down.'"[35]And although he quarreled with the Army's
plans for the Soviet campaign, he agreed with O.K.H. on the
importance of crushing Russian resistance on the frontier and
in the forward area, thereby preventing any large-scale
Russian retreat into the interior: a retreat that would
infinitely prolong the campaign.[36]

If a rapid campaign meant victory for the Germans and
defeat for the Russians, an extended campaign would reverse
the odds. For the Soviet Union, time was against her in the
short run; for her in the long run. In 1941, Russia was not
strong enough to defeat a German invasion; but her potential
resources were greater than those of her enemy. It was
essentially a question of mobilization which only time
would allow.

But even time carried a sense of urgency. Since the
Soviet Union remained a predominantly agricultural state,
she could not initially hope to match the armies of the
industrialized western powers. In the interwar period,
Stalin sought to bridge the time gap. Conscious that the
interval was short, convinced that the Soviet Union must
achieve industrial status rapidly to survive the hostile
designs of the other powers,[37]he sought the modernization
of the U.S.S.R. through successive Five-Year Plans. For
only these industrial programs could provide the indispensable
basis for a modernized army. The Soviet Union needed time:
time to prepared, time to survive. This need would be
even greater once the enemy launched his attack.

Even the most stable element of national power,
geography, initially favored the aggressor. A carefully
prepared attack could secure tactical, if not strategic,
surprise. For the border was so extensive and vulnerable

that military prediction became impossibly difficult. There
were so many points where the enemy could strike that even
Russia's vast manpower could not cover these unending
reaches with cordon defenses: "The frontier was an extremely
long one--the Finnish frontier, between the Arctic and the
Gulf of Finland about 750 miles long, and the 'German'
frontier, between a point just east of Memel on the Baltic
and the mouth of the Danube in Rumania, over 1,250 miles
long."[38] If the initial shock of attack could be absorbed,
if the Soviet Command could successfully extricate its forces
from westernmost Russia while mobilizing its reserve power
in the east, then geography would become a friend rather
than a foe. The long distances would swallow an invading
army, exhausting its forces while drawing it further and
further away from its supply centers. Allied to the long
Russian distances was the hard Russian winter. If the
enemy could be drawn slowly into the interior while the
summer passed away,[39] the winter would find him far from
home at the worst possible time.

a. The Soviet Army: Only in a Long War

At the outbreak of the Russian-German war, the Soviet
Army numbered between 150 and 180 divisions on Russia's
western frontier.[40] The Germans and their allies had
approximately 149 divisions concentrated for the attack
on Russia.[41] But this relative equality in numbers is deceptive.
For the quality and experience of the German Army was
initially superior to that of the Russians. In leadership,
equipment and morale, the German soldier had no superior in
Europe.

The officer corps of the German Army had been blooded
on the fields of Poland, Norway and France. On the uppermost
levels, it was almost uniformly good. Contrastingly, the
Russian officer corps had not recovered from the brutal
purges of 1937-1938 which had eliminated about 15,000 of
its members.[42] The effect was tantamount to professional
castration. The qualifications and professional ability
of the Russian soldier and officer sank perceptibly. The
experience of the Red Army, moreover, was far inferior to

that of the German army at this time. Accordingly, Soviet
military leaders drew the wrong conclusions on armored
warfare,[43] ignoring the lessons of the early campaigns of the
Second World War.[44] The Germans, of course, were the champions
of armored war.

In equipment, the Russian armies were also outclassed.[45]
The Soviet soldier, however, was a more formidable foe than
the German Wehrmacht had previously encountered:

> 'The Russian soldier,' Krylov had said, 'loves a
> fight and scorns death. He was given the order:
> "If you are wounded, pretend to be dead; wait until
> the Germans come up; then select one of them and
> kill him! Kill him with gun, bayonet, or knife.
> Tear his throat with your teeth. Do not die
> without leaving behind you a German corpse."'[46]

If he were ultimately a formidable opponent, he did not
perform remarkably in the early stages of the campaign. His
performance was weakened by poor training and by the effects
of the Great Purge on the Soviet officer corps. Essentially,
the Russian soldier, like the average Russian civilian, suffered
from inertia induced by long years of totalitarian immersion
under Tsars and commissars. When the German onslaught broke
over Russia, he was unprepared psychologically for the blow.
Only the resurgence of Russian patriotism and the re-assertion
of Soviet control over the average soldier saved the Red Army
from disintegration.[47] In morale, therefore, it was initially
inferior to the German Army.[48]

The Soviet Air Forces suffered from obsolescence. At
the time of the German invasion, it consisted of about
8,000 planes, the newer models merely beginning production
while the older types were markedly inferior to those of the
Germans.[49] Also, menaced by the land armies of continental
enemies, the Soviet military leaders ignored the potentialities
of strategic air offensives.[50]

    b. The Soviet Economy: The Time Lag

As the deficiencies in Soviet material indicated, the
Five Year Plans had not achieved their final objectives.
The economic gap between the essentially agricultural
eoncomy of the Soviet Union and the predominantly industrial
economies of the western powers had not been closed by the
time of the German attack. As indicated, Soviet production

still lagged.

Although the U.S.S.R.'s economic potential was great, the essential base of the Soviet production system being well established by 1940,[51] military production goals remained unachieved by the time of the German attack. Russia could not produce enough new planes and tanks in time to check the initial blow.[52] No longer a sleeping giant, Russia had not yet fully awakened.

      c. Psychological Mobilization and the Need for a Long War

By June 1941, psychological mobilization was even less advanced than economic and military mobilization. The elements of dissidence were strong throughout Russian nationalities.[53] It took the full brutality of the war, the shock of invasion, the inhuman cruelties of the Nazis and the strong appeal of the Soviet leadership to native patriotism before the Russians could be psychologically mobilized for the war.

In any swift war, therefore, the Russians would be at a marked disadvantage. Their hope for victory lay in a protracted struggle. Given their military unpreparedness, their economic shortages and the uncertain temper of the nationalities, the logical strategy would have been to prepare carefully for an extended conflict. It would have been wise for the Soviets to concentrate their forces within the interior, leaving the frontier to delaying elements which would merely harass the advancing foe, making him pay for every march forward. After wearing down their opponent, the Soviets could finally assume the offensive. Their strategy should have imitated Mao-Tse-Tung's.

However, their strategic plans and military dispositions favored their opponent. And ultimately these failures necessitated a much longer war. Before 1939, the Russian army was well positioned; it had a workable defense plan which recognized the impossibility of defending the vast borders of Russia, or of trying to be strong everywhere. One of inheritances of Field Marshal Tukhachevski, it called for a light concentration of forces in the north and for the disposition of massed Soviet mobile forces on the Dnieper. From here they could strike out at the right flank. As the

Field Marshal anticipated, the enemy would be drawn into the
desolate and extensive corridor stretching between Leningrad
and the northern reaches of the Pripet Marshes. Here the
Soviet forces could counterattack at the moment when the foe
was already feeling the effects of overextension.[54]

But on the eve of the German attack, the Russian forces
were positioned along the frontier. The Soviets had formulated
a doctrine of the general offensive: "an integrated 'steam
roller' of all arms,"[55]an irresistable wave of mass and might
rolling down upon the helpless and bewildered foe. Shaposhnikov,
Chief of the Soviet General Staff, and Zhukov were devoted
adherents to this doctrine. Moreover, it reflected the
predominantly offensive spirit of Bolshevik ideology.[56]Not
surprisingly, therefore, the Soviet military leaders were
susceptible to the fatal attractions of the attack and prone
to the foolish military dispositions[57]which led to the early
disasters. These defeats only confirmed the need to fight
a protracted war.

Russia's geographical position, the relative backwardness
of her military, economic and psychological mobilization,
militated for a long-term strategy.[58]Because the Soviets were
caught in an exposed position at the beginning of the Soviet-
German war, they were roundly beaten at the start of the campaign.
These defeats, which chewed up Russian divisions in a maelstrom
of destruction, forced the Soviets to resort to attritional
warfare while they rebuilt their forces. If they could slow
the momentum of the enemy advance, leaving him their scorched
earth, their destroyed cities and burnt crops, time was on
their side. Time to complete the mobilization of the U.S.S.R.
Time to bring the three to one superiority of the Russian
masses to bear on the Germans.[59]Time to complete the
reorganization of the Russian armies: restoring the professional
command and prestige of the officer, strengthening the morale
and the incentive of the Russian soldier,[60]more than doubling
the size of the Soviet Army by the end of 1944.[61]Time for
the initally shaken morale of the Soviet Army to heal, rise
and turn in strength.[62]Time to evacuate Russian industry
from the Central and Eastern Ukraine to the less-accesible

reaches of the Urals, the Volga, Western Siberia and Central
Asia.[63]Time for Russian industry to recover, rebuild and
expand.[64]Time for the Communist leadership to reawaken
the pride and patriotism of the Russian people. Time until
the immense but slumbering resources of the Allied nations
could be mobilized and brought to Russia's aid across the
dangerous reaches of the Arctic and the difficult and tenuous
lines of communication running through the Persian
corridor.[65]Time for the Allies to launch a second-front.[66]
Time to gain time. Time to win.

4. The United Kingdom: A Matter of Time

Like the Soviet Union, the United Kingdom required a
long war. For the British have won their wars by utilizing
a strategy which combines the attritional pressure of an
ever-tightening economic blockade with the utilization of
the massed armies of their continental allies. But economic
warfare is slow and allies are often difficult to recruit.
In 1939, Great Britain, the earliest industrial nation in
the world, could still command formidable resources in
manpower and economic potential. But these resources were
largely scatered throughout her far-flung, long-distanced
empire. Therefore, the mobilization of this reservoir of
strength was slow. However, once mobilized and allied to
the strength of others, it could be decisive.

Even in the late twenties, the Committee of Imperial
Defense had formulated a definition of the "Great War."
Although there was debate and disagreement on the meaning
of that phrase, its accepted definition was: a war
"in which the whole resources of a nation would be
engaged."[67]It would perforce be long. For, as the British
planners assumed, such a development would involve the
progressive unfolding of the nation's total strength:
military, economic, psychological. Ultimately, as
the planners realized, it would "demand the maximum of civilian

sacrifice and achieve the maximum of military striking power."[68]

Geography favored the British. Although the Channel may
be a negligible obstacle in the age of nuclear weapons, in 1940
it was a formidable anti-tank ditch, an impossible crossing
for an invader without naval or aerial supremacy. And, in the
Second World War, only airpower could offset the advantages
which this barrier, combined with British naval superiority,
conferred upon England. A short interval of space gave the
British a long interlude of time. Behind this protection, the
British could mobilize their rescources, using their naval
supremacy to wear down their foe while preparing a counterattack.[69]

There are two beginnings to British mobilization: September 3, 1939, when England declared war against Germany, and
June 1940, immediately after the fall of France. Although the
British always needed a long war for victory, time had a
different tempo in each instance. At the beginning of the
war, delay favored the Allies, for the longer the interval
between the declaration of war and the German attack the more
certain the victory. Time would allow the British and the
French an opportunity to garner their potential strength and
to convert it into military power. "'The Allies are bound
to win in the end,' declared Mr. Chamberlain, 'and the only
question is how long it will take them to achieve their
purpose.'"[70] There was no feeling of urgency during the
comfortable months of the "phony war."[71] The British thought
the war would last three years, a prediction that now seems
grossly optimistic.[72]

After Dunkirk and the Fall of France, complacency
evaporated. Everything was charged with such a terrible
sense of urgency that it would not have been surprising if
all sense of long-range timing had vanished. But the sense
of time is inexorably linked to military planning; even in
crisis and imminent disaster, British leadership did not
lose its perspective. An official historian defines the
British approach as follows:

> In that summer, when it might have semed vain
> to take thought for any but the most immediate
> of morrows, the Government was thinking and working
> in lengthening dimensions of time: the days ahead,

> the weeks and months ahead, the years ahead. In
> the short run, there was no longer any meaning in
> the old deliberate plans of mobilization for a
> three years' war; British survival depended upon
> the efforts of the next weeks and days. But as
> the immediate dangers were in rapid succession
> fended off, the forward view of work and battle
> lengthened into a future no longer closed by the
> clear horizon of three years.[73]

Victory was predictable only as a long-range goal, the gift

of a protracted war. Churchill warned the nation that the

British must "ride out the storm of war, and...outlive the

menace of tyranny, if necessary for years, if necessary alone."[74]

    a. British Military Mobilization: Present Weakness,

Future Promise

    At the outbreak of the Second World War, Britain's military,

eoncomic and psychological mobilization had merely begun. The

British still felt the effects of years of military penury,

reinforced by the ten year rule. This prediction, literally

accurate but pragmatically idiotic, was made at the end of the

First World War: "'there will be no major war for ten years.'"[75]

This assumption was the kiss of death to any military program;

and even after it was rescinded in March 1932, its deleterious

effects lingered.

    At the outbreak of war, the poor relation among the

neglected was the British Army. Its weakness was compounded

by Britain's imperial commitments which scattered military

units far from the European front.[76]In the first five weeks

of the war, the British could not send more than four divisions

to the Western Front in France. And the task of mobilizing

an effective BEF was complicated by the conscription laws.

Although conscription would ultimately expand the strength of

the British Army, its immediate effect was to handicap existing

units, thereby thwarting their effectiveness and draining

the core of professional officers needed for the training and

organization of the new units.[77]It is obvious that the British

could not supply any force powerful enough to defeat the

German Army. Any hope of victory depended on the French

Army. The British could play only an auxiliary role.

    The strength of the British Navy was still formidable,

but now subject to an undefined danger: a coalition of

naval powers: Germany, Italy and Japan.[78]Weighing this

strategic threat, the Admiralty had pressed for the adoption
of "a two power standard":[79]"a superiority of three capital
ships over Germany in home waters and of one capital ship over
Japan."[80]Since the Germans had an impressive ship-building
program, which if completed would seriously challenge British
supremacy, the war came at a fortunate time for the Royal Navy.[81]
With its natural command of the seas, Britain retained a strategic
mobility that would allow her to commit and deploy her forces
at points and times of her own choosing. Yet even here
actual power did not cover potential challenge. The destroyer
strength of the Royal Navy was notably weak for a naval force
which would have to defeat the counterblockade imposed by the
German submarine.[82]Moreover, the craft necessary for amphibious
assault across distant seas were not even on the drawing
boards. Of course, in 1939, the need for them was not apparent:
the Allies still held a front on the continent of Europe.

Even naval supremacy was no guarantee of immunity from
invasion. Air power could neutralize superior sea power.
The United Kingdom could no longer be merely protected by a
shield; it also needed a helmet. As Churchill summarized:

> Sea power, when properly understood, is a wonderful
> thing. The passage of an army across salt water
> in the face of superior fleets and flottilas is
> an almost impossible feat. Steam had added
> enormously to the power of the Navy to defend
> Great Britain....But now there was the air.
> What effect had this sovereign development
> produced upon the invasion problem? Evidently
> if the enemy could dominate the narrow seas on
> both sides of the Straits of Dover, by superior
> air power, the losses of our flottilas would
> be very heavy and might eventually be fatal.
> No one would wish, except on a supreme occasion,
> to bring heavy battleships or large cruisers into
> waters commanded by the German bombers.[83]

Aerial superiority was a necessary adjunct to naval
supremacy. But here time played a dual role, offering a
double salvation. Since the close of the First World War
and the dramatic advent of airpower, the British public
and government had anticipated that any new conflict
would open with a knock-out blow by the enemy air force,

a pre-nuclear cataclysm which would devastate Great Britain
before she could strike back.[84] The Air Staff felt that the
only proper counter strategy was massive retaliation,
the fear of which would keep the foe from attacking.[85]
The investigations which preceded and accompanied the
Munich crisis, however, pointed out the need to develop
the fighter force.[86] Unless England survived the first
attack, there would be no chance to launch a retaliatory
stroke.[87] As previously pointed out, this shift in emphasis
came in the nick of time.[88]

In a sense, therefore, only the postponement of
war, however unfortunate it may have been in other
respects, and the interlude of the 'phony war' gave the
British time to build up their Fighter Command. The
official history of the Royal Air Force analyzes the
unexpected blessing conferred by the year's delay secured
through the Munich Agreement:

> ...For the Royal Air Force, the value of a year's
> grace--not Chamberlain's intention in concluding
> the Munich agreement, but its only possible
> justification--may perhaps be seen from this:
> that in September, 1938, to oppose the German
> long-range striking force of some 1,200 modern
> bombers, Fighter Command could muster, including
> all reserves, only 93 of the new eight-gun
> fighters. All the remainder of its 666 aircraft
> were the oudated biplanes. No Spitfires
> were yet in line; and the Hurricanes, being
> without heating for their guns could not
> fight above 15,000 feet, even in summer. A
> year later, when war came, over five hundred
> of these modern fighters were immediately
> available for operations.[89]

The disaster in Flanders and the battle over Dunkirk
cut down British fighter forces.[90] But the irresolution and
unpreparedness of the Führer for the assault on England
gave the British another gift of time. By the opening
of the Battle of Britain, Fighter Command was even
stronger than on the eve of war. But, though it could prevent
defeat by frustrating the Luftwaffe's bid for aerial
supremacy, it could not attain victory. It could merely

deflect the aim of the enemy, not strike at his heart
and brain. Only Bomber Command could achieve this offensive
aim. At the outbreak of war, however, Bomber Command was
under strength, poorly equipped and totally lacking in
the navigational and operational skills necessary to carry
the attack into the enemy's heartland.[91] The Air Staff,
therefore, welcomed the respite from attack that the
"phony war" gave them. Time would be as much of a boon
to Bomber Command as to Fighter Command.

Moreover, the problem of aerial armament was complicated
by the need to provide adequate training and the need to
build up adequate reserves. Since any air offensive
could win only by the sheer weight and persistence of
its assault, front line strength was useless without
organization in depth behind it.[92] For the sake of the
future, immediate air offensives against Germany were
sacrificed. And the future held hope. Since the RAF
was better balanced, better organized than the Luftwaffe,
containing both an offensive and a defensive force,
it could in time build its strength sufficently to carry
the war back into the enemy's heartland.[93] Its strength,
however, ultimately depended upon the speed with which
British factories could turn out more, newer and better
planes. Operational deployment would depend ultimately
upon economic mobilization.

b. British Economic Mobilization: Re-armament
in Depth

A comparison between the prewar economies of Britain
and Germany would inevitably favor the latter. And, in
the minds of most observers, the early initiation of
re-armament in Germany would reinforce this advantage,[94]
leaving the United Kingdom hopelessly behind from start
to finish. But reality defeated all anticipation,
betrayed all prophecies. For surprisingly, the wartime
acceleration of munitions production was far greater
in Great Britain than in Germany. The economic historian,

Burton Klein, provides the statistics:

> In Britain...total gross national output
> increased six and one-half times between 1939
> and 1942, representing in 1942 one quarter of
> Britain's total gross national product.
> During the same period in Germany, however,
> munitions output hardly doubled, and as a
> propotion of total output reached only 11
> percent in 1942.[95]

A comparison of aircraft production is staggering.
Contrary to contemporary belief,[96] British aircraft
production overtook German aircraft production in 1940,
pushing ahead with remarkable speed and maintaining its
lead over its initially superior rival: "...Britain led
Germany in total aircraft production by 40 per cent in
1940, by 70 per cent in 1941, and by 50 per cent in
1942."[97]

But Britain's production lead extended to ground
equipment as well as to aircraft. The reasons for this
unexpected, unsuspected superiority lie in the different
aims and goals of the two powers. Since the Germans
sought to wage and win a limited continental war, they
re-armed in width: seeking to create a formidable
military force which could achieve the goals of German
policy within a short period of time. For the British,
however, the conflict was world wide and unlimited from
the start. To achieve victory, they needed a military
force, so equipped and so mobilized that it could fight
a protracted war under a multitude of conditions. They
had to re-arm in breadth.[98] The two powers and their leaders
had a totally different point of departure, based on
different estimates of the length of the war.

Re-armament in breadth, preparation for a protracted
war, meant a total mobilization of the resources of the
country, achieving an effective balance between the
claims of the armed services and the demands of industry.[99]
So the British planned and worked towards total
commitment. The Germans did not.[100] If England forfeited

time in the short run by not re-arming immediately after
Hitler's assumption of power, Germany forfeited it in the
long run by not re-arming in depth. By the time the
Germans turned to full-scale re-armament, the British
were totally mobilized and United States production was
moving full blast.

     c. British Psychological Mobilization: the Awakening

    Economic mobilization ultimately depended upon
psychological mobilization. It depended upon the realization
by the British public that war was inevitable, a realization
which did not exist until after the Munich conference.
The main purpose of early re-armament had been to preserve
the peace or to prepare for full-scale war production,
should it become necessary. M. M. Postan defines its
purpose as follows:

> Until 1935 international disarmament was still
> a popular hope and still the object of British
> foreign policy. For at least another three
> years the object of successive rearmament
> programmes was not so much preparation for war
> as the reinforcement of peace. Their purpose
> was to back up diplomatic efforts with a show
> of force and thereby to impress the would-be
> aggressors and to reassure public opinion
> at home. The early stages of rearmament
> were therefore dominated by the need for a
> 'deterrent' display--a first line strength
> impressive on paper but not necessarily backed
> by sufficient establishments or by industrial
> reserves.[101]

In the dissillusionment of the post-Munich period, most
Englishmen realized that war was inevitable. The process
of psychological mobilization had reached an initial
step, a step still guarded and muted by comfortable
assumptions on the superiority of Allies strength.
Given time, we will win.[102]

    Full psychological commitment could come only with
further realization: the war would be a long, hard
conflict in which victory was not easily assured. This
awakening came in the wake of the disasters of 1940:
then the realization grew that England was involved in

a life and death struggle. As the Chiefs of Staff had
warned in March 1940: "'Time is on our side...only if we
take the fullest possible advantage of it.'"[103]Only in this
realization was the national will finally steeled. In the
words of Hancock and Gowing:

> An agreed statement of the national interest and
> duty emerged very slowly out of the long debate
> between Government, Parliament and people;
> clarification of mind and concentration of will
> were not achieved until the great testing time
> of 1940.[104]

d. Play for Time: the Strategy of Attrition

Because her mobilization was incomplete but already
moving steadily in 1939, Britain, unlike Germany, sought
to gain a prolonged pause in which to arm and prepare.
Germany, armed in width and led by a gambler determined to
win by a throw of the dice, chose a strategy of annihilation,
designed to destroy its foe in battle before the advantages
of surprise and superiority passed. Britain, temporarily
weak but arming in depth, sought a strategy of stalemate
and attrition designed to wear down the enemy while
preparing for the ultimate counterattack.[105]Logically,
therefore, the initial strategy, drafted by the British and
French staffs, consisted of three stages:

> "We should be faced by enemies who would be
> more fully prepared than ourselves for war
> on a national scale, would have superiority
> in air and land forces, but would be inferior
> at sea and in general economic strength. In
> these circumstances, we must be prepared to
> face a major offensive directed against either
> France or Great Britain or against both. To
> defeat such an offensive we should have to
> concentrate all our initial efforts, and
> during this time our major strategy would
> be defensive....Our subsequent policy should
> be directed to holding Germany and to dealing
> decisively with Italy, while at the same time
> building up our military strength to a point
> at which we shall be in a position to undertake
> the offensive against Germany."[106]

The first period would be one of postponement and preparation,
lasting approximately three years.[107]The second period,

one of limited liability; and the third, of full-scale
counterattack. In this evaluation, drafted in the spring
of 1939, the Allies would hold their strength in reserve
while the enemy wasted his initiative; then, using their
accumulated strength, they would throw themselves
upon him.[108]

The British correctly placed their hopes for victory
upon a protracted war. But they could not anticipate
the time and effort required for the task. And they
could not anticipate that by the end of the war Britain
would have passed from full mobilization towards possible
exhaustion. The continuation of the war into 1945 imposed
severe hardships and strains on the British economy. As
John Ehrman notes, national commitment had passed its
limits:

> ...the prolongation of the war in Europe imposed
> new demands which could scarcely be met except
> by increased aid from America. It was not a
> case, as in the United States, of adjustments
> within a programme which still held a measure
> of slack; but of extracting the last ounce from
> an economy which, already pledged to war more
> fully than at any time in British history, was
> becoming steadily less competent to maintain,
> in its accustomed proportion, the operations
> of the British armed forces.[109]

For the British, the war had lasted too long.

5. The United States: the Sluggish Giant

The United States, with its seemingly inexhaustible
resources, could sustain the strain of a long war. And
yet this country has always sought to fight as rapid a
war as possible, a paradox intensified by the general
unpreparedness of the American military and economic
establishments for war, a condition which would seem to
demand a prolonged period of mobilization. Actually the
paradox is not absolute since the temporal imperative
follows two patterns or rhythms in American strategic
planning. The first asserts itself in the pre-war

period of preparation when emphasis falls on gaining
time to strengthen a nation ill prepared for the approaching crisis. With the declaration of war, the emphasis
on time reverses itself. Underneath the shift, however,
lies a basic consistency. The emphasis, whether in the
pre-war phase or during the war itself, falls on speed:
we must be quick to prepare, quick to act. "The affair
cries haste and speed must answer."[110]

    a. American Military Mobilization: A Lethargic
Awakening

    A rapid war calls for a high degree of pre-war
mobilization and preparation, which would allow a power
to deploy its forces swiftly in every theater. But even
by the end of 1941, America's preparations were incomplete,
her mobilization limited. General Eisenhower paints
a graphic pciture of these lethargic days:

> In early 1940, however, the United States Army
> mirrored the attitudes of the American people,
> as is the case today and as it was a century
> ago. The mass of officers and men lacked any
> sense of urgency. Athletics, recreation, and
> entertainment took precedence in most units
> over serious training. Some of the officers,
> in the long years of peace, had worn for
> themselves deep ruts of professional routine
> within which they were sheltered from vexing
> new ideas and troublesome problems. Others,
> bogged down in one grade for many years because
> seniority was the only basis for promotion,
> had abandoned all hope of progress. Possibly
> many of them, and many of the troops too,
> felt that the infantry-man's day had passed.[111]

It was a cross between the land of the lotus eaters and
Dante's Limbo!

    The mobilized strength of the Army had declined
throughout the twenties and the thirties. Although the
National Defense Act of 1920 allowed for a Regular Army
of 280,000 men, its strength immediately dropped to
201,918 men in 1920 and still numbered only 267,767
men by 1940.[112] The original intent of the National

Defense Act had been sound. A force of 280,000 men would be organized as a nucleus for a mass army. In an emergency, this nucleus would expand rapidly, providing maximum efficiency with minium waste. "To that end it would be composed of a maximum number of units in the form of cadres of men highly trained for expansion in emergency. This necessarily meant the minimum of men per unit in peacetime."[113]But this scheme could not survive the financial stringency of the military programs of the twenties and thirties.[114]

The more realistic mobilization plans of the thirties were attempts to assure that the Army could deploy with adequate rapidity, attempts to insure that it would be sufficiently strong to cover its own expansion. Typical were the Protective Mobilization Plans (PMP) which sought mobilization by defined stages. In the first stage, the United States Army would consist of an Initial Protective Force (IPF), a defensive force of 400,000 men which would allow the nation enough time to mobilize more fully.[115]In the second stage, initiated by the declaration of an emergency, the Army would expand rapidly to 1,000,000 men.[116]These plans, like the National Defense Act of 1920, attempted to insure that the military mobilization of the United States would not be delayed beyond the danger point.

But the problem of effectively raising an army did not end with its manpower. The financial blight which struck the military establishment left no hope that the Army would be adequately equipped for waging a modern war. As Eisenhower notes:

> The situation in weapons and equipment added little to the infantryman's esprit. The Springfield rifle was outmoded; there was no dependable defense against a modern tank or plane; troops carried wooden models of mortars and machine guns and were able to study some of our new weapons only from blueprints. Equipment of all sorts was lacking and much

of that in use had been originally produced for the national army of World War I.[117]

The American Army was a diminutive force equipped with obsolete equipment. This condition was reinforced by a genial unconcern on the part of Congress over research and development.[118]

If the equipment situation was only adequate by 1918 standards, the training situation was only adequate for the Indian warfare of the late nineteenth century. The Army was reduced to small units, whose exercises were strictly confined by the ammunition shortage.[119] In 1939, there was "no functioning corps or field army,"[120] making large-scale troop maneuvers unthinkable. Even divisional exercises were impossible because of insufficient motor transportation.[121]

Finally, reinforcing and perpetuating this condition of unpreparedness was the psychological attitude of many officers. Eisenhower admits that many of them were completely oblivious to the mounting danger, even after the fall of France in 1940:

> The commanding general of one United States division, an officer of long service and high standing, offered to bet, on the day of the French armistice, that England would not last six weeks longer--and he proposed the wager much as he would have bet on rain or shine for the morrow.[122]

The condition of the United States Army in 1939, at the outbreak of war in Europe, was so pathetic that only time could save it from its disabilities which had grown interminably in the interwar period. By 1939, time was vanishing.[123]

Although the United States Navy was far better off, its condition was relative to the challenges which the United States would face in the near future, relative to the strength of the potential enemy fleets. The strength of the American Navy did not decline as precipitously as that of the Army at the end of World War I. But

neither did it grow.[124]The Washington Naval Agreements,[125]
perfectly sensible for the twenties and completely senseless
for the thirties, eventually reduced American naval power
to a position of inferiority in the Pacific. For, although
the naval needs and responsibilities of the United States
had grown from those of a one-ocean to those of a two-ocean
navy, the Washington Disarmament Agreements limited her
to her initial status, thereby giving the Japanese local
superiority.[126]Throughout the twenties and the early thirties,
the pacifists who regarded re-armament as a mortal sin,
almost inseparable from aggression and war,[127]and the
advocates of air power, who unilaterally and infallibly
condemned surface navies as obsolescent dinosaurs fit for
the rubbish pile of history,[128]perpetuated the inequities
of the Washington Treaties. But these inequities were
even more insidious because they remained largely unnoticed.
Even on the ever of war, the Navy was still seen as an
impenetrable wall sheltering the country from enemy
attack.

But the current weaknesses of the United State Navy,
its initial vulnerability in the Second World War, lay
in the types of vessels that the Navy favored, vessels
whose future usefulness was not as great as other types
ignored by contemporary naval opinion. The emphasis was
on the battleship, not on the cruiser, carrier or destroyer.[129]
And, in naval training and maneuvers, the exercises
turned into courtly gunnery matches in which, like in
the medieval tourney, ships competed against one another
under ideal conditions.[130]These naval jousts were hardly
adequate preparation for modern naval battles.

Despite her weaknesses, apparent in the sequel, the
Navy's actual strength was greater than either the Army's
or the Air Force's strength. Moreover, her potential
development was formidable. The impetus towards new
ship construction, initially promoted by President
Franklin D. Roosevelt, always an avid Navy fan, was
strengthened and quickened by the outbreak of war in

Europe on September 3, 1939. The fleet that would carry
the United States to victory was already in the making.[131]
The new fleet would be a perfectly balanced tool for the
extension of global strategy. But time was necessary for
the completion of this two-ocean navy, capable of asserting its superiority simultaneously in the Atlantic and
the Pacific.

The sense of urgency found in the Army programs was
not evident in the Navy's new expansion plans. The major
reason is that although naval officers were aware of the
Navy's weaknesses, the extent of these weaknesses was
not as obvious then as it is today. They "envisaged
the battles of the next war as long-range gunfire
duels between battle lines, as at Jutland...."[132]

But so did everyone else. The Japanese, the Germans,
the Italians, the French: all were obsessed by the
battleship mania.[133] All identified naval strength with
capital ships, with the mass and range of fire power.
And in 1941, despite the Washington Treaties, the
United States still outweighed every fleet except the
British. The American Navy was not perfectly balanced,
nor was it sufficiently powerful for a two-ocean war.
It was, however, powerful enough to deal with any single
challenge.[134] Since all accepted the same standard of
judgment, no tell-tale comparisons were made which might
have revealed that the pressure of time was greater than
it was thought to be.

With the Army Air Force, the sense of urgency
was sharper, more imperative. As Secretary of War
Stimson told a joint congressional committee in
August 1940:

> Air power today has decided the fate of nations.
> Germany with her powerful air armadas has
> vanquished one people after another. On the
> ground, large armies have been mobilized to
> resist her, but each time it was that additional
> power in the air that decided the fate of each
> individual nation....As a consequence we are in

the midst of a great crisis. The time factor
is our principal obstacle.[135]
This sense of urgency, therefore, arose from two sources:
the American neglect of air power in the interwar period
and Germany's large scale development of her air forces,
a development even more impressive in Allied and American
imagination than in reality.[136]

The Air Force suffered even more than the Army from
the stringency of the lean years of the interwar period.
Being merely part of the Army, the Air Force received
only a thin sliver from the budget pie.[137] Only an
independent budget would solve its problems; only autonomy
would give it the chance to compete for the material and
financial resources of the nation.

The Army and the Navy were unalterably opposed to
giving the Air Force its independence.[138] The Army, which
thought of air power as merely one arm among many, an arm
whose main function should be to support ground troops in
combat,[139] sought to achieve a balance among its constituent
elements, a balance which would subordinate them to the
prime force: the infantry.[140] As the hostile Baker Board
concluded in July 1934: "'the time has arrived for the
Air Corps to become in all respects a homogenous part of
the Army, under General Staff control, and be subject to
military coordination, study, influence and operation.'"[141]

As long as the Army Air Forces failed to attain
independence,[142] or at least autonomy within the Army, its
budget would be habitually trimmed by the War Department.[143]
And within those limitations, almost any attempt at
expansion in manpower and equipment was foredoomed to
failure. Of course, in time of peace, the attempt was
doubly futile. On September 1, 1937, General Embick,
Deputy Chief of Staff, noted, with considerable irritation,
that official War Department correspondence was rampant
with the assertion that the Air Corps should be
maintained "constantly in time of peace in such a condition

of complete readiness for war that is fully prepared to
engage at once in actual hostilities."[144]Such heresy
was intolerable, particularly unthinkable because its
financial cost would mean the "complete emasculation of
our ground forces."[145]However, Embick could always rout
error with dogma: "Yet, as accepted by all informed
thought, and confirmed by the current events in Spain
and China, it is upon our ground forces that military
success must ultimately depend."[146]

But orthodoxy proved no solution to the mounting
challenge of the German Air Force. Ultimately, despite
the caution of the Army General Staff which continued to
dream of a balanced force,[147]the President set the goals
for expansion.[148]In the period remaining before American
entry into the war, the Air Force plans for expasion
mounted in harmony with the President's emphasis.
Every new challenge meant a new program. The plans for
the growth of the AAF went from twenty-four to eighty-four
groups.[149]Always necessity overtook supply. Always time
overtook capacity.

b. American Economic Mobilization: the Ultimate
Solution

Time would bring several solutions, solutions which
ultimately depended upon the economic mobilization of the
United States, the conversion of a predominantly peacetime
economy into full-time war production. On March 25, 1941,
President Roosevelt set the tone and the tempo:

> ...the urgency is now.
> We believe firmly that when our production
> output is in full swing, the democracies of
> the world will be able to prove that dictatorships
> cannot win.
> But now, now, the time element is of supreme
> importance....
> The great task of this day, the deep duty that
> rests upon each and every one of us is to move
> products from the assembly lines of our factories
> to the battle lines of democracy-NOW![150]

Shortly after the entrance of the United States into the
war, the President sounded the call again: "The task
that we Americans now face will test us to the utmost.
Never before have we been called upon for such a prodigious
effort. Never before have we had so little time in
which to do so much."[151]

The task was immense. The United States was the
technological giant of the twentieth century. It possessed
the resources and the industrial plant essential for
military strength. But this great peace economy still
had to be converted into a great war economy. The tasks
of industrial mobilization were formidable. Before
industrial strength could be converted into military
force, a weapons gap had to be crossed. An American
Army military historian, R. Elberton Smith, emphasizes
the seriousness of this problem:

> Contrary to popular feeling...superiority
> in economic resources carried no automatic
> guarantee of victory in war. As the United
> States learned to its peril, there was a wide
> and dangerous gulf between 'economic potential'
> and the capacity to deliver specific munitions
> in the quality, quantity, and time needed
> to win a major war.[152]

Given the German threat, the task was urgent. Only
two factors mitigated it: America's geographical
isolation and the continued resistance of her future
allies.[153] These factors gave the United States a breath
of borrowed time in which to build up the foundations
necessary for full-scale mobilization and for the waging
of total war.

Fortunately, there was another gift: the experience
of industrial mobilization in World War I, an experience
which had shown clearly that preparation for any future
war would demand intense prewar planning. The interwar
Industrial Mobilization Plans which attempted to meet
this potential need "were essentially the broad

recommendations of the Army and Navy as to functions
and organizations essential to effective mobilization
of the nation's resources for war production."[154]
They attempted, therefore, to anticipate two problems:
functional and organizational. Functional planning
would deal with the effective marshalling of the industrial
and material strength of the nation for war; organizational
planning, with the creation of the vast but temporary
control agencies which would conduct and command
mobilization.[155]Unlike the Army, whose command structure
could be expanded or revised, the peacetime economy could
provide no ready-made administrative hierarchy, instantly
prepared to administer this industrial task.

Obviously, in any such plans, the question of timing
was pre-eminent. When should mobilization begin? To
answer this hypothetical question, military planners
borrowed their terminology from troop mobilization
planners. In the twenties, the General Staff first
used the term "M-Day" to refer to the inception of
mobilization.[156]After 1925, this concept was also applied
to the initiation of procurement: "'M-Day for the supply
branches is the day on which they receive adequate funds
to operate; M-Day for the combatant arms is the day they
receive orders to mobilize. These two days should be
brought as close together as possible.'"[157]Eventually,
M-Day became the signal for the immediate and total
activation of industrial mobilization.[158]

This concept clearly embodied a great deal of wishful
thinking. No single day could bring forth that much force!
By the middle of the nineteen thirties realism had set in.
Planners began to think in terms of an extended period,
a transition phase consisting of three major stages.
Kreidberg and Henry summarize this more realistic
analysis:

> The successive mobilization stages, as the
> various annexes envisaged them, were:

> (1) a period of U.S. neutrality after a major
> foreign war had begun or was imminent;
> (2) a transition period of emergency during
> the first part of which the armed services
> would secretly expand their mobilization
> activities and during the latter part of which
> mobilization activities for war would be
> brought into the open; (3) the period after
> the United States entered the war when industrial
> mobilization, with all its controls, went
> into full operation.[159]

The task of industrial mobilization proved as
formidable as envisioned. As predicted, full mobilization
did not begin until after the Japanese attack at Pearl
Harbor. Until then, cars, refrigerators and washing
machines disputed the priority of planes and tanks.[160]
But, despite hesitancy, the foundations were laid. And
the time gained was crucial. As the Army's economic
historian reports: "...the eighteen months of preparation
before Pearl Harbor played a crucial if not decisive part
in the outcome of the war."[161]

    c. American Psychological Mobilization: From Apathy
to Commitment

If the major task of industrial mobilization was
the conversion of a peacetime economy to full-scale
wartime production, the major task of psychological
mobilization was the conversion of peacetime apathy
to wartime commitment. For in the nineteen thirties
the American people were generally unresponsive to
international challenges and responsibilities. The
aftermath of World War I's Great Crusade had been a
bitter awakening, and a mounting disgust against all
European adventures. And even in the late nineteen
thirties the taste of the past world war was still keen.
The fear of another entangling misalliance remained,
fed by the subterranean explorations of the Nye
Committee.

Although the American public was horrified by the

Nazi pogroms against the Jews[162] and frightened by Hitler's
exanpansion in Central Europe,[163] hostility and fear did not
shake the nation's determination to remain clear of new
European conflicts. Even after Munich and the November
1938 pogrom, the American public was 95 per cent opposed
to involvement in any war.[164]

In some respects, American public opinion was ahead
of the isolationsit block in Congress. By May 1939,
the polls showed that the public favored revisions of
the Neutrality Laws to allow the United States, in case of
war, to supply munitions to Hitler's enemies. But, when
the President tried to persuade Congress, Senatorial
opposition was still too strong to secure passage of
the proposed revisions.[165]

The shattering attack of Hitler's Germany upon Poland
found American public opinion united. Sympathy for
Poland and an intense hostility towards Germany, however,
conflicted with a fervent desire to keep out of the war.[166]
A memorandum, written shortly after the outbreak of war,
summarized American sentiment. After declaring that,
unlike 1914, there was no division in American public
opinion, it summarized the two causes for this unity:
American hatred of Nazi Germany's totalitarian system
and fear of her ambitions:

> That is the meat in the coconut so far as American
> public opinion is concerned. They realize that
> if Germany and Italy succeed in imposing the
> dictator form of government on their European
> neighbors, or become so powerful that the
> smaller states of Europe will be bullied into
> doing their will, the next and logical German
> or Italian movement, separately or in combination,
> will be against other parts of the world,--
> French Colonies, Belgian Colonies, British
> Colonies--or with equal likelihood, one or
> more of the American Republics.[167]

During the transition period from September 3, 1939
to December 7, 1941, American hostility to Hitler and to
Nazi Germany did not change. Germany was judged as the

wicked originator of the war. Moreover, American public
support for the Allied cause remained constant. These
sentiments, however, were still hedged by the hope that
the United States would stay out of the war. The variables
were the public's estimate of whether American entry was
inevitable and whether the United States should enter
the war to save the Allies from defeat.

Against this cross-current of popular feeling,
the President steered cautiously, often taking a half
tack back for every tack forward. Sometimes he seemed
to lead; sometimes, to follow. If he steered towards a
chosen port, he followed a winding course, governed by
the shoals and currents of popular sentiment. Everything
depended upon timing, upon arriving at the right spot at
the right time. And the only charts available were those
drawn by the barometers of public opinion. If war came,
it must find the American people united in their support
of the administration. Premature action, hasty commitment,
would shatter this hope. But inaction was dangerous too.
The President could either forfeit his leadership or
run the ship of state aground by passively drifting
with the tides towards disaster.[168]

As we shall demonstrate,[169] American strategy, even
in the transition stage, was thinking of waging an
offensive war which would ultimately carry United States
forces into the heartland of enemy power. Obviously,
such a strategy would require a tremendous build-up of
military power, a build-up inconceivable in 1940.
Therefore, the United States needed time to build up
the military forces which would fight a two-ocean war
and carry the offensive into the enemy's homeland, time
to arouse a still sluggish economy and transform it into
full war production, time to commit the nation to its
gigantic task. And the pressure of time was a spur
to action, an incentive to move rapidly. Although

initially governed by external necessity, this pressure
did not diminish, did not slacken as American mobilization
swung into high gear. Although U.S. resources were
vast, so vast that they could have supported American
forces for many years of war, the drive for speed never
let up. It never weakened even after the outward necessity
for it had vanished. It carried the United States to
the threshold of peace, to the Japanese surrender on the
deck of the <u>Missouri</u>.

6. Conclusion: Time is of the Essence

Time is of the essence. For all nations, success
or defeat hinges on the utilization of this vital element.
In World War II, two countries, the Soviet Union and Great
Britain, needed a prolonged war to achieve victory. Two
nations, Germany and Japan, needed a short war. Their
resources were not equal to a protracted conflict with
the major western powers. One nation, the United States,
needed a prolonged period for mobilization but then posited
her strategy on bringing the war to as rapid an end
as possible. For all, the temporal imperative was an
ineluctable master.

Since time serves as a gauge of strength, a measure
of force, its logic is unquestionable. Forming the
foundation on which the national machinery of war stands
and moves, the temporal imperative is strongly preconceptual, seldom challengeable.

Are all subject to its tyranny? Is war inescapably
caught within the confines of a time scheme, pressing
for victory within a measured period? Actually, the
temporal imperative is a product of an industrialized
society which, when fighting a total war, must seek
victory within the limits of mobilization. But an
agricultural society which does not fight war with
the weapons of modern technology is free from this
compulsion. To the Chinese, time is as infinite as

space. And space can be used to gain time, allowing a
pre-industrial state to wear down the strength of an
industrial power. In his famous strategic treatise,
"On the Protracted War," Mao Tse-tung emphasizes that the
problem is not to end the war quickly, but to keep it
going infinitely until the stronger foe wears out his
strength and reaches the limits of his mobilized powers:
"as 'a distant journey tests the strength of a horse
and a long task proves the character of a man,' guerrilla
warfare will demonstrate its enormous power in the course
of a long and ruthless war...."[170]

PART II

Time of Uncertainty

Introduction

Between 1920 and 1941, American military thinking underwent a
fundamental revolution, moving from the static defensive doctrines of
pacifistic isolationism towards the dynamic offensive doctrines of militant
interventionism. But this transition was neither clearly defined nor
completely identifiable. It was a passage through a time of uncertainty.
Therefore, the signs were often muted, ambiguous, confusing. Strategic
beliefs, reflecting and expressing our planning and preparation for future
war, were often clothed in the guarded language of the past. Although they
revealed the attitudes and trends later fully embodied in the plans of the
Allied coalition, they now moved like hesitant shadows, pausing in the
past before passing into the future.

Perhaps nothing indicates the apparent conservatism of American
strategic thinking more clearly than its obsessive emphasis upon "defense."
The most radical departures in policy and practice--the securing and
arming of advanced positions projecting towards the enemy's centers of
power--were defined as "defensive" moves. All planning for the projection
of American forces onto the planes of Europe and into the reaches of the
Western Pacific sought to secure the continent from attack, to crush any
aggressor before he could strike. The process of justification--
covering the expansion of the armed forces and increased commitment to
an Allied victory--defined every new measure as a move designed to "further
the defense of the United States." The growing emphasis upon total victory
reflected a mounting conviction that only the complete defeat of the
aggressor powers would permanently secure American security. The
persistent stress upon her need for time--and more time--expressed the need
to prepare American defenses against the expected assault of the enemy's
hostile forces.

Seeking to preserve her security, the United States prepared to wage offensive war on an unprecedented scale. For her newly defined defensive line would provide a perfect platform for attack. An emphasis upon the direct approach would provide the strategic guidelines which would allow America to hurl her forces into the heartlands of enemy power. The evolution of an emphasis upon total victory and the development of strategic bombing concepts would allow the United States to apply its full force to the complete and unconditional destruction of the enemy's strength. She would use time to prepare her forces for defense; but these same forces could easily be used to invade the enemy's empire.

Despite uncertainty and ambiguity, the revolutionary process continued, the transition occurred. Arming for defense, the United States prepared for offense. And throughout, the President, aware of the hesitations of public opinion, divided between the need for security and the desire for peace, laid the guidelines for his military planners, prodding them towards a new view, a new vision of American security and her role in the world.

Chapter VII

The Evolution of Global Defense

1. From Stonewall to Hemisphere Defense

On September 14, 1937, the President of the United States received a highly opinionated, critical memorandum on American national policy. Presumably written by Harry Woodring--then Secretary of War--it scolded those American officials who promoted a pro-British policy. The Secretary felt that such a course, unless immediately corrected, would drag the United States into war:

> ...The proponents of this policy assume that the fate of America depends upon what of the British Empire. They do not know and they do not enquire what sacrifices in American life and resources will be involved.
> 2. The argument is, of course, fallacious. The United States are a natural economic and military entity. No nation is so little dependent upon the fate of others. The strategic isolation of our position combined with our continental resources give us a unique position--one that can be defended against the remainder of the world. The technical military improvements discussed hereinafter which have lessened our capabilities to intervene overseas, have increased our capabilities for defense at home.[1]

Appalled by the prospect of another intervention, the Secretary warned that conditions had changed notably since World War I. Two causes had largely effected these changes:

> a. The re-alignments among military Powers and the changes in national military strengths.
> b. The technical developments in means of defense. These seem likely to have the far-reaching result of segregating the world into distinct strategic areas, not easily penetrable by military (including naval) force from another area.[2]

The Secretary's memorandum, therefore, envisioned a world divided into hermetically sealed compartments, self-sustaining islands of force, capable of repelling any aggressor. From the development of modern weapons, Woodring drew comfort, seeing them as increments to defensive strength--rather than threats to security. Although the Secretary's memorandum may now seem strangely anachronistic, it probably sounded logical at the time. It fitted the isolationist rationale comfortably.

Moreover, this theory was accidentally appropriate to the condition of military weakness into which the American Army had fallen. If the United States were a fortress in the 1930's, then it was merely a natural one. The weaponry from which the Secretary derived such comfort was not available. Therefore, from weakness rather than strength, the United States was committed to "passive defense" or--as Colonel J. W. Anderson of WPS christened it: "the stone-wall defense of complete isolation."[3]

To Woodring--writing in 1937--the advent of air power and the possible breakup of the British Empire posed no problem for the security of the United States. To the President of the United States, the moral was opposite. From 1937 on his concern about the dangers implicit in the development of German air power grew. From Hitler's use of bomber blackmail during the Munich crisis, and from the impact of the Luftwaffe on the fields of Poland, Flanders and France in the campaigns of 1939 and 1940, the President took warning.

Publicly he expressed his concern and his apprehension before the opening of the European war. In his State of the Union address of January 4, 1939, a speech echoing with the impact of the Bullitt report,[4] he defined the new threat:

> In our foreign relations we have learned from the past what not to do. From new wars we have learned what we must do. We have learned that effective timing of defense and the distant

points from which attacks may be launched are completely
different from what they were twenty years ago.
We have learned that survival cannot be guaranteed by arming
after the attack begins--for there is new range and speed to
offense.[5]

Almost a year and a half later, the impact of the imminent disaster

in Flanders led the President to define this new threat more precisely:

The Atlantic and Pacific Oceans were reasonably adequate defensive
barriers when fleets under sail could move at an average speed of
5 miles an hour....Later, the oceans still gave strength to our
defense when fleets and convoys propelled by steam could sail the
oceans at fifteen or twenty miles an hour. But the new element--
air navigation--steps up the speed of possible attack to two
hundred, to three hundred miles an hour.
Furthermore, it brings the new possibilities of the use of nearer
bases from which an attack or attacks on the American Continents
could be made. From the fiords of Greenland it is four hours by
air to Newfoundland; five hours to Nova Scotia, New Brunswick and
to the Province of Quebec; and only six hours to New England.
The Azores are only 2,000 miles from parts of our eastern seaboard
and if Bermuda fell into hostile hands it would be a matter of less
than three hours for modern bombers to reach our shores. [6]

After detailing the vulnerability of other areas and cities in the

United States, the President drew the natural conclusion. The events

in Europe had shown the American people "that the possibility of attack

on vital American zones" was real and pressing.[7]

And the danger from German air power accentuated the danger from the

breakup of the British Empire--so contemptuously dismissed by Woodring.

For behind this last threat lay another: the danger of German domination

in Europe. The conquest of the continent by a potentially hostile power

would, as Roosevelt foresaw, directly challenge the security of the United

States. For even before the outbreak of war in Europe, the President

understood the menace posed by an Axis triumph. In victory:

...their first act would be either to seize the British
Navy or put it out of action. Then they would establish
trade relations with Latin America, put instructors in the
armies, etc. They would probably not touch British, French,

or Dutch possessions in this hemisphere. But in a very short
time we would find ourselves surrounded by hostile states. Further,
the Japanese, who "always like to play with the big boys," would
probably go into a hard and fast alliance. The combined German
and Italian Navies were about the equal of ours and the
Japanese was about eighty percent of ours. Therefore, the
temptation to them would always be to try another quick war
with us, if we got rough about their South American penetration.[8]

Unlike Woodring, therefore, the President saw a threat to the United

States both in the development of air power and in the possible defeat

and dissolution of the British Empire. For Roosevelt America was not a

fortress which could easily be defended against "the remainder of the

world." It was not an island of freedom and strength capable of self-

preservation in the midst of a totalitarian sea. For any island of isola-

tion would soon turn into a prison of deprivation.

> Some indeed still hold to the now somewhat obvious delusion
> that we of the United States can safely permit the United
> States to become a lone island, a lone island in a world
> dominated by the philosophy of force. Such an island may be
> the dream of those who still talk and vote as isolationists.
> Such an island represents to me and to the overwhelming
> majority of Americans today a helpless nightmare of a people
> lodged in prison, handcuffed, hungry, and fed through the
> bars from day to day by the contemptuous, unpitying master
> of other continents.[9]

No continent is an island, complete unto itself.

These two factors--the threat of Axis air power and the danger of

German hegemony over Europe--led to a revised concept of national

security: a conversion of "passive" or "stonewall" defense into

"active" or "hemispheric" defense. Colonel Anderson noted this change was

revolutionary:

> Under the policy of hemisphere defense we have formulated for
> the Army a new mission that recognizes the importance of the
> initiative in war and visualizes an early need for more than
> passive defense. Under this policy we have set our mission
> as the defense, not of our territory alone, but cooperation in
> the defense of the entire western hemisphere. This mission

requires the provision of means with which we can deny the enemy
bases from which he might launch military operations against us
or any of the democratic nations of this hemisphere. This policy
is designed to reduce to a minimum the likelihood of accepting
war upon our own territory. [10]

Six weeks after the Munich Conference, Roosevelt defined it more succinctly:

"'the United States must be prepared to resist attack on the western hemisphere

from the North Pole to the South Pole, including all of North America and South

America.'" [11] This conversion from the stonewall defense of isolation to hemis-

pheric defense was, therefore, a bold radical step, accompanied by a revolutionar

change in the defined mission of the military forces of the United States.

In August, 1929, a WPD memorandum had merely defined the common missions

of American military forces as 1) the defense of American territory against

all enemies, foreign or domestic and 2) the general promotion of our

interests abroad. [12] In December, 1938, another WPD memorandum defined our

military interests in entirely different terms. It began by noting that the

rising threat of European dictatorships had "greatly increased the require-

ments for national defense." [13] Now not only must America strengthen the

"defenses of continental United States, the Panama Canal, the Hawaiian

Islands, Alaska and our island possessions in the Atlantic area", but the Army

"must be prepared to intervene instantly, and possibly unassisted, in any

portion of the Western Hemisphere where our vital interests are threatened." [14]

Ultimately, the security of the western hemisphere was assured by the

maintenance of the balance of power in Europe and Asia. In the early

twenties American officials had worried about the possible intervention

of the League of Nations under its 1924 Protocol. In the thirties, the

balance of power was threatened by the rise of militant Nazi Germany and

militaristic Japan. Against rising totalitarian power stood three walls

shielding the American continent from direct or sudden attack: the

French Army, the British Navy and the vast distances of the Atlantic and

Pacific. The 1940 threat arose from the deterioration of the balance of power in Europe and Asia and the possible destruction of the three protective walls. The first two were threatened by the potential establishment of German hegemony throughout Europe; the last, by the increasing range and scope of air power. Once the assumptions underlying the comfortable adherence to stonewall defense were undermined, the adoption of hemisphere defense was immediate and natural.

2. The Nature of the Threat

    a. Indirect Aggression

As long as the outside lines of defense held against the Axis threat, as long as Germany remained embroiled in a European conflict, the chances of a direct attack on the western hemisphere were slight. Even during the crisis of 1940, following the fall of France, the British fleet remained a formidable obstacle to any power intent upon launching an attack over the reaches of the Atlantic. But other dangers already shook the security of the Western Hemisphere. Most dangerous, because it was clothed in ambiguity, was the threat of indirect aggression, the technique for conquest utilized by Hitler in his triumph over Austria and Czechoslovakia. As Hull noted in his memoirs:

> To me the danger to the Western Hemisphere was real and imminent. It was not limited to the possibility of a military invasion. It was more acute in its indirect form of propaganda, penetration, organizing political parties, buying some adherents, and blackmailing others. We had seen the method employed with great success in Austria and in the Sudetenland. The same technique was obvious in Latin America.[15]

General Strong, then Chief of WPD, saw the danger in the same light as the Secretary of State. He realized that indirect aggression could become the vanguard for a direct attack. Moving "step by step," relentlessly "penetrating economically and politically into Central and South America,"[16] it could undermine hemispheric security before counter forces could be mobilized and applied: "Before military force replaced diplomatic negotiations, hostile nations may be firmly established on the Western Hemisphere in areas that threaten not only our national interests, but such vital areas as the Panama Canal as well."[17] As in Austria and the Sudetenland, penetration would precede and prepare for invasion.

As far as American advisers and planners could see, three types of Axis penetration--economic, political and military--were eroding the defenses of the Western Hemisphere, weakening their future victims. The economic threat arose largely from the spread of German and Italian business interests throughout Latin America and the acute economic dislocations effected by the European war.[18]

To Cordell Hull, the German threat was clear. In the prewar period, the Germans were already trying to "undermine our trade with Central and South America."[19] Their merchants were penetrating Latin American markets, "developing their businesses and digging in socially, commercially, and politically."[20] Like hordes of termites, they were undermining the foundations of independent states, "using every method possible in the line of subversive action."[21]

One of the most alarming symptoms of Nazi influence over the Latin American economy was the Axis control of important commercial airlines. From the prewar years to the close of 1941, the German CONDOR, the Italian LATI and the Vichite Air France constituted a severe threat to hemispheric defense. Besides serving as reconnaissance forces and possibly guiding German submarines to their prey, they could form an entering wedge for an invasion army.[22]

More sinister than the first threat, the spread of Axis economic influence, was the second threat: Germany and Italy's political infiltra- into Latin America. The potential force for a strong pro-Nazi movement was there. By 1940 there were at least 300,000 native Germans in Latin America, besides 1,250,000 people of German extraction.[23] The Italian population, from birth or descent, was even more substantial.[24] Naturally the Axis governments had already organized these still unassimilated groups into a potential Fifth Column: a bridgehead for penetration and subversion. Consequently Berlin strove to insulate the German population from assimilation into an alien community:[25]

> Berlin insisted that Germans in Latin American countries attend German schools, vote aboard German ships in Hitlerite plebiscites, refuse to marry non-Germans, become members of the Nazi Party and contribute to it, promote German business by all conceivable means, and gather information for the Fatherland.[26]

Like the Sudeten Germans, their allegiance should belong to their original home, not their adopted one.

Automatically these "colonies" became centers of anti-American propaganda denouncing American imperialism and intervention. Writes Hull:

> We were accused again and again of intervening in Latin American internal questions, of trying to monopolize trade with our neighbors to the south or to squeeze them in our financial tentacles, of favoring one side or the other in boundary disputes.[27]

The most alarming form of potential subversion was the political stroke, the quiet or violent coup d'état, which could depose a pro-American government and replace it with a pro-Axis clique. This possibility of an Axis-sponsored revolution haunted American political and military leaders throughout the prewar period. The rumors of coups, abortive or potential, were constant reminders of a persistent danger, most acutely felt in Brazil, Argentina, Uruguay and Mexico.[28]

The danger of revolution, moreover, was insidiously difficult to counter. It could assume such an ambiguous form that it would inhibit

American military action. As the Chief of Staff's office
saw it, the problem could pose serious difficulties in
interpretation and action:

> ...the transformation of Latin American states into
> dependencies or colonies of Germany or Italy...presents
> perhaps the most serious and delicate problem of
> all, and one which is now staring us in the face.
> In different places in Latin America, the problem
> may be presented in any variation of the following forms:
> (a) An internal overthrow of an existing government,
> without acknowledged dependence on outside support,
> resulting in an ostensibly autonomous regime.
> (b) A revolution, avowedly inspired and carried out
> by Nazi or Fascist elements, with no subsequent
> acknowledgment of allegiance to Germany or Italy.
> (c) The same sort of revolution which, when
> accomplished, announces the association of the
> country as a colony of Germany or Italy.
> (d) A gradual overturn of an existing government
> resulting in cooperation with Germany or Italy,
> without any overt revolution.[29]

The threats posed by political and economic penetration
were intensified by the third threat: Axis infiltration of
Latin American military establishments. Through the sale of
munitions and the training of South American officers, the
Axis could exert an disproportionate influence. As Stetson
Conn observes, "in most Latin American nations the military
had a large influence in the formulation and direction of
national policy."[30]

b. The Ultimate Threat

Trojan horses of indirect aggression were, however,
only the vanguard for further moves, moves intended to
undermine the independence of Latin America. Behind these
shadowy plays, American officials detected a master
conspirator. Cordell Hull writes in his memoirs:

> In general, the Nazis in Latin America,
> according to the cables I received from our
> diplomatic missions, were making no secret

of their plans and were boasting openly that Germany could easily conquer South America. Their plans run as follows:
(1) Use the British, French, Scandinavian, and other merchant fleets to carry on commerce with Latin America at rates that would put American lines out of business.
(2) Blanket Latin America with German aviation lines carrying freight and passengers at rates with which American lines could not compete.
(3) Export German and European merchandise to Latin America at whatever prices necessary to undersell American products.
(4) Overthrow any Latin American Government not favorable to Germany and substitute one that would cooperate.
(5) Then take over the Latin American countries as virtual dependencies.[31]

Hull concludes: "Had Hitler's armies and air force conquered Britain, I am convinced Germany would have tried to pursue this program to the letter."[32] Most of the President's advisers agreed, accepting indirect aggression as a serious threat.[33]

For the Latin American game was merely one play in the great drive for world conquest. Behind official nervousness over Axis penetration into the Western Hemisphere, lay the image of the enemy, the estimate formed by American leaders of the intentions and ambitions of Adolf Hitler. This estimate pictured the Fuhrer as directing a world conspiracy, aiming for total domination. If he could defeat England, capture or destroy the British and French fleets, he would launch his armies against the South American nations. But his attack against the Latin republics would merely be a prelude to his final assault against the United States.

We have already noted the President's conviction that Hitler's ambitions were unlimited and insatiable. Apparently this estimate was formed either shortly before the beginning of the war or in the early months of the conflict, becoming fairly fixed by the time the Germans launched their offensive against the Western Allies in the spring of 1940.[34] Many of the reports that reached the President's desk from American embassies abroad either stimulated or confirmed it. One particularly sensational report,

apparently relayed through Ambassador Bullitt in Paris, dramatized it
succinctly and clearly:

> Secretary of State Keppler and Director General Vogl have
> related the following: "On Wednesday, March 8th, a conference
> was held at the Fuehrer's which was attended by personalities
> from the army, economic circles, and the Party. 'Austria' was
> represented by <u>Gauleiter</u> Puerckel in addition to those mentioned
> above."[35]

After proposing the elimination of Czechoslovakia and Poland, the defeat

of France and the domination of England and the British Empire, the Fuhrer

turned to even grander designs:

> "'Thus having for the first time unified the continent of
> Europe according to a new conception, Germany will undertake
> the greatest operation in all history: with British and French
> possessions in America as a base, we will settle accounts with
> the Jews of the dollar (Dollarjuden) in the United States. We
> will exterminate this Jewish democracy and Jewish blood will
> mix itself with the dollars. Even today Americans can insult
> our people, but the day will come when, too late, they will
> bitterly regret every word they said against us.'"[36]

Apparently Ambassador Bullitt vouched for the authenticity of the

above account. As he reported to the President on September 16, 1939, he

had no reason to doubt its veracity:

> Under the circumstances, I think you ought to have studied now
> in all its aspects the military and naval problem that will
> face the United States in case France and England should be
> defeated during the next eight months. I am convinced that
> if Hitler should be able to win during this period, he would
> be able to obtain the support of the Italians and the Japanese
> and would be in a position to make the attack on South America
> which he announced to the leaders that he convoked on the
> eighth of March last. I now have in written form the statement
> which I telegraphed to you on that subject some months ago.
> The report was handed me by Otto of Japsburg. It comes from
> one of his most trusted agents in Vienna who is in the center
> of the Nazi Movement, and I consider it absolutely authentic.[37]

The United States was, therefore, menaced by the threat of ultimate

conquest and domination at the hands of an unappeasable dictator, an

insatiable dreamer with unbounded designs. Even if the President doubted the veracity of the above report--and there is no reason to believe he

did--his speeches show clearly that he accepted its major premise.

Bullitt's view was shared by the Secretary of State, Cordell Hull.
In a speech defending the Lend-Lease Bill, he warned the United States of
her danger, delineating the threat in more general terms, but dissecting
the technique of aggression as one which successively lulled and then
devoured its chosen victim, dividing and conquering one by one:

> All information which has come to me...confirms the view...
> that this nation faces real danger, and that every possible
> step for national defense should be taken with the utmost
> rapidity....This country by now should have no longer any
> illusions as to the nature or magnitude of the dangers which
> confront us....It has seen a combination of forces come into
> being which, step by step, has challenged the right of every
> nation, including our own, to exist save at the dictation of
> alien masters. In every case, the nation whose turn had not
> come up was told that there was no danger; that it needed to
> do nothing but sit still and all would be well. And with
> deadly certainty, the governments which have swallowed this
> bait have been, in their turn, destroyed. Only those which
> devoted every ounce of their energy toward immediate defense,
> and which were ready to cooperate with others, have escaped
> destruction.[38]

For Hull the lesson was obvious. The United States must take all

necessary measures to prevent a Nazi triumph:

> ...our immediate business is to see to it that the would-be
> conquerors of the world shall not be in a position in which
> they can command the seas, attack any country in this hemisphere,
> and, when they are able, attempt to deal with us as they have
> been dealing with Europe and with Asia.[39]

This initial premise of American defensive thought was also widespread
among military thinkers and planners. In a memorandum addressed to the
Chief of Staff, General Strong, Assistant Chief of Staff, WPD, saw the
threat to the United States as immediate, as a threat which would
materialize as soon as the British were swept out of the way. He
warned that "we (must) recognize the probability that we are next on

the list of victims of the Axis powers...."[40]And seven months later, on
January 27, 1941, Brigadier General Sherman iles, Chief of G-2, saw the
master conspiracy in terms of absolute alternatives: "'hitler's idea for
a new order is a world order dominated by the Germans, linked with
Japanese supremacy in the Far East.'"[41]

The subversive activities of Axis agents in Latin America were,
therefore, merely symptoms of disease. The real threat to American
security lay in the enemy's final intentions, his plan for world conquest,
his insatiable appetite, his unlimited ambitions. Therefore, every
specific threat was merely one more act in the great drama, one more
manifestation of the existence of a voracious disease.

3. The Path of the Enemy's Approach

As our planners and leaders foresaw, the ultimate attack on the
United States could take many forms, choose many paths. The approaches
to the Western Hemisphere were vulnerable, exposed to sudden assaults,
individually launched or simultaneously converging from several directions.

a. Combined Attack: Pacific and Atlantic

The maximum threat was a combined attack in which the three Axis
powers--Germany, Italy and Japan--would strike simultaneously at the
United States and its possessions. On April 21, 1939, the possibility
of such a massive assault led the Joint Planning Committee to draw some
somber conclusions.[42]As it reported, the existing naval power of the
United States could forestall an attack by the European Axis. It could
even protect United States possessions in the western lacific,if reinforced.
It could not, owever, accomplish both tasks simultaneously.[43]It was
totally inadequate for the initial prosecution of a two-ocean war; and--

in case of a concerted attack--some cruel choices would have to be made.[44]

More than a year later, when the Nazi onslaught had descended upon Western Europe, the War Plans Division was the possibility of a combined attack as one of several possible dangers:

> 1. Further imminently probable complications of today's situation are:
>   a. Nazi-inspired revolution in Brazil.
>   b. Widespread disorders with attacks on U.S. citizens in Mexico and raids along our southern border.
>   c. Japanese hostilities against the United States in the Far East.
>   d. Decisive Allied defeat, followed by German aggression in the Western Hemisphere.
>   e. All combined.[45]

b. The Threat from the Atlantic Approaches.

Far more probable than a simultaneous assault was an attack by a victorious Germany over the ranges of the Atlantic. This possibility acquired new probability with the defeat of France in June, 1940, and the mounting German preparations for the invasion of the British Isles. If Great Britain were defeated in the summer of 1940, a German attack across the Atlantic seemed certain. For the surrender of the United Kingdom would open new opportunities for aggression in the New World: it would allow the Germans to claim British, Dutch and French possessions in the Caribbean as legitimate spoils of war; and it would probably allow them to use the former British and French fleets against the American Navy. With this new opening and this new strength, the European Axis could strike either in the North or the South Atlantic.

The danger from a German controlled Allied Fleet was primary. For without command of the seas, the Axis powers could not easily seize bases in the Western Hemisphere. American leaders clearly recognized this crucial factor. In a series of conferences held on May 16, 1940, the President and his military advisers agreed that Hitler could not invade the Western Hemisphere without control of the Allied fleets. If the Germans acquired immediate access to France's African possessions, they could, of course, launch a direct air attack on South America. But without naval supremacy they could not project a ground force across the Atlantic.[46]

As the situation in the West continued to deteriorate, the alarm of the planners became more emphatic. The basic war plan formulated in the heart of the crisis, RAINBOW 4, stressed the effect that the acquisition of the two fleets would have on the position of the United States in the Atlantic. "Should that happen, Germany and Italy would soon attain a naval strength in the Atlantic equal or superior to that of the entire United States Fleet."[47]

The surrender of either fleet would have a dual effect upon American defense policy. First, it would necessitate the initiation of full-scale mobilization. Although it would probably take the Germans six months to refurbish the captured fleets, American forces were not prepared to deal with any threat to the Western Hemisphere. They would need that six month interval to mobilize, equip and train.[48] Therefore, as RAINBOW 4 warned, "'the date of the loss of the British or French Fleets automatically sets the date of our mobilization.'"[49]

Second, the loss of either fleet would threaten our naval deployment. With this monumental menace, could the American fleet remain in the Pacific? Should it be transferred to the Atlantic? On June 27, 1940, the problem was noted by the military chiefs:

> 2. If the French Fleet passes to the control of Germany, our attitude in the Pacific should be defensive for the time being. The decision to move the major portion of the United States Fleet to the Atlantic will be taken later.
> 3. If the French Fleet remains available to Great Britain,

> the United States Fleet will remain in the Pacific and our
> defensive attitude in the Pacific will be continued, pending
> further developments.[50]

The loss of either fleet would pose a formidable danger which could
only be met by extreme measures. Fortunately, the British action at
Mers-el-Kebir and the repulse of the Luftwaffe in the Battle of Britain,
thwarted this menace, allayed this fear.

The threat to European dependencies in the New World did not
materialize until the crisis of June, 1940, which--because of the
possible reversal of the naval balance of power in the Atlantic--
threatened the loss of all Allied possessions in the Western Hemisphere.
Shortly before the crisis, on March 29, 1940, WPD turned out a study
stressing the potential military value of the European possessions in
the New World. But the study admitted that this military value could
not balance the political liability and the financial cost of their
acquisition.[51] Until a definite threat materialized, the incentive was
negligible.

But the German onslaught on Western Europe and the rapid and apparently
complete disintegration of the Allied Armies eroded previous reservations,
bringing quick proposals from military planners. On May 21, 1940,
Lt. General Brooks directly related the threat of a German victory in
Europe to the danger facing European possessions in the New World. Unless
the United States acted promptly the Axis might soon entrench itself on
the approaches to the Western Hemisphere:

> In view of present world conditions, it is believed that this
> country should take immediate steps to acquire British and
> French possessions in the Atlantic. It is realized that a
> victorious Germany must first digest the territory she has
> already taken over, and arrange for the control of the civil
> population of any other subjected countries. However, it will

also be necessary for Germany to rehabilitate herself economically.
This without doubt means trade with South America; trade with
South America means trade routes thereto, and Germany will take
no chance on protecting these trade routes.
If Germany is victorious over France and England in the very
near future, it is not only possible, but highly probable that
she will take over Bermuda and many of the British and French
possessions in the Caribbean and along the South American coast.
Establishment of German air bases on certain key islands in the
Atlantic before the year is over is not a fantastic dream.[52]

The seriousness of these two threats to the Western Hemisphere
accounts for the extreme measures America was willing to adopt as counteraction.[53] For the nature of the danger emphasized the essential indivisibility
of the two hemispheres, the almost inevitable extension of the war into the
Western Hemisphere once the Axis powers defeated the Western Allies. As
Cordell Hull warned on October 26, 1940:

"There can be nothing more dangerous for our nation than for us
to assume that the avalanche of conquest could under no circumstances reach any vital portion of this hemisphere. Oceans give
the nations of this hemisphere no guarantee against the possibility
of economic, political, or military attack from abroad. Oceans are
barriers but they are also highways. Barriers of distance are
merely barriers of time. Should the would-be conquerors gain
control of the seas, of the air over the seas, and of the world's
economy; they might then be able with ships and with planes to
strike at the communication lines, the commerce, and the life
of this hemisphere; and ultimately we might find ourselves
compelled to fight on our own soil, under our own skies, in
defense of our independence and our very lives."[54]

And in the Atlantic there were two approaches, two "highways" whose
accessibility and utility were strengthened by a series of stepping stones.
Their control by the enemy would allow him to project his forces into the
Western Hemisphere.

1) The North Atlantic Highway

To the north lay the Iceland-Greenland-Newfoundland route; to the south,
the Dakar-Natal route. Seizure of either would allow the Germans to project
their military forces into the Western Hemisphere. If they seized the
northern highway, their forces would stand on the threshold of the north-

eastern industrial heartland of the United States. If they occupied the southern highway, they could, by seizing a series of advanced bases, attack the Panama Canal.[55]

In the North Atlantic, control of one position would lead almost automatically to partial control over the next objective. As Secretary of War Stimson summed it up for the President: "Whoever holds Iceland can command and control the shores of Greenland. Whoever holds the shores of Greenland is within easy bombing distance of our American outposts in Newfoundland."[56]

Obviously the control of Iceland by a hostile power would threaten the entire North Atlantic highway. As Karl Haushofer, the Nazi geopolitician, observed: "'Whoever possesses Iceland holds a pistol permanently pointed at England, America and Canada.'"[57] But its possession by the Nazis would pose a double threat. First, by occupying Iceland, Germany could advance towards the Western Hemisphere. Second, it could sever the great commercial and naval artery leading from the United States to the United Kingdom, thereby isolating two great potential allies from one another. It could menace both the territorial integrity of the Western Hemisphere and the freedom of the seas.[58] In his radio address of May 27, 1941, shortly before he ordered the Army to plan the relief of the British garrison in Iceland, the President noted the dual nature of this threat:

> You remember that most of the supplies for Britain go by a northerly route, which comes close to Greenland and the nearby island of Iceland. Germany's heaviest attack is on that route. Nazi occupation of Iceland or bases in Greenland would bring the war close to our own continental shores, because those places are stepping-stones to Labrador and Newfoundland, to Nova Scotia, yes, to the norther United States itself, including the great industrial centers of the North, the East, and the Middle West.[59]

Although the War Department originally underrated the strategic
importance of the second stepping stone, Greenland, declaring that it was
"so underdeveloped and so far on the flank of sea and air routes that its
possession by a hostile power would not constitute a significant threat",[60]
its defensive importance soon became too evident to ignore. The occupation
of Denmark by Germany on April 8-9, 1940, posed the danger of possible
Axis control over both Iceland and Greenland: "The Copenhagen Government,
under duress, might find itself compelled to give Hitler a free hand in
these Danish possessions."[61] Although the rapid occupation of Iceland by
the British and the continued naval supremacy of the United Kingdom
nullified the worst danger--full-scale military occupation-- it did not
eliminate other dangers to Greenland, however, such as German moves which
might prove the prelude to full-scale attack.

The primary concern of American planners centered around the
cryolite mines at Ivigut--essential to American and Canadian aluminum
production[62]--and the possible establishment of an enemy weather station,
a vital aid to the Germans in their operations against the United Kingdom.[63]

Closest to the threshold of the continental United States was the
third steppingstone: the island of Newfoundland. As noted by the
Permanent Joint Board on Defense, Canada-United States, on August 27, 1940:

> The Island of Newfoundland occupies a commanding position at the
> entrance of the St. Lawrence-Great Lakes waterway and on the
> flank of the sea route between the Atlantic seaboard of North
> America and Norther Europe. It is on the direct air route
> between the East Coast of the United States and Northern Europe.
> It is the point in North America, nearest to Europe, from which,
> if occupied by an enemy, further operations against the North
> American continent might be effectively initiated.[64]

But Newfoundland also played a key role in the air defense of the Western
Hemisphere and the continental United States. For the conquest of Newfoundland by the Germans would expose the major cities of the northeast to attack.

As Secretary of War Stimson warned on January 22, 1941: "In the case of
the establishment of an air base in either Newfoundland or Labrador, air
attacks would be possible upon American cities on the Eastern seaboard as
far south as Wilmington, N.C., and as far west as Detroit and Cleveland,
Ohio."[65] Finally, a successful German aerial campaign from Newfoundland
could be a prelude to a ground invasion.

2) The South Atlantic Highway

Although the northern route was more formidable in terrain and more
forbidding in weather than the southern route, it could bring an invasion
force within reach of prime targets on the North American continent.
The North Atlantic approach to the Western Hemisphere was potentially
the most rewarding, the South Atlantic the most vulnerable. An advance
along the latter route would be far easier, but it would leave the invader
away from the continental United States. It would, however, entrench
Axis forces within the Western Hemisphere, giving them a bridgehead from
which they could progressively leapfrog towards their ultimate objectives:
the Panama Canal and the continental United States.

One of the worst strategic nightmares of America's prewar period
arose from the vulnerability of this route, a vulnerability exposed after
the fall of France left the French African colonies hanging like rich
prizes before the conqueror's eyes. If Hitler chose, he could launch an
attack through Spain and Portugal--with or without Franco's blessing--
seizing Gibraltar, pouring troops into French North Africa. From there,
his forces could fan out in two directions: driving eastward towards
the Suez Canal and the Middle East land bridge; or turning southwest,

thrusting towards the naval base at Dakar, African gateway to the New
World.[66] Across the Atlantic "Narrows"--southwest of Dakar and only 1620
nautical miles away--lay Natal on the Brazilian Bulge, the most vulnerable
approach to Latin America. From there an Axis invader could launch an
attack against the United States positions in the Caribbean and ultimately
against the Panama Canal.[67]

Moreover, the distance problem made it far easier for the Axis to
establish a foothold in the Western Hemisphere than for the United States
to counter the move. As the air forces' official historians write:

> To meet an invasion of this area, U.S. planes would have to fly
> some 2,600 miles from Puerto Rico, the nearest U.S. territory.
> Since Air Corps intelligence in the spring of 1940 wrongly
> credited the Axis powers with a surplus over their European
> requirements of some 4,100 planes capable of making the Africa-
> Natal flight, the implied threat was no light one.[68]

Once the Axis established itself on the Brazilian bulge, the problems of
ejecting it would be formidable, far beyond the capacity of the Initial
Protective Mobilization Force of 1,400,000 men. With their shorter lines
of communication across the Atlantic, the enemy powers could reinforce and
expand their footholds before the United States could transport and deploy
any expeditionary force into Latin America.[69]

The South Atlantic threat to the Western Hemisphere was reinforced
by a chain of islands curving like a Saracen's dagger towards Natal.
The Atlantic Islands--the Azores, Canaries and Cape Verde Islands--
formed a ridge of potential air and naval bases, which posed a double
threat to the Western Hemisphere: a threat to maritime commerce which
could be harried and destroyed by planes and submarines operating from
Axis bases within the islands, and a threat to the territorial security
of the Americas.[70] Consequently, the expulsion of the British from the

Mediterranean, followed by the creation of a German empire in central
Africa and the seizure of the Atlantic Islands, would create a formidable
problem for the United States.[71]

c. The Threat from the Pacific

The Pacific threat to the United States was neither as pressing
nor as proximate as the Atlantic threat. Some danger existed to the
Panama Canal, whose approaches were actually far more exposed on the
Pacific than the Atlantic side.[72] But the main Japanese threat was not
to the continental United States nor to the Western Hemisphere; it was
to American interests and possessions in the Western Pacific.[73] The
approaches to the Western Hemisphere on the Pacific side were far less
accessible; the distances far longer; and the logistical problems
involved in mounting an invasion, far greater than on the Atlantic front.
Therefore, American military planners in the prewar period gave the threat
of an invasion from the west no thought.[74]

4. The Problem of Defensive Priority

The United States was, therefore, confronted by multiple strategic
threats, but no one could foretell the direction or form of the enemy's
advance. Until he struck American planners could not predict where or
when he would attack. These multiple threats posed the problem of
defensive priority in its two interrelated forms: geographical and
political. Geographical priority sought to fix America's defensive line,
to decide where she would resist and fight. Political priority sought to
define the extent and depth of America's commitment to her potential allies.
If the United States were committed to assist another country, was she
bidding for time or merely seeking to establish a holding position to
cover herself while building up her main position? Was the United States

gambling on that nation's continued resistance, or committing herself to
the preservation of that country, becoming a hostage to her future, committing the bulk of her own resources to that country's defense? Whereas
geographical priority revolved around the problem of defining where the
United States would challenge the enemy's power, political priority revolved
around the conflict between concentrating her resources on national
rearmament and expending them on foreign aid.

a. Geographical Priority: the Problem of Drawing a Defensive Line

The problem of drawing a defensive line was a difficult one; its
possible solutions almost infinite. Almost any geographical position could
form a defensive line, even a position on the frontier, on the edge of the
enemy's empire. A nation could decide that the most effective way to
thwart the enemy's threat was to choose a defensive position far from its
own shores, to wage war on another continent. Or a nation could decide
that its military forces were too inadequate for anything except a pure
citadel defense of the homeland. The question, the problem of choice,
was often complicated by the incompatability that almost invariably existed
between the ends and the means, between the policy objectives of the nation
and its military strength.[75]

Geographical priority involved two interrelated aspects: one
spatial, the other temporal. The spatial aspect revolved around the
question: What position would be defended first? The temporal aspect
dealt with adjusting priority to changes of time and circumstance. For
the question of priority arose because there were too many demands, too
few supplies. All priority choices were, therefore, temporary choices,
depending largely upon the strength and preparedness of American military

forces. Theoretically the system differentiated between the necessary and
the desirable, between essential and expendable positions and interests.
When forces were large and well equipped, and supplies ample, the
pressures of priority decisions would ease. The United States could then
defend both the desirable and the necessary. Once she could successfully
answer needs and calls from all sides, distinctions would fade.

The question first posed itself as a series of alternative choices,
conflicting and competing courses of action. They were posed most clearly
and painfully at the time of the French collapse when the inadequacies of
our defense were no longer covered by the mythical might of the fallen
army. On June 17, 1940, the Chief of Staff presented three alternatives
to the Chief of Naval Operations:

> The time is rapidly approaching when a decision covering
> possible courses of military and naval action by U.S. will
> be necessary...the United States has three alternatives for
> positive courses of action. 1st--TO MAINTAIN A STRONG POSITION
> IN THE PACIFIC. IN ORDER TO DO SO, TO AVOID ANY COMMITMENT
> ELSEWHERE, THE DEVELOPMENT OF WHICH MIGHT REQUIRE THE WEAKENING
> OF THAT POSITION....In face of the present world situation, a
> challenge to the Far Eastern interests of the U.S. is not as
> vital as a challenge to our security in the Western Hemisphere,
> to meet which our Far Eastern interests may have to be abandoned.
> 2nd--TO MAKE EVERY EFFORT, INCLUDING BELLIGERENT PARTICIPATION,
> TO SUSTAIN GREAT BRITAIN AND FRANCE IN THE EUROPEAN WAR....
> The primary purpose of American intervention in the European
> Theater would be to afford to the Allies a winning preponderance
> of force. If American intervention occurred under conditions
> such that its only effect could be to postpone the defeat of the
> Allies, the result would be to the net disadvantage of the Allies,
> and would have dissipated fruitlessly our inadequate resources,
> whereby later on to meet single-handed the inevitable conflict
> with Germany and Italy.
> The pace and extent of German success have already become so
> great that American intervention would probably be too piece-
> meal, too insignificant and too late to afford a winning
> preponderance to the Allies....3rd--TO INITIATE TIMELY OPERATIONS
> IN EFFECTIVE STRENGTH AS THE SITUATION REQUIRES, TO PREVENT OR
> OVERTHROW GERMAN OR ITALIAN DOMINATION OR LODGMENT IN THE
> WESTERN HEMISPHERE.
> This course of action involves:
> (1) Concentration of sufficient naval forces to afford effective
> naval domination of the Western, North and South Atlantic Oceans,

the Caribbean Sea, and of maritime communicati ns to the Western
Hemisphere.
(2) Readiness to deny German or Italian seizure of British,
French, Dutch or Danish possessions in the Western Hemisphere
by U.S. assumption of sovereignty over these possessions, and
protective occupation thereof in sufficient strength to defend
them against attack.
(3) Preventive occupation of the strategic areas in the
Western Hemisphere wherein German or Italian bases might be
established to manace the Panama Canal or the Continental U.S.
(4) To prevent the transformation of Latin American States into
dependencies or colonies of Germany or Italy....[76]

According to this memorandum, the United States had three defensive choices.

It could pursue the policy of Pacific first, Europe first, or Western

Hemisphere first. The choice of any one would automatically exclude the

other two.

Obviously the choice of any global priority would determine defensive

lines within competing theaters. Extensive commitment in one potential

theater of war would naturally involve retrenchment or limited commitment

in other vital areas. This dilemma was analyzed in an earlier WPD memoran-

dum dated May 22, 1940:

2. We have vital interests in three general areas:
    a. The Far East.
    b. South America.
    c. Europe.
3. There should be an immediate decision as to what major
military operations we must be prepared to conduct.
4. It is not practicable to send forces to the Far East, to
Europe, and to South America all at once, nor can we do so to
a combination of any two of these areas without dangerous
dispersion of force.
5. We cannot conduct major operations either in the Far East
or in Europe, due both to lack of means at present and because
of the resultant abandonment of the United States' interest in
the area to which we do not send forces.
6. It would appear that conditions now developing limit us for
at least a year, more or less, to the conduc of offensive-
defensive operations in South America in defense of the Western
Hemisphere and of our own vital interest; such limited offensive
operations in Mexico as the situation may require; possible
protective occupation of European possessions in the Western
Hemisphere; and the defense of the Continental United States and

> its overseas possessions East of the 180th Meridian.
> This appears to be the maximum effort of which we are capable
> today.[77]

For this anonymous analyst, the choice was obvious. It was dictated by
America's limited means. Holding a defensive line in the Pacific at the
180th Meridian, the United States should confine herself to the defense
of the Western Hemisphere. On the Atlantic front, the only question was:
where in the Western Hemisphere could she draw the line?

Even a decision to defend the Western Hemisphere still posed a
multitude of choices. For where was the frontier between the Old and
the New World? Both worlds extended into the indivisible Atlantic.
The problem of priority hung on the question of definition. But since no
outside authority could define continental frontiers in universally
accepted terms, definition became a flexible tool for rational policy.
The limits of the Western Hemisphere could be restricted or expanded
freely and fearlessly within the boundaries of the Atlantic Ocean.

The President's military advisers wanted a restricted interpretation.
Since the United States was completely unprepared for military conflict
with Nazi Germany, the Government should limit itself to the feasible.
It should not extend its limited forces, dispersing them in exposed
positions along the vulnerable ranges of the Atlantic frontier; it should
confine itself to the defense of the continent. But even this restriction
was initially contracted even further. In the famous "Basis for Immediate
Decisions Concerning the National Defense", the War Department drew the
defensive line within the South American continent: "...until December,
1940, our Army will not be in a position to undertake operations south of
the latitude of Venezuela...."[78] However, this division of Latin America
into defendable and non-defendable lands, was purely a pragmatic convenience.

No question of definition was involved. Obviously, since
Latin America was an essential part of the Western Hemisphere,
it should be defended wherever possible.

   1) The Extension of America's Defensive Line into
        the Central Atlantic

  Far more debatable and controversial was the extension of
the Western Hemisphere into the Central Atlantic, a redrawing
of the eastern American frontier accomplished by the President
to the dismay of his military advisers. The German
occupation of Denmark in April 1940 began the process of
re-definition by raising the question of the future disposition
of two Danish possessions: Greenland and Iceland.

  Greenland posed no problem. It fell naturally within the
orbit of the Monroe Doctrine,[79] a claim asserted by the United
States in April 1940. Afraid that Canada or England would
occupy Greenland to prevent its seizure by the Germans,
Cordell Hull informed the British Ambassador, Lord Lothian,
that the island was part of the Western Hemisphere:

> I stated that there is the express application of
> the Monroe Doctrine by this country regarding Green-
> land; and that there appeared to be no serious
> question about Greenland forming a general part of
> this hemisphere as contra-distinguished from the
> European side of the Atlantic.[80]

When the United States finally assumed a protectorate over
the island, it cited the Monroe Doctrine.[81]

  Whereas Greenland fell conviently within the Western
Hemisphere, Iceland did not. As Langer and Gleason note:

> In air distance Iceland was much closer to the
> British Isles and to Scandinavia than to the
> coasts of Canada and the United States; its
> trade, too, was largely with Europe.

> Whatever the Administration's views on the applicability
> of the Monroe Doctrine to Iceland, it certainly was not
> prepared at this stage to put Iceland in the same category
> as Greenland.82

Because of this debatable status, President Roosevelt did not invoke

the Monroe Doctrine when--on July 7, 1941--he ordered the landing of

American troops in Iceland. He justified his decision by reminding

the American people that German occupation of the island would threaten

the security of the New World.[83] Although by definition the President

was excluding Iceland from the Western Hemisphere, his action made

any distinction fairly academic, for its occupation by American forces

bound the island politically and militarily to the Western Hemisphere.

The extension of American protection over the northern approaches

was matched, accompanied explained and justified by an extension of

the frontier of the Western Hemisphere over the central regions of the

Atlantic. But definition was problematic and unclear. Where exactly

did the oceanic boundary lie? Seeking authoritative advice, Roosevelt

recruited the services of Dr. Isaiah Bowman, President of John Hopkins

University. In his May 9, 1941, letter to the President, Dr. Bowman

wrestled with the problem:

> Hemisphere limits have reference to territory and special
> protection: they do not restrict our sea-borne trade.
> Since the foundation of the Republic it had been our settled
> policy to uphold the right of Americans freely to go and come
> upon the seven seas in pursuit of peaceful trade....
> Territorial inviolability is a seasoned Western Hemisphere
> policy. Meanwhile, without surrendering our right to trade
> in any part of the world, it is proper that we should define
> the area within which we continue a policy of territorial
> inviolability, a policy established for a hundred years.
> Within the area so defined all merchant ships must be free to
> move in safety whatever flag they fly. Within that area all
> warships, airplanes, and submarines must be under the surveillance
> of our armed forces. Notice is given that within that area all
> armed intrusions are subject to enquiry and challenge. Self-
> defense is the ultimate law....I propose at this time to lay
> down a clear definition of hemisphere responsibility. It is

> based upon the realities of the modern world. These realities
> have been brought home to every American by the cruelties of
> successive conquests that have already spread their effects
> past the inner threshold of the Western Hemisphere.[84]

Dr. Bowman admitted that previously there had been no difficulty in
delineating the boundaries of the Western Hemisphere. The cartographers
drew up purely conventional limits along the lines of 20 degrees west
longitude and 160 degrees east longitude.

> However, when it comes to international questions in our modern
> age, it is not cartographic convenience that we consult but the
> facts of history and the new meaning which modern armament and
> aviation give to maritime outposts of unquestionable concern....
> For fifty years our eastern and western approaches have gained
> in importance as we have more sharply realized that island
> footholds of power may strongly affect continental destiny.[85]

Dr. Bowman advised the President against choosing any permanent line.
It would be more advantageous to retain complete freedom of action,
defining the limits of the Western Hemisphere as need indicated.[86]

But this advice was a bit late. A month earlier, on April 10,
1941, the President had drawn a mid-ocean line at the twenty-fifth
meridian of longitude, withdrawing to the twenty-sixth meridian only
a few days later. The ocean west of that line became the Neutrality
Zone,[87] a definition promulgated unequivocally by Navy Operation Plan
No. 3.[88] But even this stand was modified by new needs. Since the
twenty-sixth meridian passed to the west of Iceland, the landing of
American forces on the island necessitated a re-interpretation which
would progressively extend the boundaries of the Western Hemisphere
until they covered all approaches to Iceland.[89]

Although this redefinition covered the Northern and Central Atlantic,
it did not enclose or protect the southern approaches stretching from
Northwest Africa and the Atlantic Islands to the exposed Natal Bulge.
Wishing to defend all roads to the hemisphere, the President thought

of extending the Monroe Doctrine until it covered the African coast.
Both Secretary Hull and Secretary Stimson were appalled by the proposal;
and Roosevelt quietly dropped it, though there is little doubt that it
appealed to him enormously.[90]

By a series of acts, the President had redefined the limits of
the Western Hemisphere, pushing the line of defense far into the
Atlantic and establishing a protective wall which would cover most of the
approaches to the American continent. Although his geographical expertise
postponed the adoption of an even bolder measure--the initiation of
full-scale convoy between the United States and England--it projected
American forces and commitments far beyond the limits recommended by
military planners in the spring crisis of 1940, far beyond the limits
that American unpreparedness allowed. It projected them away from the
third alternative--exclusive concentration on the defense of the Western
Hemisphere--recommended by the Chief of Staff in his June 17, 1940,
memorandum, "Decisions as to National Actions."[91] It progressively
pushed the United States towards the second alternative--full-scale
support of anti-Nazi forces in Europe. America was moving back full
circle. Her interwar security had depended upon the European wall of
resistance formed by the French Army and the British fleet. Now,
when the integrity of the New World was threatened, the United States
moved to preserve and restore the partly shattered strength which had
once sheltered her.

2) The Extension of America's Defensive line into the Western

Pacific

In the Pacific, the problem of drawing a defensive line was
neither as imperative nor as complicated as in the Atlantic. Here the

frontiers of the Western Hemisphere were clearly understood, firmly
established on the International Date Line or the 180 meridian. [92] The
Line adequately and completely covered America's chief defensive
position in the Pacific: the strategic triangle extending between
Alaska, Hawaii and Panama. In turn the strategic triangle shielded the
Pacific coast from direct attack.

Although there were three theoretical lines of defense in the Pacific--[93]
the Philippines, the strategic triangle and the western coast of the United
States--the second position was preferred by Army planners. They felt
that it was the most natural, most effective line of defense in the Pacific.
There was never any proposal to voluntarily withdraw American forces from
the strategic triangle to the west coast; and initially there was no
serious plan for the indefinite defense of the Philippines. America's
exposed position in the western Pacific was repeatedly condemned, denounced
as a liability which could be eliminated by the withdrawal of United States
forces. [94]

Actually the political and military logic of the prewar years reinforced
the case for withdrawal from the western Pacific. Six essential causes and
developments strengthened this argument: the consistent emphasis on the
defense of Hawaii in the strategic plans and military decisions of the
first decade of the twentieth century, the improvement of Japan's strategic
position after World War I, the commitment of American policy to the
independence of the Philippines by the Tydings-McDuffie Act, the rising
threat posed by the European Axis, the failure to reinforce Guam, and the
weakness of the existing defenses along the strategic triangle. [95]

By 1938 the above developments had remolded the original ORANGE plan
for a Pacific war against Japan. This plan had undergone radical

transformations, some more implicit that explicit, more inherent than stated.

The initial assumption governing the defense of the Philippines was that the Archipelago could be held until the relief and rescue expedition fought its way from Hawaii to Manila Bay.[96] With every subsequent revision of the war plan, more and more emphasis fell upon the military difficulties of conquering and securing the extensive line of communications between Pearl Harbor and the Philippines.[97] As the tenuousness of the American position in the Pacific became apparent,[98] the rescue of the Philippine garrison became increasingly doubtful. What had initially seemed like a weekend Jaunt, became a major enterprise stretching into years of effort and achievement.[99] Although Army planners never successfully imprisoned the Navy within the confines of the eastern Pacific, they succeeded--in the 1938 ORANGE plan--in placing the major emphasis upon the security of the strategic triangle.[100]

The difference between the Army and Navy over Pacific defense was the defference between the advocates of vertical and horizontal defense. The Army thought primarily in terms of defending a consolidated position, a line extending from and contiguous to the Western Hemisphere. By taking its stand on the strategic triangle, the United States could insure the security of the New World. The Navy thought primarily in terms of defending its Pacific bases and their interconnecting system of communications, a network whose retention would serve to launch offensive operations. While the former sought to protect the home ground, the base of operations, the latter thought to flank Japan's lines of communication.

This disparity was reinforced by the differences between the two geographical positions, the two lines of defense over which military leaders clashed so emphatically in the late 1930's. The strategic triangle formed

a solid block, a continuous extension of the continental United States.
Occupying and controlling it, American forces would hold to a consolidated
line. But the Philippines formed a solid wedge, cutting across the
enemy's lines of communication stretching from Japan to the mandated
islands of the Central Pacific. Moreover, it formed the great peak of
the British, Dutch and American position in the western Pacific, capping
the island range formed by the Netherlands East Indies and the Malay
Barrier. A menacing blade, it pointed towards the enemy's guts. As a
defensive position, it was a liability; as an offensive platform, it
could be an asset. Only as protection for our widely scattered interests
in the western Pacific could it possibly be classified as defensive. But
ironically, it could only achieve this undertaking by wide-scale offensive
operations which would hinder and possibly thwart Japan's southward
expansion.

This realization that the Philippines could be defended by offensive
operations soon led to hope and to a dramatic reversal of War Department
policy on the defense of the Archipelago.[101]

Although a modest reinforcement policy began in December, 1940,[102] no
radical shift occurred until July 31, 1941--five days after the appointment
of General Douglas MacArthur to the command of USSAFFE[103] Then General
Marshall announced to members of his staff that: "'it was the policy of
the United States to defend the Philippines. This defense will not be
permitted to jeopardize the success of the major efforts made in the
theater of the Atlantic. "[104] Since this initial reinforcement policy was
limited in its provisions and its aims, seeking to reinforce the Philippine
Islands without disturbing the existing priorities, it held few hopes.[105]

Since the President and the Secretary of War were unwilling to abandon the Philippine garrison, to admit the indefensibility of the Archipelago, they sought for means to implement its defense, finally finding salvation in the B-17 reinforcement policy.[106] Subsequently, it broadened the strategic mission of the Philippine forces; ultimately, it awakened wild optimism in Washington and Manila on the defensibility of the "indefensible" Archipelago.

The original mission of the Philippine garrison was, throughout the strategic planning of the 20's and 30's, a modest and limited one. It was to hold the entrances to Manila Bay, preventing the use of the port by the Japanese until the naval rescue task force could bring reinforcements and supplies from Hawaii.[107]

Gradually, the mounting realization that this enterprise was far more difficult and time-consuming than originally estimated led military planners to further limit the mission of the garrison. The Philippine forces were merely to stage a glorious, ultimately foredoomed, holding operation.[108] In both the original and the modified concept, the assignment of the force was confined to the defense of Manila Bay.

Now, however, the rush of reinforcements into this previously neglected theater and the advent of the B-17 opened new vistas. On October 1, 1941, General MacArthur alerted the War Department to the need for a revision of the conservative provisions of RAINBOW 5, dealing with the strategic mission of the Philippine forces:

> The strategic mission, as formerly visualized, of defending merely the entrance to Manila Bay by a citadel type defense with a small token force, should be broadened to include the defense of the Philippine Islands. There can be no adequate defense of Manila Bay nor of the Island of Luzon if an enemy is permitted to seize and operate from land bases on the

islands immediately south thereof. The wide scope of possible
enemy operations, especially aviation, now makes imperative the
broadening of the concept of Philippine defense; and the strength
and composition of the defense forces projected here are believed
to be sufficient to accomplish such a mission.[109]

The War Department was convinced. Even the Chief of WPD, Lt. Gen.
L. T. Gerow, became infected with enthusiasm, seeing a multitude of
strategic advantages in the retention and total defense of the Philippine
Islands. His October 8, 1941, memorandum to the Secretary of War clearly
reveals the strategic euphoria then permeating the War Department:

> The Philippine Islands are in the path of any Japanese movement
> to the south. If Japan should attempt to bypass these islands
> to the west, her lines of advance and supply will be under
> constant threat of air bombardment and naval attack. If she
> moves by the eastern route she must keep east of the Pelews in
> order to be beyond range of Philippine-based aviation and her
> lines of advance will then be subject to attack by the United
> States Pacific Fleet. Even if Japan were successful in by-
> passing the Philippines, she would still be confronted with the
> combined aviation of the Associated Powers operating from
> British and Dutch bases.
> The removal of the Philippines as an obstacle to her advance
> south, would be a hazardous military operation if opposed by
> strong aviation forces (United States and Associated Powers.)
> For air support of such an attack on the Philippines, Japan
> must rely on carrier-based aviation and intermittent support
> from long-range aircraft based on Taiwan. The cost of this
> operation would be so great that Japan will hesitate to make
> the effort except as a last resort.[110]

On November 21, 1941, RAINBOW 5 was revised; it now called for the defense
of the entire Archipelago and the conduct of offensive air operations against
enemy forces and bases.[111]

As in the Atlantic, American defensive thinking in the Pacific had
come full circle. From a pessimistic position which advocated strategic
retrenchment, which sought to disengage from the non-essential and
concentrate on the vital, the military planners, especially Army, had
moved to an optimistic advocation of full-scale strategic involvement.

On all fronts the line of defense was drawn in an advanced position,
pushing close to Europe in the Atlantic, and nearly touching the coast of
China in the Far East. American forces were as dispersed and extended as
her commitments and interests. In no sense did her global deployment on
the eve of war correspond to the dream of the isolationist, who thought
of the United States as a self-contained, self-defending natural fortress,
invulnerable because it was aloof and free from world politics.

   b. Political Priority: Rearmament versus Foreign Aid

   But American commitments at the time of Pearl Harbor extended far
beyond any military positions in the Atlantic and the Pacific. Actually
the United States had underwritten the continued resistance and the
eventual victory of the anti-Axis forces. Since America's real security
lay in the continued resistance of the Allied forces, her lines of defense
stretched from the fields of China and the plains of Russia to the shores
of Britain. Only full-scale aid, the adoption of all measures short of
war, could sustain and maintain these advanced positions.

   Although the President quickly realized the advantages of this
policy, commitment and conviction did not come automatically or immediately
to American military leaders and planners. As they favored conferring
absolute priority of the defense of the Western Hemisphere, so they
favored national rearmament to military foreign aid. [112] This preference
was the logistical and political corollary to their geo-strategic choice.
For American forces to be adequately prepared to execute their mission
and defend the Americas against all attacks, they must be adequately
armed, even at the cost of denying arms to all others.

   Their opposition to foreign aid crystallized under the impact of the
Allied disaster in Flanders and France. In the late spring and early

summer of 1940, most American military experts expected that the fall of
France would be quickly followed by the defeat of Great Britain. The
Joint Planning Committee, when questioned by the President in June, 1940,
was clearly skeptical on Britain's chances of survival:

> On the crucial point--the fate of Great Britain six months
> hence--they found it doubtful that Great Britain, as
> distinguished from the British Empire, would by that time
> "continue to be an active combatant." Germany had the intention,
> the equipment and forces, and the bases for powerful air attacks
> on British "port and naval bases, facilities, railway communica-
> tions, air bases, munitions depots and factories." Continuous
> air and submarine operations against British sea communications
> would result in heavy casualties and food shortages in England.
> "The actual invasion and overrunning of England by German
> military forces" appeared to be "within the range of possibility."[113]

Since any equipment furnished to the Allies could ultimately fall
into the hands of the Axis, the conclusion was inescapable. As the
service chiefs wrote to the President in the first edition of the "Basis
for Immediate Decisions Concerning the National Defense", all future
military aid to doomed Britain was dangerous and futile: "to release
to Great Britain additional war material now in the hands of the armed
forces...will seriously weaken our present state of defense and will not
materially assist the British forces."[114]

The President's reaction when this study was presented to him on
June 22, 1940, was unexpected. Although he worded his reservations in
a diplomatic manner, it was obvious that his assumptions and attitudes
were diametrically opposed to those of his planners. For unlike his
military advisers, he felt that the British had a good chance of surviving,
at least until the end of the year. To Admiral Stark and General Marshall
he expressed his decision to continue aid to the British:

> He stated that a decision in this matter would have to depend
> on the situation; that if, for example, the British displayed
> an ability to withstand the German assault, and it appeared

> that a little help might carry them through to the end of the
> year, then we might find it desirable from the point of view
> of our defense, to turn over other material that apparently
> would exercise an important effect on the action....That
> orders for munitions for Great Britain be accepted as long
> as the material can be employed to damage the German effort,
> and without seriously retarding procurement programs of our
> own Army and Navy....[115]

"The Basis for an Immediate Decision Concerning the National Defense"

was consequently toned down. And although the second edition (June 27,

1940) still reflected the planners' pessimism, it contained an escape

clause:

> The further release of war material now in the hands of our
> armed forces will seriously weaken our present state of defense.
> Therefore, in general, further commitments for the sale of
> military equipment of the armed forces of the United States will
> be made only if the situation should indicate that Great Britain
> displayed such an ability to withstand the German assault, and
> that the release of such equipment as we could find it possible
> to spare would exercise an important effect in enabling Great
> Britain to resist until the first of the year.[116]

The rather ambiguous wording of the above document conceals one of the

most momentous decisions of the prewar period, a decision previously

announced on June 10, 1940. At Charlottesville, Virginia, the President

had clearly enunciated his aim:

> ...we will extend to the opponents of force the material
> resources of this nation and, at the same time, we will
> harness and speed up the use of these resources in order
> that we ourselves in the Americas may have equipment and
> training equal to the task of any emergency and every defense.[117]

Naturally, when the President was informed by his military advisers at

the meeting of June 22, 1940, that his two objectives--rearmament and

foreign aid--were incompatible, he refused to make a choice. Faced with

these two alternatives, he still chose both, refusing to acknowledge their

"incompatability."

He recognized that England was "the last remaining line of defense...
beyond our own shores."[118] Therefore, its preservation was "vital to the
defense of the United States."[119] But the President's decision was
basically a calculated gamble, an act of faith. The victory of the RAF
in the Battle of Britain and Hitler's failure to invade England in the
summer of 1940, confirmed its wisdom. By the fall of 1940 even the
skeptical Army officers were converted. They now realized that continued
aid to the British would complement, rather than compete, with hemisphere
defense. Since the United States did not have enough forces for the defense
of the New World, aid to Britain made military sense. The wall that had
once seemed on the verge of crumbling, now seemed stable and strong.[120]
By reinforcing it, America could defend herself by proxy. In their
September 25, 1940, estimate, therefore, the joint planners accepted the
assumption that the President had followed on June 22. They assumed that
the United States had a twelve month interval of grace since it would
take the Axis six months to defeat Great Britain and assert its control
over the eastern Atlantic and another six months to mount a trans-Atlantic
offensive operation.[121]

By the end of the year this conviction had deepened. Marshall and
Stark were convinced that the United States could not allow Great Britain
to lose the war, even at the cost of Allied intervention or a full-scale
American ground offensive in Europe. In his famous Plan Dog memorandum,
Admiral Stark tied the security of the Western Hemisphere and the preserva-
tion of the British Empire together:

> I believe that the continued existence of the British Empire,
> combined with building up a strong protection in our home areas,
> will do most to assure the status quo in the Western Hemisphere,
> and to promote our principal national interests. As I have

previously stated, I also believe that Great Britain requires from us very great help in the Atlantic, and possibly even on the continents of Europe and Africa if she is to be enabled to survive.[122]

The Army planners and their Chief, General Marshall, agreed.[123]

The issue of rearmament versus foreign aid did not end with the President's decision. It merely took another form. Whereas the issue was first fought on an "either or" basis, it now became a question of logistic priority. "How much can we allocate here; how much, there?" Perhaps most typical, certainly most important, was the struggle over the allocation of airplanes. Here the competition between the needs of the British and those of the Army Air Forces became particularly savage. By the summer of 1940 the AAF was committed to the 54-group program, considered absolutely minimal for the needs of hemisphere defense.[124] When, therefore, the President proposed an equal division of aircraft production between the AAF and the British, the AAF howled.[125] It fought savagely for its own minimal needs, seeking to postpone the allocation of aircraft to Great Britain until these needs were satisfied. But the President overruled its appeals. He felt that the emphasis should fall on aid to the British: their units were actually engaging the enemy. Throughout 1941, therefore, the staffs and experts of the AAF agonized over percentage figures and allocation formulae which would satisfy the needs of the British without totally sacrificing their own future. At the outbreak of war, the possible strength of the AAF had been reduced considerably by a national allocation policy which favored foreign aid over rearmament.[126]

The debate continued, however, repeatedly refired by two factors, two uncertainties, which plagued all prewar planning: the impossibility of

predicting the date of American entry into the war and the impossibility
of permanently relying on the resistance of the British Empire. The first
factor persistently worried the service planners. If America entered the
war suddenly and without fulfilling her minimal military needs, then her
situation would be precarious, the role of her forces as limited as her
power. But the continuing uncertainty over England's fate was even more
alarming. Although the Battle of Britain temporarily healed the June,
1940, jitters of the War Department, American military planners did not
then realize that this German defeat was permanent and decisive. Until
the invasion of the Soviet Union in June, 1941--to a certain extent even
beyond that date--the fear persisted that the Germans could and would
invade the British Isles. This anxiety was strengthened in early 1941
by the knowledge that the Allies were turning a critical corner. The
coming year would provide the Germans with their last opportunity to
invade England. As the chief of the Army planning division reported:

> It is, therefore, assumed that the greatest danger which the
> British Commonwealth must face during the present year is
> greatly intensified air, surface, and subsurface activity
> coincident with or followed by an attempted invasion.
> During this critical period, the United States cannot afford
> to base its military program on the assumption that the
> British Isles will not succumb as a result of blockade, or
> that they cannot be successfully invaded.[12]

If United States military planners had known that the British would hold
indefinitely, and that American intervention would be postponed, they
would have accepted the emphasis on foreign aid with more ease. But
unfortunately the present provides no horoscope for the convenience of
decision makers and advisers.

The turning point came with the passage of the Lend-Lease Bill on
March 8, 1941. Although the immediate basis for Lend-Lease was the

128

financial crisis of the British Empire, the impact of its implications carried far beyond. The passage of this bill meant that the presidential policy of aid to Britain and other anti-Axis nations had become national policy confirmed by Congessional sanction. It identified the resistance of these nations with the defense of the United States.

This identity of purpose between American and British forces, this vital fusion of interests, was clearly noted by the Acting Army Intelligence Chief, Sherman Miles. He also diagnosed the transformation that this policy effected in our "neutrality" status:

> I understand the present basic policy of our Government to be "All aid to Great Britain short of war." The Secretary's directive that for supply purposes, British forces are to be considered as an American expeditionary Force seems merely to implement the basic Aid-to-Britain policy in our existing period of so-called "neutrality."[129]

The Lend-Lease progam was originally conceived as a policy for the rescue and preservation of the British Empire. But, the President wanted to encourage all anti-Axis forces by extending aid to all present and future victims of aggression. Anticipating this broadening of Lend-Lease, President Roosevelt refused to restrict its applicability. With the extensive authority delegated into his hands by Congress, he could subsequently extend Lend-Lease even to undemocratic, but anti-Axis, nations: to China in the spring of 1941, to the USSR in October, 1941.[130]

America's geographical and political commitments also met in a more specific manner. The political extension of her defensive line led to the redefinition of her military position in the Far East. More than six months before the attack on Pearl Harbor, the United States was virtually committed to the Allied position in the western Pacific, to the defense of the Netherlands East Indies, the Malay Barrier and portions of Southeast

Asia. This unannounced and unpublicized defensive line was defined in the
American-Dutch-British (ADB) Report summarizing the military consultations
and decisions reached at Singapore in April, 1941. The conference
summarized the conditions under which the three powers would fight Japan:

> A "direct act of war" by Japanese armed forces against American,
> British or Dutch territory. A movement of Japanese forces into
> Thailand west of the meridian of Bangkok or south of the Kra
> Isthmus. Ocupation of Portugese Timor or the Loyalty Islands
> off New Caledonia.[131]

As America's Far Eastern commitments matured and developed, the
retention of this line became more and more imperative. Its seizure
would seriously threaten her defensive posture in the western Pacific,
dooming the Philippines to isolation and defeat. Any failure to support
the British and the Dutch would fatally disrupt the coalition of
interests and powers in the Far East.

When the Far Eastern crisis came to a climax in December, 1941,
this defensive line was generally accepted as inviolable and non-
negotiable. The United States would fight to maintain it. Its defense
was the unannounced _sine qua non_ of American policy in the western
Pacific. As the service chiefs reminded the President on November 27,
1941, it was the only position for which the United States should fight
without question, without hesitation:

> ...United States, British, and Dutch military authorities in
> the Far East agreed that joint military counteraction against
> Japan should be undertaken only in case Japan attacks or
> directly threatens the territory or mandated territory of the
> United States, the British Commonwealth, or the Netherlands
> East Indies, or should the Japanese move forces into Thailand
> West of 100° East or south of 10° North, Portugese Timor,
> New Caledonia, or the Loyalty Islands. Japanese involvement
> in Yunnan or Thailand up to a certain extent is advantageous,
> since it leads to further dispersion, longer lines of communi-
> cation, and an additional burden on communications. However,

a Japanese advance to the west of 100° East or south of 10°
North, immediately becomes a threat to Burma and Singapore.[132]

In the Atlantic and Pacific, political commitments reinforced America's
geographical line of defense. But there were differences in emphasis.
In the Atlantic, political commitments extended her geographical positions.
In the Pacific, her military position in the Philippines capped and
culminated her political pledge to defend the Netherlands East Indies and
the Malay Barrier. In both theaters American global lines of defense
touched the frontiers of the enemy's empire.

5. Conclusions

a. From Hemisphere Defense to Global Defense.

What were the implications of these multiple, extended lines of
defense? America's geographical and political commitments were proof
that she had moved far beyond stonewall defense, far beyond hemisphere
defense. By the outbreak of war on December 7, 1941, she was committed
to global defense. She identified her security neither with the protection
of a continent nor the safety of a nation. She identified her security
with the world situation, the world condition. More and more the
President realized that aggression could not be confined by arbitrary
boundaries or artificial frontiers. It was an infection against which,
no announced barrier could permanently hold. Like President Woodrow
Wilson--who in 1917 had identified American security with a global applica-
[133]
tion of the Monroe Doctrine--Roosevelt realized that continental sanctuaries
were no longer defendable.

b. The Consistent Core: The Interdependence of America and Defense
with Global Security

This development was accompanied by a persistent and permanent emphasis. Every move forward, every expansion of her commitments, every extension of her position, was designed to accomplish a single aim: to strengthen American security. From the RAINBOW plans to the ABC agreements and the Victory Program, the first clause, the first task, was always the same. When the Joint Board weighed the alternative strategies that the United States should pursue and evolved the five situations, it made RAINBOW No. 1 the core case around which the other four plans revolved. This plan fused the defense of the continental United States with that of the Western Hemisphere. Moreover, it announced the primary mission which all five plans must perform before they could carry out any extended or additional operations. As described by a JPD planner the essential mission was to

> RAINBOW No. 1: Protect the possessions of the United States, the Western Hemisphere north of latitude 13 degrees south, and United States sea-borne trade, against hostile aggression or violation of the letter or spirit of the Monroe Doctrine.[134]

All other projected plans echoed this refrain: "carry out the missions of RAINBOW 1"[135], "as in RAINBOW No. 1"[136], "like RAINBOW No. 1."[137]

This emphasis continued when America engaged in coalition planning with the British. As the ABC-1 Report--the first British-American "war plan"--clearly enunciated, the primary "strategic defense policy" of the United States was the defense of the Western Hemisphere: "The paramount territorial interests of the United States are in the Western Hemisphere. The United States must, in all eventualities, maintain such dispositions as will prevent the extension in the Western Hemisphere of European or Asiatic political or military power."[138] This precise terminology was reincarnated in Joint Army and Navy Basic War Plan--RAINBOW No. 5.[139]

Throughout the entire prewar period, American defensive thinking
moved in a continually expanding direction, progressively pushing
forwared her military frontiers until the distinction between offensive
and defensive positions was obscured. But the appeal made by planners
and leaders remained the same. Every extension of the line, every
occupation of an advanced position was justified on defensive grounds,
was presented as a move designed to insure the security of the continental
United States and the Western Hemisphere. The prewar revolution in
American military thinking which moved her from stonewall to global
defense represents, therefore, a progressive reidentification of its
defensive stance. Before Pearl Harbor this process or tendency had
reached its ultimate stage: American defense was now inextricably bound
to the maintenance of an advanced global position against the Axis.

Throughout this entire process, however, lay a basic thread of
consistency underlying every development, undercutting every ambiguity:
the interdependence of American and world security, the inextricable
identification between the defense of the United States and the stability
of international conditions. From the beginning of its national existence,
the security of the American nation had depended largely upon the international situation. Even during the isolationist era, world security was
the precondition to national withdrawal. Any major European war, any
threat to the stability of the European or Asiatic balance of power
inevitably involved the United States.

American isolationism was, therefore, a myth. Once the challenge
arose and the major international barriers protecting the Western
Hemisphere collapsed, the United States could no longer remain aloof.
She was compelled to move into the strategic vacuum, to shore up the

eroding situation, to try to salvage and save. Stonewall or even hemisphere defense was only possible when other powers were preserving and maintaining global defense. Once they failed or faltered, however, the United States had to reconvert herself, to extend her strength beyond her own shores, seeking in the midst of the general deterioration to save or re-establish or create a secure world. The defensive-offensive complex eventually embraced all the alternatives of the June 17, 1940, "Decisions as to National Action": hemisphere defense, the maintenance of an advance position in the Pacific and full support for the Allies. The circle of security that the United States built around the Americas had a constantly expanding circumference; but its preconceptual core was consistent. The safety of the United States ultimately depended upon the stability and security of world conditions.

Chapter VIII

The Evolution of Strategic Priority

1. Production versus Participation.

Although, in the prewar period, the United States assumed a position of advanced defense, although it committed itself to the defeat of the Axis and the victory of the Allies, it stopped short of full-scale involvement. By December, 1941, it had reached a half-way house between the withdrawal of the isolationist and the complete involvement of the interventionist. The United States had become the arsenal of the anti-Axis nations; it had assumed major responsibility for the security of the Atlantic and the Pacific. But even after the passage and implementation of Lend-Lease the official debate over her global role continued. This time the debate fell between those who believed that production alone could secure victory and those who believed that only full-scale American involvement would insure the triumph of the anti-Axis forces. If the interventionists won the debate, their victory would mean more than the assumption of a new line of defense: it would mark a passage from the defense to the offense. For the resolution of the debate over Lend-Lease had narrowed the alternatives.

The old question of aid-to-England or exclusive concentration on national rearmament had been relegated to the files. Now the problem was: could we win by merely adhering to a policy of defense by proxy? Could the British win for us if we supplied them to the hilt? Or was victory only possible if the United States hurled her own forces into battle? If the latter solution was adopted, the United States would still have to

choose the form of its intervention, the path of its approach. What foe
would the United States strike first? Where? If she chose the direct
approach, where would it lead? And, finally, how would the United States
deliver her attack?

The issue of intervention did not arise seriously until after the
crisis of June, 1940. Though some of the planning documents of that
fearful period did propose intervention as an alternative, it was merely
theoretical, and soon dismissed.[1] On June 13, 1940, the President startled
his planners by predicting what the strategic situation would be in the
fall. He prophecied that the United States would then be engaged in
limited action against the Axis, "'active in the war, but with naval
and air forces only.'"[2] The planners were shocked by this hypothetical
situation. As they saw it, American intervention would be too premature
and too weak to be effective. She would find herself alone, divested of
Allies, unprepared to meet the Axis threat:

> 'Belligerent entry by the United States in the next few
> months would not only disperse and waste our inadequate
> means, but would result in leaving the United States as the
> one belligerent to oppose the almost inevitable political,
> economic and military aggression of totalitarian powers.'[3]

During the balance of the interwar period, the military planners
debated the question of participation repeatedly, shifting their views
according to the changing military situation.

At first everything turned on the question of British resistance.
In the summer of 1940, the United States sent an exploratory group--
the Emmons-Strong-Ghormley mission--to Great Britain.[4] Its main purpose
was to discover the strength of British resistance and to explore the
"devious" byways of an "alien" strategy to whose support American
policy was increasingly committed. During the August 31 meeting with

the British Chiefs of Staff, Admiral Ghormley asked the crucial question:
If Germany is the main enemy, how do you expect to defeat her? Although
Sir Cyril L. Newall, Chief of the Air Staff, admitted that the "'coup de
grace'"[5] could only be delivered by a ground invasion of the continent,
he strongly hoped that British power would fatally weaken the German
Army before launching this final stroke.[6] Unwittingly, the Chief of
the Air Staff had conjured the problem which would weigh the scales
for American intervention. Was Great Britain sufficiently strong--
when reinforced by American production--to defeat Germany? If she were,
then American production would suffice. If not, full-scale participation
by the United States would be imperative.

Admiral Stark drew the implications into the open. In his Plan Dog
memorandum[7] he challenged the belief that the British could win the war
without American participation. For the English, vast empire and all,
had neither the manpower nor the material strength to do the final job,
to carry out the invasion of the continent. Since only a ground
offensive would knock Germany down, "the United States, in addition to
sending naval assistance, would also need to send large air and land
forces to Europe or Africa or both, and need to participate strongly in
this land offensive."[8]

But Admiral Stark's memorandum dealt with long-range requirements,
with the demand of a strategy for victory. Most of the military planners
dealt with the question of intervention on a day-to-day basis. Their
usual question was: should we enter the war now? The April, 1941,
crisis over the convoy question threatened to explode into war. A
debate over intervention ensued. For General Marshall's benefit, the
War Plans Division produced an analysis of the pros and cons of an

immediate American entry into the European war.[9] While WPD thought that

we should postpone any early intervention, it recognized its ultimate

inevitability. It also stressed the paramount importance of preserving

the British Isles against German conquest:

> 'Upon the assumption, which appears reasonable, that the
> United States will enter the present war sooner or later,
> it appears to the War Plans Division highly desirable that
> our entry be made sufficiently soon to avoid either the loss
> of the British Isles or a material change in the attitude of
> the British Government directed toward appeasement.
> In contrast to this view, it must be recognized that the Army
> can, at the present time, accomplish extremely limited military
> support to a war effort, and from this point of view it is
> highly desirable that we withhold active participation as
> long as possible.'[10]

General Embick--summoned to Washington especially to advise on this

crisis--disagreed sharply with this analysis. Detecting the pro-interventionist

tone of the memorandum, he launched out violently against it. "He declared

that he himself would not advise entering the war and believed that to do

so 'would be wrong in a military and naval sense' and unjust 'to the

American people.'"[11] Despite this verbal assault, the WPD planners stuck

to their argument, Colonel McNarney even reiterating and strengthening

the case for intervention:

> '...anything that would tend to cause the fall of the British
> Isles would tend to put the whole load on the United States;
> that it is important that we start reducing the war-making
> ability of Germany. We do have a Navy in being and can do
> something. If we wait, we will end up standing alone, and
> internal disturbances may bring on communism. I may be called
> a fire-eater, but something must be done.'[12]

The German attack on the Soviet Union eased the crisis. Since an

immediate German invasion of the British Isles was now unlikely, the

WPD planners swung towards the anti-interventionist stand taken by Embick.

The shifts in the War Department's attitude were quite remarkable.

In June, 1940, England's plight had held one warning: the United States

must not be sucked down the drain. She must preserve her strength, not give it away. Now, when the April crisis in the Atlantic sounded another prelude to disaster, WPD preached full-scale intervention to save the British Isles. This shift, moreover, did not reflect any substantial expansion of American military strength, but rather reflected the new estimate now placed within the circles of the War Department on the value of continued British resistance.

The German involvement in Russia did not change this estimate. It did, however, remove the urgency for intervention. With the heat off, its disadvantages became only too apparent. Perhaps nothing reveals this more clearly than the War Department's reaction to the "General Strategy Review" presented by the British Chiefs of Staff at the Argentia Conference.[13] This extensive strategic study (dated July 31, 1941), hailed the prospect of American intervention as an unmitigated boon:

> 'At sea the situation would immediately be relieved, and this should be reflected in reduced shipping losses. Even if Japan intervened, the balance of the advantage would still be with us. American forces might be able to prevent enemy penetration in Morocco and West Africa, and could take over potential commitments in the Atlantic Islands.
> It is clear, however, that if intervention is to come, the longer it is delayed the greater will be the leeway to be made up in every direction.'[14]

The prospect of American intervention excited the British planners; it appalled the Americans. When General Marshall offered the review to the War Plans Division, the result was an explosion of memoranda which flayed the British approach unmercifully.[15] Particularly exasperating to the American planners was the certainty with which the British announced the blessings of intervention: "'The intervention of the United States would revolutionize the whole situation,'"[16] or "'United States intervention would not only made the victory certain, but might also make it swift.'"[17]

This attitude seemed like the impertinence of overassurance. [18]

Gradually the question of participation began to separate from the question of intervention. The United States could enter the war against the Axis without full-scale involvement. Participation could take several forms. America could commit herself fully, engaging the mass of her forces into the conflict, pouring her troops on the European battlefield; or she could restrict her commitment to air and naval forces while concentrating her emphasis on the mass production of the articles of war. Participation, therefore, could assume two forms: limited or total. [19]

Paradoxically, the War Department planners opposing intervention were the strongest advocates of full-scale participation once America entered the war. Actually, it is not surprising. Since these military planners thought in terms of a massive commitment of forces, since they believed that only large-scale ground operations would bring victory, they opposed any premature commitment, any intervention before American forces were fully trained, equipped and mobilized. If they opposed any immediate entry into the war, it was largely because they realized the full magnitude of their task.

The conflict between the champions of victory through production and the advocates of full-scale participation came to a climax with the Victory Program. [20] This monumental strategic and logistic study and estimate of the probable cost of intervention was unwittingly initiated by President Roosevelt. On July 9, 1941, the President sent a letter to Stimson and Knox, asking them for a study of "'the overall production

requirements required to defeat our potential enemies.'"
Although the demands seemed broad, the tone of the letter and
its contents showed, in the opinion of Coakley and Leighton,
that Roosevelt's main interest was to discover how the United
States could outproduce her enemies:

> The President was not concerned with the strategic
> concept or plans that might govern eventual American
> participation in the war, nor with the American forces
> that might be required. The whole tenor of the
> request implied, in fact, that whether or not the
> United States became a belligerent, it would continue
> to serve primarily as an arsenal for the nations
> actively fighting the Axis. His basic assumption,
> made explicit in a supplementary message a few
> weeks later was that 'the reservoir of munitions
> power available to the United States and her
> friends is sufficiently superior to that available
> to the Axis to insure the defeat of the latter.[21]

To Army planners, this view was heresy. As General Gerow
reminded Assistant Secretary McCloy: "'It would be unwise to
assume...that we can defeat Germany simply by outproducing her.'"[22]
Only balanced military power can produce victory: "'sound
strategy, implemented by well-trained forces which are
adequately and effectively equipped.'"[23] Not surprisingly,
the Victory Program was radically different than what the
President had ordered. Instead of acquiring a compact volume,
he received, _gratis_, an entire library.

The Joint Board's "Estimate of United States Over-all
Production Requirements" was a key document of the Program.[24]
Unequivocally, it stated the need for full-scale participation:

> '...it is the opinion of the Joint Board that
> Germany and her European satellites cannot be
> defeated by the European Powers now fighting
> against her. Therefore, if our Europen enemies
> are to be defeated, it will be necessary for
> the United States to enter the war, and to employ
> a part of its armed forces offensively in the
> Eastern Atlantic and in Europe or Africa.'[25]

Although this Estimate was generally vague about the form that full-scale
participation would assume, other documents in the Victory Program file
fill out the outline, amplifying it in several partially complementary,
partially contradictory directions.[26] The contradictions merely reflect
the composite nature of the program, the contemporary medium of uncertainty in which planning took place, and the failure to fuse
service viewpoints into a coherent whole.[27]

The Army's "Ultimate Requirements Program" contemplated a full-scale
assault on the European continent:

> 'We must prepare to fight Germany by actually coming to grips
> with and defeating her ground forces and definitely breaking
> her will to combat....Air and sea forces will make important
> contributions, but effective and adequate ground forces must
> be available to close with and destroy the enemy within his
> citadel.'[28]

The Navy's view on participation was embodied in the "Joint Board Estimate".
It favored a strategy strikingly similar to that advocated by the British
at the Atlantic Conference and later during the wartime conferences.

> 'The Navy considers that, since the principal strength of the
> Associated Powers is at present in naval and air categories,
> the strategy which they should adopt should be based on the
> effective employment of these forces, and the employment of
> land forces in regions where Germany cannot exert the full
> power of her land armies.[29]

The Army Air Force expressed its views on strategy in AWPD/1: its
Victory Program. Here it proudly proclaimed that victory could be
achieved through air power alone, thereby nullifying the need for a
ground offensive against the Axis. But this key air force doctrine--
which would also have eliminated the need for a large Army--was heresy
to the more orthodox Army officers. So the air planners guarded their
program by making allowances for close tactical support of land armies
in the field.[30]

To summarize, three major interpretations of the term "participation"
emerged from the Victory Program. Full-scale participation could mean the
concentrated application of air power, the application of sea and air
power without the maximum utilization or mobilization o: land armies,
or finally, the mobilization and engagement of massive ground forces in
an assault upon the centers of Axis strength. Obviously only the first
two interpretations were compatible with the President's advocacy of a
strategy based on production rather than participation.[31]

Was there any consistency or basic agreement among this welter of
interpretations? Only one thread held them together: the belief that
whatever course was followed, whatever degree of participation was
involved, full-scale or limited, the force and power of the Allies
would be concentrated against the major enemy, not dispersed against
a multitude of foes. The implications of this basic agreement will be
further explored when we study the evolution of the "Germany first"
doctrine.

At the time, however, the President was unconverted by the impressive
statistics of the Army's Victory Program. For the views of the Production
advocates still reigned. To Secretary of War Stimson, Roosevelt confessed
his hope that the United States could avoid full-scale involvement. He
disliked "the implications of all-out war--that is...the ultimate
necessity of American forces invading and crushing Germany."[32]

As the nation moved towards Pearl Harbor, the tempo of rearmament
actually slowed down. The belief that the United States should, or
would, participate by fully committing its ground forces to a massive
invasion of the European continent, weakened. Correspondingly, the

pressure grew to commit more aid to the Allies and less equipment to
American ground forces, thereby limiting future participation of the
United States to naval and air forces. On the eve of Pearl Harbor
anti-Axis foreign nations were still receiving the largest amount of
munitions. As the logistic historians of the Army have noted, there
was a good chance that in any purely Atlantic war the United States
would confine its role to production: "On the eve of Pearl Harbor the
prospects were that America's contribution to the war would be in
weapons, not armies."[33]

In intermittent, spasmodic steps, the United States military,
particularly the Army, moved far from its earlier conviction that
the nation should remain aloof, uncommitted to any objective except the
defense of the Western Hemisphere. Its conversion to full-scale
participation arose from several causes. It grew partly from the
modification of the objectives of national policy by the President,[34]
but it also arose from the Army's mounting realization that the security
of the United States was directly tied to the maintenance of the British
Empire and the defeat of the Axis. Since the latter objective could not
be attained without the intervention and full participation of American
forces, the question of American entry became merely a matter of time.
But production versus participation also laid the foundations for
controversies between direct and indirect approaches. For if the
United States restricted itself to being the arsenal for anti-Axis
resistance, only an indirect strategy would be feasible. If she became
an active participant, the degree of her participation would determine
whether the Allied powers could adopt a direct or an indirect approach.
If her participation was limited to the use of air and naval forces, the

Allies would have to adopt an indirect strategy against the main enemy,
Germany. If her participation included the use of massed armies, the
Allies could mount a direct assault on the citadel of enemy power.

2. Avenues for the Strategic Offensive

The controversies between these conflicting interpretations of
participation arose partly from the service rivalries within the American
military establishment, and partly from the conflicts between British
and American views on strategy. But their ultimate foundation lay in
the geographical position of the United States, placed in a roughly
central position between the power centers of its potential foes.
America's geographical position exposed her to multitudinous lines of
approach--lines of defense which could easily become lines of offense.
They and their relationship to the enemy's nexus of strength traced the
avenues of approach that competing, conflicting strategies could take.

a. The North Atlantic Approach

The North Atlantic lifeline--leading from the eastern ports of the
United States to the shores of the United Kingdom--formed a gigantic
logistic channel moving from a chief base of operations to a major
advanced position, from the arsenal to the prime battlefield. For
the United Kingdom would ultimately form an ideal springboard for an
assault against the European Axis. Here the demands of the defense and
the needs of the offense blended together. As Secretary of War Stimson
constantly reiterated, the North Atlantic was the main lifeline to the
35
British Isles; its security would protect America's last line of
defense outside the Western Hemisphere. But its security, its relative
freedom from attack and disruption, meant far more than the mere denial

of offensive bases to the Axis. It meant control of an
oceanic route over which American and British supplies could
freely move. It meant that the United States was building
a line of communications, laying the basis for the projection
of Allied forces against the enemy's heartland. The northern
approach was, therefore, not only the most threatening avenue,
but also the most promising: "'the direct line of our
strategical route towards victory.'"[36]

b. The South Atlantic Approach

The South Atlantic approach was also a dual highway.
If it could serve as an avenue for the conquest of Latin
America, it could also expose the southern expanses of
the Axis empire to attack. Every major defensive move
in the South Atlantic would open offensive possibilities.
The seizure of the Atlantic Islands, "'preliminary operations'" which would strengthen our position in the Western
Hemisphere,'"[37] would "'prepare the way for further action
in Europe or Africa when the situation warrants.'"[38] The
Army planners felt increasingly that the Atlantic Islands
project had more offensive than defensive value.

Perhaps the boldest defensive move of the United States
in the prewar period, according to Coakley and Leighton, would
have been the occupation of Dakar. This action would have
provided "the most effective riposte to a German move into
northeast Africa,"[39] insulating the Brazilian bulge against
German attack. It would also have furnished a major
supporting base for any subsequent attack against French
Morocco;[40] and it would have given the United States a
bridgehead on the southern fringes of the enemy's empire.

c. Pacific Approaches:

In the Pacific, the United States simultaneously sought
to defend the approaches to the American continent and to
preserve its advanced, exposed positions in the western
ocean. These positions, posing a threat to the enemy's lines
of communication, were essentially offensive. Their retention
would thwart any Japanese consolidation in the Western Pacific.[41]
Successful defense would lay the basis for subsequent offense.
The loss of this region, however, would not threaten American
security.

4. "Germany First": The Evolution of the Direct Approach

The complexity of approaches in the Pacific reflected
the problems of applying the direct approach on a global
scale. The ease with which the direct approach could be
applied stood in inverse proportion to the complexity of the
challenge. In a single theater war, the problem of application
was relatively simple. Once a weak position was found in
the enemy's front, an army could launch a massive assault;
or, selecting the enemy's vital center, it could strike one
blow after another until he collapsed. The direct approach,
therefore, sought to disrupt the enemy's power, to draw
his military strength into battle and smash it by a massive
application of force. Napoleonic in conception, it was
suited to the continental warfare of the early 19th century.

It was not so easily adaptable to the challenges of
20th century global warfare. As the field of war broadened,
objectives proliferated. Confronted by multiplying threats,
descending from widely separated directions, a nation could
no longer seek a single center. It was presented with

multiple objectives: the enemy's territory, his military
forces, his economy, his morale. These manifold objectives
converted modern warfare into siege warfare on a previously
inconceivable scale. No threatening avenue of approach
could be totally ignored; no promising target of attack,
totally bypassed.

Therefore, the first task of global siege warfare in
World War II was defensive containment; its second task,
offensive concentration. Neither could be successfully
accomplished without the establishment and maintenance
of priorities. Defensive priorities attempted to define
the relative importance of one area as opposed to another:
to decide which should be defended first. But while they
established a scale of relative values, it was not
maintained.   Planners finally recognized that the defense
of the priority position depended upon the defense of the
subsidiary position.

The attempt to establish offensive priorities was
also marked by ambiguity. Theoretically, the problem
seemed simple, solvable in two ways. The first solution
was to classify a theater as offensive or defensive,
noting the priority of the former. The second solution
was to divide an offensive or defensive theater into
primary and subsidiary areas, subordinating the latter
to the former. This system would create a hierarchy of
values which could be used to apportion the claims of
war. Moreover, the creation of this system would lay
the basis for the direct approach. By restricting
supplies and forces flowing in one direction, it would

free them for concentration in another. It would create a
global framework for the application of the strategy of
disruption. It would meet the needs of siege warfare while
creating the opportunity for a classic confrontation with
the main strength of the enemy.

The above implications were not clearly understood in
the prewar period when they remained implicit and tentative.
Only the war crisis, when the conflict and struggle for
supplies and forces swelled to epic proportions, made them
explicit.

In the prewar period, however, the major decision was
already sealed. The United States and its Allies would
concentrate on the defeat of Germany before launching a
major offensive against Japan. The Atlantic would be the
theater for the offense; the Pacific, for the defense. The
acceptance of this priority division was accompanied by the
evolution of a general concept of the direct approach.
The second process, the division of theaters into secondary
and primary areas, however, could not take place until the
United States entered the war.

a. ORANGE Strategy: Single War in a Single Theater

Even the first solution to the problem of priority
came relatively late. Actually, during most of the interwar period, American planners exercised their ingenuity
upon war plans which evaded the problem altogether. Since
these war plans dealt with single offensives in a
single theater, the Pacific, against a single enemy, Japan,

they posed fewer problems in definition and in choice. Even War Plan ORANGE--the only plan of the early interwar period which was more than an academic exercise--was generally unplagued by priority problems.

There were three possible objectives for the ORANGE plan: the destruction of the Japanese fleet, the rescue or liberation of the Philippines and the invasion of the Japanese homeland. Any direct approach would depend on which objective was chosen as the goal of the Pacific war. In the various versions of War Plan ORANGE the first two objectives predominated. The third was given only intermittent thought. Actually, the first two goals were not mutually exclusive, but were complimentary. The liberation or rescue of the Philippine Islands, the geographical objective, would present the United States with the opportunity to destroy the Japanese fleet, the force objective. The earliest plans had emphasized this interrelatedness: the Pacific Fleet would first relieve the besieged but unconquered Philippine garrison; then, commanding the facilities of the Archipelago, American naval forces would launch their offensive against the Japanese fleet.[42]

In the numerous revisions of ORANGE, stretching from the 1924 to the final 1938 plan, the interrelatedness of these two objectives remained paramount. However, there was a subtle shift of emphasis. Although American plans originally assumed that the retention of the Philippines was essential and possible,[43] it became increasingly obvious that the islands, almost automatically engulfed in a Japanese sea once the war began, could not be held. Although lip service was long paid to the prior belief,[44] the advance to the Philippines was imperceptibly transformed from a rescue into a liberation mission.

Moreover, this shift of emphasis was accompanied by another transformation. As it became more and more obvious that the advance into
the western Pacific would present immense difficulties, the importance
of the approach route became increasingly evident. More attention was
placed on securing the Navy's lines of communication into the western
Pacific. Increasingly, in the minds of the planners, this operation
grew more difficult, more time consuming.[45]

The contrast between the 1924 and the 1938 plans was startling.
In the former, all emphasis fell upon the attainment of a geographical
objective: the Philippine Islands. Scant attention was placed on
studying the difficulties of the direct approach to this distant
objective. In the 1938 plan, the emphasis fell totally upon the
approach to the enemy, almost divesting the plan of any geographical
center. Even the force objective, the destruction of the Japanese
fleet, was left purposely undefined. Obviously, any advance into the
western Pacific would involve a confrontation with Japanese naval power.

Even the emphasis upon the Pacific offensive was subsidiary,
conditioned by the paramount importance of retaining and securing the
strategic triangle. By 1938 the assumptions and conditions under which
the earlier plan was evolved were completely altered. Although the plan
still conceived of a single war fought in one theater, it was now
formulated in a world threatened by global conflict. This possibility
eliminated the basic assumption of any ORANGE plan: that the United
States would concentrate its massive strength on the Pacific. Now the
problem of priority asserted itself, revealing that the time for planning
single theater wars was ending.

The third possible objective of any ORANGE plan, the invasion of the
Japanese homeland, also implicitly involved both a geographical and a
force objective. For any assault upon the former would automatically
entail the destruction of the Japanese Army. Perhaps it would constitute
the only effective means of drawing the latter to full-scale battle.
But though these implications seem obvious now, they were barely revealed
in the prewar ORANGE plans. For the major ORANGE strategy was primarily
naval; it was one of attrition rather than annihilation. Until the late
1930's the consensus among the planners was that this strategy would
probably suffice to effect the defeat of Japan. The individual plans
left the question open and vague.

In the 1924 ORANGE plan, the Joint Board conceded that the
establishment of American power in the western Pacific and the subsequent
attrition of Japanese communications might not defeat the enemy. However,
the choice of a subsequent course of action was postponed for the occasion:

> Should it at any time become apparent that operations of
> the nature of those stated above will not be sufficient
> to bring about a successful termination of the war,
> decision will then be made as to what further action is
> necessary or desirable to that end.[46]

Although it merely implied the ultimate goal of the Pacific war,
the 1935 ORANGE plan was more specific concerning the approach to the
main objective. Among other measures, it recommended 'the seizure,
occupation and defense of additional outlying advance bases, successively
closer to the ORANGE MAIN ISLANDS."[47]

No serious doubts on the adequacy of attritional strategy were
heard, however, until Maj in Craig, Chief of Staff, 1935-1939, questioned
the effectiveness of the accepted plan. Among other weaknesses, he
charged that ORANGE's strategy was inflexible and unrealistic:

a. It offers a single course of action only, without any
alternative whatever.

b. Its avowed purpose is to bring ORANGE to her knees
primarily by naval action, in spite of the fact that
history does not record a single instance of any first-
class military-naval power having ever been subdued
primarily by such action.[48]

The Army's rejection of the doctrine of victory through sea power

dominated the second 1937 split report. Here the clash between service

views was clearly expressed in the section defining "the concept of the War":

> Army Draft
> The defeat of ORANGE through military and economic pressure,
> consonant with the existing situation and made progressively
> more severe until the national objective is attained. The
> initial operations will be primarily naval in character,
> coupled with measures designed to insure the security of
> Continental United States, Alaska, Oahu, and Panama. They
> will be followed by such other military and naval operations
> as may be necessary. The latter operations may ultimately
> require the maximum effort of the two services.
> Navy Draft
> An offensive war, primarily naval, designed to exhaust ORANGE,
> while conserving the resources and institutions of the United
> States.[49]

Neither the geographical nor force objective were named or defined; they

could merely be deduced logically from the Army's premise that the defeat

of Japan would require more than a strategy of attrition. Surprisingly,

however, the 1938 plan returned to the original assumption: the defeat

of the enemy through naval action, coupled with an advance into the

western Pacific.[50]

The third possible objective of an ORANGE war was, therefore, never

explicitly embodied in any version of the plan. Nowhere is there a

direct reference to the necessity for an invasion of the Japanese

home islands. For the earlier versions, this objective was unnecessary;

for the final version, it was academic. The rising priority of the

Atlantic theater made such long-range schemes visionary.

b. RED-ORANGE: Early Concept of a Two-Front War

The ORANGE plans were, until 1937, largely untroubled by priority conflicts, but not all Pacific planning was as free from encumbrances. The most complex, the most dangerous challenge envisioned by the planners was a RED-ORANGE war, a two-front war against Japan and Great Britain.[51] The dual threat posed by such a simultaneous attack immediately posed the problem of choice. Where would we concentrate our forces? Louis Morton writes:

> As the planners viewed this problem, the strategic choices open to the United States were limited. Certainly the United States did not have the naval strength to conduct offensive operations simultaneously in both the Atlantic and Pacific Oceans; it must adopt a strategic offensive on both fronts or else assume the strategic offensive in one theater while standing on the defensive in the other. The recommended solution to this problem--and it was only a recommended solution, for no joint war plan was ever adopted--was "to concentrate on obtaining a favorable decision" in the Atlantic and to stand on the defensive in the Pacific with minimum forces.[52]

This choice obviated all the assumptions and expectations of the ORANGE plans. It condemned the American garrison in the western Pacific to inevitable defeat and conquest by the Japanese.[53] It also, more hopefully, challenged the need for any extensive offensive operations in the Pacific. For the defeat of RED in the Atlantic might force ORANGE to sue for peace.[54] America's first two-ocean war plan, therefore, readily, almost automatically, asserted the priority of the Atlantic as a strategic theater. In this basic respect, it resembled RAINBOW 5 with its similar emphasis upon the defeat of the European enemy.

c. RAINBOW 2 and 3: Reversed Priority

All the RAINBOW plans, developed under the pressure of the imminent

threat of war in Europe, dealt with the basic priority choice of global
strategy: Atlantic versus Pacific. But no two plans found the same
answer to the puzzle. Two variants, RAINBOW 2 and 3, developed a
reversed priority: American power should fall on the Pacific, not
the Atlantic.[55]

Significantly, from the demise of ORANGE to the evolution of
RAINBOW 4 and 5, from early 1939 through the end of the phony war on
the Western Front, this reversed priority prevailed. RAINBOW 2 and 3,
evolved and developed before the German onslaught had overturned the
defenses of the Allied powers in western Europe,[56] emphasized major American
operations in the Pacific:

> 2. Rainbow No. 2: Under the assumption that the United
> States, Great Britain and France are acting in concert,
> carry out the missions of Rainbow No. 1, and in addition,
> carry out the terms of agreement whereby the United
> States does not provide maximum participation in continental
> Europe, but undertakes, as its major share in the concerted
> effort, to sustain the interests of the Democratic Powers
> in the Pacific. Under this plan, Great Britain and France
> would be relied on for naval support in the Atlantic,
> but the principal assistance to be expected from them in
> the Western Pacific would be the use of their Asiatic bases,
> notably Singapore. The timely reinforcement of the
> Philippines, to assure its availability as an operating
> base, would be of paramount strategic importance. The
> plan would call for a major effort by both Army and Navy.
> 3. Rainbow No. 3: This plan is similar to Rainbow No. 2, with
> the important difference that the United States is acting
> wholly unsupported. Hence the objective with respect to the
> Western Pacific is to sustain United States interests alone
> and to exercise control of the Western Pacific, and in this
> task no reliance can be placed on use of British or French
> bases. With respect to the protection of the Western
> Hemisphere, no reliance is to be placed on British or French
> support in the Atlantic. This plan would call for a major
> effort of far greater magnitude and difficulty than Rainbow
> No. 2. For the Navy as well as for the Army, available
> forces would be inadequate to bring all necessary operations
> to a successful conclusion.[57]

Obviously, the assumptions of RAINBOW 2 were more realistic than those of

RAINBOW 3. Without Allies, it was doubtful that the United States could ever adopt a "Pacific First" strategy.[58]

d. From Plan Dog to the Victory Program

The German onslaught followed by their triumph in the West obliterated the reversed priority. American military planners initially preferred the adoption of a merely defensive stance and the surrender of both alternatives, hoping to concentrate all military resources on the defense of the Western Hemisphere.[59] But the President's decision to aid England and the successful outcome of the Battle of Britain reintroduced the possibility of an Atlantic First strategy.

1) Plan Dog

The evolution of RAINBOW 5 did not begin until November, 1940, when Admiral Stark submitted his celebrated Plan Dog Memorandum.[60] The Pacific-conscious Navy, not the Atlantic-minded Army, re-introduced the basic priority division of the war. Actually, this fact is not surprising. The Navy habitually thought in terms of global strategy Not confined to any ocean or continent, ir peace or war, it thought naturally of world-wide operations.[61] Second, Navy planners knew that any early assumption of the offensive in the Pacific depended upon continued military and naval quiescence in the Atlantic. Since the combined fleets of the British Empire and the French Republic were formidable compared to those of Germany and Italy, they relied upon the European Allies to contain Germany and Italy while the United States tackled Japan. Once this assumption, this expectation, was challenged, naval thinking veered in the other direction.

The reliance upon allied aid was reinforced by a secret "agreement"

between British and American naval officials. Almost two years before the
opening of the war in Europe, in December, 1937, an informal, unsigned
and totally unbinding understanding had been reached by American and
British naval experts. The Director of the Navy War Plans Division,
Captain Royal E. Ingersoll, went to London to discuss possible wartime
collaboration against Japan. In the course of the discussion, the
possibility, and consequent implications, of a two-ocean war was raised.
The British proposed a division of strategic responsibility: the French
would hold the western Mediterranean; the British, the Atlantic; and the
United States, the Pacific.[62] Possibly this "understanding" underlay the
persistent "indifference" of the Navy with the situation in the Atlantic,
an "indifference" which lasted throughout the latter half of the thirties.

But the defeat and destruction of the French army, the military
isolation of Great Britain and the possibility that Hitler might acquire
or seize both Allied fleets,[63] eliminated the assumptions of the 1937
"understanding." It confronted the United States Navy with a strategic
nightmare: the possibility of being outnumbered and outgunned by the
combined naval forces of Germany, Japan and Italy. This new situation
threatened the United States with a two-ocean confrontation and posed a
problem of choice.

Plan "Dog" presented the priority alternatives as a series of questions:

    A. Shall our principal military effort be directed toward
        hemisphere defense and security in both oceans?
    B. Shall we prepare for a full offensive against Japan,
        premised on assistance from the British and Dutch forces
        in the Far East and remain on the strict defensive in the
        Atlantic?
    C. Shall we plan for sending the strongest possible military
        assistance both to the British in Europe and to the British,
        Dutch and Chinese in the Far East?

> D. Shall we direct our efforts toward an eventual strong
> offensive in the Atlantic as an ally of the British,
> and a defensive in the Pacific?[64]

Admiral Stark rejected all variants of alternative B. As he saw it, even
a limited war against Japan might weaken America's ability to concentrate
her resources against Germany.[65] He rejected course C. as overly ambitious,
and admitted course A. was the most appropriate strategy while the United
States remained at peace. But only course D., the alternative to be
adopted when America went to war, would bring an Allied victory.[66] So the
priority choice was evident to Stark: the United States should assume the
strategic defensive in the Pacific and concentrate on the offensive in the
Atlantic. But he went further. He saw that America's effort and commitment would involve a massive ground offensive.[67] Although the objectives
of this power drive were not drawn out in specific geographic terms, the
first and second premises of the direct approach had been cast.

2) The ABC Agreement

These two premises, concentration in the Atlantic and the ground
offensive, gradually embedded themselves in American and Allied coalition
planning. Even before the outbreak of war, the United States had
committed itself firmly to the first premise, implicitly to the second.
The first was established by the President in his usual indirect manner.
In a White House Conference on January 16, 1941, Roosevelt avoided any
explicit definition or approval of global priority.[68] But he did declare
that the United States would maintain the defensive in the Pacific,
basing the fleet on Hawaii, and making no effort to save the Philippines.[69]
By eliminating one alternative, he left his planners "free" to choose the
other.

They did. Before the opening of the ABC Conversations, the Chief of

Staff and the Chief of Naval Operations drew up a memorandum on national

policy, which was subsequently amended by the President. As finally

delivered, the statement, though tentative and conditional, set the main

priority, committing the United States to a major effort in the Atlantic-

Mediterranean-European theater.[70]

The ABC Conversations and the subsequent ABC-1 Report incorporated

this "Germany First" decision into the framework of coalition strategy:[71]

> (a) Since Germany is the predominant member of the Axis Powers,
> the Atlantic and European area is considered to be the
> decisive theatre. The principal United States Military
> effort will be exerted in that theatre and operations of
> United States forces in other theatres will be conducted
> in such a manner as to facilitate that effort.
> (b) Owing to the threat to the sea communications of the
> United Kingdom, the principal task of United States naval
> forces in the Atlantic will be the protection of shipping
> of the Associated Powers, the center of gravity of the
> United States effort being concentrated in the Northwestern
> Approaches to the United Kingdom. Under this conception,
> the United States naval effort in the Mediterranean will
> initially be considered of secondary importance....
> (d) Even if Japan were not initially to enter the war on the
> side of the Axis Powers, it would still be necessary for
> the Associated Powers to deploy their forces in a manner
> to guard against eventual Japanese intervention. If
> Japan does enter the war, the Military strategy in the
> Far East will be defensive. The United States does not
> intend to add to its present Military strength in the Far
> East but will employ the United States Fleet offensively
> in the manner best calculated to weaken Japanese economic
> power...[72]

Premise one was clearly stated. Premise two was ambiguous. Two of the

principal strategic policies demanded "the buildup of the necessary forces

for an eventual offensive against Germany" and "the capture of positions

from which to launch the eventual offensive."[73]

3) RAINBOW 5

Joint War Plan RAINBOW 5 incorporated the above phrasing, thereby

establishing a continuity between the agreements of coalition strategy and the agreements of the two services.[74] From Plan Dog to RAINBOW 5, the first two premises of the direct approach had been set and tentatively confirmed. However, neither RAINBOW 5 nor ABC-1 were as emphatic as Plan Dog on the necessity for a ground offensive against Germany.[75]

　　4)　The Victory Program

This emphasis returned in the Army Victory Program which interpreted full-scale participation as a massive projection of American land power against the enemy's continental center.[76] The Victory Program, however, was a step forward in definition, for the Army planners were not merely content to state the need for a ground offensive, which could be anything from a peripheral operation to a massive power drive. They clearly announced that only the latter would do the job. As the planners warned: "'It should be recognized as an almost invariable rule that only land armies can finally win war.'"[77] This power drive would strike at the center, not the periphery of enemy power: "'it may be necessary to come to grips with the German armies on the continent of Europe.'"[78]

　　e.　Transition: Defense to Offense: the Foundations of the Direct
Approach

American strategic thinking had altered considerably since the early ORANGE plans. It now revolved around the problem of waging a two-ocean war. Within that framework the President and his military advisers had established the major priority and begun to develop the logic of the direct approach. Although the United States was establishing the foundations for future offensives, she was still technically on the defensive. Actually the logic of the offense developed naturally from the assumptions of the defense. Offensive priorities being merely a natural extension of

defensive priorities.[79] Since the enemy was a master conspirator lusting
for world conquest, only his final defeat could secure the safety of the [80]
United States. And since his defeat could only be consummated by an [81]
Allied drive, supported and mounted by full-scale American participation, [82]
even a transition to a major offensive, even America's entry into the
war would serve a defensive purpose.

Since this transition was natural, the translation of one form of
priority into its equivalent opposite was axiomatic. For every assesment
made in 1940 and early 1941 assumed that Germany posed the greater
threat to the security of the United States. [83] Therefore, American
involvement would automatically mean a greater concentration of power
against Germany. The greater the defensive need, the greater the
offensive compulsion.

5. The Evolution of the Indirect Approach

With the Victory Program of September, 1941, the global framework
for American strategy had been expounded and the major priority decision
established. Finally a ground offensive had been advocated as the only
certain avenue to victory. But there it ended. America's plans and
prewar priority choices readily assumed that the division of emphasis
between the offensive in the Atlantic and the defensive in the Pacific
could be secured by an anticipatory policy decision. There was no
realization, no anticipation of the eruption of events which would
temporarily erode the basis for the "Atlantic First" policy, creating
secondary priorities in the Atlantic and Pacific.

Moreover, the basis for the direct approach grew out of the policy
and planning decisions of the prewar period. But this development seemed
neither inevitable nor automatic at the time. The two initial premises
of the direct attack, concentration in the Atlantic and the necessity
for a ground offensive, could be variously interpreted. Actually, they

could form the basis for an indirect strategy. For in the prewar plans
the two strategic approaches intertwined with one another, almost unaware
of their essential incompatability.

a. The Impact of British Strategic Thinking

The indirect approach intruded into American strategic thinking
from without and from within, from the influence of British strategic
thinking and from the impact of Navy and Army Air Force views. To
some extent the two effectively reinforced one another. The British
strategists found that they already had allies within the American
camp.

But not always. They could influence the composition of ABC-1,
but could not move their American peers by their massive exposition of
strategy at the Atlantic Conference.[84] A comparison of the two documents
demonstrates the extent and the limitations of British influence.

ABC-1 did advocate the preparation and adoption of "an eventual
offensive against Germany."[85] But this recommendation was merely one
among many. The other recommended strategies were:

> (a) Application of economic pressure by naval, land, and air
> forces and all other means, including the control of
> commodities and their source by diplomatic and financial
> measures.
>
> (b) A sustained air offensive against German Military power,
> supplemented by air offensives against other regions under
> enemy control which contribute to that power.
>
> (c) The early elimination of Italy as an active partner in the
> Axis.
>
> (d) The employment of the air, land, and naval forces of the
> Associated Powers, at every opportunity, in raids and
> minor offensives against Axis Military strength.
>
> (e) The support of neutrals, and of Allies of the United
> Kingdom, Associates of the United States, and populations
> in Axis-occupied territory in resistance to the Axis Powers.[86]

To summarize: blockade, air attrition, hit-and-run operations,
subversion and an emphasis on the early defeat of Italy. Taken together,

these recommended strategies involved a progressive strangulation of the foe, a whittling process which would wear the enemy down before polishing him off. However, these "principal offensive policies against the Axis powers"[87] were fortunately vague; and were not arranged into any specific sequence. They, therefore, did not exclude an eventual massive ground offensive.

The July 31, 1941, "General Strategy Review by the British Chiefs of Staff" held a far more specific definition of the indirect approach. Superficially it resembled ABC-1, advocating similar measures of blockade, a strategic air offensive, subversion and propaganda, combining economic and psychological warfare. However, it not only listed strategies, but also predicted their effect. They would erode the power of the Axis, leaving Hitler's Europe vulnerable to invasion and defeat:

> '...if these methods are applied on a vast scale, the whole structure upon which the German forces are based...will be destroyed, and.. whatever their present strength, the armed forces of Germany would suffer such a radical decline in fighting value and mobility that a direct attack would once more become possible....
> It may be that the methods described above will by themselves be enough to make Germany sue for peace....We must, however, be prepared to accelerate victory by landing forces on the Continent to...strike into Germany itself.'[88]

This final, tangential invasion would not be a massive power drive. It would be launched by a select, well-equipped professional force: "'We do not foresee vast armies of infantry as in 1914-18. The forces we employ will be armored divisions with the most modern equipment.'"[89] Reinforcements would come from local "'patriot forces.'"[90] Here was a specific formula for victory which predicted that a strategy of attrition could destroy the Axis. Finally, this strategy, seeking to undermine rather than confront, would attempt to overthrow the enemy by attacking his civilian morale and economic power. It would avoid his military forces while eroding his national strength.

American reaction was violent. Basic criticisms fell on the British planners' predilection for civilian targets, on their optimism over the effectiveness of an indirect attack. Moreover, the American planners saw this choice of civilian targets as a contravention of ABC-1.[91] Not surprisingly, Wedemeyer was most vitriolic:

> The British indicate that they expect to win the war by creating conditions in Germany which will permit them to invade the continent with ground forces. They expect to bring about these conditions by bombing German industrial areas, military centers, lines of communication and transportation facilities. The British do not really believe this is possible of accomplishment. Their courageous and dogged defense against a numerically stronger enemy last year, is cogent proof, that a nation cannot be brought to her knees through bombardment of essential installations. The Germans employed mass air concentrations under much more favorable conditions...than would be possible operating bombardment planes against Germany from British Isles Bases.[92]

Brigadier General Kibler, General Gerow and Colonel Burly agreed emphatically.[93]

In one case, therefore, British strategic views were largely accepted and incorporated into the framework of Anglo-American planning. In another case, they were rejected and castigated with all the fury which the orthodox reserve for more devout heretics. Actually both papers advocated similar strategic measures. But whereas the first merely listed them, the second anchored them, predicting their effectiveness and excluding any massive power offensive against the ground forces of the European Axis. The exclusion of such an offensive would reduce American forces to a subsidiary strategic role: mere reinforcement and support of the British.

While American planners were willing to adopt British methods,
they were unwilling to adopt them to the exclusion of their own.

b. The Indirect Approach in American Strategic Thought

Significantly the American critiques were the work of
Army officers. Navy and air force officers were not shocked
by British theory. For the British Strategy Review stressed
naval and air action. Despite their hostility to theories of
victory through air power,[94] navy strategists would support the
British planners' emphasis upon naval blockade and interediction.
And, as the AAF official historians stress, the Review's
emphasis upon the bomber offensive was "a point of view which
could be regarded...sympathetically by the Air Staff."[95]

Many American planners, therefore, sympathized with
the advocates of the indirect approach. The Navy and the
Air Force supported strategies which resembled the British
program for victory. In War Plan ORANGE the Navy advocated
a war of attrition against Japan; in the Victory Program,
it proposed limited action against Germany. And the Army
Air Force, which gave little thought to the Pacific,
believed that Germany could be defeated by air power. Only
the Army remained hostile. The Review antagonized Army
planners because its approach was exclusive. Unlike
ABC-1, its wording did not comprise all interests.[96]

1) American Naval Strategy: ORANGE

Initially there was little dispute over the applicability
of the indirect approach in the Pacific. The Navy fervently
believed that Japan could be defeated by the
application of seapower. This belief was entrenched
in most versions of War Plan ORANGE, and even

Army planners willingly conceded that any Pacific war would inevitably,
almost automatically, become a naval war. If America avoided any serious
entanglement on the Asiatic mainland, operations could be projected across
the almost inexhaustible, unending reaches of the Pacific. Geography
reinforced Japan's vulnerability to seapower strategy. In Europe the
Atlantic would form the strategic periphery of the continent; but in the
Pacific the mainland would form the strategic periphery of the ocean.
Once it conquered the continent, Germany could solidly enclose herself
within the casing of her conquests, but Japan was an island--open and
exposed to attack from the east. On its western front, it was sufficiently
sheltered by Manchuria and occupied China. On its ocean front, it could
only be protected by the establishment of a sheath of outposts from
which the Japanese could establish and maintain zones of maritime control,[97]
protecting their lines of communication and their access to the Southern
Resources Area. If these zones could be pierced and shattered by naval
power, Japan's defensive position would be fatally disrupted.

The initial offensive task of ORANGE strategy, according to the
original 1924 plan, was the establishment of American seapower in the
western Pacific after a direct thrust into the Philippines.[98] Then the
"second phase" would begin: the progressive harassment and strangulation
of Japan's economic and military strength, "the period during which
operations are primarily directed toward the isolation and harassment of
Japan through control of her vital sea communications and through
offensive sea and air operations against her naval forces and economic
life."[99] Although provisions were made for further operations,[100] it
was generally expected that this relentless application of indirect

pressure would overthrow Japanese resistance. Since the initial and second phases depended upon the full-scale utilization of seapower, it is no wonder that the "concept of the war" was defined in naval terms:

> AN OFFENSIVE WAR, PRIMARILY NAVAL, DIRECTED TOWARD THE ISOLATION AND HARASSMENT OF JAPAN, THROUGH CONTROL OF HER VITAL SEA COMMUNICATIONS AND THROUGH OFFENSIVE SEA AND AIR OPERATIONS AGAINST HER NAVAL FORCES AND ECONOMIC LIFE: FOLLOWED, IF NECESSARY, BY SUCH FURTHER ACTION AS MAY BE REQUIRED TO WIN THE WAR. [101]

Although the Army later challenged some of the above assumptions, particularly in the final 1937 split report,[102] the final version of ORANGE, the 1938 plan, returned to the concept of a predominantly naval war in which indirect pressure or remorseless attrition would inevitably overthrow the enemy.[103]

Apparently this strategic approach also appealed to the political leadership. Figuratively, it promised a large return for a small investment. A memorandum written by Admiral Yarnell to Admiral Leahy, then Chief of Naval Operations, on October 15, 1937, painted the advantages of such a strategy in quick and easy strokes. After warning that the United States must avoid the "costly mistakes of 1917-1918,"[104] the Admiral expounded his version of the next general war with an ease which appealed to the President:[105]

> Such a war, from our point of view, as well as the others, must be an economical war. The gross extravagance of the last war was responsible for the present economic dislocation throughout the world and the United States is neither in a position nor of a mind to incur a repetition of such conditions. An economical war could be best conducted in this case--and in this case it is particularly appropriate--by economic methods. With our allies we would control roughly ninety percent of the world's reserves of iron, coal and oil as well as a major portion of other raw war essentials, notably copper, wool, rubber, aluminum, tin and food stuffs. By virtue of a heavy supremacy of combined shipping, we would also have free access

to neutral sources and markets. These factors give us an
economic superiority which would make possible an economical
prosecution of the war with reasonably early victory, without
the financial burdens of the last war....
Such an economic, and therefore economical war, must be one of
strangulation, in short, an almost purely naval war in the
Pacific as far as we are concerned. The military situation in
Europe makes this premise possible, with Russia, supported by
England, well able to occupy Germany to the extent that France,
supported by her Little Entente, could successfully meet Italy
and still defend her German frontier. Held, also, that British
and French naval strength can contain Germany in the North Sea
and Italy in the Mediterranean, which gives us control of the
Atlantic and able to exercise a rapidly developed superiority
in the Pacific. Such superiority in the Pacific would be
greatly augmented, not only by the base facilities of our
allies, but in all probability by a quickly accelerated
support of British light forces....
Such a naval superiority in the Pacific would enable us
to conduct the naval war in the Pacific largely in the
manner of our own choice, which would mean complete severance
of Japanese lines of commerce to the rest of the world,
excepting China from the Yangtze north. This would be quite
feasible operating from a main line of bases, Dutch Harbor,
Hawaii, Guam, the Philippines, Java and Singapore, with
scattered minor bases....
In other words, it will be a naval war, with only enough
soldiers to garrison such bases as may be occupied....The
old-dyed-in-the-wool strategists declare that a naval war
cannot bring a country to terms; that there must be
invasion of the enemy territory and defeat of his armies.
This may be true of some countries, but does not hold in the
Pacific. Some nations can be strangled to death. The
invasion theory is a legacy from Clausewitz who was writing
from the European standpoint of 100 years ago with self-
contained countries and permanent armies.[106]

The above strategy would have appealed to the British since its assumptions

and objectives closely paralleled theirs. It envisioned a war won primarily

by attritional pressure, without heavy land engagements, without the need

for expending lives on the grand scale, without the need for raising large

armies. It envisioned a war won by economic preponderance and superiority

of materiel.

2) American Air Strategy: AWFD/1

The Navy and its leaders could advocate an independent strategic
approach, thereby relegating the Army to secondary tasks. The Army Air
Forces, however, could not afford the delightful luxury of reducing its
competitors to menial satraps. Since the messianic days of General William
Mitchell, the AAF had learned to live within the structure of the Army.
Its leaders, like General Arnold, were passionate advocates of the theories
of strategic air power; but they had learned to subordinate their enthusiasm,
to wait for their opportunity, to strive for autonomy rather than independence.[107]
Therefore, their strategic war plan, AWFD/1,[108] combined the direct approach
advocated by the Army with the indirect approach cherished by the disciples
of "Billy" Mitchell, Douhet and Trenchard.

AWFD/1 began with a global assignment of forces, stating that the
AAF had three basic jobs: defense of the hemisphere, maintenance of the
defensive in the Pacific and a concentrated strategic air campaign against
Germany and occupied Europe. Scorning the first two tasks, the Army Air
Forces clung to the third. Their real aim, they maintained, was "'the
application of air power for the breakdown of the industrial and economic
structure of Germany.[109] Here the AAF would play an independent role,
disguised as a subordinate task. For they could achieve victory through
air power while ostensibly preparing the way for a land invasion of the
continent. By supporting the Army's strategic position, they could assure
themselves of a powerful ally, thereby laying the foundations for a valid
test of their doctrines. Not surprisingly, therefore, AWPD/1 contained
the following assignment of tasks for the AAF:

> 'a. Destroy the industrial war making capacity of Germany.
> b. Restrict Axis air operations.
> c. Permit and support a final invasion of Germany.'[110]

Objectives a and b were essentially air force tasks which would test, and possibly prove, the theories of Mitchell. Moreover, they were interdependent. The first mission could hardly be achieved without the second. The third task remained an army mission, the air forces playing a subordinate rather than an independent role. However, the accomplishment of the initial missions could obviate the necessity for any invasion.[111] Victory through air power might be attained while laying the foundations for victory through ground power.

The extraordinary purpose behind the plan was exposed in the modest program adopted by the AAF for the implementation of its first task: the destruction of German war industry:

'No. Selected Targets	Result :
50	Disrupt electric power.
47	Disrupt transportation.
27	Disrupt 80% synthetic petroleum.
18	Destroy airplane assembly plants.
6	Destroy 90% aluminum.
6	Destroy magnesium
154	Total targets to destroy and keep destroyed to accomplish the task.'[112]

Obviously, if results measured with anticipations, the strategic air offensive would batter Germany into an industrial corpse, blasting her war-making capacity out of existence. It was doubtful that she could use her modern mechanized army after suffering this monumental devastation. As the British General Strategy Review predicted, Germany could be defeated by attrition alone.

6. A Core of Agreement Beneath Strategic Dissension

The Army Air Forces, the Army and the Navy, therefore, could advocate

separate strategies for the defeat of the enemy. Clearly these
strategies revolved around the individual services, arrogating the
primary role to themselves. Was there any thread of consistency
within this tissue of contradictory and conflicting opirions?
Our clue lies in the evolution of the primary priority: the decision
to defeat Germany first.

This choice was not made by a single service; it was accepted and
supported by all three. Although agreement did not bring any further
definition and clarification, although no final and conscious choice
was made between the indirect and direct strategies, although the degree
of participation was indeterminate, all three services could agree on the
main enemy. The "Germany first" priority was initially proposed by the
Navy, immediately accepted by the Army and concurred in by the Air Forces.
All three had different motives for agreement. The Navy--although its
major prewar emphasis had fallen on the Pacific where the main enemy
could only be defeated by naval warfare--was profoundly alarmed by the
deterioration of the preponderance of Allied naval power in the Atlantic
and probably anxious to reassert command of the ocean. The Army,
thinking in terms of wider participation, felt that the only effective
and decisive action lay in a continental ground offensive against the
chief enemy. The Army Air Forces, committed to the destruction and
obliteration of industrial complexes, felt that Germany was an ideal
proving ground for the successful demonstration of strategic air power.

Behind their specific and individual motives, however, lay a
deeper reason for agreement. All three services accepted the principle
of concentration. Although each differed on the degree of participation

that the others should contribute, all felt that their service should
be fully engaged. The Navy, despite its reluctance to move its major
units from the Pearl Harbor base, realized that a major Atlantic threat
would have to be met by an undivided fleet. The Army still thought in
single theater terms fearing military dispersion. The Army Air Forces
advocated a massive strategic offensive against a single national
complex, fearing the scatterization of air power in subsidiary tactical
tasks. All three services, therefore, were devotees of the principle of
concentration; all three feared strategic dispersal. All could agree
that the main force should and must be brought against the major danger:
Germany.

But the decision to concentrate against Germany had further consequences
which many ignored but some foresaw. Given the balance of forces and the
inability of the existing Allied coalition to defeat Germany, the eventual
full-scale commitment of American ground troops was inevitable. In the
long run, the agreement to concentrate on the defeat of Germany committed
the United States to a massive land offensive, binding the Air Forces and
the Navy to the support of Army strategy, elevating a service view into a
national cause.

7. Conclusion: the Indeterminate Condition of American Planning in the
Prewar Period

These developments, however, were still in the future. In the prewar
period most strategic plans did not explicitly choose between the direct
and the indirect strategic approaches. ABC-1, RAINBOW 5, and the Victory
Program were composite programs including the basis for both strategies.
Although American planners rejected outrightly any unequivocally attritional

strategy, they readily accepted more guarded, conditional phrasings of the same program. This conduct contrasted sharply with the vehemence with which they later assailed the indirect approach and the stubbornness with which they defended the necessity for a power drive to the core of the enemy's strength.

There were three major reasons for the indeterminate condition of military planning in the prewar period. First, the United States was not a participant, Great Britain was. Therefore, coalition planning would automatically reflect the views of the combatant. These strategic ideas would inevitably influence America's contingent plans for participation.

Second, American forces were not yet mobilized. Since the implementation of any massive assault would require the participation of a still non-existing force, the possible adoption of any direct approach lay deep in the future. The indirect approach of closing the ring was temporarily far more feasible.

Third, American strategic plans reflected the diverse views of the separate services in all their contrasting complexity. Until the entrance of the United States into the war, the Army and the Navy could afford the luxury of phraseological dissension. But later, when American planners had to meet the British regularly to coordinate their strategic plans, the internal dissensions among them were healed by compromise and trading. To the British they could then present a solid front, concealing the conceptual and jurisdictional disputes that still divided them, joining forces to present their apparently uniform stand. Then the relationships between the separate service strategies would be welded into one forged under the hammer of war. Only then, when the Army assumed dominance in strategic planning for the European war, would the subpriorities upon which the evolution of the direct approach depended, fall into place.

Plans for the Atlantic theater, particularly the Army's Victory Program and the Plan Dog Memorandum, anticipated the future development of American strategy. In the Pacific nothing was firm or fixed. Beyond the general proviso which reduced it to a secondary defensive priority, there was little indication of the course and direction American strategy would take. There was a definite time lag between the development of American strategy against Germany and Japan, a time lag which was not overcome despite the mounting inevitability of an early showdown.

The reasons are apparent. After ORANGE was discarded, the Pacific fell into secondary status. Attention temporarily shifted to the Atlantic where the menace was greater, while the Pacific remained relatively quiescent. America was supported by the assumptions which sheltered her thinking and insulated her planning.

The most comfortable assumption was the belief that the United States fleet would enter the war intact and untouched. Therefore, it could bring its force to bear almost as soon as hostilities began. This illusion was reinforced by the belief that Pearl Harbor, our strongest position in the Pacific, was unassailable.[114] The "unsinkable" fleet was guaranteed by the invulnerable fortress.

But these easy assumptions were strengthened by the attitudes held about the defensive line in the western Pacific. Whether they assumed that the Philippines were indefensible or defendable, whether they drew the line at the strategic triangle or at the western Pacific, the Army planners did not make any realistic estimate of a feasible line of

defense within the Southwest Pacific. Nor was there any realization that
a situation might arise when the United States could neither retreat
totally, nor hold indefinitely. [115]

The reduction of the Pacific to a secondary theater inhibited the
development of strategic planning. Since achievement waited upon the
defeat of Germany, since military thinking was restricted to planning
for the defensive (or at the most for limited offensives) no attention
fell on the direct approach. Moreover, none of the RAINBOW plans
provided the Allied forces with a Pacific objective beyond the Philippine
Islands and the Malay Barrier. Until the defeat of the European Axis,
there would presumably be no occasion for the application of the direct
approach to the Pacific. All offensive action would be strictly limited
to the support of defensive purpose.

But the destruction of American assumptions in the disaster that
accompanied and followed Pearl Harbor would shake and almost shatter
the simple priority formula with which the globe was divided into
offensive and defensive spheres. The cost of the defensive would rise
monumentally in the Pacific, challenging this major decision, threatening the application of strategic power in the European theater as well.
By December 7, 1941, the foundations of the direct approach had been
formulated; but they had not settled into any solid base.

Chapter IX

From Isolationism to Interventionism:
the Genesis of American National-Military Policy

1. Introduction.

War being a continuation of policy by other means, the determination
of military priority and the evolution of the direct approach ultimately
depends upon decisions of national policy. Beyond the ultimate military
objective of victory, limited or total, lie the political objectives of
the national leadership. Strategy is an extension of politics.

The soldier and the statesman, however, look at national security
problems from different worlds. The soldier, conservative and cautious,
deals within the limitations of actual power, measuring action by the
yardstick of national mobilization. The statesman, more optimistic and
more daring, lives within a world of multiple, often impossible and
incompatible objectives. Whereas the soldier seeks the possible and the
practicable, the statesman concentrates on the desirable. Although the
latter acknowledges the supremacy of the former, approaches and objectives
are often hopelessly at variance.

2. Study in Incompatability: the Debate over the Philippines

Perhaps the most obvious interwar case history exemplifying the
incompatability between political optimism and military conservatism,
is the debate over the Philippine Islands. Here military means and
political ends were hopelessly divided. The objectives of national
policy could be brought into line with the available military resources
in two ways: retrenchment or reinforcement. The United States could
either withdraw its forces to the strategic triangle or pour reinforcements

into the western Pacific, fortifying its bases, expanding its commitments. Politically, however, the United States could do neither. The influence and control of isolationism was too strong for the latter course; the pull of American interests in the western Pacific was too compulsive for the former. We were, therefore, committed to defend the indefensible.[2]

The debate over the Philippine Islands was conducted on the levels of strategy and policy. The military arguments for strategic retrenchment followed a definite, logical pattern. Since the United States did not have the means to defend the Philippines, it was military folly to leave the American garrison on the Archipelago--a prisoner to fate, a hostage to fortune. Therefore, the United States should abandon this unfeasible position and withdraw.[3] But the Army and Navy planners did not confine themselves to military arguments. Since they invariably invoked their particular interpretation of American national policy, the issue of the Philippines soon developed into a full-scale policy fight between the advocates of retrenchment and the champions of retention.

The Army planners reinforced their military arguments by invoking the logic of isolationism. Since the United States did not have any vital interests in the area, the retention of American positions in the Western Pacific was irrational. One typical case will exemplify the Army's attitude. On October 28, 1935, Colonel Walter Krueger reduced American claims to absurdity. The United States had acquired the Philippines by accident, assuming that acquisition would confer great economic and military advantages. But this hope was mere

delusion. Actually, the American annexation of the Philippines was
an historical abberation, a "'departure which might and in all probability
would produce a clash with a power into whose natural domain of expansion
we had accidentally strayed.'" [4] Krueger curtly dismissed the resounding
phrases sounded by American diplomats to defend expansion into the Western
Pacific: "phrases like the 'open door', 'American interests', and 'trade
expansion' had become mere repetition and dogma which guided our policy."[5]

Krueger then bolstered his political arguments with a comparative
analysis contrasting the geographical-strategic position of the United
States and Great Britain. The latter, a maritime imperial power with
world-wide commitments, needed a vast network of bases to support its
interests and defend its extensive trade-routes. The United States,
a continental power blessed with internal lines of communication, did
not need any base in the western Pacific. She should, therefore, cut
her commitments and confine herself to the blessings of geographical
immunity:

> 'Properly directed, the energies of our people can be fully
> absorbed in that hemisphere for many generations to come.
> It is practically self-supporting and could be assailed
> from overseas with the greatest difficulty only. Granted
> reasonable naval and military preparedness on our part,
> it is virtually invulnerable.'[6]

The Army's definition of America's national interest did not
correspond to either the Navy's or the State Department's. To the
Navy's General Board, America's outlying bases in the Western Pacific
were not superfluities to be abandoned, but were essential supports
for foreign policy. Their abandonment was a surrender of American
interests. On December 17, 1935, Commander Arthur Carpenter gave the
following exegesis for the JPC:

" Policy	Purpose
Participation in the Pacific	To maintain the status quo and preserve the general peace and balance of power in the Pacific.
Integrity of China	To maintain the rights, interests, and territorial integrity of China.
Open Door in China	To promote intercourse between China and other powers on the basis of equal opportunity.
League of Nations mandate	To protect the rights of the United States regarding joint rights in mandates; to prevent the assumption of sovereignty by states holding mandates.
Limitations of armaments	To eliminate naval competition and further peace by an equitable ratio and removal of friction and fear.
Freedom of the seas	To safeguard our rights at sea in accordance with existing international law.
Neutrality	To preserve the rights of the neutral under existing international law.
Political isolation	To prevent entangling alliances."[7]

The Navy was unequivocally opposed to the abandonment of any objective. Injecting a racist note, it warned that strategic retrenchment would unleash an uncontrollable flood: "...the yellow race's usurpation of the white man's place in the Far East."[8] Exposing British positions to Japanese attack, this policy would destroy American interests in the Far East and erode her power and prestige in Europe and Latin America.[9] Finally, as the Navy planners warned, the American people would never tolerate the abandonment of the Philippines.[10]

The State Department agreed. In his meetings with the Joint Planning Committee, Dr. Stanley Hornbeck, Hull's expert on Far Eastern affairs, persistently refused to agree to the withdrawal of American forces from the Philippines which he warned "would lower American prestige in the Far East, and encourage Japan to further aggression."[11]Ironically, the

State Department later opposed the fortification of Guam, the only move which would have made the defense of the Philippines feasible.[12]

The basic problem is evident. In the interwar period, the United States had world interests but not the means to defend and preserve them. Isolationism, the final national objective listed by the naval planners, vitiated other policies. Essentially, the split between means and ends reflected the deeper split within national policy.

3. The Isolation of the Military Planners

The civil-military split was reinforced by the isolation of the U.S. military planners. There were no overall directives. No coordinating agency directed and corrected the planners' work within the context of American foreign policy commitments. As Professor Ernest May points out, the development of coordination between the State Department and the planners depended upon the internal evolution of these agencies: "Until a Joint Board of the Army and Navy and the State Department, too, perfected their internal workings, the coordination of strategy and policy could only be haphazard."[13] And organizational maturity had to be accompanied by an external equalization of power, dependent upon a mutual recognition of the interdependence of war and policy.

The early decades of the twentieth century were conducive to neither. The early Joint Board did not have the maturity or the power to play an important role; and the State Department was more interested in the total secrecy of its operations and interests than in an effective interchange

of civil-military information.[14]The early Joint Board was
an advisory agency with no power to initiate discussions or
to give commands. Its recommendations had no weight unless
supported by the Service Secretaries.[15]At the end of World
War I, the Joint Board was reorganized, emerging as a far
stronger body. Although it was still an advisory agency,
all matters involving interservice coordination were now
referred to it.[16]Also, the creation of a subsidiary planning
agency, the Joint Planning Committee, increased its power
to investigate and formulate.[17]

The early ineffectiveness of the Joint Board reflected
a larger problem: the failure of communication between the
civil and the military authorities which vitiated coordination
and mutual understanding. During the first decade of the
twentieth century, the State Department treated the War and
Navy Departments with the studied circumspection that it
would adopt towards a hostile foreign power. In their
correspondence, the three secretaries practiced the fine
art of interdepartmental deception.[18]Since the military
planners foresaw the necessity of civil-military coordination,
they often sought the advice of the Department of State.[19]
But these civilian experts snubbed proposals for concerted
action.[20]They could not understand the requirements of
military planning, or its basic dependence upon national
policy. This blindness was dramatically revealed by
President Woodrow Wilson's reaction to the "sinister"
activities of the American General Staff. General Tasker
H. Bliss narrates this blowup:

"It was early in the autumn of 1915. I was Acting Chief of Staff. Mr. Breckinridge was, for a day or two, Acting Secretary of War. He came into my office early one morning and said that the President had summoned him a few minutes before. He found him holding a copy of the Baltimore Sun in his hand, 'trembling and white with passion.' The President pointed to a little paragraph of two lines in an out-of-the-way part of the sheet, evidently put in just to fill space. It read something like this: 'It is understood that the General Staff is preparing a plan in case of war with Germany.' The President asked Mr. Breckinridge if he supposed that was true. Mr. Breckinridge said that he did not know. The President directed him to make an immediate investigation and if it proved true, to relieve at once every officer of the General Staff and order him out of Washington. Mr. Breckinridge put the investigation up to me. I told him that the law creating the General Staff made it its duty 'To prepare plans for the national defense'; that I was President of the War College when the General Staff was organized in 1903; that from that time till then the College had studied over and over again plans for war with Germany, England, France, Italy, Japan, Mexico, etc. I said that if the President took the action threatened, it would only make patent to everybody what everybody already knew and would create a great political row, and finally, it would be absurd." [21]

Although the President cooled down, the damage had been done. General Tasker H. Bliss has recorded the outcome:"'...Mr. Breckinridge directed me to caution the War College to 'camouflage' its work. This resulted in practically no further official studies.'" [22] The incident clearly emphasized the monumental breakdown of communication between the President and his military advisers.

World War I revealed rather clearly that there was a dual need for coordination: first, between the military planners of the two services, and second, between the civil and military authorities. The former need was partially answered by the creation of the stronger Joint Board; the latter was recognized by perceptive civil and military officials, but never officially acknowledged by any administration. [23]

Although the isolation of State, Navy and War Departments was matched and partly balanced by contacts and associations at lower levels, [24]

this latter collaboration made no difference in major national decisions
in the 1920's or the early 1930's.[25]   Until 1935 even Roosevelt and his
Secretary of State, Cordell Hull, did nothing to end this situation.
The President, however, understood civil-military problems far more
clearly than his predecessors, and mounting dangers in Europe and Asia
brought a realisation of the need for understanding and collaboration.
As Secretary Hull admitted, he quickly discovered that his dealings with
Axis diplomats were directly affected by their estimate of American
military strength: "'I soon discovered...that they were looking over
my shoulder at our Navy and our Army and that our diplomatic strength...
goes up or down with their estimate of what that amounts to.'"[26]

In the remaining prewar years stretching from 1935 to 1941, civil-
military coordination reached a new high. Consultation between State,
War and Navy departments became far more frequent although still marked
by an institutional informality that limited their long-range effectiveness. There were three important attempts at collaboration: Hornbeck's
tenure as political adviser to the Joint Planning Committee, the Standing
Liason Committee and the War Council. None of these ad hoc arrangements
proved effective or lasting.

Merely revealing the basic cleavages between the Army and the Navy
over Far Eastern policy, cleavages reinforced by the attitude of the
State Department, Hornbeck's discussions with the Joint Planning
Committee did not resolve the underlying split between national policy
and military force.[27] This experiment in civil-military collaboration,
therefore, resulted in a discovery of mutual incompatability.

The Standing Liason Committee was established in April, 1938,

bringing together the Undersecretary of State, the Chief of Staff and
the Chief of Naval Operations. [28] Although this organization was a marked
improvement over previous efforts at interdepartmental coordination, it
was limited in scope and effectiveness. Theoretically, it could settle
all questions affecting the three departments; actually, it dealt mostly
with Latin American problems. [29] Theoretically, it could serve as a channel
of communication between the Army, Navy and State Departments; actually,
its members were too harried and pressed by more important jobs and
concerns. Consultation was therefore minimal. [30]

The final prewar coordinating agency was the War Council, composed
of the Secretary of War, the Secretary of the Navy, the Secretary of
State, the Chief of Staff and the Chief of Naval Operations. Theoretically,
this group could discuss all issues of national policy; [31] actually, it
served more as a platform for the President who used it to announce the
decisions previously made with his Chiefs of Staff. [32]

With the declaration of war, the process of civil-military consultation effected a complete reversal. Hull was now exiled from the War
Council. [33] The military who at one time were administrative outcasts of
federal bureaucracy moved within the inner circle of decision making.
The civilian leaders of the State Department who could once shut the door
on civil-military collaboration were exiled from the favored clique. [34]

One may well wonder why collaboration did not develop more effectively
during Franklin Roosevelt's administration, particularly since he had
formerly proposed a comprehensive reform scheme giving institutional
backbone to civil-military consultation. [35] Why didn't the intermittent
and informal systems of consultation provide the foundation for more

permanent and effective systems? Why did the national emergency inhibit
rather than develop this promising beginning?

President Roosevelt was certainly conscious of the interactions of
war and politics, and the close relationship between diplomacy and force.
But his entire administrative style, his policy of consulting many advisers
while reserving his final decisions, militated against permanent institutional methods or organizations.[36] By adopting this procedure, President
Roosevelt left all effective civil-military coordination in his own hands.

The prewar systems of coordination led nowhere primarily because
they had no institutional strength. They were mostly transient arrangements, informal organizations whose members were too busy to give the
job the time or attention it deserved. Before civil-military coordination could receive its due, it would have to permanently institutionalize.

4. The Consequences of Isolation

The administrative isolation of military planners in the interwar
period left a marked effect on their views of national policy. It led
to the stubborn opposition of Army planners to all attempts from Congress
and newspapers to establish a set national policy for the United States.
Also, the Army planners defined national objectives for themselves; and
were conservative in formulating strategic plans and professional opinions,
advising against the pursuit of objectives for which military means were
evidently inadequate. Though their concept of national policy lagged
behind the President's and seldom anticipated his innovations, they
ultimately followed his lead.

a. The Military's Opposition to any Final Definition of National Policy

The military's opposition to the formulation of a definite and inflexible set of national policy objectives was founded upon two basic premises.

Their recognition that the formulation of national policy was not their concern; and a belief that a rigid, determined definition would be inflexible and dangerous, committing the United States to a single course of action whose feasibility could be vitiated by changing events. Since the prewar years moved with growing uncertainty and mounting alarm, it is not surprising that several attempts were made to enunciate an articulate, consistent national policy.

An article by George Fielding Eliot, "Wanted a Military Policy", profoundly alarmed an anonymous planner to whom Mr. Eliot's suggestions were neither proper nor desirable:

> Running through Mr. Eliot's paper are two clear implications which should be brought out in the open and brought under consideration. One of these implications is that it is the responsibility of the War and Navy Departments to establish the military policy of the United States. The other implication is that one and one only military policy is essential.[37]

These suggestions could be repudiated on constitutional and pragmatic grounds:

> With regard to the first of these implications, the responsible officials of the War and Navy Departments never overlook the fact that in essence the military policy of the United States is established by the people of the United States, acting through Congress and through the Executive. With regard to the second implication, it is necessarily true, whether or not the fact is ideal, that in this country military policy must follow and can not lead national policy. National policy in turn is determined by people of the United States acting through Congress and through the Executive. As is well known, this national policy changes from time to time, sometimes quite gradually and at other times abruptly.[38]

As the planner pointed out, this situation had an inevitable effect upon the formulation of military plans:

> Recognizing this fact, the War and Navy Departments have found it necessary to formulate and agree upon alternative plans to meet the possible variations of national policy, with such readiness as the nation will permit to deal with any given

emergency, in accordance with the form of national policy that
may be found to prevail at the time. This is obviously a very
different thing from the German coordination of national and
military policy pointing directly toward a pre-determined
objective over a period of years, with no necessity for
deviation other than that directed by the one mind who dictates
the entire national effort of Germany.[39]

The opposition of the military planners to definitive formulations

was also directed against several Congressional efforts to set up

committees which would define American military aims in inflexible

terms. Senate Resolution 46, formulated in the spring of 1940, called

for the selection of a committee which would "formulate a military policy

for the United States."[40] This suggestion was rejected by Louis Johnson,

then Acting Secretary of War, with the same arguments with which military

planners had previously rejected the advice of George Fielding Eliot:

> The War Department is of the opinion that the enactment of
> the subject Resolution could serve no useful purpose. The
> formulation of the military policy of the United States is
> dependent primarily upon the foreign policy of this country.
> The foreign policy of the United States changes from time to
> time and the military policy must necessarily change with it.
> In view of this fact, the War Department questions the wisdom
> of establishing a military policy which, in a short time, might
> become unresponsive to the foreign policy and act as more of a
> detriment than an asset in developing National Defense.[41]

On the grounds of constitutional impropriety and pragmatism, the Army

planners and the War Department rejected all attempts to formulate a

consistent, comprehensive national policy.

b. National Policy: the Planners' Version

For purposes of planning, however, the military needed some defini-

tion of national policy objectives. Their administrative isolation

prevented any regular interchange with the State Department. Therefore,

as noted in the debate over the retention of the Philippines, they

formulated their own definitions. Fred Greene summarizes:

> The absence of over-all directives and the failure to establish
> a formal coordinating agency...compelled the military planners
> to fall back on their own resources in defining our national
> policy, national interests, and position in international
> affairs.[42]

Although the Navy's definitions were comparatively broader and bolder,
all military formulations were essentially conservative. The two
services could agree on the sanctity of the Western Hemisphere and
non-entanglement in Europe, but they emphatically disagreed on America's
national interests in the Far East.

Though the Army consistently stressed the pre-eminence of the
Monroe Doctrine and the policy of non-involvement,[43] it recognized that
America's involvement in the western Pacific and her expanding trade
interests[44] did not fit neatly into this definition. These commitments
were the greatest source of danger for any policy of non-entanglement.
Perhaps it was the realization of this fundamental inconsistency,
accompanied by the mounting Japanese menace in the Far East and the
continued weakness of the armed forces which provoked the Army planners'
attempt to cut short its commitments to the Philippines. For they
redefined American national policy, divesting it of any ultimate interest
in the fate or future of the western Pacific area.[45]

Despite its desire for strategic retrenchment, the Army was not
blind to American dependence upon foreign events; it was aware that
her continued non-involvement depended on the maintenance of the
European balance of power.[46] Recognizing their subordinate position,
however, Army planners wrote flexible and conditional definitions of
national policy, leaving them open to amendment and alteration. In
January, 1940, the War Department, under the impact of Congressional
prodding, produced a brief statement:

> The fundamental defense policy for the United States,
> as it relates to the Army may be stated as follows:
> In relation to world conditions, to maintain the
> military forces and to provide the installations and
> specialized military equipment essential--
> 1. To protect the United States and its overseas
>   possessions against external attack.
> 2. To prevent the domination or occupation of any of
>   the independent states of the Western Hemisphere
>   by any state outside this Hemisphere.
> 3. To be prepared to raise, rapidly and effectively,
>   the forces required for a military effort of
>   whatever magnitude, necessary to accomplish a
>   purpose decided on by the Government of the
>   United States.
> 4. To protect the United States from internal
>   disorder and insurrection.[47]

With the third clause, the Army defined its constitutional
position and maintained its flexibility.

The Navy's definitions of national policy were more
inclusive and static, insisting that all American interests
were essential. Unlike the Army, it felt that "the maintenance
of national sovereignty and independence required a 'closed
cycle of industry,' encompassing agriculture, mining,
manufacturing, and transport and cable services among the
different elements."[48] This dependence vitiated pure isolationism. Although it did not compel the United States to adopt a
policy of territorial imperialism, it "meant an ability to
deny control of Latin America to a major enemy as far south as
the mouth of the Amazon and an offensive capability against
the ocean trade routes of any aggressive power."[49]

In its preparations for the Washington Conference
(1921-1922), the Navy General Board studied the foreign
policies of all major powers. It catalogued the four main
American policies as "no entangling alliances, the Monroe
Doctrine, the Open Door, and the recently developed exclusion
of Asiatics."[50] As Fred Greene notes, the Open Door contradicted
the policy of isolationism:

> The Open Door was understood to include China's territorial
> and political integrity and equal commercial and industrial
> opportunities there for all nations. The navy held that
> the Monroe Doctrine and the Open Door had a vital feature
> in common--respect for national sovereignty.[51]

c. The Attempt to Balance Ends and Means

In the twenties and the early thirties, Army conservatism harmonized
with the times; in the late thirties, it became increasingly inadequate.
It opposed the adoption of any objective beyond the defense of the
Western Hemisphere, and even this was overly ambitious in the crisis
and shortage years. It was an irreducible imperative of policy, both
national and military. Since the planners were cautiously seeking to
balance ends and means, they would not advocate any extension of
American commitments until primary national needs were met. Therefore,
they initially rejected the idea that security could be guarded through
an extension of commitments and the projection of a defensive line
towards the coast of Europe and the reaches of the western Pacific.

5. Prewar Civil-Military Conflicts

This lack of synchronized coordination, reflecting a general
imbalance between political ends and military means led to a series
of civil-military conflicts. In each of these exchanges, the Army
planners advocated a cautious course, restricting their positive support
to the most limited objectives.

Actually the President and his military advisers split over two
aspects of the problem of involvement. The planners advised strongly
against the adoption of any commitment beyond hemisphere defense; but,
paradoxically, insisted that commitments once made would inevitably lead

to full-scale involvement. The paradox, however, held a central core
of consistency. Unlike the President, the planners saw that the cost
of additional involvement would be heavy and realized that commitments
could not often be contained within strict limits. The President,
however, could not follow this restrictive logic. He had to balance
the opposite needs of his foreign policy: the external need to shore
up the lines of defense against Axis aggression, and the internal need
to secure domestic support for his policy without alarming the isolationist
watchdogs in Congress. Therefore, he tried to adopt comfortable solutions
answering inconsistent impulses, assuring victory without full-scale
intervention.

Because of their anxiety over America's military inadequacies, the
planners fought against the extension of the defensive line in the
Atlantic and Pacivic, argued against the occupation of the Azores and
other Atlantic Islands, opposed the decision to occupy Iceland,
advocated the abandonment of foreign aid and warned against the dangers
of challenging Japanese power in the Western Pacific. Once their
restrictive arguments were rejected, they switched emphasis. They
then warned the President against the dangers of underestimating the
immense task ahead, prophecied that Allied victory was impossible
without American participation, decried any exclusive reliance on
panacea weapons, like the bomber offensive, and advocated the build-up
of a balanced force capable of carrying war to the enemy's vital centers.

a. Conflict over the Occupation of the Atlantic Islands

The debate over the occupation of the Azores and other Atlantic
Islands was prolonged but intermittent throughout 1940 and 1941.[52]

In the spring of 1940 President Roosevelt became fearful that the Axis
would seize the Azores.[53] The defeat of France, which opened the possibility
of an enemy advance through Spain and North Africa, exposed the Atlantic
Islands to German aggression.[54] Although Army and Navy advisers made
preliminary plans in the fall of 1940,[55] the real impetus for an Azores
expedition came from the President. On May 22, 1941, he issued a
directive ordering the Army and Navy to prepare a joint plan for the
occupation of the islands. Seven days later the plan was drafted and
submitted to the Joint Board, receiving the latter's blessing.[56] Code-
named GRAY, it called for an occupation of the Azores by an expeditionary
force composed of the 1st Army and the 1st Marine divisions.[57] Although
the plan was approved by the President on June 4, 1941, his subsequent
decision to send a garrison to reinforce the British in Iceland
cancelled any chances for GRAY's success.[58] However, interest in the
project did not falter; and planning and strategic debates consequently
dragged on for the rest of the year.[59]

The President and his military advisers stood in opposite corners
throughout. The Chief Executive saw the occupation of the Atlantic
Islands as a sound defensive move shielding Latin America from any Axis
ground or air assault and protecting the South Atlantic sea lanes from
U-boat attack.[60] He also probably gauged their offensive capabilities.[61]
The planners vigorously dissented. Logically the Army leaders felt
that the most effective counteraction against any German occupation of
Northwest Africa would be the seizure of Dakar, a currently impossible
operation. Without its control, conquest of the Atlantic Islands would
be futile and dangerous: "the Canary and Cape Verde Islands could not

be held, even if taken."[62] And the Azores, though easier to occupy, were
equally perilous. They would be difficult to defend against enemy air
power based either in France or in the Iberian Peninsula, and their
seizure would not forestall any German move against Dakar since they
were too far north.[63] Beneath these reasons, however, lay a far more
serious and determining factor: the total lack of means. Perhaps
nothing clarified this lesson more dramatically than the abortive Azores
plan of May, 1941. As American planners then discovered, an expeditionary
force would absorb the major resources and shipping capacity of the
United States. It would leave her without the means of countering
other, more dangerous Axis moves. Planning for the Azores expedition
re-emphasized America's military weakness:

> It...emphasized...the fact that, a year after the launching
> of the defense mobilization program, an expedition involving
> some twenty-five thousand miscellaneous Army troops, with
> only three battalion landing teams, represented a maximum
> effort.[64]

Some officials were even more perceptive and prophetic.
Secretary of War Stimson opposed the Atlantic Island project as he
opposed every move to deploy American forces into the southern periphery
of the enemy's empire. To him all these projects were dangerous
diversions leading away from the main theater of war, the north
Atlantic: "the direct line of our strategical route towards victory."[65]
Long before Operation TORCH emerged from the fertile imagination of
Winston Churchill, the Secretary of War shrank from the prospect of
any African or Mediterranean adventure.

Keenly conscious of the meagerness of their resources, doubting
the value of the Atlantic islands to the security of the Western
Hemisphere, the Army planners opposed all South Atlantic projects.
They felt that the security of the Americas could be effected by the

placement of a small security force on the Brazilian bulge.[66] Rejecting

any extension of our commitments, they fought to keep American forces

close to home base.[67]

b. The Debate over Pacific Strategy

On the issue of Pacific strategy and resistance to Japanese

expansion, the Army and Navy planners differed sharply with the

President. Some echoed the sentiments of the isolationist press and

of Walter Lippmann who urged an understanding with the Japanese

Government.[68] General Embick was exceptionally candid:

> "What seems to me of first importance at present is definitely
> to accept the fact that we cannot carry out the plan for the
> defense of the Western Hemisphere and also intervene in the
> Far East. Lippmann's article of yesterday, advocating an
> understanding with Japan is the plainest kind of common sense.
> I hope our State Department and the Senate Foreign Affairs
> Committee can be made to see that a reversal of their past
> provocative attitude is a military essential of first
> importance in the new World situation."[69]

1) The Decision to Base the Fleet at Pearl Harbor

Most military personnel did not express themselves as freely as

Embick, but consistently advised against the adoption of any measure

which could provoke a Japanese attack. Roosevelt's decision to base

the Pacific fleet at Pearl Harbor, announced by Admiral Stark on

May 27, 1940,[70] provides an illustrative case. The President saw this

move as a powerful deterrent to Japanese aggression. As Admiral

Stark informed Admiral James O. Richardson, the Pacific Fleet commander:

"'You are there because of the deterrent effect which it is thought

your presence may have on the Japs going into the East Indies.'"[71]

The Army planners doubted that this would work. They were afraid that

the Japanese Government would interpret this action as a provocative challenge. The move in itself was militarily worthless:

> Its effect on short-range policy was to give the Japanese
> Government the option of ignoring the implied challenge or
> accepting it on the most favorable terms. The Army planners
> believed that the United States should either withdraw the
> fleet from Pearl Harbor or prepare seriously for hostilities,
> consciously deciding 'to maintain a strong position in the
> Pacific,' and 'in order to do so, to avoid any commitment
> elsewhere, the development of which might require the
> weakening of that position.' The retention of the fleet in
> the Pacific might cause Japanese leaders to review and revise
> their plans, but it would act as a deterrent 'only so long
> as other manifestations of government policy do not let it
> appear that the location of the Fleet is only a bluff.'"[72]

The subsequent commitment of the United States to an "Atlantic First"[73]

strategy confirmed the planners' estimate that the United States should

pursue a cautious policy in the Pacific, without overextending her

meager means to cover infinite aims.

    2) The Decision to Impose an Oil Embargo on Japan

The debate over Pacific strategy reached its climax over the

"oil embargo." The administration could most effectively impose this

embargo by freezing all Japanese assets within the United States. If

the British and Dutch followed suit, the Japanese would be unable to

purchase any oil.[74]

These successive acts would present an ultimatum: unless Japan

desisted from aggression, she would suffer economic starvation. The

Japanese had a choice of responses: they could pull their forces out

of China; or descend on the Netherlands East Indies, precipitating

a Pacific war.[75]

Since American military planners thought that war was far more

probable than surrender, they conscientiously opposed every move towards

the imposition of an "oil embargo." Although Marshall and Stark
objected, their reactions were different in tone and emphasis.
Marshall's opposition was neither clearly articulated nor
unequivocal; but he agreed with Stark in opposing the "oil
embargo." Keenly conscious of America's military unpreparedness,
he wanted to delay any confrontation with the enemy. However,
his testimony before the Pearl Harbor Enquiry was vague.
Roberta Wohlstetter analyzes the General's stand:

> This vagueness may be partly explained by Marshall's
> general reticence as a witness. But it can also be
> laid to the Army's traditional lack of interest in
> economic or diplomatic events and their implications
> for foreign policy. These areas were left to the
> State Department and the White House. Marshall, for
> example, when questioned as to how he felt in 1941
> about the effect of embargoes on American-Japanese
> relations, said he could add no comment to the
> wording in the joint dispatch of July 25. He did
> remark, however, that during this period 'our state
> of mind...I am referring now to both Stark and
> myself--was to do all in our power here at the
> home, with the State Department or otherwise, to try
> to delay this break to the last moment, because of
> our state of unpreparedness, and because of our
> involvement in other parts of the world.'...
> Whatever the case, he made no recorded objection
> to the Embargo Act.[76]

The Army's doubts were veiled; the Navy's outspoken.
When President Roosevelt consulted with Admiral Stark before
the imposition of the embargo, Stark directed his chief
planner to prepare a study on the impact of this policy.
On July 20, 1941, he forwarded a memorandum by Richard Kelly
Turner to the President. Echoing the Navy's anxiety about
the Atlantic and its fears of strategic diversion in the
Pacific, this study predicted that Japan would not expand
beyond French Indo-China unless the United States
imposed an oil embargo. It clearly delineated

the danger of this uncompromising challenge to Japanese interests:

    5 (e) An embargo on exports will have an immediate severe psychological reaction in Japan against the United States. It is almost certain to intensify the determination of those now in power to continue their present course. Furthermore it seems certain that, if Japan should then take military measures against the British and Dutch, she would also include military action against the Philippines, which would immediately involve us in a Pacific war. Whether or not such action will be taken immediately will doubtless depend on Japan's situation at that time with respect to Siberia....

    7 (c) An embargo would probably result in a fairly early attack by Japan on Malaya and the Netherlands East Indies, and possibly would involve the United States in early war in the Pacific. If war in the Pacific is to be accepted by the United States, actions leading up to it should, if practicable, be postponed until Japan is engaged in a war in Siberia. It may well be that Japan had decided against an early attack on the British and Dutch, but has decided to occupy Indo-China and to strengthen her position there, also to attack the Russians in Siberia. Should this prove to be the case, it seems probable that the United States could engage in war in the Atlantic, and that Japan would not intervene for the time being, even against the British.

    8   <u>Recommendations</u>—That trade with Japan not be embargoed at this time.[77]

Admiral Stark not only forwarded Kelley's study to the President, but also underwrote it: "I concur in general. Is this the kind of picture you wanted?"[78]

If the Turner memorandum had been dispatched three weeks earlier, it would have corresponded closely to the President's estimate and approach. He was then relying on delay and caution, hoping to avoid any confrontation in the Pacific, and to promote some settlement with the Japanese Government. As long as he felt that the Japanese were not irrevocably committed to the policy of southern expansion, he hesitated to take any precipitate steps that would provoke them. He apparently felt that an embargo would challenge the Japanese Government, pushing it into the hands of the extreme militarists and unleashing a general war in the South Pacific.[79] This initial estimate was forcefully expressed in Roosevelt's July 1, 1941, letter to Harold Ickes. The Secretary of the Interior had been assuring the President that the Japanese would not strike in the Pacific until Germany had decisively defeated the USSR, even if the United States imposed an embargo. But the President remained skeptical:

> I think it will interest you to know that the Japs are having a real drag-down and knock-out fight among themselves and have been for the past week--trying to decide which way they are going to jump--attack Russia, attack the South Seas (thus throwing in their lot definitely with Germany) or whether they will sit on the fence and be more friendly with us. No one knows what the decision will be but, as you know, it is terribly important for the control of the Atlantic for us to keep peace in the Pacific. I simply have not got enough Navy to go round--and every little episode in the Pacific means fewer ships in the Atlantic.[80]

The President's original doubts were removed, however, when he received irrefutable evidence that the Japanese were poised to push aggressively into the southern resources area. On July 8, 1941, a week after he dispatched his unusually frank letter to Harold Ickes, a Japanese code (MAGIC) message to Berlin was placed before the President. A single sentence revealed the futility of the policy of delay and caution: "'Preparations for southward advance shall be reenforced and the policy already decided upon with reference to French Indo-China and Thailand shall be executed.'"[81] His view changed radically. Since the Japanese had already chosen their course of action, the embargo could no longer act as a provocation.

This conclusion was confirmed by a July 14 MAGIC intercept. Sent by officials of the Japanese Southern Army to military attaches, it unequivocally defined Japan's purpose:

> "The immediate object of our occupation of French Indo-China will be to achieve our purpose there. Secondly, its purpose is, when the international situation is suitable, to launch therefrom a rapid attack...next on our schedule the sending of an ultimatum to the Netherlands Indies. In the seizing of Singapore the Navy will play a principal part."[82]

After this message, it was impossible for even the most obtuse members of the State Department to dismiss the Japanese moves into Indo-China as isolated actions. If Japan was already committed to a southward advance, she was beyond provocation.

The President was, therefore, converted to the hard-line policy long advocated by Stimson, Knox, Ickes and Morgenthau.[83] Since the imposition of the "oil embargo" would not necessarily lead to war, the best method of preserving peace in the Pacific was to apply force.[84] When Secretary of the Treasury, Morgenthau joshed the President at the cabinet meeting of July 24, 1941, quoting Roosevelt's former assumption about the Japanese reaction to an embargo, the President revealed his new estimate of the situation:

> I raised the question as to whether or not this type of order which upon its first publication would indicate to Japan that it could not get further supplies of oil from this country might not force it to take action in the Far East which we had tried to forestall during the past year. The President said that he did not think so, that he was inclined to go ahead with the order in the regular way and grant licenses for the shipment of petroleum as the applications are presented to the Treasury.[85]

The President thereby fully repudiated the policy of caution and delay long advocated and supported by his military advisers and by the State Department: a policy based on the assumption that the United

States could worry and weary the Japanese Government into a change of heart and a change of course, a policy partly dictated by the lack of means in the Pacific and the pull of events in the Atlantic. He now felt that the United States had no choice except to confront the challenge which it could not forestall. Though the means were scarce, the ends were imperative.

Throughout the above debates--over the Azores, rearmament versus foreign aid and containment of the Japanese--the military planners understandably approached all questions of policy from a conservative vantage. They had lived in a period of prolonged scarcity when America's military forces were cut beyond the bone, when they learned to ask for little and expected less. The interwar period had been, moreover, an era of isolationism in which the poverty of the military establishment harmonized with the national policy of diplomatic retrenchment. Now national policy was being revolutionized, but the means to support this revolution towards intervention were still unavailable.

6. Panacea Solution versus Calculated Cost

a. The Cost of Full-Scale Involvement

From July 1941 on, after the initiation of the economic sanctions against Japan, the emphasis of the planners changed. Their conservatism remained, but their attention now shifted to the ultimate cost of defeating the Axis powers. Now the roles between the President and his military advisers were reversed. The President--reluctant, at least publicly, to admit that the entry of the United States into the war was vitally necessary for Allied victory--clung to the theory that the United States could confine herself to being the arsenal of democracy; the planners--certain that full-scale commitment of forces into a massive invasion of the enemy's homeland was a necessity--repeatedly warned that there was no easy road to success, no cheap solution which could exonerate us from playing a major role and paying a heavy price for Allied victory.[86]

b. Panacea Weapons versus Balanced Forces.

The planners also took a firm stand against the belief that any panacea weapon, or weapon system, could bring victory cheaply or exclusively. Their clearest opposition emerged in the Atlantic Conference when they criticized the British for their hope that victory could ride through the expansion and application of air power.[87]

But this outburst was merely the most spectacular expression of the planners' opposition to quick, cheap solutions. Actually, in earlier, protracted debates over rearmament, the planners had opposed the President on the development of air power. For they favored the creation of a balanced force of all arms, capable of performing conventional and unorthodox tasks.

The early 1938 rearmament plans of the Army called for a balanced methodical rearmament whose tempo would be geared to the speed of munitions production.[88] No special emphasis was then placed on the expansion of the air forces,[89] though belated support was finally given in the fall of 1938.[90] The problem of balance was also emphasized, the construction of a powerful air force meaning far more than the mere

flow of planes from an assembly line. Mark Watson analyzes
the AAF position:

> But among the advocates of air expansion, who felt
> sure that the President was in agreement with them,
> there was equal certainty that there should be a
> large immediate increase in the numbers of airplanes
> on hand and in the provision for many more in the
> visible future. There was equally persuasive argument
> for the installation of grand-scale maintenance and
> training facilities, on the sound reasoning that it
> would take as long to train efficient crews and pilots
> as to build efficient planes.[91]

The adoption of a balanced program would necessitate a
methodical development of all elements, keeping the expansion
of airplane production within bounds.

The President, however, was interested in immediate
expansion, not in steady progression. In a "momentous
White House meeting,"[92] held on November 14, 1938, Roosevelt
launched his program:

> His stated objectives were: (1) production over a
> two-year period of 10,000 planes as described, of
> which 8,000 would come from existing commercial
> plants and 2,000 from new plants to be built with
> government funds and (2) the creation of an unused
> plant capacity for producing 10,000 planes annually.[94]

The emphasis fell entirely upon more airplanes. Nothing was
said about equipment, pilots, maintenance units or the
development of a balanced force.[95]

The War Department vigorously disagreed. On November 15,
1938, Louis Johnson, Acting Secretary of War, instructed the
Chief of Staff to prepare a two year budget. The following
objectives would achieved a balanced program for the air forces:

> "1. An Army airplane strength of 10,000 planes
>   balanced as to types, 50 percent of them
>   to be maintained on an operating basis,
>   including personnel, installations, materials,

50 percent to be kept in storage.
2. Provision for seven government aircraft factories each with
   an average annual production of 1,200 planes, buildings to
   be constructed from relief funds but machinery and operation
   to be provided from Army funds.
3. Necessary supporting materials and services--Ordnance,
   Quartermaster, Signal Corps, and so on."[96]

At the same time, the Acting Secretary sought to balance the needs of

the air force with those of the ground troops. He asked for an

estimate of the cost of supplying the Army under the Protective

Mobilization Plan. The fulfilment of this need would call for:

"1. Completion of the educational orders program.
2. Equipping the existing government arsenals with modern machinery.
3. Completing plans for the factory output of critical supplies.
4. Acceleration of the industrial mobilization program by
   completing the current surveys and specifications.
5. Providing a reserve of special machinery for the making of
   essential munitions.
6. Providing stock piles of critical raw materials."[97]

Under the energetic prompting of the Deputy Chief of Staff, the

program rolled. The final product was a December 17th message from the

Chief of Staff to the Assistant Secretary of War:

1. A total of 5,620 combat planes, 3,750 trainers, and 630 other
   planes....Also 8,040 additional planes by the end of 1941...
   attainable by the proposed erection of seven government-
   operated plants with 10,000 annual output. Also 7,900
   officers, 1,200 cadets, and 73,000 enlisted men....
2. An increase of 58,000 in the Ground Forces.
3. An increase of 36,000 in the National Guard.
4. Materiel for a PMP M-Day force of 730,000, plus 270,000
   M-Day-plus-5-months reinforcements; this would take one
   year to produce.[98]

The difference between the Chief of Staff's program and that of

the President's directive was obvious. At his November 14 conference

the President had asked for a totally different air force, splitting

its components into "2,500 training planes, 3,750 line combat and

3,750 reserve planes."[99] The Chief of Staff had shifted the components

in favor of a more balanced all-purpose force. The President had
ordered a two-year program for the production of planes; the Chief of
Staff advocated a three-year program, placing his emphasis on methodical,
systematic rearmament rather that immediate production.[100]

The difference between the Chief of Staff's proposals and the
President's order went further. The Chief of Staff also pressed for an
expansion of the Army as a whole, not merely for the air forces. He
wanted a Regular Army capable of carrying out expeditionary tasks in
defense of the Western Hemisphere; a National Guard, capable of
re-enforcing and strengthening the Regular Army; and enough materiel
for an all-purpose military force.[101]

The President, soon alerted to the schemes of his military advisers,
summoned them for an educational session at the White House. When
Roosevelt insisted that he wanted only airplanes and that the Army
was selling him everything else, his military advisers emphasized the
need to balance the military establishment.[102] After a number of
compromises, the President's demands were reduced to 6,000 planes,[103]
while the rearming of the Regular Army proceeded with the expansion of
the air forces.[104] To a greatly limited extent, both programs were initiated.

This dual perpetuation gave to the American rearmament race "a
confusion of aims",[105] mirroring the basic conflict between the President
and the military establishment. Roosevelt was interested in panacea
solutions which would reconcile the needs of national security with the
restraints of isolationism. He saw in the expansion of airplane production a means to expand America's military capacity while providing
increased aid to the Allies. Obviously, if the arms were intended

primarily for foreign export, the need for balance was secondary.

The military had an entirely different view: they thought not of aid, but of rearmament. Their main purpose was to strengthen the national forces for ultimate participation on the field of battle. To prepare for this role, the ground troops would have to be as well-equipped as the air forces.

Finally, this split between the President and his military advisers was probably strengthened by conflicting attitudes towards air power. Roosevelt saw the airplane as unique and formidable; the military, as one weapon among others, its ultimate use to support the operations and aims of more conventional forces.

At an early stage, therefore, the military planners were assessing the full cost of possible involvement. Although their projections responded directly to the mounting, apparently imminent, threat to Latin America, they already anticipated the emphasis of the Victory Program.

7. The Nexus of Civil-Military Relations

War and policy, therefore, always mirror the relationship between civil and military authority, a relationship governed by a division of functions. The political leadership defines the national policy (sets the ends); the military leadership implements it (determines the means). "'The work of the statesman and the soldier...are...coordinate; where the first leaves off the other takes hold.'"[106] This simple division assigns a subordinate but not a subservient role to the soldier, for his sphere of action, although circumscribed, remains autonomous. Policy remains the realm of the political leader; operations, the world of the military commander.

This model of civil-military relations, tenaciously held by the
military in the interwar period, was partly produced by the isolation
of the soldier within a semi-hostile, semi-indifferent society, an
isolation which emphasized and ultimately encouraged military pro-
107
fessionalism, teaching loyalty to the state while asserting the freedom
of the soldier from unwarranted and habitual interference at the hands
of civilian amateurs.

Originally the division between policy maker and military leader
did not exist. Throughout the eighteenth century and in the early
decades of the nineteenth, the supreme military commander was often
the head of the state. Moreover, the planning and direction of any
military campaign originated on the field itself, from the tent of
the leader who would direct operations and appraise the situation,
making the necessary command decisions. Policy, strategy, and tactics
flowed from a single source.

But the nineteenth century revolution in military management and
108
communications altered and destroyed this unity.   Bringing the soldier
into the council chamber, it ultimately retired the ruler from the
battlefield. The growing complexity of war necessitated the growth
of specialization and division of function. Even though the political
109
leader might retain the supreme role in politics and war, he was increasingly dependent upon his military advisers. Since it became more difficult to fill both roles adequately, war and politics became increasingly
autonomous.

Autonomous but not independent. For specialization and separation
of functions did not lead to the evolution of two worlds, isolated from
one another. Actually civil and military functions developed like two

emerging nations, plagued by an ill-defined but common frontier. Where did strategy begin and policy end? Where did the control of the civilian authority yield to the command of military power?

Even in a democratic society--where civilian supremacy is entrenched by tradition and constitutional law--the precise intersection of the two boundaries remains uncertain. Here the military planners have no authority to modify or directly challenge the existing definition of national policy. They can merely warn that its objectives are beyond present strength, that the means are incomensurate with the ends. If their arguments are persuasive, they may convince a political leader to alter his more extravagent plans. But if their arguments are overruled, they must make the best of a bad situation, loyally applying the military means at their disposal to the achievement of the objectives of an objectionable or debatable national policy.

The final decision belongs to the civilian leader; but his [110] effectiveness depends ultimately upon his strength and determination, for a power vacuum can create the opportunity for institutional imperialism. If control is not direct and continual, the military will automatically move, though unconsciously and often reluctantly, into the unoccupied territory. Though war is the tool of politics, the needs of the military are not always subordinated to the imperatives of political action. In time of war, especially, they tend to dominate, emerging as autonomous demands whose imperatives overrule those of its master. Political desirability often yields to military feasibility. So the simple relationship between means and ends--a relationship that assures the dominance of one and the subordination of the other--is not always maintained, nor maintainable.

In times of peace the normal relationship between policy and
strategy is easier to preserve. But then the advantage is reversed.
For then the soldier is a negligible quantity in American society and
political leaders tend to interfere, to intrude into his cloistered
world, exerting strict financial control over his professional life.

The hypothetical separation of means and ends, praised as the
ideal division of civil-military authority, is bureaucratically feasible
but functionally impossible. The separation of functions is due to the
increasing complexity of civil and military affairs, not to their
inherent differences. As noted by Professor Louis Morton:

> In the world of today there are no purely military or
> political solutions to the complex problems that face the
> great powers. To draw a sharp line of demarcation between
> the political and military, the economic and psychological
> elements of policy, to put each in a separate compartment
> and attempt to deal with it alone would not only be absurd
> but dangerous as well.[111]

But although the dangers of compartmentalization are now clearly
recognized, they were not always so evident. Only World War II and
the subsequent failure of peace dramatized the issue in an inescapable
manner.

The worlds of the politician and the soldier cannot be described
as fundamentally different. They both deal with ends and means, and
differ only in approach, not content.

Military leaders, insofar as they adopt a professional attitude,
insist that ends and means balance. A nation's policy should be guided
by her available power and circumscribed by her existing strength. A
nation should avoid political adventures and commitments which cannot
be maintained autonomously. If means are non-existent, the end should

be abandoned. A military planner feels very strongly that he can only
112
advise, supporting only what he considers possible. Occupying a
totally different position, the political leader takes an opposite
view; rather than advise, he commands and mobilizes, creating resources
totally unavailable to the planner. As a national leader one of his
chief functions is the preservation of national unity, necessarily
appealing to diverse and contradictory impulses and dreams. He welds
together incompatible needs and pressures, conflicting groups and
antagonistic interests, into a coalition of compromises--difficult to
maintain, essential to preserve. He realizes that needs cannot be
tailored to accomodate means simply by fitting them within some
Procrustean pattern.

His approach to international politics often mirrors his attitude
to domestic problems. Recognizing instinctively and often immediately
that means never balance with needs, he knows never-the-less that these
needs cannot be denied and ignored. Therefore, a political leader often
seeks to do the impossible with the available, like a magician creating
something out of nothing. Military advisers concentrate on limitations,
politicians on the uncommitted wealth of potential power. The military
assumes the worst, painting the international situation in its most
somber colors; the political leader sees present difficulties as
ultimately solvable. One looks into the pit of disaster; the other,
towards the sunrise of hope.

8. Conclusion

Throughout the prewar years, President Roosevelt allowed the
military to function autonomously, to plan without a set or definite

formulation of national policies. But this allowance was merely a temporary license, strictly controlled. Roosevelt preferred to let the military present its own professional estimates and advice without coordination and often without consultation. His technique in dealing with the military reflected his general approach to command, his flair for control by division.[113]

To maintain this ficticious autonomy, the President moved warily towards strategic commitment. Nothing marked his adeptness more clearly than his reaction to ABC-1 and RAINBOW 5 which were never formally approved, though he had not hesitated to initial similar strategic plans.[114] Although he informed General Marshall that he understood both plans and that they should be returned to him in case of war, Roosevelt still reserved final, official approval.[115] By the clever and deliberate utilization of this procedure, the President managed the manipulization of two worlds, allowing his planners to proceed with their work while partially disassociating himself from their endeavors.

Left to themselves the planners proceeded from antiquated premises: casting national policy in an isolationist mold, seeking to disassociate the defense of the United States from all European and Western Pacific commitments. The President corrected, at times overruled, his planners, gradually educating them concerning the ends of national policy. But he always avoided definitive and conclusive formulation, refusing to imprison his aims in rigid terms. He thereby assured his ultimate freedom to reformulate national objectives. While he was educating the military, they were educating him. But they were not too successful.

The President still refused to face the implications of full-scale
participation. Only the opening of the war, which automatically
obliterated the possibility of panacea solutions, forced the
President to assess the full cost of military involvement.

Chapter X

The Foundations of the Just War

In defining the Axis threat and the problem of security, President
Roosevelt diagnosed the major threat and the enemy's plan for world
conquest. His emphasis, often more moralistic than political,
established the grounds for justification, formed the logic for the
crusade and sowed the seeds of a full-scale total war long before actual
American intervention.

1. The Problem of Justification

The problem of justification was simple in theory, difficult in
application. Every offensive move was justified as a defensive play,
designed to preserve the security and neutrality of the nation. While
straddling that twilight region between war and peace, American policy
and strategy were described as attempts to preserve territorial
integrity and maintain peace in the hemisphere. Even bold, offensive
moves were purely defensive, basically peaceful.

The chief assumption of the United States was the belief that
the enemy was a master conspirator with insatiable aims,[1] and this belief
accelerated the offensive-defensive transition, removing all sense of
ambiguity. Since aggression was always a potentiality, the occupation
of outlying positions was considered defendable and justifiable. All
aid to belligerent nations was designed to shore up the dam and hold
back the floodwaters of aggression and war. No nation quibbles at
technical or legal distinctions when confronted by an infinitely malign,
dangerous and relentless adversary.

The development of justification, therefore, paralleled and accompanied the extension of the defensive perimeter of the United States. There was a difference, however, dictated primarily by the distinction between private and public debate. In making all final security decisions, the President could invoke his prerogative as Commander-in-Chief. The military centered their arguments on technical grounds and were concerned over whether we could, not over whether we should act. Although they could delineate the pitfalls and intrinsic difficulties of any international course, they could not question its political validity. In the ultimate outcome, the President could override all professional arguments with perfect impunity.

In private debates with his advisers, the President would define and expound policies and possible courses of decision and action. While some projects were rejected or discarded, others were simply forgotten. These deliberations were held in secret and professional honor and practice bound everyone to discretion. Therefore, discarded plans could be eliminated and forgotten without ever raising the question of justification. Once decisions were made or actions taken, however, the problem of justification arose. Now the President had to convince, not merely command. He now had to explain and defend, persuade and prevail with those who could limit and ultimately define his power: the United States Congress and the American people. As political leader rather than head of the administration and Commander-in-Chief of the military establishment, he had to reconcile contradictory forces, conflicting interests of the coalition which put him into power and could ultimately depose him.

As a political leader he had to find the common denominator of public opinion with which to persuade and capture the majority, identifying his cause and policy with their interests and sympathies. National security and peace were universally appealing causes, incontrovertible and incontestable. The identification of these two themes into an inextricable whole allowed the President to reverse some of the basic antipathies of the American people. The defense of involvement and intervention by an appeal to security and peace was a master stroke which only an extraordinarily capable and flexible politician could have successfully accomplished.

2. The Nexus of Justification.

The true test of the President's ability to persuade and convert lay in his success in overcoming some of the deepest antipathies of his people and of the Congress. Involved in this process was the reversal of well-established traditions.

We can most clearly perceive the President's technique for justification by investigating and delineating the arguments he used to push through two controversial, revolutionary policies: conscription, upsetting the tradition of no draft in peacetime, and foreign aid, reversing the policy of non-entanglement.

In both cases, the President ran against powerful opposition. He therefore mobilized every possible argument to tie his cause with that of the American people, eventually fusing together self-interest with national and world interest.

3. The Battle over Conscription

a. The Debate over the Burke-Wadsworth Bill

Ironically the President initially played a minor and contradictory role in the controversy over the first draft legislation, the Burke-Wadsworth Bill, not supporting it publicly until the eleventh hour.[2] His leadership was temporarily quiescent, though ultimately effective.

The original proposal came from Grenville Clark, a leader of the Military Training Camps Association.[3] On May 8, 1940, he urged a preparedness campaign implemented by universal and compulsory military service.[4] A National Emergency Committee, established under Clark's chairmanship, immediately but unsuccessfully began to canvass administration and official support.[5]

From the Chief of Staff the Committee received only opposition, objections or silence. The austere Marshall was not opposed to the draft in principle; but, like most soldiers, favored it:

> It is unlikely that anybody acquainted with a major war's requirements in manpower, as evidenced years before in World War I, doubted the necessity of selective service for development of a large army. The Staff's Brief Account of 1939 had referred to it as "the only sound measure" in such an emergency, and the wish for a draft act at the right time was probably more acute in the General Staff than in any other institution.[6]

But here the wish could not father the deed. A Selective Service Act might be theoretically imperative, but practically impossible.

Marshall could cite several immediate and long-range reasons for his inability to support Grenville Clark's project. The immediate reasons were bound with the Army's training plans,[7] its fears of a hemispheric attack by Axis forces,[8] and his concern over the Army's appropriation bills in the Congress.[9] The long-range reasons revolved around the problems of legal and moral justification.

The final reason was decisive, for General Marshall would have discarded immediate objections to the draft if he had felt that it was politically saleable. His long-range objections mirrored the effects of the military neglect which soldiers had suffered throughout the interwar period.

He was also sharply aware of the limitations which domestic politics imposed upon military programs.[10] Since any attempted justification would run against a long tradition, the opposition of Americans to a peacetime draft, it would be a bold experiment, certain to rouse the ire of tradition-alists and isolationists. As an official Army historian points out, the political climate was not encouraging:

> If the White House and Army alike erred in their judgment of what the 1940 Congress would do in the light of Blitzkrieg's towering flames, it must be remembered (1) that thus far Congress had been reluctant to go the full distance in other respects, (2) that there was an active pacifist movement in America, and (3) that the Congressional and President-ial elections were only a few months distant, and the Democratic National Convention (where the third term would be a dominant issue) was almost at hand.[12]

If political tradition and climate were opposed to an immediate enactment of the draft, constitutional discretion prohibited the Army from raising the issue or from associating itself openly with its fate. The General Staff felt that overt championship would raise the specter of militarism, which isolationist leaders would exploit.[13]

Finally, Marshall was scrupulously aware of the prerogatives of civilian leadership and knew that the decision was not his. As Mark Skinner Watson notes:

> The question of supporting a prewar draft was a matter of national policy in which not even the military Chief of the Army had the power of decision, and upon which at such a time he could not with propriety even give expression publicly to his own professional views, save with approval of his civilian superior, the Secretary of War and, more especially, the President.[14]

Roosevelt was hardly enthusiastic.

Meeting with Marshall and the Chief of Naval Operations on June 22,[15] 1940, the President flatly and unequivocally disassociated himself from the current legislative efforts to pass a selective service act, and also rejected the Chiefs' own mobilization plans.[16] He was consistently cautious when facing his congressional opponents, certain that the draft would surely arouse the righteous anger of the isolationist gang. The rub, therefore, was not public opposition, but Congressional[17] obduracy. Justification stood or fell before the majority of both houses.

The President remained as silent as the proverbial sphinx until his renomination by the Democratic National Convention. Then, in his acceptance speech delivered on July 19, 1940, he finally but cautiously supported the draft: "...most right thinking persons are agreed that some form of selection is as necessary and fair today as it was in 1917 and 1918."[18] Lost to many observers was the astuteness with which the President used the selective service proposal to introduce his decision for a third term:

> Lying awake as I have, on many nights, I have asked myself whether I have the right, as Commander-in-Chief of the Army and Navy, to call on men and women to serve their country or to train themselves to serve and, at the same time, decline to serve my country in my own personal capacity, if I am called upon to do so by the people of my country.[19]

By association and identitication, the President's speech supported

both "drafts": his own for a third term and the draft of selectees for
military service.[20]

Then the President climatically developed his major thesis,
reiterating again and again in defense of selective service: the draft
in both senses was an absolute necessity produced by the violent and
dangerous world in which Americans lived and feared:

> In times like these--in times of great tension, of great crisis--
> the compass of the world narrows to a single fact. The fact
> which dominates our world is the fact of armed aggression,
> aimed at the form of Government, the kind of society that we
> in the United States have chosen and established for ourselves.
> It is a fact which no one longer doubts--which no one is
> longer able to ignore.
> It is not an ordinary war. It is a revolution imposed by force of arms
> which threatens all men everywhere. It is a revolution which
> proposes not to set men free but to reduce them to slavery--to
> reduce them to slavery in the interest of a dictatorship which
> had already shown the nature and the extent of the advantage which
> it hopes to obtain.[21]

With this depiction of an increasingly threatened world tormented by a
counterrevolution of force and slavery, Roosevelt established the
justification for selective service legislation, as well as his acceptance
of a third term.

He waited until the dedication of the Great Smoky Mountains National
Park on September 2, 1940, to throw the full power of his undivided
eloquence behind the draft and to carefully delineate its justification:

> Today we no longer face Indians and hard and lonely struggles
> with nature--but today we have grown soft in many ways.
> If we are to survive, we cannot be soft in a world in which
> there are dangers that threaten Americans--dangers far more
> deadly than were those that the frontiersman had to face.
> The earth has been so shrunk by the airplane and the radio
> that Europe is closer to America today than was one side
> of these mountains to the other side when the pioneers toiled
> through the primeval forest. The arrow, the tomahawk and the
> scalping knife have been replaced by the airplane, the bomb,
> the tank, and the machine gun. Their threat is as close to

> us today as was the threat to the frontiersmen when hostile
> Indians were lurking on the other side of the gap.
> Therefore, to meet the threat--to ward off these dangers--
> the Congress of the United States and the Chief Executive
> of the United States are establishing by law the obligation
> inherent in our citizenship to serve our forces for defense
> through training in many capacities. [22]

This statement was Roosevelt's strongest stand in defense of the Selective
Service Act. Straightforward, unequivocal and unambiguous, it put the
President on the line.

Then, after acknowledging the hardships that the draft would inflict
on many individuals and families, the President linked the theme of the
occasion with that of the current world crisis: the conservation of
natural resources with that of freedom and civilization. The United
States was preserving the past and the future against the dangers of
the present:

> If the spirit of God is not in us, and if we will not prepare
> to give all that we have and all that we are to preserve
> Christian civilization in our land, we shall go to destruction.
> It is good and right that we should conserve these mountain
> heights of the old frontier for the benefit of the American
> people. But in this hour we have to safeguard a greater
> thing: the right of the people of this country to live as
> free men. Our vital task of conservation is to preserve the
> freedom that our forefathers won in this land, and the liberties
> that were proclaimed in our Declaration of Independence and
> embodied in our Constitution.[23]

But the President reserved his most moving eloquence, his most
touching appeal to idealistic patriotism till the end of his speech.
Again identifying the modern American with the frontiersman, he blessed
the former. For the modern American had a mission to defend:

> ...the good earth of this land, our homes, our families--
> yes, and far more. We shall be defending a way of life
> which has given more freedom to the soul and body of man
> than ever has been realized in the world before, a way of

> life that has let men scale whatever heights they could
> scale without hurting their fellows, a way of life that has
> let men hold up their heads and admit no master but God.
> That way of life is manaced. We can meet the threat. We
> can meet it with the old frontier spirit. We can forge our
> weapons, train ourselves to shoot, meet fire with fire, and
> with the courage and the unity of the frontiersmen.[24]

Here the President defended the draft by stressing its importance to the

defense of the United States, her people and traditions. While mainly

defining his justification on the basis of self-defense, he also

strengthened his argument by an appeal to tradition. The draft would

not be a violation of American rights, but a fulfilment of American

responsibilities.

This second basis for justification, the argument that the

draft was fully democratic and totally compatible with the traditions

of free men, was fully proclaimed by the President when the Selective

Service Act was finally passed by the United States Congress:

> In thus providing for national defense, we have not carved
> a new and uncharted trail in the history of our democratic
> institutions. On the contrary, we have merely reasserted an
> old and accepted principle of democratic Government. The
> militia system, the self-armed citizenry with the obligation
> of military service incumbent upon every free man, has its
> roots in the old common law. It was brought to this continent
> by our forefathers. It was an accepted institution in
> colonial days. At the time of the adoption of the Federal
> Constitution, nine of the thirteen States explicitly provided
> for universal service in their basic laws.[25]

In his speech on Registration Day, October 16, 1940, Roosevelt

introduced the maintenance of peace as a third theme or argument for

draft justification: "to that cause...we Americans today devote our

national will and our national spirit and our national strength."[26]

A tardy advocate of selective service, the President was unparalleled

in its defense or definition. He drew the themes of justification

together, appealing strongly to the American public while silencing
most effectively the voice of opposition and the clamorous carping of
the isolationists.

Each of the Roosevelt themes—defense, democracy and peace—was
challenged and reversed by his isolationist critics. They flayed the
President, depicting the enactment of the bill as a triumph of militarism
over democratic institutions, a commitment to intervention and war in
Europe.[27] The specter of 1917 haunted them.

But most Americans accepted his arguments, seeing in the enactment
of the bill a necessary safeguard for the Western Hemisphere, rejecting
the theory that the bill was an authorization for an American expeditionary force. Possibly the current view was well expressed, with all the
tones of contemporary anti-European prejudice, by General Hugh Johnson,
radio commentator:

> "We will never again be fools enough to send a single
> American mother's son to double-crossing Europe. It
> isn't a question of that now. It is a question of double-
> crossing Europe threatening us. With our strength of men
> and resources we can take a defensive position which no
> body will ever dare threaten."[28]

b. The Debate over the Extension of Selective Service

The debate over conscription did not end with the passage of the
Burke-Wadsworth Act. When the Administration sought to extend Selective
Service, it faced the same hurdles, mobilized many of the same argu-
ments and was opposed on the same grounds. This time, however, the
case for justification negotiated an even narrower passage. Fortunately,
President Roosevelt and General Marshall, principle advocate of the War
Department's case, plied a more consistent, a more clearly chartered
course.[29]

Throughout the debate that followed, General Marshall, who was
highly esteemed by most Congressmen, bore the brunt of the fight.[30]
Sensitive to their prerogatives, he sought to justify the measure
on strictly professional grounds. The extension of selective service
would improve the "'efficiency'" of the armed forces, while its
defeat would "'be catastrophic.'"[31] He tried to disarm Congressional
opposition by insisting that he did not contemplate any great increase
in forces: "'My principal concern is with the efficiency of the
numbers we now have rather than with a great expansion with a possible
superficial result.'"[32] His emphasis sought to assuage the fear of
militarism prevelant in legislative circles.

The President of the United States could easily base his arguments
on broader grounds than the Chief of Staff. In a major speech delivered
on July 21, 1941, he began by stressing the same basic argument as Marshall:

> ...if and when an organized and integrated company, battalion,
> regiment, or division is compelled to send two-thirds of its
> members home, those who return to civilian life, if called to
> the colors later on, would have to go through a new period of
> organization and integration before the new unit to which
> they were assigned could be depended on for service. The
> risks and the weaknesses caused by dissolving a trained army
> in times of national peril were pointed out by George
> Washington over and over again in his Messages to the Continen-
> tal Congress.[33]

He then drew the full implications of the existing threat to national
security. Evoking the image of the master conspirator, he depicted the
dangerous situation surrounding the country, thereby fully developing
his justification:

> ...it is the well-nigh unanimous opinion of those who are
> daily cognizant, as military and naval officers and as
> government servants in the field of international relations,
> that schemes and plans of aggressor Nations against American
> security are so evident that the United States and the rest

of the Americas are definitely imperiled in their national
interests. That is why reluctantly, and only after a
careful weighing of all facts and all events, I recently
proclaimed that an unlimited national emergency exists....
I must refer again to the sequence of conquests--German
conquests or attacks--which have continued uninterruptedly
throughout several years--all the way from the coup against
Austria to the present campaign against Russia.
Every move up and down and across Europe, and into Asia, and
into Africa, has been conducted according to a time schedule
utilizing in every case an overwhelming superiority not only
in materiel but in trained men as well. Each campaign has
been based on a preliminary assurance of safety or non-
aggression to the intended victim. Each campaign had been
based on disarming fear and gaining time until the German
Government was fully ready to throw treaties and pacts to
the winds and simultaneously to launch an attack in overwhelming force.
Each elimination of a victim has brought the issue of Nazi
domination closer and closer to this hemisphere, while month
by month their intrigues of propaganda and conspirace have
sought to weaken every link in the community of interests
that should bind the Americas into a great western family.[34]

The President concentrated his case on the pressing danger to

United States security. He did not evoke his earlier argument that

the draft was essentially a defense of peace. Possibly, he now doubted

that the two incompatible poles of his policy--commitment to the Allied

cause and continued neutrality--could be reconciled. Perhaps he merely

felt that the best way of pushing the Congress in the right direction

was to emphasize the mounting danger.

The arguments of the opposition echoed previous stands. Although

there weren't many protracted prophecies about the decline and fall of

American democracy, there were plenty of outcries that the recommended

measures would authorize an American expeditionary force, consequently

triggering war.[35] But the most serious obstacle to justification was

political, nesting in the nature of American democracy itself. Many

Congressmen felt that the extension of the term of service would be

tantamount to "a breach of contract with the conscripted men."[36] This
action would be so unpopular among the disaffected soldiers[37] and their
relatives that it would cost any elected official his political future:

> A good many Congressmen were evidently willing to take a
> long chance to escape the odium of voting to keep their
> constituents and the constituents' offspring in camp. As
> one of them wrote to his colleagues before the roll call:
> 'If you don't watch your step, your political hide, which
> is very near and dear to you, will be tanning on the barn
> door.'[38]

The imperatives of domestic politics seemed more important and relevant
than the necessities of international politics.

This factor made the problem of justification far more difficult
in 1941 than it had been in 1940. Although the international situation
was manifestly more critical and the need for extension evident to most,
including many who voted against the draft,[39] the bill authorizing the
extension of military service passed by a narrow margin: 45 to 30 in
the Senate and 203 to 202 in the House.[40] It had won, four months before
Pearl Harbor, by a majority of one!

The final vote revealed that the problem of justification was not
solved by late 1941. The sense of emergency was not strong enough to
definitely and clearly outweigh the suspicions and doubts of Congress.
Many still suspected the motives of the Administration and feared their
domestic supporters far more than their foreign adversaries. The sense
of crisis had not suppressed partisan divisions or brought forth a
sense of national unity. Although Senator Burton K. Wheeler was
hardly an objective commentator, his judgment did illuminate the
distances the Administration would have to travel before it could
convince Congress that the country was in mortal danger:

"This vote clearly indicates that the Administration could not get a resolution through the Congress for a declaration of war. It is notice to the War Department that the Congress does not approve of their breaking faith with the draftees. It is also notice that the Congress does not take seriously the cry of the Administration that the so-called emergency is greater now than it was a year ago."[41]

Obviously even such an exaggerated evaluation would make the President, always extremely sensitive to the rise and fall of the public barometer and to the obstructions of the isolationists, hesitate. Although he had established the tradition of the peacetime draft, he had maintained it with difficulty. He still could not rely on overwhelming bipartisan support for his conscription measures, designed to ready the American forces for war.

4. The Debate over Foreign Aid

Americans questioned and debated the peacetime draft and had mixed, confused and inconsistent feelings over foreign aid. For this policy was a challenge and reversal of the hallowed tradition of non-entanglement. Today we find it difficult to recapture this belief. Living in a world in which international interdependence is obvious and accepted, we forget the time in which it was considered challengeable and dangerous. Whereas most informed Americans now bewail the scuttling of the League of Nations by the United States Senate as a great national tragedy, the entire Wilsonian "experiment" was formerly denounced as an aberration, a radical departure from sound and safe practice. By 1937 most Americans regarded their country's entry into the First World War as a major error.[42]

The most serious damage to Wilsonian internationalism was inflicted by the notorious Nye Committee. Firmly committed to the conspiracy theory of history, this Committee investigated the activities of munition makers and bankers in World War I. It came to an extraordinary conclusion.

America's entry had been triggered by the nefarious machinations
of the "Merchants of Death." Seeking to protect their
investments whose solvency depended on Allied victory over
Germany, these sinister peddlars had engineered U.S. intervention.
This theory had the virtue of being straight-forward. Moreover,
it offered the hope that peace could be maintained and
involvement avoided by a simple expedient. Dourselle,
the diplomatic historian, acidly summarizes this attitude:

> To conclude that the United States entry into the
> war in 1917 had come about in this way was to
> believe in the existence of a simple mechanism which
> appropriate measures would eliminate: since the
> United States had gone to war to obtain the repayment
> of credits, it would suffice not to grant credits to
> any belligerent, aggressor or victim. If one
> consistently put an embargo on all shipments of arms
> and munitions to belligerents there would be no
> cause for the arms industry to be interested in
> the success of either camp....[43]

Legislation would serve as a massive preventive arrest, placing
all potential criminals behind the walls of the Neutrality Laws.

These laws, passed between 1935 and 1937, sought to
prevent any recurrence of the 1917 involvement. In case of war,
the President would proclaim an embargo on arms and munitions
to all belligerents, forbid the travel of Americans aboard
belligerent vessels and prevent all private loans or credits
to the participants.[44] "Seemingly no loophole had been left
through which the country could again be drawn into the
conflicts of other nations."[45]

These laws and public support for them constituted
formidable barriers against foreign aid to the Allies. Any
justification would have to defeat a powerful, entrenched tradition

against America's former intervention.

Naturally these thorough Neutrality Laws could not survive the
opening of the Second World War. They could not survive our increasing
realization that their enforcement would deny essential military
supplies and munitions to the Allies. By November 4, 1939, a new
neutrality act was passed and signed into law allowing the Allies to
purchase arms and munitions on a "cash and carry" basis. [46] The antipathy
of the American public to the Nazi regime, its mounting dread of an
Axis victory, allowed the President and his Congressional supporters
to negotiate this important revision.

But if the American public and its political representatives were
willing to forgo rigid neutrality, they were not willing to risk
involvement nor financial commitment to Allied victory. The memory of
unpaid debts also inhibited measures designed to furnish arms and munitions on any long-range credit basis. The "cash and carry" rule was
designed to prevent a recurrence of any indebtedness commitment. The
success of this new legislation would depend on Allied ability to pay.

Despite the President's Charlottesville pledge, the financial
restrictions of the Neutrality Act held throughout the spring crisis of
1940. This pledge ultimately formed the nucleus of the President's
developing policy of aid to England; but, in the summer of 1940, it was
totally unimplemented. Its significance was its promise that the United
States would not abandon the Allies merely to concentrate on national
rearmament. [47] So far, however, the promise was unkept.

But a vital problem of justification emerged as the United States
moved from neutrality towards war, seeking to choose between these two

great inconsistencies: the maintenance of peace and the support of the
Allied cause. Here, two great decisions mirrored the problems and
achievement of justification: the destroyer deal[48] and Lend-Lease.[49]

In both cases, the President keenly sensed the difficulties of
preserving and selling revolutionary decisions to the public and the
Congress. In both decisions the President waited to convert the public
before challenging Congress. In the first case, though he initially
managed to circumvent the hurdle of Congressional approval, he still
had to gain a post-facto blessing. In the second case, he had to carry
the issue into the legislature, converting enough opponents to assure its
passage. In both, he departed from traditional definitions of neutrality
and brought the United States closer to involvement, overthrowing strong
traditions of non-entanglement.

a. The Destroyer Deal

America's legislators failed to recognize or admit the relativity
of their neutrality. They suffered from a common delusion: the belief
that they could legislate an absolute policy of neutrality and that its
enactment and application would suffice to keep us out of war.

The sanctity of these illusions crumbled under the rising menace
of the Axis powers, finally shattering with the fall of France and the
threatened invasion of England. The walls were leveled, but the illusions
held. To move his country closer to involvement, the President had to
convince his fellow citizens that the old belief was a dangerous delusion.
To aid the British, he ultimately had to justify distinctly unneutral
actions.

The destroyer exchange was a definite step in the direction of

American involvement. The problem was first brought to Roosevelt's attention by Prime Minister Churchill in his famous May 15, 1940, message:

> 'First of all, the loan of forty or fifty of your older destroyers to bridge the gap between what we have now and the large new construction we put in hand at the beginning of the war. This time next year we shall have plenty. But if in the interval Italy comes in against us with another one hundred submarines, we may be strained to the breaking-point.'[50]

The implications of this move and its motives were fairly apparent. Churchill recognized the necessity for American intervention, realizing it would insure Allied victory. But if the United States would not immediately enter the war, then extensive aid would be an effective substitute: "'non-belligerency...would mean that you would help us with everything short of actually engaging armed forces.'"[51] Actually, the alternative was illusionary; extensive aid would be an initial step to full-scale involvement.

To achieve either end, Churchill had a powerful bargaining asset: the British Fleet. He knew that its fate was of major concern to the American Government.[52] Therefore, it would be invaluable in securing American aid and reminding the United States of its strategic dependence upon Great Britain.[53] As a literal and symbolic token of American agreement and participation, Churchill suggested the loan of fifty destroyers. President Roosevelt was sympathetic. But before he could justify this proposal to the nation, he would have to clear many military, legal and political obstacles.

The military problem was obvious. The United States needed these destroyers for her own defense.[54] Because of extensive commitments and general unpreparedness, the Navy was reluctant to make the transfer.[55]

But this obstacle paled before the legal difficulties involved.
There were several laws which explicitly blocked the destroyer exchange,
making it manifestly illegal. They were summarized by the State
Department's Legal Adviser, Green H. Hackworth:

> Section 23, Title 18, of the United States Code makes it
> unlawful to fil out and arm or to procure to be fitted out
> and armed, or knowingly to be concerned in 'furnishing,
> fitting out, or arming of any vessel, with intent that such
> vessel shall be employed in the service of any foreign prince,
> or state' etc., to cruise or commit hostilities against the
> subjects, citizens, or property of any foreign prince, or
> state, etc., with which the United States is at peace.
> Section 33 of the same Title of the Code provides that
> during a war in which the United States is neutral it
> shall be unlawful to send out of the jurisdiction of the
> United States any vessel built, armed, or equipped as a
> vessel of war, with any intent or under any agreement or
> contract, written or oral, that such vessel shall be delivered
> to a belligerent nation, or to an agent, officer, or citizen
> of such nation, or with reasonable cause to believe that the
> said vessel shall or will be employed in the service of such
> belligerent nation after its departure from the jurisdiction
> of the United States.
> Section 14 (a) of the act entitled 'An Act to expedite
> national defense, and for other purposes' (Public--no. 671--
> 76th Congress), approved June 28, 1940, provides that
> 'notwithstanding the provisions of any other law, no military
> or naval weapon, ship, boat, aircraft, munitions, supplies,
> or equipment, to which the United States has title, in whole
> or in part, or which have been contracted for, shall hereafter
> be transferred, exchanged, sold, or otherwise disposed of in
> any manner whatever unless the Chief of Naval Operations in
> the case of naval material, and the Chief of Staff of the
> Army in the case of military material, shall first certify that
> such material is not essential to the defense of the United States.[56]

Not only did the destroyer exchange violate Federal laws, it also contro-
verted international law. The United States was a signatory to the
Hague Convention whose Article VI flatly contradicted and nullified such
a transaction: "'The supply in any manner, directly or indirectly, by
a neutral Power to a belligerent Power of warships, ammunition, or war
materials of any kind whatever is forbidden.'"[57] Whether or not the State

Department took such a prohibition seriously, considering the nature of
our potential opponent, was besides the point. The prohibition must be
dealt with.[58]

Behind the legal obstacles stood the firm opposition of a Congress
dominated by isolationists. The danger signs were evident; they had
been dramatized by the uproar over the proposed transfer of twenty Elco
torpedo boats, an incident which led to the enactment of the June 28th
prohibition on any transfer of military equipment without the certifica-
tion of the military chiefs.[59] Certainly this exchange between the White
House and the Hill was inauspicious, promising no returns for an open
policy of aid to England.

Moreover, this political block was strengthened by the uncertainties
of the 1940 presidential election. If the President transferred the
destroyers to the United Kingdom, his political opponent, Wendell Wilkie,
could challenge and denounce the transaction as dangerous to American
interests. This stand would be particularly tempting since it would
receive the overwhelming support of the isolationist branch of the
Republican party, unifying the quarrelling party members under a single
banner.

Against such strong arguments--military, legal and political--the
problem of justification would be formidable. Mr. Roosevelt had to
prove that the transfer would strengthen the defense of the United States,
and that it did not violate constitutional or Congressional law. He
also had to neutralize the fury of the opposition and convert Wendell
Wilkie.[60]

The ideal solution was discovered by the Century Group in a series
of memoranda drawn up in July, 1940. This organization, the most radical

group in William Allen White's Committee to Defend America by Aiding
the Allies, openly favored American intervention on the side of Britain.[61]
Convinced that England's defeat would automatically be followed by an
Axis attack against the Western Hemisphere, it passionately advocated
American aid to the Allies even at the risk of war. However, its
leaders were realistic; they grasped the difficulties of selling aid
projects to the American public and the problems of neutralizing
Congressional opposition. Their July proposals were designed to
accomplish this end while overcoming all problems of justification.

On the issue of the transfer the Century Group was clear.
Accepting columnist Joseph Alsop's estimate that continued destroyer
losses would expose Great Britain to invasion, the Group drafted a
memorandum in which it delineated the close identification between
national interest and the survival of Great Britain:

> 'The most valuable sector in the American defense line is the
> North Atlantic. Consequently the primary immediate responsi-
> bility of the...Government is to insure adequate defense in
> that area. If Germany wins control of the North Atlantic,
> the period prior to the completion of our two-ocean Navy will
> be a period of acute danger for us. During that period the
> United States could be invaded from the Atlantic. The most
> certain preventive (until our two-ocean Navy is built) is the
> continued existence of the British Fleet. And the fate of
> the British Fleet will be settled by the battle for the control
> of the North Atlantic, which is about to begin on the shores
> of England, Scotland and Ireland. The British chances of
> success are at present doubtful; but responsible British
> officials believe that they could successfully withstand
> invasion if they had one hundred more destroyers.'[62]

Here was long-range justification for a policy of full-scale aid, indeed
for a policy of intervention. But the Century Group realized that most
Americans did not share their assumptions, did not accept their diagnosis
of the mounting danger. Therefore, more solid, more immediate reasons

should be offered. In return for the transfer of one hundred destroyers, the United States should secure the following concessions:

> '...the United States should ask for some guarantee that the British Fleet should neither be scuttled nor surrendered, but in case of a successful German invasion of England, should operate thereafter from Canadian and-or American bases, or... these destroyers should be offered to Britain in exchange for immediate naval and air concessions in British possessions in the Western Hemisphere.'[63]

Here was the formula the President needed. The transfer must be transformed into a "deal" in which the United States would obtain a concrete asset. Moreover, such an exchange would have a tremendous advantage. Since the isolationists had been clamoring for years for the acquisition [64] of European bases in the Western Hemisphere, it would literally seize the fire from their hands.

The President quickly seized upon the possibilities of this proposal. By August 2, 1940, his decision had crystallized, his strategy had clarified. At the Cabinet meeting dealing with the possible acquisition of British bases, Roosevelt's predominant emphasis was on the transfer of the destroyers and the securing of an assurance from the British on the future disposition of the Fleet. This emphasis shows that the President's basic interest was in aiding the British, not in acquiring new defensive positions. The grounds for justification were laid. Since the defense of Great Britain was vital to the United States, she should receive the destroyers. But all provisions must be made to prevent them [65] from falling into German hands if England subsequently capitulated.

The problem of neutralizing Republican opposition was also stressed and a preliminary strategy of contact and approach worked out. Through an indirect liaison with Wilkie and the Republican leaders in Congress, the President hoped to remove the issue from partisan politics. [66]

This strategy for justification, however, depended upon Congressional approval. Without the active cooperation of the Republican members of the legislative branch, the laws blocking the transfer could not be amended. But the foundation for the President's strategy was shaken when Wendell Wilkie, known to favor the transfer, refused to commit himself or his party publicly or unequivocally. [67] This refusal put Roosevelt in a bind.

While the President hesitated, the campaign continued. The Committee to Defend America built up a tremendous propaganda line. Two main arguments were reiterated time and again: the destroyer transfer was defined as a defensive measure and defended as a peaceful move designed to keep the United States out of war. [68]

But active propaganda could not allay Congressional opposition or diminish the prospect of a stunning defeat if the Administration attempted to amend the existing laws. [69] Since the President was overly circumspect in his dealings with Congress, and perhaps too anxious about the strength of isolationist opposition, everything stood at a perfect stalemate.

If Congressional action were blocked, perhaps another path to justification could be found. This possibility was first proposed by four lawyers--Charles C. Burlingham, Thomas D. Thacher, George Rublee and Dean Acheson--in an August 11, 1940, letter to The New York Times. Arguing that a proper interpretation of the prohibitory laws revealed no real barrier to the destroyer transfer, these eminent lawyers urged the President to act independently. Roosevelt could effect the transfer by executive action alone, [70] circumventing isolationist opposition.

But although Roosevelt could bypass Congress, he knew that he needed its ultimate support. [71] That support, whether formally requested or informally evoked, could only be secured if presented as an irresistably

advantageous bargain. With this realization, the President turned in
two directions simultaneously. He asked the Attorney General for his
opinion of the legality of such an executive act and sought a deal with
the Prime Minister.

In his negotiations with Churchill, the President adopted the
proposed strategy advocated by the Century Group. The transfer would
be effected as part of a mutual exchange. As explained to Churchill on
August 13, 1940, the deal would assume the following form:

> 'It is my belief that it may be possible to furnish to the
> British Government as immediate assistance at least 50
> destroyers, the motor torpedo boats heretofore referred to,
> and insofar as airplanes are concerned, five planes of each
> of the categories mentioned, the latter to be furnished for
> war testing purposes. Such assistance, as I am sure you will
> understand, would only be furnished if the American people
> and the Congress frankly recognized that in return therefor
> the national defense and security of the United States would
> be enhanced. For that reason it would be necessary, in the
> event that it proves possible to release the materiel above
> mentioned, that the British Government find itself able and
> willing to take the two following steps:
> 1. Assurance on the part of the Prime Minister that in the
> event that the waters of Great Britain become untenable for
> British ships of war, the latter would not be turned over to
> the Germans or sunk, but would be sent to other parts of the
> Empire for continued defense of the Empire.
> 2. An agreement on the part of Great Britain that the British
> Government would authorize the use of Newfoundland, Bermuda,
> the Bahamas, Jamaica, St. Lucia, Trinidad and British Guinea
> as naval and air bases by the United States in the event of
> an attack on the American hemisphere by any non-American
> nation; and in the meantime the United States to have the
> right to establish such bases and to use them for training
> and exercise purposes with the understanding that the land
> necessary for the above could be acquired by the United
> States through purchase or through a 99-year lease.'[72]

Churchill's reply was prompt and decisive. Delighted that the
President was so cooperative, he raised few difficulties, merely informing
him that a lease of the naval and air bases was immeasurably preferable
to a sale and urging him to use the assurance about the Fleet in a tactful

and discreet manner, thereby avoiding any impression that England's
situation was desperate.[73]

By then the President's hand was strengthened by the assurances of
his Attorney General that the transaction was legal and within executive
power.[74] It now seemed apparent that the entire deal could be reduced to
an amicable exchange of letters between the British Ambassador to the
United States, Lord Lothian, and the Secretary of State, Cordell Hull.[75]
Unfortunately the techniques of justification have no trans-Atlantic
visa. What would make the deal palpable to the American public would
make it noxious to the British. What could be flouted as a good sharp
trade in Congress, would be denounced as a sell-out in Parliament.
Mr. Roosevelt could trade the destroyers, not give them. Mr. Churchill
could give the bases, not exchange them.[76] He explained to the President
on August 22nd : "I see difficulties, and even risks...in admitting in
any way that the munitions which you send us are a payment for the
facilities. Once this idea is accepted, people will contrast on each
side what is given and received. The money value of the armaments
would be computed and set against the facilities, and some would think
one thing about it and some another."[77] The destroyer transfer should
also "'be entirely a spontaneous act.'"[78]

For a while everything locked in an impasse. The President could
not ignore the provisions of the law requiring the Chief of Staff and
the Chief of Naval Operations to certify that the transferable materiel
was not essential to American defense. Mr. Churchill could never
present "a one-sided horse trade.'"[79] to the British public or Parliament.

Finally on August 26th the Department of State and the Department
of Justice proposed a compromise dividing the facilities into two
categories: one consisting of bases offered as a free gift; the other

80.
of bases offered in exchange. Here was a workable formula for justification.

Now the President could act. Presenting the transaction as a
fait accomplit to the United States Congress on September 3, 1940,
and defending it at a subsequent press conference, Roosevelt interlayed
his presentation with several arguments. The exchange, not a war
measure, reinforced America's defensive position in the Western
Hemisphere. Also the use of an executive agreement was consistent with
past tradition. This final point was strengthened by comparing the deal
with the Louisiana Purchase: "This is the most important action in the
reinforcement of our national defense...since the Louisiana Purchase....
The value to the Western Hemisphere of these outposts of security is
beyond calculation...Their consequent importance in hemispheric defense
is obvious."[81] Defense, peace and tradition—their appeal was designed
to silence the opposition, and negate the charges of war-monger and
dictator often hurled at the President by his most bitter critics.

By the use of his flexible authority as Commander-in-Chief, and
by a liberal interpretation of the existing laws, the President could
neutralize the opposing arguments.[82] Finally, by turning the destroyer
exchange into a "deal" he could neutralize the rabid criticisms of the
inveterate isolationists. By a combination of shrewdness and diplomatic
astuteness, and a good deal of non-professional aid from the White
Committee and the Century Group, he managed to overcome all hurdles, to
effect the apparently impossible.

Throughout the battle for justification, Roosevelt carefully
avoided creating any impression that his action was either revolutionary

or unorthodox. He ultimately justified it by appealing to precedent, presenting it as an action implementing national defense and preserving peace in this hemisphere.

Actually the destroyer deal was a bold act moving the United States towards intervention. Although the President and his Attorney General skirted the issue of its effect upon American neutrality and its compata-bility with international law,[83] although the Prime Minister then dampened any suggestion that the exchange held far reaching implications,[84] its revolutionary nature was obvious. It was a transaction more appropriate to two Allied nations than to a belligerent and a neutral. It gave the United States a physical stake in the survival of the British Fleet. It stretched the interpretation of both "neutrality" and "defense" far beyond the literal letter of the law. As later summarized by Churchill:

> The transfer to Great Britain of fifty American warships was a decidedly unneutral act by the United States. It would, according to all the standards of history, have justified the German Government in declaring war upon them. The President judged that there was no danger, and I felt there was no hope, of this simple solution of many difficulties. It was Hitler's interest and method to strike his opponents down one by one. The last thing he wished was to be drawn into war with the United States before he had finished with Britain. Neverthe-less the transfer of destroyers to Britain in August, 1940, was an event which brought the United States definitely nearer to us and to the war, and it was the first of a long succession of increasingly unneutral acts in the Atlantic which were of the utmost service to us. It marked the passage of the United States from being neutral to being non-belligerent. Although Hitler could not afford to resent it, all the world, as will be seen, understood the significance of the gesture.[85]

Although we masked our move by appealing to the status quo, our action marked a definite step towards inter national involvement and commitment.

    b. Lend-Lease

        1) Significance

The destroyer deal was a revolutionary act; but it was a single commitment beginning and ending in itself. Indicating the direction in which America was travelling, it did not commit her to a single course. Moreover, the break with the past was never publicly admitted by the Administration, and the entire transaction was accomplished by a sleight of hand, not determined and reasoned debate and decision. Although the President had plenty of public support for his move, he avoided a head-on collision with his political opponents.

The destroyer deal appears like the clever trick of a master manipulator who seeks to win the game by the speed and skill of his hands, not by the strength of his pack. In contrast the successful enactment of Lend-Lease was a masterful act of creative statesmanship, Mr. Roosevelt's finest and boldest hour. Unlike the destroyer deal, it was pushed through the House of Representatives and the Senate. Its implications were, therefore, fully explored and carefully debated. Moreover, unlike the destroyer deal, it was presented as a new departure attended with a considerable degree of risk, though inaction was far more dangerous. In justifying its course, the Administration had to identify the security of the United States with England's continued resistance, while still allaying some of the same fears and removing some of the same barriers that had previously inhibited the destroyer deal. But this time these barriers were struck down, not maneuvered around. With the ultimate passage of Lend Lease, the American public and their representatives sanctioned the President's interpretation of defense commitments. It signalled the end of American non-entanglement and marked the beginning of intervention.

2) The Churchill Messages

Lend Lease began with Churchill's famous May 15th message. At its
close the British Prime Minister had indicated the scope of England's
future problem and the implications of America's coming choice: "'We
shall go on paying dollars for as long as we can, but I should like to
feel reasonably sure that when we can pay no more, you will give us the
stuff all the same.'" Here the reefs were chartered, the challenge was
cast. But the problem still seemed remote. By December, 1940, it was
imminent.

On December 8, Churchill, in a masterfully persuasive presentation
of the State of the British Union, delineated the problem and its
interconnections with the expanding fury and cost of war. Churchill
began by enunciating the major premise of present Anglo-American policy:

> '...the safety of the United States, as well as the future of
> our two Democracies and the kind of civilization for which
> they stand, is bound up with the survival and independence
> of the British Commonwealth of Nations. Only thus can
> those bastions of sea-power, upon which the control of the
> Atlantic and Indian Oceans depend, be preserved in faithful
> and friendly hands. The control of the Pacific by the United
> States Navy and of the Atlantic by the British Navy is
> indispensable to the security and trade routes of both our
> countries, and the surest means of preventing war from reach-
> ing the shore of the United States.'[87]

By stating the premise and its corollary, the preservation of peace in
the Western Hemisphere, the Prime Minister skillfully strengthened his case.

He then turned to another aspect, another solid bond of self-interest
linking the two countries together. Since the United States had just
begun it rearmament, British resistance provided the necessary time
barrier behind which America could carry out its military program without
danger or interruption: "'It is our British duty in the common interest,

as also for our own survival, to hold the front and grapple with the
Nazi power until the preparations of the United States are complete.'" [88]

Having established a mutual bond of interest, Churchill then

delineated the present danger in which the British stood. Disclaiming [89]

any need or desire for a large American expeditionary force, he

underlined the major need, the increasing danger: "'Shipping, not men,

is the limiting factor, and the power to transport munitions and supplies

claims priority over the movement by sea of large numbers of soldiers.'" [90]

Imminent assault had been replaced by the threat of economic and military

paralysis:

> 'The danger of Great Britain being destroyed by a swift,
> overwhelming blow has for the time being very greatly receded.
> In its place there is a long, gradually maturing danger, less
> sudden and less spectacular, but equally deadly. This mortal
> danger is the steady and increasing diminuition of sea tonnage....
> The decision for 1941 lies upon the seas. Unless we can
> establish our ability to feed this island, to import the muni-
> tions of all kinds which we need, unless we can move our armies
> to the various theatres where Hitler and his confederate
> Mussolini must be met, and maintain them there, and do all this
> with the assurance of being able to carry it on till the spirit
> of the Continental Dictators is broken, we may fall by the way,
> and the time needed by the United States to complete her defen-
> sive preparations may not be forthcoming. It is, therefore, in
> shipping and in the power to transport across the oceans,
> particularly the Atlantic Ocean, that in 1941 the crunch of the
> whole war will be found. [91]

Having established the Atlantic threat as a major and mutual danger, the

Prime Minister continued by specifically noting and analyzing the current [92]

difficulties of the shipping crisis.

After this elaborate diagnosis, Churchill launched into an exegesis

of possible remedies, propounding either "'the reassertion by the United States

of the doctrine of freedom of the seas,'" [93] the escort of American vessels

into British ports by American naval vessels, [94] or the transfer of

additional vessels, especially destroyers, to the British Navy. [95] These

recommendations all had a single object: "'to reduce to manageable pro-

portions the present destructive losses at sea.'" [96] But more was needed.
The extensive nature of the war, its far flung commitments, necessitated
far more merchant tonnage than Great Britain could possibly produce:
"'Only the United States can supply this need.'" [97]

The need for additional plane production was equally vital. Without
air supremacy victory over Germany was impossible: "'In order to achieve [98]
such superiority, it is plain that we shall need the greatest production
of aircraft which the United States of America is capable of sending us.'" [99]
There were still further needs involved in the equipping of armies, needs
already generously answered by the United States and whose magnitude
would rise as the tide of fortune turned against the Axis: "'...when
the tide of dictatorship begins to recede, many countries trying to
regain their freedom may be asking for arms, and there is no source to
which they can look except the factories of the United States.'" [100]

The need for munitions were pressing, complex and multitudinous;
but Churchill was merely preparing his main case, laying the foundations
for his chief plea. At the core of the circle of reasoning, at the
base of the complex pyramid of purchasing, lay the question of finances.
If this problem were not solved, the entire edifice of supply, the
structure of the British war effort, the precondition of British
strategic plans, would crumble. Everything was a prelude to the final
demand, to the ultimate need:

> 'Last of all, I come to the question of Finance. The more
> rapid and abundant the flow of munitions and ships which you
> are able to send us, the sooner will our dollar credits be
> exhausted. They are already, as you know, very heavily drawn
> upon by the payments we have made to date. Indeed, as you know,
> the orders already placed or under negotiation, including the

expenditure settled or pending for creating munitions factories
in the United States, many times exceed the total exchange
resources remaining at the disposal of Great Britain. The
moment approaches when we shall no longer be able to pay cash
for shipping and other supplies. While we will do our utmost,
and shrink from no proper sacrifice to make payments across
the Exchange, I believe you will agree that it would be wrong
in principle and mutually disadvantageous in effect if at the
height of this struggle Great Britain were to be divested of
all saleable assets, so that after the victory was won with
our blood, civilization saved, and the time gained for the
United States to be fully armed against all eventualities,
we should stand stripped to the bone.'[101]

The letter then closed with a masterful definition of its appeal "'as a

statement of the minimum action necessary to achieve our common purpose.'" [102]

The advocate had made his case. Step by step he had outlined Britain's

needs, skillfully identifying them as imperative, compatible and indispen-

sible to the United States and the United Kingdom. Churchill had adeptly

avoided stirring or affronting the President's deep desire to keep his

country out of war, stressing that even the most provocative actions would
[103]
fail to antagonize Hitler sufficiently to attack America.   Underlying

the entire letter, moreover, was an implied, never stated threat: If

you cannot solve these problems, England will fall; and the United States

would have to assume the entire burden of defense. Mr. Churchill was far

too astute a diplomat to even suggest this conclusion; but he knew that

it was inevitable.

3) The Obstacles to Justification

If the interests of the United States and Britain were mutual and

interdependent, if America's best defense was the continued resistance

of the British Empire, then Mr. Churchill's plea was logical and

inescapable. America must either underwrite Allied victory or wait

complacently for the Empire to fall. The latter course was unthinkable.

The former, difficult to justify. The legal and political obstacles which could be circumvented in the destroyer deal could no longer be evaded.

The military obstacle was also still evident. Obviously any aid to the British was a calculated gamble. If they survived and threw back Hitler's assault, the risk would pay off. If they succumbed, then any American equipment captured by the Germans would probably be turned against the United States. However, this obstacle was now no hurdle to either the department chiefs or their service advisers because of three major reasons.

First, since the Administration had already emphatically defined and implemented its commitment towards England,[104] strategy now superseded and replaced political considerations. The second and the third reasons were more positive. Marshall and Stark were now committed to the British cause. Even if England fell, the program of continued assistance would be militarily valid. As the Chief of Staff pointed out in a December 10 Conference at the Treasury:

> Standardization had done its work. The airplanes, tanks, and ordinance the British needed would be indispensable for American defense if England fell, as would the new capacity for their manufacture.[105]

Since the next six months would determine the fate of the United Kingdom,[106] the possibility of the newly ordered equipment falling into enemy hands was negligible.

The third reason was the new position of the service chiefs. Although they had previously favored hemispheric isolation,[107] they were now fully committed to global defense. Even the threat of British defeat did not

change their new estimation. They were now convinced that
the United States should not allow England to fall into
enemy hands. Certain that war was inevitable,[108] they were
willing to take drastic action to save Great Britain.[109]

However, there were formidable legal and political
obstacles, largely unaffected by previous aid policies:
"The British were running out of dollar exchange and the
hands of the Americans were tied by statute."[110] The two
principal objections were the Johnson Act and the amended
Neutrality Law.

The former law forbade "the floating of loans in this
country by nations that were in default on their war debts."[111]
The latter ruled that transactions between belligerent nations
and the United States should be governed by "Cash and Carry."[112]
Behind this law lay an established concept. According to
Edward Stettinius, this doctrine was:

> ...the doctrine of neutrality which had been evolved
> during the 19th century in response to the desire of
> nations to continue normal commercial trade with
> belligerents. The law was a complicated compromise
> between this desire to trade and the natural desire
> of a warring enemy to cut off its enemy from all
> outside sources of supplies....As a part of all this,
> the doctrine was evolved that wars are neither good
> nor bad; they just exist. No distinction was to
> be made by non-belligerent governments between the
> side that was in the right and the side that was in
> the wrong.[113]

Technically, the new Neutrality Law subscribed to that formula:
munitions could be purchased by any nation capable of
buying and transporting them. Practically, since the
British and the French ruled the seas, only the Allied
coalition could buy military supplies in the American

market. But, despite this obvious favoritism, the restrictions of both
acts held. Munitions could not be given to the British, nor could they
be subsidized by loans.
                                                    114
    Although there were other legal obstacles, none was as generally
effective as these two. And, since only Congressional action could
remove or supersede them, the Administration could only win by facing
and defeating its political opposition in Congress. By the late fall
of 1940 a great majority of Americans favored continued, extended aid
                   115
to Great Britain. But the margin of those willing to risk war was
       116
thinner, and Isolationist strength was greater in the legislature than
                                      117
in the country at large.

    4) The Process of Justification

    The process of justification, therefore, faced an extended and
complex task. Before the successful enactment of the Lend-Lease Bill,
it would pass through four separate, successive and interdependent
stages: 1. the preliminary justification of the British case to the
Administration and ultimately to the American public; 2. the presentation of the Lend-Lease program by the President; 3. the preparation and
presentation of the Administration's case to Congress; and 4. the debate
and battle in the House and Senate.

    a) The British Case

    The first task was immensely difficult. The British had to prove
the desperateness of their economic plight to the United States. Most
Americans could not imagine that the rich, powerful British Empire was
so close to financial insolvency. As the British Ambassador, Lord Lothian,
reported to his Government: "'American public opinion...remained

'saturated with illusions...that we have vast resources available that
we have not yet disclosed...and that we ought to empty this vast
hypothetical barrel before we ask for assistance.'"[118]

This skepticism was not confined to the public. Some members of
the Administration, notably Cordell Hull,[119] were initially incredulous.
Fortunately the key figure, Secretary of the Treasury Morgenthau, knew
the British problem and understood its ramifications. But he also
appreciated the political difficulties involved. Congress and the
American public must be completely convinced or the necessary legislation
would never pass.

If the British expected to win American aid after their dollar
resources dried up, they had to sacrifice. The suggestions made by
the President and the Secretary of the Treasury were specific and
thorough. "...Britain was expected to aid herself by selling all her
foreign assets, including South America securities and 'direct investments' in the United States."[120] As Lord Lothian reported, shortly before
the fall election, the United States Congress would require a strict
accounting. As a precondition to any aid policy, it would insist on
the preliminary exhaustion of all British investments in the United
States and Latin America.[121] He also warned that the Administration
might strengthen its Congressional hand by asking "for a share in
United Kingdom tin and rubber investments in Malaya."[122]

The British Government found the problem of divesting far more
difficult than any outsider could appreciate. It was easy for the
United States Government to urge the United Kingdom to sell these
assets and securities, but far more difficult for the British Government

to market them at a reasonable price.[123]The gold reserves of the
British and their Allies were more accessible. A British
official historian summarizes the forthcoming demand: "It
was clear that the Americans would expect the United Kingdom
to use all the Allied gold upon which hands could be laid."[124]
But even here there were problems. Although the British
collaborated splendidly in the depletion of their gold reserves,
the supplies of her Allies posed a thornier problem. Only the
Czechs parted graciously with their reserves. Despite extensive
sacrifices and fervent explanations, some members of the
Administration were still unconvinced.[126]They believed that
the British had billions stashed away in secret hordes.[127]
But the British had done enough: they sacrificed what they
could and persuaded Morgenthau and Roosevelt that they could
do no more.

    b) The President's Case

The second stage in the battle for justification was the
President's presentation of Lend-Lease. It was delivered on
three separate occasions: at the press conference of December
17, 1940; during the fireside chat of December 29; and during
the State of the Union address of January 6, 1941.

The President returned from his Caribbean cruise aboard
the Tuscaloosa, during which, prompted by Churchill's December
8 letter, he developed the Lend-Lease program.[128]The thought
which Mr. Roosevelt lavished on this concept was evident by
the directness of his press conference. The President began
with a common sense argument, stressing the value of British
military orders for the buildup of American defense:

> ...I go back to the idea that the one thing necessary
> for American national defense is additional productive
> facilities; and the more we increase these facilities--

factories, shipbuilding ways, munitions plants, et cetera, and so on--the stronger American national defense is.[129]

Then he popped his solution for the British dollar crisis, tying it firmly with the national policy of the United States:

> It is possible...for the United States to take over British orders, and because they are essentially the same kind of munitions that we use ourselves, turn them into American orders. We have enough money to do it. And thereupon, as to such portion of them as the military events of the future determine to be right and proper for us to allow to go to the other side, either lease or sell the materials, subject to mortgage, to the people on the other side. That would be on the general theory that it may still prove true that the best defense of Great Britain is the best defense of the United States, and therefore that these materials would be more useful to the defense of the United States if they were used in Great Britain, than if they were kept in storage here.[130]

After declaring that he sought "to eliminate the dollar sign,"[131] the President illustrated, defined and defended his novel proposal by the use of a familiar homey image:

> Well, let me give you an illustration: Suppose my neighbor's home catches fire, and I have a length of garden hose four or five hundred feet away. If he can take my garden hose and connect it up with his hydrant, I may help him to put out his fire. Now, what do I do? I don't say to him before that operation, "Neighbor, my garden hose cost me $15; you have to pay me $15 for it." What is the transaction that goes on? I don't want $15--I want my garden hose back after the fire is over. All right. If it goes through the fire all right, intact, without any damage to it, he gives it back to me and thanks me very much for the use of it. But suppose it gets smashed up--holes in it--during the fire; we don't have to have too much formality about it, but I say to him, "I was glad to lend you that hose; I see I can't use it any more, it's all smashed up." He says, "How many feet of it were there?" I tell him, "There were 150 feet of it." He says, "All right, I will replace it." Now, if I get a nice garden hose back, I am in pretty good shape.[132]

Roosevelt had crystallized his case. Lend-Lease was represented as a friendly exchange between neighbors, a good will transaction which could be enacted with profit and honor for both.[133]

Having settled on a solution, Mr. Roosevelt proceeded to convert
the public. In his fireside chat on December 29, 1940, he made his
strongest appeal, his most cogent presentation. He began by invoking
the trinity summoned so frequently by the Administration to justify
its policy: national defense, the preservation of American values and
the maintenance of peace:

> This is not a fireside chat on war. It is a talk on national
> security; because the nub of the whole purpose of your Presi-
> dent is to keep you now and your children later, and your
> grandchildren much later, out of a last-ditch war for the
> preservation of American independence and all of the things
> that American independence means to you and to me and to ours.[134]

After delineating the master conspiracy of the Axis,[135] the President
stressed American military dependence upon the continued resistance of
the Allies: "...it is a matter of most vital concern to us that European
and Asiatic war-makers should not gain control of the oceans which lead
to this hemisphere.[136] Having established his initial premise, the defense
of Great Britain and her Allies as essential to American defense, the
President engaged in an historical exegesis of the Monroe Doctrine,
admitting that its successful application had been largely due to British
maritime supremacy.[137] This natural collaboration between American aims
and British policy would not be duplicated if Germany won the war:

> It is no exaggeration to say that all of us in the Americas
> would be living at the point of a gun--a gun loaded with
> explosive bullets, economic as well as military. We should
> enter upon a new and terrible era in which the whole world,
> our hemisphere included, would be run by threats of brute
> force. To survive in such a world, we would have to convert
> ourselves permanently into a militaristic power on a basis of
> war economy.[138]

Having conjured that fearful spectacle--the world converted to
totalitarianism and the United States subverted to militarism--the

President rejected the theory that the Atlantic and Pacific Oceans provided a wide belt of safety. He stressed the impact of modern technology over former barriers of time and distance.[139] He ridiculed a telegram which begged him not to alarm the nation; for "frankly and definitely there is danger ahead—danger against which we must prepare. But we well know that we cannot escape danger, or the fear of it, by crawling into bed and pulling the covers over our heads."[140]

Then the President discredited the complacency of the isolationists, citing the numerous violations of neutrality by Nazi Germany, excoriating the pious excuses given by the Nazi leaders for every new act of conquest.[141] He compared captive Belgium, used as a base of operations by the Germans against England, to the South American republics and the Azores. If victimized by the insatiable world gangster, these areas could be used as a platform for aggression against the United States.[142] Against such a foe, the wishful thinking of the isolationists provided no security:

> ...the vast resources and wealth of this hemisphere constitute the most tempting loot in all the world. Let us no longer blind ourselves to the undeniable fact that the evil forces which have crushed and undermined and corrupted so many others are already within our own gates.[143]

Then after denouncing the American isolationists,[144] ridiculing the possibility of a negotiated peace with Hitler,[145] and defining the New Order as "an unholy alliance of power and pelf to dominate and enslave the human race,"[146] President Roosevelt identified the British cause with the preservation of security and peace in the Western Hemisphere:

> Thinking in terms of today and tomorrow, I make the direct statement to the American people that there is far less chance of the United States getting into war if we do all we can now to support the nations defending themselves against attack by the Axis than if we acquiesce in their defeat, submit tamely to an Axis victory and wait our turn to be the object of attack

in another war later on....The people of Europe who are
defending themselves do not ask us to do their fighting.
They ask us for the implements of war, the planes, the
tanks, the guns, the freighters, which will enable them to
fight for their liberty and our security. Emphatically we
must get these weapons to them in sufficient volume and
quickly enough, so that we and our children will be saved
the agony and suffering which others have had to endure.[147]

The President then explained the need for the integration of Allied
[148]
war needs, thereby allowing the Administration to decide where to use
[149]
its ever mounting stocks of munitions "to defend this hemisphere."[150]

Finally, he swept on to his phraseological and thematic climax: "We

must be the great arsenal of democracy. For us this is an emergency as

serious as war itself. We must apply ourselves to our task with the

same resolution, the same sense of urgency, the same spirit of patriotism
[151]
and sacrifice, as we would show were we at war."

The last presentation of his Lend-Lease program was his State of

the Union Address, delivered before Congress on January 6, 1941. He

then reasserted in briefer terms the major arguments of his "arsenal

of democracy" speech, identifying the resistance of the anti-Axis forces
[152]
with the defense of the United States, asserting that Lend-Lease would

give Americans the flexibility to choose between those munitions which
[153]
they would reserve for themselves, and those which would be sent abroad,

exhorting all groups and interests to national unity and denying that
[154]
the program would be an act of war.

The President had carefully prepared his case and systematically

enunciated the major themes which colored the defense of Lend-Lease

throughout the public and political debate that preceded its enactment.

Astute politician, he appealed to all shades of American opinion except

to the intransigent isolationists. In a sense his speeches formed a

mirror, reflecting the contradictions of public opinion in the
winter of 1940-1941. They reflected mounting anxiety over
national security, a determination to help the British and a
continued fear of involvement. Although Roosevelt admitted
the risks and the mounting uncertainties of the future which
called for increasing sacrifice, he still assured his fellow
citizens that they could reconcile the demands of peace with
the needs of security. Lend-Lease was defended as involving
"the least risk now,"[155] as not "unneutral,"[156] as an action which
would spare Americans from "the agony and suffering of war
which others have had to endure."[157] The freedom of American
traditions, the security of the hemisphere, the peace of the
United States and the future peace of the world would be
preserved and extended. Even in his moment of greatest
decision, the President never forgot that he was a politician,
and that he could justify his policy only by reconciling the
incompatible demands of the public. Revolution became
conservation.

  c) The Administration's Case

Members of the Administration took their cue from the
President. The third stage of justification, the presentation
of the Administration's case before Congress, was orchestrated
by the members of the cabinet who elaborated on the President's
arguments, substantiating his case.

Procedure was carefully planned and the strategy of
presentation governed by a division of tasks among several
members of the Administration. Mr. Hull would define the
current crisis, linking American and British interests.
Mr. Morgenthau would dwell on Britain's financial plight,

emphasizing its desperateness. Mr. Stimson would defend the
measure as necessary for the American defense establishment,
reconciling previously conflicting demands of separate
procurement services; Mr. Knox would dwell on the role of the
British Fleet in maintaining American security. In every case,
Administration spokesmen would reconcile the demands of security
with the maintenance of peace.

The Secretary of State delivered "unexpectedly strong and
positive testimony."[158] After recapitulating the march of aggression
in the Far East and Europe and recounting American peace moves
the Secretary stressed the unique nature of the present conflict:

> ...it has become increasingly apparent that mankind
> is today face to face...with an organized, ruthless
> and implacable movement of steadily expanding conquest.
> We are in the presence of forces which are not restrained
> by considerations of law or principles of morality;
> which have fixed no limits for their program of conquest;
> which have spread over large areas on land and are
> desperately struggling now to seize control of the
> oceans as an essential means of achieving and main-
> taining their conquest of the other continents. Control
> of the high seas by law-abiding nations is the key
> to the security of the Western Hemisphere in the
> present-day world situation.[159]

Anticipating the isolationist argument that the Atlantic
provides an insulating wall protecting the New World from the
predators of the Old, the Secretary naturally and automatically
linked the defense of Britain with the security of the United
States, warning of the serious consequences which would ensue if
England should fall.[160] He prophesied that the Axis would
concentrate on the vulnerable regions of the Western Hemisphere,
undermining security from within before attacking.[161] This
effort would be reinforced considerably "if control of
the high seas were to pass into the hands of the would-be
attackers."[162] Obviously, passive resistance would

offer no protection, so the only alternative was aggressive "self-defense." [163]

As long as the Axis flouted the rules of international law, its chosen

victims could not adhere rigidly to established codes. [164] The Secretary

ended his prepared statement with an endorsement of Lend-Lease:

> The great problem of democracy is to organize and to use its
> strength with sufficient speed and completeness. The proposed
> legislation is an essential measure for that purpose. This
> bill will make it possible for us to allocate our resources
> in ways best calculated to provide for the security of this
> Nation and of this continent in the complex and many-sided
> conditions of danger with which we are, and are likely to
> be confronted. Above all, it will enable us to do all these
> things in the speediest possible manner. And, overwhelmingly,
> speed is our greatest need today.[165]

The next witness was the Secretary of the Treasury. Morgenthau

concentrated on the financial aspects, presenting the British justifica-

tion for Lend-Lease in statistical detail. Submitting extensive tables,

clearly revealing the dollar crisis and projecting a $1464 million deficit

by the end of 1941, he summed up England's tremendus financial contribu- [166]

tion to the war: "the British people are not only dodging the bombs and

fighting for their existence, but...are also making a stupendous effort

to pay for this war by themselves." [167] When questioned on British assets,

he consistently reiterated and reformulated his answer that the British

could not afford to liquidate any more of their assets: "they just have [168]

not got it." [169]

The third Administration witness, Secretary of War, Henry L. Stimson,

contrasted the present emergency with the 1917 crisis, stressing the

immeasurably greater dangers of the present:

> ...let me point out how much more acute is the present
> emergency and how much more dangerous is the situation of
> our own country with reference to the time element in the
> production of munitions of defense than it was in 1917....
> Then...there was a stable front line in France, safely held
> by the Allies against Germany. Italy and Japan were arrayed
> against Germany on the side of Britain and France. The

> British, French, Italian and Japanese fleets were in
> practically complete control of all of the oceans of the world.
> Today Italy and Japan are members of the German axis. France
> is conquered and her fleet is incapable of opposing the Central
> Powers. The British fleet today stands alone as an obstacle to
> German control of the Atlantic.[170]

Related to this critical strategic situation was the dangerous munitions

status of the United States. She could no longer depend on those arsenals

which had produced for her in the previous crisis. Now they were providing

for Germany and her allies. So the task of outproducing the Axis was now

far more formidable.[171] Having set the overall framework for his presentation,

the Secretary of War concentrated on the procurement benefits of Lend-Lease.

Substituting a single purchasing system for a multitude of competing

claimants, centralizing authority in the hands of the President, it

would allow the Administration to use American production in a flexible

manner:

> ...I feel that the proposed bill is a forthright and clear
> grant of power which will enable the President to place in
> operation the best and simplest plan to carry out a national
> policy many times stated and endorsed. It substantially
> assists us in the job of caring for our own needs and the
> needs of those whose defense is a matter of vital importance
> to us. But it leaves in our hands the power to determine at
> the time when the munitions are completed the country which
> shall receive them, and thus to insure that this vital
> decision is made solely in the interest of the defense of the
> United States.[172]

The fourth witness, Secretary of the Navy, Frank Knox, concentrated

his case on the implied maritime and diplomatic dependence of the United

States on Great Britain. Historically the two powers had implicitly

collaborated in confining aggression to the Old World and in maintaining

the inviolability of the Atlantic and Pacific.[173] Inevitably the new

European tyrants would turn their attention and designs towards America:

> Like all its predecessors, the Nazi regime has found that the
> power of its armies alone cannot establish that rule, because
> Europe is not self-supporting in raw materials, and the Nazi
> armies are powerless to obtain these materials unless they have
> control of the seas.[174]

Reminding his listeners that Great Britain had preserved her indepen-

dence by controlling the narrow seas and vanquished aggressor nations

by cutting them off from sources of raw materials, the Secretary expounded

the lesson of history and naval power:

> The struggle now going on is, fundamentally, an attempt by
> Germany to seize control of the sea from Great Britain. That
> is the reason why, from a military viewpoint, the war has so
> vital an interest to the United States. Our nation has evolved
> without particular hindrance from Britain's control of a large
> part of the sea. But I believe it would be very different
> were control to pass to Germany, and were she able to send her
> armies into other parts of the world, and there lay tribute of
> raw materials for further building up her powers of oppression.[175]

Then, predicting that Nazi control of the Atlantic would mean the rapid

establishment of Axis power in Latin America, he declared that the

British fleet "holds the Nazis in Europe."[176]

The Administration's case had been presented and defined by the four

key cabinet members.[177] The justification for Lend-Lease lay basically in

the unprecedented nature of the Axis threat. Totally chaotic and immoral,

it knew no respect for the rules of international law and morality. There-

fore, the rules and distinctions of the calmer, more reasonable age, which

had produced the orthodox concepts of neutrality, were useless. By

setting aside literal neutrality, she could possibly save and salvage

those very ideals which neutrality sought to conserve from the ravages

of conquest, war and tyranny: security, peace, and freedom.

Unprepared, confronted with an unprecedented danger, the United

States should service and supply the foes of totalitarian oppression

throughout the world: the British, the Greeks, and the Chinese. Their struggle was America's. It not only preserved the United States from inevitable attack, but gave her time to rearm. Once their means were exhausted, America should share and shoulder the burden of battle by furnishing munitions and a flow of production. This in turn would increase national preparedness and strengthen military potential.

d) The Congressional Debate.

The case was prepared, witnesses selected, and the jury was still deliberating. The final stage of justification was enacted in the halls of Congress, newspaper offices, coffee shops, bar rooms, and drug stores of the nation. Each side summoned its tally of respectable experts: lawyers, diplomats, educators, aviators. Each side orated and roared, quoted and prophesied, gesticulated and articulated its opinions, its commitments and its prejudices. Each side exaggerated its case, seeing either salvation or disaster in the passage of H.R. 1776. Neither was totally honest; neither totally prescient.

A close coverage of the Congressional passage of Lend-Lease illustrates the major arguments of the legislative belligerents, charges and counter-charges echoing throughout the nation.[178] After summoning its quota of experts and prophets, the House Committee on Foreign affairs released H.R. 1776.[179] It submitted a majority report favoring Lend-Lease, and a minority view condemning it.[180] The former began by defining the foreign policy of the United States:

> From these hearings and the public discussion and debate on the bill, it has been clear to your committee that our national policy is and should be: (a) To keep out of war; and (b) for our own national security, to aid Britain and those other nations

> whose defense is vital to the defense of the United States by
> supplying them as quickly and as efficiently as possible with
> defense articles in a manner consistent with our democratic
> procedures.[181]

The Majority Report then declared that Lend-Lease perfectly guarded and
maintained American objectives: "the probable effect of the bill will be
to keep us out of war rather than to get us into it."[182]

The Minority Report, presented by Hamilton Fish, supported aid to
England but bitterly opposed Lend-Lease. It denounced its "dictatorial"[183]
implications and denied that America was in danger of attack by any power.
It also rejected the frequent comparison between central Europe and the
United States , climaxing its dissent with an uncompromising denunciation:

> Under this bill we surrender our democratic way of life now,
> for fear of a future threat to our democratic way of life.
> The oldest and the last constitutional democracy surrenders
> its freedom under the pretext of avoiding war, with the
> probable result that the newest dictatorship will soon go
> to war.[184]

The Senate Majority Report closely paralleled the House's in
reasoning and presentation, in definition and assumption. But there
was one major difference. Whereas the House report had merely defined
present United States policy, the Senate defined our foreign policy in
immutable terms, conferring upon recent definitions the sanctification
of tradition.[185]

The Minority opinion, presented by Senator Johnson of California,
quickly challenged the assumptions and conclusions of the majority. It
denounced Lend-Lease as a bill which neither provided additional aid
for Britain nor increased the defense status of the United States.[186]
It was castigated as a disguised attempt of the President to grab
tremendous power: "It makes the Chief Executive a dictator and worse,

a dictator with power to take us into war."[187] The proposed legislation
would transfer the war-making powers of the Congress to the President,[188]
allowing him to identify and define aggressor nations,[189] committing the
United States to a predetermined route: "For once embarked on a course
it will be necessary for the people to follow through."[190]

Released from the Senate and House Committees, Lend-Lease was now
presented to Congress. The debate on the floor followed the set arguments
of the Majority and Minority Reports of the two houses. But it was far
more colorful. Skillful and time-consuming oratory from both sides
replaced the business-like assesments of the committees. The bill's
supporters reiterated the trinity of arguments favoring the passage of
the bill: freedom, defense, peace. Their emphasis, however, was not
totally consistent. Some Congressmen merely parroted the Administration
line; others recognized that the United States was drawing close to the
time of choice when she would have to choose either intervention or
neutrality.

The sponsor of the bill in the House of Representatives, John W.
McCormack, stuck fairly close to the Administration line:

> In the face of a greater danger--destruction in all probability--
> we are compelled then to react in a contrary direction to what
> our natural instincts prompt us to do. That is why there are
> two aspects involved, one of which is to keep the country out
> of war--that is the easiest thing we have to do. All we have
> to do is nothing, but if we do nothing, does your judgment tell
> you that we are keeping war from our shores later? In order
> to keep our country out of war, as I see it, in the face of
> the imminent danger that confronts us, to prevent that danger
> from becoming actual we have to take affirmative steps of some
> kind to prevent the war later coming to our shores.[191]

In the Senate the most eloquent supporter of Lend-Lease was also its
sponsor, Senator Alben Barkley of Kentucky. When he introduced the measure

on the floor of the Senate for debate, on February 17, 1941, he began

by citing the determination of the American nation to preserve its

freedom and neutrality, intimating, however, that the people of the

United States would never choose peace over freedom.[192] He then spelled

out the meaning of totalitarianism and the nature of the enemy, conjuring

the nightmare of a Nazi triumph:

> It is a war of ideas, a war of philosophies, a war to impose
> upon the world a system of moral, economic, and political
> control to which it has never been subjected in all its history.
> These controls are diametrically opposed to the theory of free-
> dom and democracy. They are opposed to the doctrine of self-
> government. They are avowedly antagonistic to Christianity
> or any other form of religion except the worship of the state;
> the state to be under the autocratic domination of authoritarian
> theories and actions which deny the people any voice in their
> government or their society....It is impossible to have
> intellectual freedom where the soul of man is enslaved. It
> is impossible to have economic freedom where the political
> rights of man are trampled under foot.
> Can there be any doubt of the intention of Hitler to impose
> this revolting system upon the whole world, including the
> United States? [193]

After outlining Hitler's repeated violations of neutrality in almost

rhythmic prose, he swept on to his conclusion: "If Hitler should win,

we will face...not only a hostile Germany, but a hostile world."[194]

If the Administration spokesmen agily reconciled the claims of

self-defense with the maintenance of peace, other Congressmen and

Senators were franker and clearer about the necessity for choice.

Senator Claude Pepper of Florida felt that the alternatives were

unmistakable:

> ...we have had to come to the decision that one or the other
> shall live, totalitarianism or democracy, tyranny or freedom,
> and that it is as impossible for the two to live in the same
> world as it is for darkness and light to inhabit the same
> space at the same time....America will not let England fall

to Hitler. If the action now proposed will not save England, we will save it anyway. Watch American opinion, and see if what I say is not true.[195]

But even he defined Lend-Lease as "the only way possible to stay out of war."[196]

The opponents of the bill attacked it as a sinister measure designed to destroy republican freedoms, to create a Roosevelt dictatorship and to lead us into war. Opinions varied considerably, running from the avid rejection of the avowed Anglo-phobes to the milder opposition of Congressmen who supported England but preferred other measures. But the opposition was united in its fear that the enactment of Lend-Lease would yield unprecedented power to the President.[197]

The most thorough and windy denunciation came from Senator Nye, arch investigator of imaginary conspiracies. In speech after speech, he challenged and attacked the assumptions of Lend-Lease. Two particularly honored arguments attracted his special scorn. He challenged the belief that 1) there was a distinct difference, morally and politically, between the British and the Germans; and that 2) the United States was in danger of attack and invasion from a victorious Germany.

His hatred for President Roosevelt was only matched by his detestation of the English. In one blistering speech after another, he denounced the iniquities of Britain's past, cataloging the massacres, injustices, and oppressions of the British system,[198] quoting Churchill against Churchill,[199] until the uninformed would swear that the horrors of Nazi Germany were kindergarten games compared to the excrescent record of the British Empire. To him there was no valid distinction, no difference in value, between the two belligerents. He summarized it: "...we encounter this awful hatred towards the aggressor, and the feeling that we must help stop the aggressor. As our ally in this stupendous course we choose the most aggressive aggressor the world has ever known, Great Britain."[200]

But the Senator's scorn also targeted on the invasion hypothesis which he categorically condemned as a fabrication, "a bogey".[201] Having comfortably disposed of present fears and future dangers, Senator Nye quickly dismissed the assumption that a German victory would threaten either the security or interests of the United States.[202]

The legislative contestants had, therefore, drawn their battle for justification or condemnation around the long-range implications and effects of the enactment of Lend-Lease. Its supporters, like the Administration and its spokesmen, had insisted that the Bill would defend and extend America's freedom, secure the Western Hemisphere, and maintain peace. Its most vigorous opponents had insisted, with equal vigor and emphasis, that it would decree the end of all treasured American values, erecting a dictatorship which would lead us inevitably and immediately into war. The product of a sinister mind, Lend-Lease did not answer either the needs of America's defense--for the "danger" of invasion was mere fraud--or the need to aid England--which could be met fairly well by lesser measures.

The passage of the Bill was not secured merely by the use of justifying arguments, but was attained through legislative compromise, the President's willingness to relinquish some powers originally sought, and his agreement to limit some of its provisions.[203]

5. The Implications of Lend-Lease.

The implications of Lend-Lease went far beyond all the articulated
arguments of its supporters. For emphasis fell largely upon the conserv-
ing aspects of the Bill, not upon its revolutionary impact. It was
mainly represented as a measure designed to save the future by preserving
the past. Its ultimate impact, however, was to usher in an entirely
new world, an entirely new destiny for the United States. We can
now see its effects stretching through World War II, leading ultimately
to full-scale involvement in international affairs. We can see the
Marshall Plan, Point Four and the innumerable foreign aid programs of
the post-war decade as the natural heirs of Lend-Lease.

Hindsight always uncovers implications hidden to the most astute
contemporary. However, the revolutionary nature of Lend-Lease was recognized by some of its supporters. Particularly prescient were the
interventionist cabinet members: Stimson, Knox and Morgenthau. On
December 1, 1940, the Secretary of the Treasury outlined the problems
of the British economy to his fellow interventionists. Secretary Knox
turning to Morgenthau, drew the obvious conclusion: "'We are going to
pay for the war from now on, are we?'"[204] With the passage of Lend-Lease,
therefore, the United States underwrote Allied victory. She would pay
everything required for the defeat of the Axis. As Stimson summarized,
Lend-Lease was a "'declaration of economic war.'"[205]

The economic implications of Lend-Lease entailed political
consequences of even greater force. If the fall of Britain still
seemed imminent and inevitable, logic would dictate and necessitate
further steps towards intervention. The enactment of the Bill meant

commitment to the survival of England.[206]

Perhaps nothing emphasized this implication more clearly than the issue so frequently cited and discussed during the Lend-Lease debate, escort of convoy to the British Isles. The opposition leaders were fast to grasp the connection. As Representative Usher Burdick of North Dakota noted:

> All-out aid to Britain may mean anything. To sell her supplies is one thing--that we are doing now--...to sell her supplies and convoy them to England is another thing; to have these convoys sunk by German submarines and mines is another thing; to have actual war is the last thing. But the first thing and the last thing are in close proximity--the last thing is inevitable from the first thing.[207]

Two champions of Lend-Lease, Stimson and Knox, were fairly clear on the implications and desirability of convoying. Even before the President proposed his program, the Secretary of War had deduced its necessity. To him the logic and its conclusions were clear. To save England, the United States must secure the North Atlantic lifeline leading from the Western Hemisphere to the British Isles. As Stimson summarized, England must be saved by "assistance from us by convoy in the Atlantic."[208] But Roosevelt was not as adamant, fearing any direct confrontation with Congress over this question.[209]

Secretary of the Navy, Frank Knox, apparently agreed with Stimson,[210] but was publicly more cautious.[211] When questioned by the Senate Foreign Relations Committee on the desirability and the meaning of any convoy action, he opposed its adoption.[212] And when Senator Nye pressed him by asking "You look upon it as an act of war?" the Secretary confessed it was "substantially" that.[213] He merely added that he would obey if the President ordered him to carry out convoying.[214]

Although Roosevelt never formally and fully adopted escort of convoy, a measure requiring specific Congressional approval, [215] he enacted it informally and partially, sufficiently to aid the British in their struggle with the German U-boat. The redefinition and extension of the Western Hemisphere to the mid-ocean point, [216] the adoption of patrolling measures which allowed the United States Navy to report the presence of German submarines to the British, [217] the practice of trans-Atlantic hitch-hiking by belligerent merchant ships--[218] these measures were all significant substitutes for full-scale convoy. For the passage of Lend-Lease had implicitly committed the United States to supply and deliver munitions. If these partial measures had failed, the President would inevitably have turned to full and complete adoption of escort-of-convoy. [219]

With the passage of Lend-Lease, the battle over justification reached its decisive turn. The United States had moved towards full-scale intervention by a declaration of economic war against Nazi Germany. Overcoming the antipathy of the American public against a peacetime draft and foreign aid, the Roosevelt administration had effectively undercut the foundations of isolationism. Throughout the debates of the prewar period, however, revolutionary changes of policy and practice had been justified by consistently conservative arguments. The Roosevelt administration had repeatedly reinforced its case by solemnly declaring that every move strengthened American defense, preserved the peace and reinforced tradition. But each step moved in the opposite direction. Selective Service, the destroyer deal and Lend-Lease broke long sanctified traditions and directed the United States closer to intervention and war. Appealing to the past, the President evoked the forces of the future.

Chapter XI

The Seeds of the Crusade

1. The Automatic Transition

The transition from the just war to the crusade--automatic, immediate and almost unconscious--was a reflex action. The foundations and premises of both doctrines were established long before the Japanese attack on Pearl Harbor, and were initially the same. Specific acts of aggression were mere symptoms of the deeper disease: the nature of totalitarianism. Since the existence of aggressive, totalitarian systems constituted a threat to American security, the only solution and ultimate protection was their defeat and destruction. Strategically, defensive needs could only be secured by a full-scale offensive against their power centers. Morally, the righteous war could only be justified by the destruction of the aggressor's system and the eradication of his ideology.

The American crusade found two prominent forms: the demand for total victory and the decision to conduct a direct assault against the enemy's industrial and military potential, "unconditional surrender" and the massive use of air power against "civilian" objectives. Although their implications were clearly foreseeable, these two pursuits, so dominant during the Second World War were mere tendencies in the prewar years.

a. The Genesis of Total Victory: No Negotiated Peace

1) "You Can't Do Business with Hitler"

The isolationist case against Lend-Lease was partly based on the belief that the best solution to the European conflict was a negotiated settlement yielding victory to neither side. Colonel Lindbergh, in his testimony before the House Committee on Foreign Affairs, emphasized the advantages of an impartial, balanced peace: "a complete victory on either side would result in prostration in Europe such as we have never seen."[1] His conviction, maintained with considerable courage and stubborness, was based primarily upon his assessment of American strategic strength and his evaluation of new weapons, especially air power. The colonel did not believe that total triumph over the Axis powers was possible. Even the intervention of the United States would not insure the one operation essential to victory: a successful invasion of the continent. Air power was supremely a defensive weapon, and its utilization by the Axis powers would frustrate all massive land offensives by the Allies.[2] It was also an impartial one, giving immunity to the enemy as well as to the Americans.[3] Since total solutions were neither desirable nor possible, a negotiated settlement was preferable and inevitable.

Actually, Lindbergh's defense of a negotiated peace was in reply to President Roosevelt's earlier denunciation. In his December 29, 1940, fireside address, the President had clearly condemned any negotiated settlement with the Nazis. The history of appeasement proved the futility of such a solution. The burden of Roosevelt's message could be epitomized by the popular phrase of the time: "You can't do business with Hitler.":

> The experience of the past two years has proven beyond doubt that no nation can appease the Nazis. No man can tame a tiger into a kitten by stroking it. There can be no appeasement with ruthlessness. There can be no reasoning with an incendiary bomb. We know now that a nation can have peace with the Nazis only at the price of total surrender....The American appeasers ignore the warning to be found in the fate of Austria, Czechoslovakia, Poland, Norway, Belgium, the Netherlands, Denmark, and France. They tell you that the Axis powers are going to win anyway; that all this bloodshed in the world could be saved; and that the United States might just as well throw its influence into the scale of a dictated peace, and get the best out of it that we can.
> They call it a "negotiated peace". Nonsense! Is it a

> negotiated peace if a gang of outlaws surrounds your
> community and on threat of extermination makes you pay
> tribute to save your own skins? Such a dictated peace
> would be no peace at all. It would be only another
> armistice, leading to the most gigantic armament race and
> the most devastating trade wars in history. And in these
> contests the Americas would offer the only real resistance
> to the Axis powers.[4]

Here was the logic for the President's early opposition to a negotiated

peace: since it was merely another act of appeasement, it could bring

no permanent peace to the world. Most crucially, a negotiated settlement

would favor the Nazi camp, leaving them with only one major opponent on

the world scene: America. Negotiated peace, appeasement, armistice,

Nazi victory: one formula captured and combined these elements into a

single whole.

All traditional explanations of the "unconditional surrender" policy

have emphasized Roosevelt's determination not to repeat Woodrow Wilson's

"mistake" at the end of World War I. When Wilson received the German

Government's bid for a settlement based on the "fourteen points", he

ostensibly accepted a negotiated peace hedged with preconditions protecting

the Germans against a Carthaginian end. But the Versailles Conference

produced a treaty far harsher than they expected. Disillusioned and

disgusted, they felt that they had been tricked into laying down their

arms long before they were militarily beaten. Wilson's decision gave

the Germans an alibi for defeat, and ultimately an excuse for new

aggressions, conquests, and campaigns. According to Sherwood, Wilson's

"mistake" haunted Roosevelt:

> The tragedy of Wilson was always somewhere within the rim of
> his consciousness. Roosevelt could never forget Wilson's
> mistakes, which had been made with the noblest will in the
> world, impelled by the purest concept of the Christian ethic.
> Wilson had advocated "peace without victory," he had produced

the Fourteen Points as a basis on which Germany could surrender honorably. The violation of these principles had plagued the postwar world, had led to the rise of Hitler and a Second World War, and there was no motivating force in all of Roosevelt's wartime political policy stronger than the determination to prevent repetition of the same mistakes.[5]

Although Sherwood's passage suffers from a number of historical errors, especially on the original purpose of the Fourteen Points, it clearly depicts Roosevelt's attitude. The President's position, however, was not simply derived from this single cause. Its development and motivations, as Sherwood acknowledges, were far more complex than usually assumed. Moreover, his position was inextricably interwoven with the Allied attitude towards a peace settlement with the German Government.

a) The Fear of Another Munich

According to Sherwood, Roosevelt's major fear at the beginning of the Second World War was that the Allies would quickly tire and negotiate "another Munich,"[6] a fear deepened by Hitler's attempts to settle the war immediately after the fall of Poland. Roosevelt felt that Hitler desired peace only because of the substantial advantages it offered:

(1) It would further strengthen his position in Germany, providing conclusive proof to the German people that he could hoodwink Britain and France into selling another small country into slavery (in this case Poland) rather than risk actual war.
(2) It would give Germany time to consolidate her gains in Czechoslovakia and Poland and further to increase her rearmament, particularly in the building of submarines, airplanes and the Siegfried Line.
(3) It would tend to push public sentiment in Britain and France--and most of all in the United States--back into the peacetime isolationist ruts, and thereby retard if not nullify all efforts in the democracies to prepare for war.
(4) It would convince the Russians--and the Japanese--that the Western democracies were completely spineless and decadent, as Hitler and Mussolini had so lond and so loudly proclaimed them to be.[7]

During the opening months of the war, The President was already opposed to any settlement short of an Allied victory.

b) The Welles Mission

Surprisingly, Roosevelt temporarily modified his attitude in the early months of 1940, on the eve of the great German offensive in the West. He then sent Undersecretary of State Sumner Welles on a quiet peace mission to the capitals of Europe.[8] But his assignment was severly conditioned and limited by circumstances and instructions.

While briefing Welles, the President clearly revealed why he no longer opposed Allied negotiations with Hitler's regime:

> ...he had been asking himself whether there still remained any step which he...could take to avert the dangers that would so clearly confront the people of this country, as well as of the civilized world, if the European war continued. It seemed to him that, if the long-expected all-out offensive by Germany upon the Western powers should take place, the results of the war would be unpredictable. With its continuation there would be ever greater danger that the United States would be involved. Even though by some miracle that might be avoided, one of two major dangers would be inevitable. The first: a victory by Hitler would immediately imperil the vital interests of the United States. The other: an eventual victory of the Western powers could probably be won only after a long and desperately fought contest which would bring Europe to total economic and social collapse, with disastrous effects upon the American people.[9]

Obviously, the President feared a quick German victory. Reports from Ambassadors Bullitt in Paris and Kennedy in London were deeply pessimistic in tone and theme, stressing the deplorable morale and military weaknesses of the Allied powers.[10] While those from the United States Consul General in Berlin, Raymond Geist, emphasized Germany's determination and military strength, stressing the unity between the Fuehrer and the German people.[11] A quick German victory seemed, therefore, increasingly probably; and would immediately threaten the security of the United States, overthrowing the last barriers between Germany and the Western Hemisphere. Sensing that the Allies were totally

unprepared to meet the expected offensive in the West, the

President felt "that a peace negotiated with Hitler was at

least preferable to a peace dictated by him."[12]

However, despite his preference, the President hedged the

Welles mission with restrictive conditions. The Undersecretary

of State was neither a negotiator nor an initiator since he

"would offer no proposals and no suggestions."[13] Instead he

would canvass opinion in Rome, Berlin, Paris and London, seeking

official views on a "just and permanent peace."[14] The President

made his position immediately clear: he wanted no armistice

which would inevitably lead to a renewal of hostilities.[15]

The United States could not be committed to mediation or

negotiation, and certainly not to intervention. Welles' mission,

therefore, was foredomed. According to Welles, even the

President realized its hopelessness:

> The President...had been canvassing the possibilities
> still open to him. He admitted frankly that the
> chances seemed to him about one in a thousand that
> anything at all could be done to change the course
> of events. On the other hand, he felt that no
> possibility, however remote and however improbable,
> should be overlooked. He believed that his
> obligations to the American people made it imperative
> of him to leave no stone unturned.[16]

The Welles mission maintained this quality of unreality

throughout its course. It was a mission without a mission,

an attempt to initiate negotiations without negotiating,

to induce mediation without mediating.

It was, however, a revealing mission. Fortunately for us,

the Undersecretary wrote an articulate and witty report

which, rich in its detail and diplomatic insights,

presents snapshot views of the European leaders and their opinions on
war and peace in the twilight months of the phony war. It also clearly shows
the complete imcompatability of Allied and Axis views, revealing that the
opportunity for a negotiated settlement did not exist even in the early 1940
months.[17]

Welles discovered that there were two interrelated, but not identical
issues dividing the belligerents: territory and security. The nexus of
the problem was that the first issue could not be settled independently
from the second. At first the territorial issue seemed solvable. The
stated demands of the Fuehrer were deceptively "moderate", not totally
incompatible with the Allied terms. Even the differences were not
irreconcilable if the desire for compromise existed.

Hitler's definition of terms seemed "moderate." There was enough
logic for a sincere or naive observer to see a reasonable chance of a
settlement with Germany if, following the conclusion of the agreement,
the Axis willingly remained satisfied and glutted with present glory.
Hitler fully outlined his aims to Sumner Welles. There were, however,
certain clear indications that the settlement would be far more than a
territorial adjustment. Still a well-wishing observer might find enough
ground for settlement, dismissing all other intimations as inconsequential:

> Hitler then said that Germany's aims and objectives were
> simple and that he would outline them to me; he would classify
> them as (a) historical, (b) political and (c) economic.
> From the historical aspect Germany had existed as an empire
> five hundred years before Columbus had discovered the western
> world. The German people had every right to demand that their
> historical position of a thousand years should be restored
> to them; Germany had no ambition and no aim other than the
> return by the German people to the territorial position which
> was historically theirs.
> Germany's political aims were coordinate. Germany could not
> tolerate the existence of a State such as Czechoslovakia

which constituted an enclave created by Versailles solely for
strategic reasons. No great power could exist under such
conditions. Germany did not desire to dominate non-German
peoples, and it such peoples adjacent to German boundaries
did not constitute a military or political threat to the
German people, Germany had no desire permanently to destroy,
nor to prejudice, the independent lives of such peoples.
From the economic standpoint, Germany must claim the right
to profit to the fullest extent through trade with the
nations close to her in Central and Southeastern Europe.
She would no longer permit that the western powers of Europe
infringe or impair Germany's preferential situation in this
regard.
In brief, the German people intended to maintain the unity
which he had now achieved for them; they intended to prevent
any State on Germany's eastern frontier from constituting again
a military or strategic threat against German security and,
finally, Germany intended to obtain recognition for her
economic priority in Eastern and Southeastern Europe.
Germany, further, would insist that the colonies stolen from
her at Versailles be returned to her. Germany had not
obtained these colonies through military conquest; she had
obtained them through purchase or through pacific negotiation;
she had never utilized her colonies for military purposes.
She now required them in order to obtain for the German
people raw materials which could not be produced in Germany,
and as a field for German emigration. Such a demand, Hitler
felt, was not only reasonable, but just.[18]

Self-determination, national security, restoration of lost property,

natural resources: what could be more reasonable? What could be more

honorable? Even the provisions dealing with the establishment of a

German sphere of influence in Central and Southeastern Europe were

understandable. Germany, like the United States, England and France,

wanted her place in the sun, a place she naturally deserved since she

was a great power.

To the innocent observer, therefore, there appeared to be some

hope for reaching a sensible agreement. And this conviction would be

strengthened by travel to Paris and London. The French held a highly

reasonable view of the peace settlement, one which could be reconciled

to Hitler's claims. Mr. Daladier, the French Prime Minister, was willing

to concede partial justice to the German claims. He summarized his
theory for Sumner Welles:

> ...obviously neither France nor England could agree...to any
> peace which did not provide for the restoration of an independent
> Poland and for the independence of the Czech people....German
> peoples of Central Europe should live under German rule, pro-
> vided they so desired. The City of Danzig was clearly a German
> city, and...the Germans of the Sudetenland or of Western Poland
> should be afforded the opportunity of uniting with the Reich if
> they so desired. That...had been his point of view at the time
> of the Munich Agreement.[19]

The French Prime Minister assured the American Undersecretary that "he
did not believe that political or territorial adjustments would create
any insuperable difficulty in reaching peace."[20]

Even in London, where morale and determination were far stiffer,
territorial questions posed no insuperable obstacle to the Chamberlain
Government. Although there were conflicting attitudes from such men
as Winston Churchill and Sir Dudley Pound, Mr. Chamberlain was the spokes-
man for England, and his position was reasonable and reconcilable, his
conditions similar to Daladier's. It was apparent that a territorial
peace posed no genuine difficulty.

Sumner Welles immediately saw that these issues were merely
symptomatic and superficial. Inextricably and interminably, they were
linked to the real problem: security. In the long conversations which
he conducted with the heads of the Great European states, the two issues
were often indistinguishable. Therefore, his diagnosis was emphatic:

> The basic problem...is the problem of security, inseparably
> linked to the problem of disarmament. I believe there is a
> slight chance for the negotiation of a lasting peace if the
> attack for peace is made upon the issue of security. If the
> great powers of Europe--even exclusive of Russia--could be
> shown a practical means of obtaining security and disarmament,
> neither the political peace required, nor the essential economic
> basis for a real peace, would, in my judgment, offer any insuper-
> able obstacles.[21]

But there was no remaining chance for peace in early 1940: the sense
of security was already shattered. Welles could diagnose the disease,
but could not suggest any viable cure.

The last attempt to define and hold security had shattered with
the failure of the Munich pact. The awakening aftermath had destroyed
any hope or trust that the Allied nations held in Hitler's word, reason-
ableness or moderation.[22] Now the mask was off, and the conqueror's
devouring hunger was horribly apparent.[23] If Hitler's future plans were
boundless, no assurances would be binding or territorial settlements final.
Any agreement would be merely another armistice.[24]

The Allied leaders did not forecast or foretell the exact pattern
of Hitler's schemes of expansion. But after their experiences at Munich
they grasped its essential dynamism. They knew they were confronted
not with a conservative statesman with reasonable appetites, but by a
revolutionary expansionist; not by Bismarck, but by Genghis Khan. With
this type of man and program there could be no security, no negotiation.

There was no feasable alternative to Adolf Hitler's dictatorial
rule over Germany. As Wells concluded, the nation was fatally imprisoned
by its common illusions: "The German people are living a life which
seems the existence of people on another planet. To them lies have
become truth; evil, good; and aggression, self-defense."[25] The
attainment of security was, therefore, impossible as long as the Fuhrer
reigned.[26] And since he had convinced his people that their existence
depended upon him, his overthrow was unlikely. The hope for a negotiated
settlement did not die during the spring offensive of 1940, but had
already disappeared in the disillusioning aftermath of Munich.

The Welles mission was crucial in several respects. It was the President's only attempt, however tentative and conditional, to encourage a negotiated settlement. Although it ended in total failure, it clearly established the impossibility of achieving any solution with the Nazi leadership. Moreover, it confirmed the President in his previous conviction: Europe could never achieve permanent stability while Germany remained powerful. The only solution was the destruction of Hitler's regime and the defeat of the German nation. The initial emphasis on total victory originated with the Western Allies, not with Roosevelt; for they were already convinced that it was absolutely imperative. Lord Halifax summarized the situation to Welles:

> ...no lasting peace could be made in Europe so long as the Nazi regime dominated Germany, and controlled German policy. Peace could not be made except on the basis of confidence, and what confidence could be placed in the plighted word of a Government that was pursuing a policy of open and brutal aggression, and that had repeatedly and openly violated its solemn contractural obligations?[27]

Roosevelt inherited this problem and its irresolvable nature from the Allies. In Halifax's rhetorical question, lay the genesis of unconditional surrender.

In his first speech as Prime Minister, Mr. Churchill defined his aim as "victory at all costs."[28] There was no longer any talk of compromise or of possible, though improbable, settlements. The British were struggling for self-preservation, waging their war of survival. Now no terrible resolution was possible. Hitler was not only totally unreliable; he was also too powerful and successful. The totality of his triumph insured the rejection of his peace bid to the English at the end of the Battle of France.[29]

2) The Hopelessness of Hope.

The failure of the Welles mission and the fall of France ended the slight hope that had governed Roosevelt's single, ambiguous peace effort. He quickly returned to his former conviction that any negotiated settlement was impossible. An armistice would now give a strong Germany an even greater chance to gather and consolidate her strength for further wars.

Underlying, reinforcing and perhaps preceding the President's political logic was his moral antipathy against Naziism. In his Labor Day speech delivered on September 1, 1941, he based his rejection of a negotiated settlement on a moral imperative:

> I give solemn warning to those who think that Hitler has been blocked and halted, that they are making a very dangerous assumption. When in any war your enemy seems to be making slower progress than he did the year before, that is the very moment to strike with redoubled force--to throw more energy into the job of defeating him--to end for all time the menace of world conquest and thereby end all talk or thought of any peace founded on a compromise with evil itself.[30]

Did the conclusions of the Welles mission rule out any alternative to the Hitler regime? And, if the opposition did overthrow the Fuhrer, could the Allies negotiate a peace settlement with a non-Nazi German government? Was the war merely directed against a regime, or was it directed against a nation? To what degree did the Allies and the United States identify the nation with its leaders? Theoretically, this identification was repugnant and unacceptable. A democratic nation cannot assume that the designs of a corrupt tyrant mirror the desires and aspirations of an entire country. Individual men may be perverted and evil, but not an entire people.

But what is theoretically unacceptable may be practically inescapable.

If there is no viable opposition to the existing regime, if the tyrant's control, particularly over the police and the channels of public information, is complete, if his propaganda builds an impenetrable wall of insulation, isolating his nation from the outside world, then the identification is sealed. Although never admitted, it forms the basis of planning. If there is no believable opposition to the regime, then no current plans can be based on the possibility of developing, sustaining and utilizing an alternative force. No specific group or organization can be recognized as the "real nation", the "real Germany," opposed to the false, usurping clique of power-driven masters.[31]

During the Welles mission, the Nazi hierarchy continually identified the German people with the aims and achievements of their leadership. Only the interview with Dr. Schacht, Germany's economic wizard, revealed any alternative. To the Undersecretary, Dr. Schacht confided the existence of an anti-Hitler faction in the General Staff. He then emphasized that the removal of the Fuhrer depended upon the future assurances of the Allies:

> Then, leaning over and talking in a whisper, he said, "If what I am going to tell you now is known, I will be dead within a week." He gave me to understand that a movement was under way, headed by leading generals, to supplant the Hitler regime. He said that the one obstacle which stood in the path of the accomplishment of this objective was the lack of assurance on the part of these generals that, if such a movement took place, the Allies would give positive guarantees to Germany that Germany would be permitted to regain her rightful place in the world, and that Germany would be not treated as she had been in 1918. If such a guarantee as this could be obtained, he said, the movement would be pushed to a successful conclusion.[32]

Since the main obstacle to negotiation was the continued existence of

the Hitler regime, an alternative German government would presumably
have been welcomed by the Allies.[33] It would have represented the possibility of viable negotiations.

But the belief in this possibility was fairly weak. Despite his
conversations with Schacht, the Undersecretary did not note the likelihood of either an anti-Nazi German government or the successful overthrow
of Hitler and his gang. Apparently, he was not convinced by Dr. Schacht's
exposition or his logic. Moreover, the assumption that haunted his
report, that no negotiations would be possible once a war of devastation
exploded, ruled out successful negotiations with any German government
after the opening of the 1940 campaign.

There were several reasons why the Allied leaders and the American
government did not seriously consider negotiations with an alternative
German government. First, as indicated by Dr. Schacht, even an anti-
German government would insist on a negotiated peace which would leave
Germany strong. Later the "opposition" peace terms were clearly revealed.
The anti-Nazi leadership would demand the retention of Hitler's bloodless
conquests.[34] Secondly, the possibility of such a settlement was rapidly
doomed to failure. Any incentive to a compromise peace disappeared
once the war escalated and when the milk-toast leadership of Chamberlain
was replaced by the impassioned, committed leadership of Churchill.
Finally the failure of the conspirators to act, their failure to forestall the offensive and to overthrow Hitler, would reduce the credibility
and desirability of any anti-Nazi German alternative.

In the Victory Program's "Joint Board Estimate of United States Overall Production Requirements"[35] the planners spelled out the strategy that

the United States and its Allies should follow upon America's entry into
the war. Their rejection of a negotiated settlement echoed the President's
logic:

> 'An inconclusive peace between Germany and her present active
> military enemies would be likely to give Germany an opportunity
> to reorganize continental Europe and to replenish her strength.
> Even though the British Commonwealth and Russia were completely
> defeated, there would be important reasons for the United States
> to continue the war against Germany in spite of the greatly
> increased difficulty of obtaining victory.'[36]

The impossibility of a negotiated peace was also clearly tied to the
beliefs that no anti-Hitler movement could succeed, and that no German
regime would propound acceptable peace terms:

> 'It is believed that the overthrow of the Nazi regime by action
> of the people of Germany is unlikely in the near future, and
> will not occur until Germany is upon the point of military
> defeat. Even were a new regime to be established, it is not
> at all certain that such a regime would agree to peace terms
> acceptable to the United States.'[37]

Several months before the Japanese attack at Pearl Harbor, therefore,
the Administration was fully convinced that negotiations with Germany
were impossible. This conviction was embodied in American thought,
enunciated in American policy, articulated in American military plans.
There were, of course, long established historical reasons for the
rejection of negotiation, such as the memory of the failure of the last
armistice. But essentially it was based on the estimate formed by the
Allies and the United States of the nature, power and intentions of the
enemy.

German society was monolithic; no alternative existed to the Nazi
state; no opposition movement could ever succeed. Therefore, the
theoretical split between the immoral leadership and the misguided, but
basically redeemable, German people was inoperable. This police state
could only be overthrown from without, not from within.

b. Japan: the Uncertain Image

Although American plans had hardened against any negotiated peace
with Germany, there was no similar prohibition against a settlement
with the Japanese Government. The "Joint Board Estimate of United
States Over-all Production Requirements" was as specific on this
possibility as it was on the hopelessness of negotiating with the Nazi
regime. Contemplating a two-ocean war and a primary concentration of
offensive force against Germany, it foresaw the likelihood of a quick
Japanese collapse following the defeat of Germany:

> '...it is probable that Japan could be forced to give up
> much of her territorial gains, unless she had already firmly
> established herself in such strength that the United States
> and its Associates could not afford the energy to continue
> the war against her.'[38]

Whether it be Allied supremacy or strategic stalemate the resolution
of the Pacific war was through negotiation, not through total victory.

Actually, this emphasis was part of the prewar planning for an
ORANGE, or an ORANGE-RED war. The varied versions of the ORANGE plan
concentrated on the retention or liberation of the Philippines;[39] only
incidentally, and often merely intermittently, did they intimate that
the invasion of the Japanese home islands was an essential prerequisite
to victory. The United States would wage war, not to assure the complete
defeat of the enemy, but to strengthen her own strategic position in the
Pacific. For example, the final ORANGE plan contemplated the progressive
application of offensive power against the Japanese Empire, thereby
defeating the enemy and securing "a settlement that would assure the
peace and safeguard American interests in the Far East."[40]

The RED-ORANGE plan was even more detailed on a possible peace
settlement with Japan in the event that Great Britain should be defeated

by the United States:

> ...the forces raised in the process of producing a favorable
> decision in the Atlantic would give the United States such a
> superiority that Japan might well negotiate rather than fight
> the United States alone. 'It is not unreasonable to hope,'
> the planners observed, 'that the situation at the end of the
> struggle with RED may be such as to induce ORANGE to yield
> rather than face a war carried to the Western Pacific.'[41]

That American military planners in the interwar period should

contemplate a limited war, resolved by negotiation rather than strategic

surrender, was not surprising. What was more startling was the continued

emphasis on a negotiated settlement with Japan in September 1941. Why

did the United States already pressing for the unconditional defeat of

Germany still contemplate such a solution? The reasons revolved around

America's national commitments in the Pacific and her estimate of the

enemy's purpose.[42]

1) The Total Solution: Conversion

The varied versions of the ORANGE plan, ultimately designed to

re-establish American power in the Western Pacific, confined national

interests to that area. Here the threat fell on America's territorial

possessions, not on her basic security and independence. Therefore,

her impulse towards total war and the crusade was far weaker in the

Pacific than in the more vital, more vulnerable Atlantic. Japan could

threaten and capture America's territorial possessions, but could not

seriously menace her continental position. Since the issue was far

more serious between the United States and Germany, the demand for

victory was far more compulsive.

But ultimately the belief that the United States could negotiate

with Japan--embodied in prewar plans and reflected in the long drawn-out

negotiations with the Japanese envoys in Washington--was based on the

belief that there was an alternative to Japanese militarism. The face of the enemy could change decisively: the war lords could

vanish and be replaced by more amenable statesmen. As Herbert

Feis notes, throughout most of the thirties,

> ...the government nurtured patient hope. Before the
> Manchurian venture (1931) Japanese diplomacy had been
> calm and seemingly in rhythm with western ideals.
> Some of the leaders who made it so had lost position.
> Some had died. Some had been killed because of
> their beliefs. But a chance remained that, if not
> deeply hurt or offended, Japan might...turn again
> to men of the same kind. There were elements in
> Japan, influential elements, who were known to have
> great doubts about and dislike for what their
> country was doing. A few revered elder statesmen
> were spreading caution. There was open worry among
> those bankers, traders, and industrialists who foresaw
> the opposition Japan would meet. Senior naval officers
> were talking informed sense. They had seen much of
> the outside world and knew how large were the seas
> which the advocates of expansion wished to bring
> under Japanese rule. The continued resistance of
> China was counted on....Sometime, the American
> authorities hoped, the Japanese people would grow
> weary of the effort and cost; the Navy would grow
> impatient at the drain upon Japan's stregnth;
> resistance to Army domination would spread. Then a
> more temperate group could regain control of
> Japanese affairs. With them a just ending of the
> quarrel in the Pacific might be arranged.[43]

The possibility of this alternative government had two

interrelated aspects: credibility and desirability. The

United States would only believe in the possibility of change

if she felt it were desirable and would favor her strategic

position. But the two aspects were not identical or static.

Credibility could become increasingly minimal while desirability

remained, or became, maximal. This formula describes the

altering attitude of the United States towards Japan

throughout the late thirties and early forties.

Theoretically, the best solution was the replacement of

the militarists by the liberals and the war lords by the pacificists.

But this possibility steadily declined. Moreover, its chances were

always long-range, never immediate; since only the complete bankruptcy
of Japanese expansionism could overturn the virtually independent power
of the militaristic clique.

In a December 1, 1939, evaluation, Joseph C. Grew--American Ambassador
to Japan--rejected this optimistic myth. He disregarded and deflated
it as a mirage produced by sheer wishfulness:

> To await the hoped-for discrediting in Japan of the Japanese
> Army and the Japanese military system is to await the millennium.
> The Japanese Army is not a protuberance like the tail of a dog
> which might be cut off to prevent the tail from wagging the
> dog; it is inextricably bound up with the fabric of the entire
> nation; its ramifications are far too deep for any effective
> amputation, or any effective withering through discredit....
> that the Army can be discredited in the eyes of the people to
> a degree where its power and prestige will become so effectively
> undermined as to deprive the Army of its control or at least of
> its preponderant influence in shaping national policy is a
> hypothesis which, I believe, no one intimately conversant with
> Japan and the Japanese would for a moment entertain. It is
> reluctantly felt that the entertaining of such a hypothesis
> is unfortunately but unquestionably a cause of the wish being
> father to the thought. Should any coup d'etat occur in Japan
> through social upheavel, there is little doubt that it would
> immediately lead to a ruthless military dictatorship.[44]

The President and the Secretary of State apparently shared this
realistic estimate, discounting the hope and dream of another Japan.
Hull traced the illusion to its most probable source, the Japanese
Liberals in the Government who regretted Japan's jingoistic course and
anticipated and projected the return of the "moderates" to power.[45]

2) The Alternatives of the Alternative

Since the war lords were too firmly entrenched in the structure
and substance of Japanese Government, total conversion was unlikely.
But there were still open alternatives or images of the Japanese Government which were promising, provided that inducement was combined with
force. The first possibility was that the Japanese moderates could

restrain the extremists, inhibiting their imperial adventures and restraining their recklessness. The second possibility was that the Japanese
Government had neither the means nor the will to pursue its plans once
its advances were checked by the firm resistance of the United
States. Either because of internal political division or because
of timidity, the Japanese could not, or would not, pursue their imperial
schemes, their plans to establish a Greater East Asia Co-Prosperity Sphere.

   a) The Divided Foe.

The first image--of a Japan divided between the moderates and the
extremists--was a fairly thin prospect by 1940. It was still held,
however, by leading officials of the State Department, Hull and Sumner
Welles, who favored a patient policy of economic and military moderation
in the Far East: "restraint would bolster the position of the moderate
group...still thought to exist within Japan and...capable...of overcoming
the die-hards."[46] This hope flickered in the early months of the European
war, dying long before the State Department abandoned its moderate and
forebearing attitude.[47] By the spring of 1941 the State Department had
few expectations of inducing any restraint or change in Japan. Then
Hull thought "that there was not one chance of success in twenty or one
in fifty or even one in a hundred."[48]

   b) The Timid Foe

The second alternative image--of a blustering and bluffing Japan,
too timid or cautious to strike against the firm opposition of the United
States--was more positive and deter: ining. It was held by the hard line
members of the Administration: Stanley Hornbeck--State Department
expert on the Far East--Harold Ickes, Henry Stimson and Morgenthau.[49]

These advocates of the strong stand were convinced that Japan was bluffing, that she would never challenge the military and naval might of the United States. When it came to a showdown, Japan would retreat.

During the first debate in June, 1940, over the imposition of an embargo,[50] Stimson cited Japanese retrenchment in Siberia as a perfect proof of her diplomatic timidity. He communicated the tale and elaborated the moral to the Secretary of the Treasury:

> 'I thought of a precedent that would be very interesting in this situation....In 1918, you may remember that the Japanese got very uppy in Siberia....They acted in a very rough way and it looked as if they were there to stay...the United States got rather alarmed at it...because it looked as if they were going off on what they've done since and the War Trade Board took it in hand....And they laid restrictions upon licenses for the export of cotton to Japan and for the import of silk from Japan....By gum...the Japs took their army and got out of there in no time....Our friend from the State Department... had better have that shown to him.'[51]

In an October 1940 memorandum the moral was fully and confidently enunciated:

> 'Japan has historically shown that she can misinterpret a pacifistic policy of the United States for weakness. She has also historically shown that when the United States indicates by clear language and bold actions that she intends to carry out a clear and affirmative policy in the Far East, Japan will yield to that policy even though it conflicts with her own Asiatic policy and conceived interests. For the United States now to indicate either by soft words or inconsistent actions that she has no such clear and definite policy towards the Far East will only encourage Japan to bolder action.'[52]

3) The Image Hardens: The Alternatives Vanish, but the Need for Negotiation Remains

The American image of the Japanese enemy was neither as frightening nor as consistently evil as that of the Nazi. If he could not be redeemed, he could be restrained. In any case a policy of containment was forseeable in the Pacific whereas it was inconceivable in Europe. Negotiations were essential with Japan, dangerous and impossible with Germany.

Although this logic held until mid-1941, its assumptions
steadily deteriorated throughout the twilight period leading into
war. Eventually the mirage of hope and illusion evaporated and the
image of the foe hardened. Although no great public crystallization
occured until Pearl Harbor, the seeds for a total war in the Pacific
were already planted. Freedom of choice had already disappeared.

In the Far East a classic stalemate had deadlocked any possibility
of diplomatic progress. The objectives of American and Japanese policy
had frozen in permanent opposition. Tragically the irresistable force
had met the immovable obstacle: Japanese expansion versus American
determination. It was "unthinkable" for Japan to abandon its adventure
in China, or for the United States to abandon its sanctions and return
to a policy of Asiatic appeasment. Increasingly, in the mirror of the
deciphered Japanese code, MAGIC, this truth became apparent and inescapable. The image of an alternative Japanese government was no longer
credible in any form, and the possibility of solution through negotiation
was ended.

But not its desirability. Negotiations still remained essential.
There was another rationale in American efforts to negotiate, a more
realistic and almost pessimistic assessment of Japanese intentions and
plans. This assessment assumed that the Japanese could not be converted
or reformed, that they could not be pressured or deterred through any
show of force. American policy could not influence the composition of
their government, nor alter their plans for conquest. It could merely
avoid provocation, hoping to gain time. Negotiations could not achieve
any strategic objective, but could gain a tactical interlude in which the
United States could prepare its forces for an almost certain collision.

a) The First Embargo Proposal

Although the State Department occasionally flirted with the hope
that the moderates might restrain the militarists, it essentially
pursued its cautious course fearing the consequences of bolder action.
It assumed that the Japanese would pursue their plans regardless of
American reaction. This belief and these fears were clearly expressed
in the State Department reaction to the Morgenthau-Stimson proposal for
a total embargo over all oil and scrap iron to Japan.[53]

Confronted with this plan, the State Department panicked, forseeing
only disaster. Since Hull had left for the Inter-American Conference
in Havana, Sumner Welles lad the State Department counterattack. His
arguments reflected its pessimistic estimate, its feeling that deterence
would automatically fail because the war lords would not change course:

> If the United States, he advised, did anything just then that
> bore vitally upon Japan's power to carry on the war in China,
> the result could not be predicted. A total ban on oil
> shipments would force it into a decision. Rather than desist,
> Japan, using our action as cause and reason, might move
> against the Indies. Should that happen, it was doubtful
> whether the American people would support the government in
> any counter military action. Most of them would judge the oil
> embargo to have been an injudicious act towards war. [54]

The Japanese Government should not be forced into a decision. The
United States should avoid retaliatory measures hoping Japan would
desist from further aggressions. Behind the curious logic of caution
lay the image of the formidable, determined foe--unconverted, unrestrain-
able, easily provoked, totally untrustworthy.

b) The Impact of the Tripartite Act: National Association

by Guilt.

This image persisted as a motivating force in State Department policy,
hardening into certainty as Japan's intentions became more apparent, as

her ambitions became inescapably clear. The chief crystallizer, the action that created a national association by guilt, was the Tripartite Act of September 27, 1940.

The State Department's official or public reaction was blandly mild:

> 'The reported agreement of alliance does not, in the view of the Government of the United States, substantially alter a situation which had existed for several years. Announcement of the alliance merely makes clear to all a relationship which has long existed in effect and to which this Government has repeatedly called attention. That such an agreement has been in process of conclusion had been known for some time, and that fact had been fully taken into account by the Government of the United States in the determining of this country's policies.' [55]

Despite this smug omniscience, the Government of the United States was shocked and surprised, seeing the Tripartite Pact as full-scale collusion between the major Axis powers. The conclusion of the alliance was a definite change, substantially altering the relationship between the United States and Japan and ending the patient tolerance of the State Department. Ambassador Grew summed up its impact succinctly: "Now that the Tripartite Alliance has been concluded, we can no longer regard and treat with Japan as an individual nation. She has become a member of a team, and our attitude toward Japan must be our attitude toward the team as a whole." [56]

Even the patient equanimity of the Secretary of State was shaken; he now saw a sinister and consistent pattern in the development of events. The separate threads were being woven into a single design, embodying the master plan for aggression. As he explained to the British Ambassador on September 30, 1940:

> ...the relations between Germany, Italy and Japan, each having a common objective of conquering certain areas of the world and each pursuing identical policies of force, devastation and seizure, have been during recent years on

a basis of complete understanding and of mutual cooperation
for all purposes mutually desirable and reasonably
practicable, with the result that the recent announcement
was part and parcel of the chain of related events.[57]

The announcement of the Tripartite Pact by consistently active col-

laborators was merely one element in the total plan. "Everybody

agreed that the purpose of the three Axis powers was to scare us out

of giving material aid to Great Britain."[58] This was the general consensus

in the President's cabinet.

Japan's continued adherence to the Axis pact became the symbol of

her perversity. The only possibility of her regeneration lay in

renouncing the Tripartite Pact. It became the touchstone for renewed

faith that negotiations could be ultimately fruitful. But Japan's

continued failure to renounce her Axis association made the situation

hopeless. As Hull disclosed:

> Our primary problem, therefore, was to obtain unequivocal
> evidence from Japan that she honestly wished to abandon her
> course of aggression and to resume a peaceful policy. Until
> we had secured this evidence, any agreement with Japan would
> have been worth less than the ink expended in signing it.
> We had repeatedly pointed out to Japan that her position with
> regard to the Axis Alliance and her professed desire for
> peace with the United States in the Pacific were in open
> contrast. Even had we worked out an agreement for peace in
> the Pacific in the most minute detail, that peace could have
> been shattered if Hitler chose to make our measures of self-
> defense a cause for war and Japan had felt obliged to observe
> the Axis Alliance pact. Japan wanted to make herself the sole
> judge as to what constituted self-defense on our part. [59]

Now both enemies had merely one face, and only a total victory in the

Atlantic and Pacific would remove the existing threat to the security

and ideals of the United States.

Though the State Department had neither expectations nor hope,

it continued to pursue the intricate, time-consuming and wearisome negotiations. The complications and commitments of the European war, the threat of Nazi Germany and the unpreparedness of American forces maintained the desirability of negotiations and sustained the hope of a miraculous alternative long after reason and experience discredited all probability.

But these closing negotiations were not meant to effect a final settlement, for no acceptable solution was then possible. They were merely designed to delay the inevitable, forestalling until the United States would be better prepared; and also to preserve the status quo in the Far East until America could more effectively meet the challenge of Japanese imperialism.

4) Conclusion.

If, in summary, we seek to relate the image of the enemy to the belief in negotiation and persuasion, we will discover that there was no absolute bond between the two. The belief that the enemy was unredeemable, unshakably committed to a ruinous and arbitrary course, was used to justify negotiations and confrontation. The belief that the enemy was divided, capable of restraint and even redemption, was used to justify a policy of firmness as well as one of patient forebearance. But although the nature of the enemy did not foreclose or free, it did determine the character of any negotiation, the purpose of any diplomatic détente. Some negotiations were posited towards a strategic settlement, a permanent and effective change; and depended on the hope for a regeneration of the enemy, a redemption of his purposes, and an abandonment of his aggressive ambitions. Other negotiations were posited

towards a tactical détente, a temporary breathing space or advantage,
and did not depend on Japanese conversion; they merely hoped for his
restraint and depended on his wisdom.

By Pearl Harbor, only tactical negotiations remained a possibility.
For the final image of the Japanese clung closely to that of the Nazis.
The Japanese militarists were so firmly in the saddle that they could
not be dislodged from power in the foreseeable future. Their ambitions
and schemes were totally incompatible with either American intentions
or principles. Their dream for the creation of an Asiatic and Pacific
Empire was ineluctable. Although their plans were not as world-wide
as those of their Nazi associates, their relationship with the latter
mired them in the same scheme and made them part of the wider conspiracy.
Since final negotiations were impossible, the Japanese militarists must
be uprooted and destroyed like their Nazi colleagues.

2. Attack against Civilian Targets: the Basis for Democratic Rationalization

Theoretically, a democratic nation is not ideologically conditioned
to the mass use of air power against civilian targets. It is not
conditioned to terror bombardment consciously designed and systematically
applied to break the morale of the enemy population by the indiscriminate
slaughter of men, women and children. An ideology which always distinguishes
the guilty few from the innocent masses, the rulers from the ruled, cannot
view with any equanimity the extermination of innocent multitudes.

This basic belief in the goodness of man, the moral correlative to
the political belief in the equality of man, militates against any crusade
directed against a nationality as a nationality, a race as a race. America
can wage war against a system, not against a national population; against

evil principles, not against an entire people. She cannot emphasize indiscriminate attacks on the innocent populus in retaliation for the misdeeds of their leaders or the crimes of their compatriots.

But this moral rejection of mass attack runs against the tendency and logic of total war, against the natural assumptions of the military mind. Since the entire nation is now engaged in war, since the national structure is inexorably and fatally united as a single military objective, any specific target is militarily legitimate--especially if its destruction weakens the resistance of the enemy, bending and ultimately overthrowing his will. If objectives discarded on humanitarian or ideological grounds form the Achilles heel of the war effort, and if their destruction could ultimately destroy enemy resistance, then they should be attacked. In this instance, ideological prohibitions conflict sharply and completely with military effectiveness.

To wage war effectively and freely, therefore, air strategists must remove moral obstacles to the full application of air power. But they must be removed gradually, subtly, by dilution and compromise, not by outright rejection and denial. In the twenties and thirties the attempt to reconcile these contradictory needs led to the evolution of American strategic air doctrine, an evolution of which refined the originally total character of the air offensive, wedding morality with efficiency.[60]

a. Original Vision: Justification of Apocalyptic Strategy

The original prophets and champions of air power assumed that mass attacks against civilian centers were justifiable. The enemy was no longer the opposing army, but an enemy nation whose economic and military interdependence eliminated the old distinction between civilian and military objectives.[61] As General William Mitchell explained:

> War is the attempt of one nation to impress its will on
> another nation by force after all other means of arriving at
> an adjustment of a dispute have failed. The attempt of one
> combatant, therefore, is to so control the vital centers of
> the other that it will be powerless to defend itself. The
> vital areas consist of cities where the people live, areas
> where their food and supplies are produced and the transport
> lines that carry these supplies from place to place.[62]

The object of war therefore legitimized the attack against any vulnerable

link in the national structure, and practical justification and target

selection would presumably be determined by military effectiveness.

So the question of mass bombardment was reduced to the question

of strategic expediency. Would an attack against population centers

disrupt and destroy the enemy's will to war? None of the early theorists

doubted it. Their rationale was expounded by Captain Basil H. Liddell-Hart

in his treatise, _Paris: Or the Future of War_, published in 1925.[63] Seeing,

like Mitchell, the true objective of war as the defeat of the enemy's

will, he advocated an indirect strategy aimed at the weakest link in the

enemy's structure, civilian morale:

> Liddell-Hart insisted that the enemy's will could be conquered
> by a method shrewder than frontal attack--one that would strike
> the vulnerable points of the enemy's armor. Referring to the
> classic example of the Trojan warrior, Paris, who struck his
> shaft into the vulnerable heel of Achilles, he called for
> direct action against the hostile population. Such action
> might include a food blockade, disintegration of the economic
> system, or disruption of the normal activities of civilized
> life. Captain Liddell-Hart asserted that the best way of
> subjecting the enemy's will was so to disturb (or threaten to
> disturb) the normal life of a people that they would prefer
> the lesser evil of surrendering their policy. He discounted
> the possibility of a "fight to the death" by the civilian popu-
> lation. Normal men, he asserted, would not continue a struggle
> after it was seen to be hopeless; they would surrender to _force
> majeur_.[64]

The most vivid apostle of apocalyptic strategy was the Italian theorist, Giulio Douhet. To him the vulnerability of civilian morale, its susceptibility to terrorization from the air, was an article of faith. In graphic images he described the systematic terrorization of a modern city from the air and the consequent collapse of all morale:

> ...take the center of a large city and imagine what would happen among the civilian population during a single attack by a single bombing unit. For my part, I have no doubt that its impact upon the people would be terrible. Here is what would be likely to happen to the center of the city within the radius of about 250 meters: Within a few minutes some 20 tons of high-explosive, incendiary, and gas bombs would rain down. First would come explosions, then fires, then deadly gases floating on the surface and preventing any approach to the stricken area. As the hours passed and night advanced, the fires would spread while the poison gas paralyzed all life. By the following day the life of the city would be suspended; and if it happened to be a junction on some important artery of communication traffic would be suspended.
> What could happen to a single city in a single day could also happen to ten, twenty, fifty cities. And since news travels fast, even without telegraph, telephone, or radio, what, I ask you, would be the effect upon civilians of other cities, not yet stricken but equally subject to bombing attacks? What civil or military authority could keep order, public service functioning and production going under such a threat? And even if a semblance of order was maintained and some work done, would not the sight of a single enemy plane be enough to stampede the population into panic? In short, normal life would be impossible in this constant nightmare of imminent death and destruction. And if on the second day another ten, twenty, or fifty cities were bombed, who could keep all those lost, panic stricken people from fleeing to the open countryside to escape this terror from the air? A complete breakdown of the social structure cannot but take place in a country subjected to this kind of merciless pounding from the air. The time would soon come when...the people themselves, driven by the instinct for self-preservation, would rise up and demand an end to the war--this before their army and navy had time to mobilize at all.' 65

A veritable Apocalypse of fire and terror sweeping enemy resistance into nothingness!

Although Douhet's influence over the majority of American air
strategists was largely second-hand,[66] and probably peripheral, his ideas
closely corresponded to those of leading American theorists whose
influence was more direct. Mitchell also saw airpower as an apocalyptic
weapon. Although he wrote and spoke about attacking industrial systems
<u>and</u> population centers, he never questioned the morality of such a strategy.
Never indicating whether the attack on morale would merely accompany an
offensive against the industrial resources of the nation, or whether it
would constitute a totally independent campaign, Mitchell clearly and
emphatically defended its effectiveness:

> In future the mere threat of bombing a town by an air force
> will cause it to be evacuated, and all work in factories to
> be stopped. To gain a lasting victory in war, the hostile
> nations' power to make war must be destroyed, the means of
> communication, the food producers, even the farms, the fuel
> and oil supplies, and the places where people live and carry
> on their daily lives. Aircraft operating in the heart of an
> enemy's country will accomplish this objective in an incredibly
> short space of time.[67]

Mass attacks were, therefore, legitimate and effective means for the
accomplishment of a legitimate end: the destruction of the enemy's
capacity to wage war.

Mitchell, court-martialled in 1926, was not the sole American
prophet of air power. Many others shared his assumptions and faith.
For example, Major General Mason M. Patrick--Chief of the Air Service
from October 15, 1921, to December 14, 1927--was as fully convinced of
the effectiveness of morale bombardment as Mitchell and Douhet. His
lectures were often saturated with quotations from the leading military
authorities--foreign and domestic--who advocated the advancement of
independent air power and who bowed to the theory of mass attacks.[68]

In a lecture delivered before the Army War College on November 9, 1925,
General Patrick regaled his audience with a vision of the impact of
mass attacks:

> Patrick...saw the air arm as the perfect weapon for waging
> war in the proper fashion, for the airplane alone could
> "jump over" enemy armies and strike directly the "seat of
> the opposition will and policy." Air supremacy...was the
> easiest and surest way of breaking the hostile morale.
> Asking his audience of ranking officers to imagine the effect
> of the destruction of an enemy's industrial establishments,
> munitions factories, and communications, plus "drenching with
> gas," Patrick left it to them to estimate how long the enemy
> would fight.[69]

According to the leading lights, therefore, there was no question as
to the validity or legitimacy of air attacks against civilian morale.

It was also argued that air power, compared to the prolonged
engagement of military forces in ground warfare, was the more humane
and less destructive method of breaking National will. Assuming that
the horrors of the protracted stalemate in World War I would repeat
themselves in any future global conflict, they saw air bombardment as
a merciful escape.

Captain Liddell-Hart, revolted by the barbarism of the protracted
slaughter on the western front in World War I, felt that the indirect
strategy of aerial demolition would avoid a repetition of this "terrible
sacrifice of blood and money."[70] And General Mitchell prophecied that
the destruction of enemy morale would be mercifully quick:

> Once command of the air was secured, the objective of
> interior destruction could be achieved in an "incredibly
> short time." Thus...the months and years of ground fighting,
> with its toll of millions of lives, would be eliminated in
> the future.[71]

Although Mitchell and his colleagues were overly optimistic about
the rapidity with which an aerial offensive would attain its effects,[72]

they saw more clearly than their critics that modern technology had destroyed the humanitarian safeguards and distinctions of the past.

b. From Morale Bombardment to Precision Bombardment.

In his 1919 Annual Report, the Secretary of War, Newton D. Baker, scathingly denounced the legality and effectiveness of mass air attacks, condemning them as "'an abandonment of the time honored practice among civilized peoples of restricting bombardment to fortified places or to places from which the population had an opportunity to be removed.'"[73] Such malevolent practices, according to Mr. Baker, were unfit for civilized men. In the past war, they typified the ruthlessness of the Central Powers:

> 'The practice was a part of the ruthlessness with which the Central Empires sought to terrify England and France into submission. Instead it may be said that the willingness of the enemy casually to slaughter women and children, and to destroy property of no military value or use, demonstrated to England and France, the necessity of beating so brutal a foe, and it is most likely that history will record these manifestations of inhumanity as the most powerful aids to recruitment in the nations against which they were made.'[74]

To the non-believer, therefore, air attacks against civilian populations were ineffective and merely reinforced their victim's will to fight.

Baker's views echoed those of the majority of Americans. This moral block[75] had a decisive effect on the development of air doctrine in the interwar period, virtually suppressing any public discussion or advocation of area bombardment by the defenders of air power. Though Mitchell and the earlier champions wer frank and direct, their followers, particularly those in office, moved away from morale bombardment, refining and redefining their concepts in more acceptable terms. As noted by Dr. Greer: "An openly advocated program of mass bombardment would have found virtually no support in the United States."[76]

This moral scruple had three effects upon the development of air power doctrine. It led the advocates of air power to stress the possibility of enemy air attacks upon American urban centers.[77]Also, the justification for long-range air forces was predilected on their usefulness against purely military objectives: enemy vessels and bases.[78] But the most important effect of all was the development of precision bombardment,[79] a refinement of theory which led the second generation of air advocates away from the theories of Douhet, William Mitchell and Liddell-Hart.

1) The Gorrell Plan

Actually the doctrine of precision or selective bombing ante-dated Mitchell. It was first expressed in the strategic air plan prepared by Lt. Col. Edgar S. Gorrell in 1917. As Chief of the Strategical Aviation Branch of the Air Service in the Zone of Advance, he was the Service's chief strategic planner.[80] His plan became the guide for American air strategy in World War I.[81]

The Gorrell plan began with a frightening assumption. The Germans were ready to initiate large scale strategic air attacks on the Allies. In anticipation the United States air forces should develop their own plan: "'not only to wreck Germany's manufacturing centers but wreck them more completely than she will wreck our's next year.'"[82] The emphasis was squarely placed on industrial and transportation targets: "'strategic bombing against commercial centers and lines of communications, with a view to causing the cessation of supplies to the German front.'"[83] But the plan did not end with this general exhortation to destruction. It then listed the specific targets within the industrial and transportation complex with the Allied Air Forces should attempt to disrupt and destroy.

The Gorrell plan defined four main target centers: Mannheim-
Ludwigshaven, Cologne, the Saar Valley and the Dusseldorf complex.[84]
Here was the genesis of specific target selection. But Gorrell fused
the principles of selective destruction with those of area attack and
morale bombardment, advocating the total annihilation of the designated
targets:

> Gorrell agreed with Trenchard on the importance of combined
> day and night operations against these areas. He passed
> over the various arguments for and against each method, insist-
> ing that only by continuous attacks could the Germans be
> deprived of rest and hindered in making necessary repairs.
> In the beginning, Gorrell allowed, the Allies should use
> whatever type of bombing equipment they had, but ultimately,
> round-the-clock operations would be essential. The plan did
> not follow Trenchard's concept of widely spread, light attacks.
> It proposed, rather, that all available planes be concentrated
> on a single target each day, with the aim of its complete
> destruction. Gorrell believed that such tactics would result
> in the maximum damage, both moral and physical to the enemy.
> He thought that in face of such an assault the defenses would
> be overwhelmed; the "manufacturing works would be wrecked and
> the morale of the workment would be shattered.'[85]

Gorrell envisioned selective saturation attacks, the total destruction
of certain geographic, not economic, targets. Therefore, his plan,
though sophisticated for his time, did not forsee the application of
precision bombardment.

2) Development of Doctrine at the Air Corps Tactical School

The doctrines of precision bombardment were developed at the Air
Corps Tactical School--originally established in 1920 at Langley Field,
Virginia; but moved to Maxwell Field, Alabama, in 1931. Here the
exigency of modern war was reconciled with the morality of democratic
ideology. By 1941 the full doctrine of daylight precision bombardment
was developed and established within the rank and file of the general

officers in the Army Air Corps, many of whom had either attended or
taught at the Air Corps Tactical School.[86]

Unlike Douhet, Mitchell and the older generation of theorists, the
defenders of precision bombardment advocated an assault on the National
Economic Structure[87]--not on the nation as a whole. The nation's economy
was particularly vulnerable, because its operation depended on the
harmonious functioning of its multitudinous systems. Interdependence
meant vulnerability:

> 'Modern war with its extravagent material factors places an
> especial importance upon a nation's economic structure and
> particularly upon its "industrial web." A nation may be defeated
> simply by the interruption of the delicate balance of this
> complex organization, which is vulnerable to the air arm and
> directly to neither of the other arms. It is possible that
> a moral collapse brought about by disturbances in this close-
> knit web may be sufficient to force an enemy to surrender, but
> the real target is industry itself, not national morale.'[88]

The effectiveness of precision bombardment was its justification.
Accuracy would allow airmen to hit at objectives more directly related
to the national war effort, crippling and killing, using a minimum
amount of discriminating slaughter. It would allow strategic air forces
to practice "pickel barrel" bombing.[89]

Throughout the teaching and development of theory at the Air Corps
Tactical School, attention was repeatedly drawn to certain examples,
illuminating microcosoms of the vulnerability of an integrated economy
to precision attack. One of the innovators of the theory, Major General
Donald Wilson, fastened on the example of the railroad system:

> The problem...was to selec' targets whose destruction would
> disrupt the entire fabric of an enemy's economy and thereby
> to discommode the civilian population in its normal day-to-
> day existence and to break its faith in the military establish-
> ment to such an extent that public clamor would force the
> government to sue for peace. From his experience as a
> civilian with American railroads, Wilson was aware that the

destruction of a few vital links would disrupt an entire
railroad system. If this was true of railroads, might not
the same be true for other industries? [90]

But the classic example of the vulnerability of a modern economy

to precision attacks came from the field of aviation itself. Major

General Haywood S. Hansell, Jr.--closely associated with the Air Corps

Tactical School from 1934-1938--used a single example to crystallize

and dramatize the potentialities of the new approach. After describing

the studies made at the school demonstrating the interdependence of a

highly specialized industrial economy, he fastened on the crucial

discovery: the realization that specialization existed within single

industries:

> 'One factory may make all the hardware for a number of
> automobile manufacturers. Another may make all the frames;
> still another all the transmissions. A small group of
> factories may make all the ball bearings for a great many
> industries. A few machine tool manufacturers may make tools
> on which all industries are dependent. And serving this
> specialization or these groups of specialities, are certain
> great services: the rail transportation system, the electric
> power system, the telephone and the telegraph communications
> system. An analysis of this great complexity indicates that
> munitions industries are especially sensitive to a relatively
> small number of plants, which make specialized parts, or
> systems which provide specialized service. The classic
> example of the type of specialization, and hence vulnerability,
> literally fell into our laps. We discovered in one day that
> we were taking delivery on new airplanes, flying them to their
> point of reception, removing the propellers, shipping the
> propellers back to the factories, and ferrying out additional
> airplanes. The delivery of controllable pitch propellers had
> fallen down. Inquiries showed that the propeller manufacturer
> was not behind schedule. Actually it was a relatively simple
> but highly specialized spring that was lacking, and we found
> that all the springs made for all the controllable pitch
> propellers of that variety in the United States came from
> one plant and that that plant in Pittsburgh had suffered from
> a flood. There was a perfect and classic example. To all
> intents and purposes a very large portion of the entire air-
> craft industry in the United States had been nullified just
> as effectively as if a great many airplanes had been individ-
> ually shot up, or a considerable number of factories had been

> hit. That practical example set the pattern for the ideal
> selection of precision targets in the United States Tactical
> doctrine for bombardment. That was the kind of thing that
> was sought in every economy....' [91]

For the want of a nail! For the minimum amount of effort, the maximum

amount of effect and disruption. The havoc inflicted accidently could

be deliberately created, systematically exploited.

Precision would, therefore, reverse and control the tendency of

total war. For the interdependent national economy could be disrupted

without the indiscriminate slaughter of civilians. Although the absolute

distinction between soldier and civilian could not be restored, [92] new

differences could be drawn between essential and nonessential targets.

Precision bombardment was humane as well as militarily effective. The

disruption of the national economy provoked by the systematic destruc-

tion of a few predetermined targets would inevitably affect the life of

the average citizen and ultimately subvert his resistance. [93] It would

achieve the ends of area bombardment without resorting to the means.

3) The Impact of Combat.

Until the outbreak of World War II in China and Europe, precision

bombardment held the field in the Army Air Corps. It combined maximum

efficiency with minimal inhumanity. With the beginning of the war

attitudes began to shift to an imperceptible degree. At first the

stoic conduct of civilian populations under air attack merely confirmed

the airman's belief in the superiority of precision bombing. In his

lecture of November 9, 1939, [94] Major Fairchild used a contemporary example

to dramatize the military ineffectiveness of general morale bombardment:

> He asked what was meant by attack on the national economic
> structure. Did it mean bombing and gassing of the civilian
> population? This, he answered, was one recognized method

of attack on an enemy nation, and the European powers
appeared to be preparing for such action. Fairchild
raised certain objections, other than the obvious humanitarian ones, to this method. Most important, said he, was
that no one know (sic) how hard such an attack had to be in
order to break civilian morale. The experience in China
suggested that Japanese bombing had actually strengthened,
rather than weakened the Chinese will to resist. At best,
Fairchild concluded, such methods seemed likely to achieve
results that were temporary and noncumulative. "For all
these reasons the School advocates an entirely different
method of attack." 95

Fairchild's scepticism was shared by American critics of the British

Grand Strategy Review.[96] Here, however, rejection was intensified by the

particular fury of Army officers against all air power panaceas.

But the war, even before Pearl Harbor, wore away part of the

climate of inhibition which had blocked any defense of morale

bombardment by the Army Air Corps. The major prewar plan of the AAF,

AWPD/1,[97] was clearly predicated upon the systematic destruction of a

number of specific targets. A minor note, however, supplemented and

accompanied the major theme. The emphasis was on precision bombardment,

but the plan allowed for "area bombing of civilian concentrations"[98] once

Germany's morale began to crack. Although the number of morale targets

was not specified, this previously rejected strategy would constitute

the final coup de grace, the culminating blow delivered against an

already disintegrating structure.

The precision formula allowed the United States Army Air Force to

reconcile military strategy with ideology. But there were several reasons

why it did not foreclose the possible adoption of massive attacks on

population centers. First, precision bombardment was developed in

peacetime when inhibitions against the use of terror attacks were at

their peak. Second, the basic assumption of the new air strategy was

that it was operationally feasible and that it could effectively crush
open enemy resistance. Third, it assumed that the final phase of area
bombardment could be effectively timed so as to coincide with the erosion
of the foe. Living in a fairly artificial atmosphere--immune from the
direct influence of battlefield operations and from the passions of war--
aerial strategists did not realize that the fury of conflict and the
operational difficulties of precision bombing would ultimately overthrow
all ideological inhibitions on the use of air power against civilian
population centers. The magic bottle could only contain, notextinguish
the genie of death that would release the devestating attacks against
Dresden, Tokyo, Hiroshima and Nagasaki.

3. "The First Shot"

By Pearl Harbor the process of justification had matured fully.
The United States was committed to a course which brought her increasingly
closer to the challenge of the war in Europe and which made involvement
merely a matter of time. The extension of the purely defensive into
the undeclared offensive had been justified to the American people. If
support of England led eventually to war, the Administration could readily
convince the public that the cause was just and involvement necessary.
The United States had undergone a revolution towards international
interventionism, though the transition was achieved only by an appeal
to tradition.

But until the attack on Pearl Harbor justification remained incomplete, suspended. Final persuasion depended on the enemy's move.
Justification could only go so far, but it could not complete the argument, seal the final phase, or convert the conflict into a crusade.
Only the enemy could. At the end the United States lost the initiative,
waiting passively for the enemy to act. She could approach the brink,

but not take the final plunge.

The last argument turned on the question of the "first shot."
Possibly the logic of justification, spawned by the threat of a Nazi
or Japanese triumph, called for an early declaration of war by the
United States against Germany. But the difficulties of American
politics barred any such conclusion. President Roosevelt felt that
he could not present the issue directly to Congress, asking them to
make the choice between war and peace. Therefore, the decision
remained in the hands of the enemy.

The final act must be conclusive: dramatic, sweeping, totally
unambiguous--not only a challenge to our interests but a direct attack
upon them. If the President had sought a flimsy pretext, as his
critics have often charged, if he had merely wanted an excuse, he could
easily have found one. But a weak or unconvincing case would have had
a disastrous political effect. A declaration of war could have been
passed through Congress only after a bitter and prolonged fight. The
public would have remained uncertain, bitterly divided in its support.
Only an unequivocal act would provide the unity necessary for the waging
of total war.

a. The Undeclared War in the Atlantic

Initially, it seemed that the "first shot" would be fired in the
Atlantic, that the President's bold use of American power would provoke
the inevitable German reaction. But although blows were exchanged,
although American ships were attacked and sunk, there was no clear-cut
confrontation. The President took retaliatory measures, but he did not
ask Congress for a declaration of war. A study of the several incidents

and the President's reaction clarifies the reasons for this hesitancy.

   1) The "Attack" on the Niblack

The first incident was a German U-boat "attack" on the American
destroyer Niblack. The intentions of the enemy were not, however,
totally evident, reasonably clear. On April 10, 1941, in Icelandic waters:

> ...when closing the coast, Niblack picked up three boatloads
> of survivors from a torpedoed Natherlands freighter. Just
> as the last men were being pulled on board, Niblack's sound
> operator made contact on a submarine evidently approaching
> for attack. Commander D. L. Ryan, the division commander,
> ordered Niblack to attack with depth charges. He did, and
> the U-boat retired. [99]

This incident occured while the President was weighing the possibility
of adopting escort of convoy.[100] He was balancing the merits of Hemisphere
Defense Plans No. 1 and No. 2.

The former was bolder, more challenging: "It provided for denial
of the newly defined waters of the hemisphere to Axis vessels and aircraft by force if necessary. It frankly envisioned naval escort of
convoy for merchant shipping along the Atlantic sea lanes as far as the
twenty-sixth meridian of longitude."[101]

Hemisphere Plan No. 2 was far more cautious. While still condemning
the entry of Axis vessels into the newly defined boundaries of the Western
Hemisphere as possibly "motivated by ...'unfriendly interest,'"[102] it did
not order their immediate destruction. It merely commanded "'American
forces...to follow Axis warships along the shipping lanes, broadcasting
their positions to the British and generally rendering their operations
as hazardous as possible within the limits imposed by the rule that
American ships were not to shoot first.'"[103]

Finally choosing Hemisphere Defense Plan No. 2, the President
decided to ignore the Niblack incident. The reason was obvious. It

was an ambiguous encounter raising the prospect of conflicting
interpretations. The President's opponents in Congress--who were
then planning to limit his authority to order escort of convoy--could[104]
interpret it in the worst possible light. Since the Niblack had depth-
charged a German submarine before being fired on, this incident could
lend"substance to the isolationist charge that the President sought to
provoke war."[105]

2) The Sinking of the Robin Moor

The second incident, the sinking of the Robin Moor on May 21, 1941,
was fairly unequivocal. As Secretary of State Cordell Hull described it:

> The sinking was atrocious because the German submarine
> commander knew from the Robin Moor markings, flag, and the
> statements of her crew that she was American enroute from
> New York to Capetown, with a general cargo none of which
> was war materials.[106]

When the news of the incident reached Harry Hopkins, the Presidential
adviser strongly urged Roosevelt to take retaliatory action:

> 'The sinking of the Robin Moor violated international law
> at sea...The present observation patrol of the Navy for
> observing and reporting the movement of ships that are
> potential aggressors should be changed to a security patrol
> charged with the duty of providing security for all American
> flag ships traveling on the seas outside of the danger zone.
> It occurred to me that your instructions to the Navy Depart-
> ment could be that the United States Atlantic patrol forces,
> to be specific are to, in effect, establish the freedom of
> the seas, leaving it to the judgment of the Navy as to what
> measures of security are required to achieve that objective.[107]

But Roosevelt refused,[108] contenting himself with a general denunciation
and limited retaliatory acts. To Congress, he issued the following
warning epitaph: "We must take the sinking of the Robin Moor as a
warning to the United States not to resist the Nazi movement of world
conquest. It is a warning that the United States may use the high
seas of the world only with Nazi consent."[109]

The retaliatory acts were confined to the freezing of the assets of Germany, Italy and some occupied countries; the closing of Axis[110] consulates[111] and a warning to the American Republics to exclude Axis personnel.[112] These actions, although ostensibly severe, were weak medicine. compared to the strong remedies proposed by Hopkins, Stimson and the other hard-line advocates in the Administration.[113]

Why did the President hesitate to make a _casus belli_ out of an incident which seemed fit to order, a classic case of unprovoked aggression on the high seas? Why didn't he seize upon the opportunity to order escort of convoy, a move which he had clearly intimated in his declaration of "unlimited emergency"?[114] Several developments could have stalled the President's decision. He knew that the country was still hesitating, still unwilling to unequivocally advocate or adopt a policy of full-scale escort.[115] Moreover, on June 9, 1941--two days before the President received his first report on the sinking of the _Robin Moor_-- columnists Alsop and Kintner and published a startling and sinister report in the _Washington Post_. Describing an incident closely paralleling the "attack" on the _Niblack_, Alsop and Kintner charged publicly "that in a recent encounter between an American destroyer and what was believed to be a German submarine, the destroyer had attacked."[116] But the account was less sinister than the imputed motive. "According to the two journalists, the President and his advisers, while saying nothing, were hoping the Atlantic patrol would produce an incident 'to serve as a pretext for really strong action by this country.'"[117] Because of the fears released by this report, the President could not fully exploit the _Robin Moor_ incident without confirming the worst predictions of the isolationists.[118]

3) The Attack on the U.S.S. _Greer_

The third incident, the U-boat attack on the U.S.S. _Greer_, a far

more ambiguous event, produced a far stronger and more effective
development of policy. The incident developed as follows:

> U.S.S. Greer, carrying the pennant of Commander G. W. Johnson
> and commanded by Lieutenant Commander L. H. Frost, was
> proceeding independently toward Iceland on 4 September 1941...
> at a speed of 17½ knots. At 0840 a British plane signaled
> to her that a submarine U-boat lay athwart her course some
> ten miles ahead. Greer commenced zigzagging, increased speed
> to twenty knots, went to general quarters, laid a course for
> the reported position, and on reaching it slowed to ten knots
> in order to allow her sound gear to operate with full efficiency.
> She made sound contact with the submarine and maintained it for
> over three hours, keeping the submerged U-652 always on her
> bow but not attacking. At 1000 the British plane captain
> inquired whether Greer intended to attack, and was answered
> in the negative. He then dropped his depth charges more or
> less at random, and returned to base to refuel. At 1240 the
> submarine headed toward the American destroyer and launched
> a torpedo, which was sighted early enough to be dodged. Greer
> counterattacked with depth charges, and at 1300 the U-boat
> shot a second torpedo, which was also avoided. Unable to
> re-establish sound contact, Greer discontinued the search at
> 1416 and resumed course for Iceland.[119]

The President's reaction was ferocious. Burning with indignation
at this not totally unprovoked attack, he scathingly denounced Nazi
"piracy" in his September 11, 1941, speech. He made the most of it:
"the German submarine fired first upon this American destroyer without
warning and with deliberate design to sink her."[120] Now recalling and
invoking the previous destruction of American ships--including the
Robin Moor--he conjured the vision of the Nazi world conspiracy, charging
that these actions were merely part of a deliberate, calculated plot.[121]
He then defined the scope and purpose of our reaction, beginning by
protesting our innocence:

> We have sought no shooting war with Hitler. We do not seek
> it now. But neither do we want peace so much that we are
> willing to pay for it by permitting him to attack our naval
> and merchant ships while they are on legitimate business.[122]

Considering the context of the Greer incident, the above definition was

not altogether appropriate. Then the President came to the key point:

> Do not let us be hair-splitters. Let us not ask ourselves
> whether the Americas should begin to defend themselves after
> the first attack, or the fifth attack, or the tenth attack,
> or the twentieth attack. The time for active defense is now....
> If submarines or raiders attack in distant waters, they can
> attack equally well within sight of our own shores. Their
> very presence in any waters which America deems vital to its
> defense constitutes an attack....our patrolling vessels and
> planes will protect all merchant ships--not only American
> ships but ships of any flag--engaged in commerce in our
> defensive waters. They will protect them from submarines;
> they will protect them from surface raiders.[123]

Roosevelt climaxed his presentation by declaring war against all German

submarines in western waters, denying that these orders were commands

to aggression:

> It is no act of war on our part when we decide to protect the
> seas that are vital to American defense. The aggression is
> not ours. Ours is solely defense. But let this warning be
> clear. From now on, if German or Italian vessels of war
> enter the waters, the protection of which is necessary for
> American defense, they do so at their own peril....The sole
> responsibility rests upon Germany. There will be no shooting
> unless Germany continues to seek it.[124]

Why did the President pick up the gauntlet over the attempted

torpedoing of the Greer by an obviously harassed U-boat commander while

he had failed to answer the challenge of the barbaric sinking of the

Robin Moor? The reason is fairly obvious. The attempted torpedoing

of the Greer occurred at a propitious moment. The President was now

committed to the mid-ocean convoy arrangements made with Prime Minister

Churchill at the Atlantic meeting. He would soon have to publicly

announce his decision, though already anticipating the horrified

denunciations which would be hurled by the isolationists. The Greer

incident gave him the perfect cover story, the convenient alibi for a decision already taken.[125]

4) The Torpedoing of the U.S.S. _Kearney_

The President had merely used the attempted torpedoing of the _Greer_ to explain his adoption of the mid-ocean convoy. He did not develop the exchange into a demand for full-scale confrontation. The next incident, the torpedoing of the U.S.S. Kearney on October 17, 1941, provided a further challenge which the President utilized in classic style. The circumstances of the torpedoing were hardly innocent. On October 15, 1941, Slow Convoy, SC-48 was attacked by a group of German submarines. Three ships were destroyed. The _Kearney_ was one of five U.S. destroyers sent in an appeal for help. After several attacks, having dumped depth charges and carried out harassing actions against the German submarine force, the _Kearney_ was : "...struck ...on the starboard side, about the turn of the bilge. She suffered many casualites, but was able to turn her engines over about ten minutes after the torpedo hit and to reach Iceland under her own power, escorted by _Greer_.[126]

From a naval point of view the torpedoing of the _Kearny_ was understandable, having occurred in the heat of battle while fully and deliberately engaged. But the official reaction to the incident was surprisingly violent. The President exploited it as fully as he had exploited the attempted torpedoing of the _Greer_. In a speech delivered on October 27, 1941--a speech ringing with righteous fury--the President denounced the act, while omitting the context and circumstances:

> We have wished to avoid shooting. But the shooting has
> started. And history has recorded who fired the first shot.
> In the long run, however, all that will matter is who fired
> the last shot.[127]

Then he drew the moral, relating the significance of the torpedoing

of the Kearny to the American nation:

> America has been attacked. The U.S.S. Kearny is not just a
> Navy ship. She belongs to every man, woman, and child in this
> Nation. Illinois, Alabama, California, North Carolina, Ohio,
> Louisiana, Texas, Pennsylvania, Georgia, Arkansas, New York,
> and Virginia--those are the home states of the honored dead
> and wounded of the Kearny. Hitler's torpedo was directed at
> every American, whether he lives on our sea coasts or in the
> innermost part of the country, far from the seas and far from
> the guns and tanks of the marching hordes of would-be
> conquerors of the world.[128]

Then, after having reinvoked the vision of the Nazi world conspiracy,[129]

he announced our determination to stop the march of Hitlerism.[130] Quoting

his orders to "shoot on sight",[131] the President closed his speech by re-

awakening the identification between the Kearny and the American nation

so skillfully introduced earlier:

> Today, in the face of this newest and greatest challenge
> of them all, we Americans have cleared our decks and taken
> our battle stations. We stand ready in the defense of our
> Nation and in the faith of our fathers to do what God had
> given us the power to see as our full duty.[132]

This Navy Day speech was a call to arms, an exhortation to prepare

for the inevitable. But, according to Robert E. Sherwood, the appeal

fell on deaf ears.[133] The majority of Americans remained fairly unconcerned

over the entire incident, taking it as a matter of course.

Since the entire context of the torpedoing was so obviously tangled,

one may well wonder why the President chose to make it a summons to battle.

There were probably two reasons: one immediate, the other long-range.

The immediate incentive was to further the Administration's case for the

repeal of certain sections of the Neutrality Law, the President deriving

as much ammunition as possible for his legislative battle.[134] His long-

range purpose may be surmised. According to Judge Samuel I. Rosenman,

the President was convinced by October 27, 1941, that American entry into

the war was inevitable.[135]The President was, therefore, preparing the
nation for an inescapable confrontation with the Axis powers.

But the expected climax did not materialize, the American challenge
led to no formal declaration of war by Nazi Germany. And the subsequent
incident--the sinking of the Reuben Jones on October 31, 1941, in the[136]
North Atlantic--created no stir, provoked no Presidential denunciation
and no new decision.

5) Presidential Caution

The first shot was fired in the Atlantic; American ships
were attacked and sunk by German submarines. But the President was
satisfied with limited measures, using these incidents as a propaganda
windfall to strengthen public and political support for his policy and
applying specific "retaliatory" measures, limited and often deceptive.
Unlike his predecessor, Woodrow Wilson, he did not take his stand on
any broad principle.

The President's failure to take a moral stand, for which we would
intervene, irritated the interventionists. Secretary of War, Henry L.
Stimson, was especially annoyed by Roosevelt's abdication of the initiative
to irresponsible subordinates on either side, by his apparent passivity
in the midst of crisis. Before the shooting incidents took place,
the Secretary of War reflected grimly about the President's leadership
in the "short of war" crisis:

> I am worried...because the President shows evidence of waiting
> for the accidental shot of some irresponsible captain on either
> side to be the occasion of his going to war. I think he ought
> to be considering the deep principles which underline the
> issues in the world and has divided the world into two camps,
> one of which he is the leader....[137]

In a May 24, 1941, letter, Stimson warned Roosevelt that the course of
history could be determined by an accident or mistake rather than by
the defense of basic principles:

> The American people should not be asked to make the momentous decision of opposing forcefully the actions of the evil leaders of the other half of the world possibly because of some accident or mistake....They must be brought to that momentous realization by your leadership in explaining why any other course than such forceful resistance would be forever hopeless and abhorrent to every honored principle of American independence and democracy.[138]

This dutiful exhortation was accompanied by the draft of a message to Congress recommending that the President be authorized to use American armed forces for the defense of certain basic principles: freedom of the seas, reinforcement of anti-Axis forces and the defense of the Western Hemisphere.[139] Stimson justified the use of American military force by accusing the Axis of violating the most elemental and sacred rights of humanity and civilization.[140] To the Secretary of War, it was simply a question of principle.

Despite his fears, the President publicly supported the principles enunciated by Stimson, justifying his retaliatory actions by citing them at length.[141] But he never applied them consistently and openly, letting his actions follow from his principles, in the manner or style advocated by the Secretary of War. Rather he played the game by ear, improvising as he moved along, incident to incident, always alternating bold advance with cautious withdrawal. He moved in the direction advocated by Stimson, but in a much more circuitous and circumspect manner.

Underlying the President's hesitation and caution were several factors—three major causes: the political impossibility of going to war merely on the basis of sacred principles; the difficulty of obtaining any declaration of war through Congress; and the impossibility of isolating the war in the Atlantic.

Of the three principles defined by the Secretary of War--the freedom
of the seas, the commitment to the victory of the anti-Axis forces and
the defense of the Western Hemisphere--only the last commanded enough
allegiance to become a casus belli for all parties and groups in the
United States. Freedom of the seas, eloquently defined and defended
by the President, had formed the basis for Wilson's decision to declare
war against the Central Powers in 1917. But in 1940 and 1941--
until the last month before Pearl Harbor--freedom of the seas was curtailed[142]
and confined by the provisions of the Neutrality Law. It was impossible
for the United States to make an ultimate stand on a principle which we
legally renounced. Finally, though committed to the victory of the anti-
Axis forces, the United States was unwilling to take the final step
towards involvement, unwilling to surrender her last illusion: a hope
that she could stay at peace.

To the moment of the Pearl Harbor attack, therefore, opinion in
America--Congressional and public--remained uncertain. Even in November,
1941, the President doubted his ability to secure Congressional
declaration of war unless national security was directly and unequivocally
challenged.[143] Langer and Gleason concluded:

> It may well be argued...that by November 13, 1941, the
> President, the Congress and the country had made the
> decision to accept war. No doubt, if Mr. Roosevelt had
> taken up the challenge thrown down by his opponents and had
> asked Congress for a formal declaration of war, he would
> have been voted down. As it was, the revision of the
> Neutrality Act gave him substantially what he and his advisers
> had come to recognize as essential in view of the world situa-
> tion, namely, acceptance by the nation of genuine involvement
> in the world conflict. Although one can rarely be apodictic
> about such matters, the evidence suggests that the American
> people, perhaps more surely than their representatives,
> "knew the score." Generally speaking they had come to realize
> that they could not permit a Nazi victory and must therefore

371.

sustain Britain at all costs. They did not want war and
shunned that ugly word as much as ever. But they were
willing to accept the reality in thin disguise and probably
found the President's gradualism and artifice more palatable
than the frank and forthright leadership for which Mr. Roosevelt's
friends so often clamored.[144]

The third reason for Presidential caution was the impossibility of
isolating the war in the Atlantic. The Tripartite Pact, which sealed
the partnership of the three conspirators,[145] clearly implied that an act
of war in the Atlantic, if initiated by the United States, would lead to
a Japanese declaration of war. This probability was unequivocally voiced
in Article #3:

> "Germany, Italy and Japan....undertake to assist one
> another with all political, economic and military means if
> one of the three Contracting Powers is attacked by a Power
> at present not involved in the European War or in the
> Chinese–Japanese conflict."[146]

Article #3, however, did not commit Japan to declare war against the
United States if the first shot was fired by the Germans. Therefore,
if America wished to check Hitler without confronting Japan, she would
have to leave the initiative in the enemy's hands. As Ambassador Grew
telegraphed the State Department on May 13, 1941:

> "It would appear reasonable to suppose that if a German
> attack on an American war ship or any other American vessel
> should bring about war, the Japanese Government would take
> the position that Germany had taken provocative action and
> had given the casus belli. On the other hand, the obligation
> of Japan under Article III might in good faith be made effective
> if an American warship fired the first shot."[147]

The first shot was fired and no declaration of war ensued. A single
incident, a single shot, was totally insufficient. It must be an occurence
frightful enough, total enough to provoke a complete reaction, jolting
the country from its condition of undeclared, limited war in the Atlantic
to full commitment, to a crusade.

b. The Pacific Dilemma

The problem of allowing the enemy to fire the first shot
was also dominant in the Pacific. Through the last days of
peace, the nuances of justification worried the President.
It was evident that a Japanese attack on Dutch or British
possessions in the Far East was imminent. This attack, as the
President told Hopkins, should be answered by an American
declaration of war. [148] A southward offensive would be a vital
threat to American interests. [149] If the Japanese wanted to place
the United States in an impossible position, they could leave
the choice of war and peace in American hands. This strategy
would be their most effective play, forcing the Roosevelt
Administration into a difficult choice. The President could
sit still and let the Japanese destroy America's strategic
situation in the Far East, isolating the Philippines and
Guam in a hostile sea; or he could ask Congress for a
declaration of war. Should Congress reject this decision,
the President and the nation would lose face and position.
Robert E. Sherwood summarizes Roosevelt's problem:

> This then was Roosevelt's dilemma:
> The Japanese were about to strike at British or Dutch
> possession or both--and what could he do about it?
> The British and the Dutch were hopelessly unable to
> defend themselves and so were the exposed Dominions
> of Australia and New Zealand. Singapore might hold
> out for a while, but it and Manila would be rendered
> inoperative as bases with the Japanese in control of
> the air above them and the seas around them. Without
> formidable American intervention, the Japanese
> would be able to conquer and exploit an empire,
> rich in resources, stretching from the Aleutian
> Islands to India or even to the Middle East; and it
> was idle to assume, and Roosevelt knew it better
> than anyone else, that there could be any formidable
> American intervention without the full, final,
> irrevocable plunging of the entire nation into war.
> And what were the chances of that when the Japanese
> landed on the Kra Peninsula? What would the
> President have to say to Congress in that event?
> ....

In 1939, with a traditional enemy in armed force on
the very frontier of France, the French isolationists
--most of whom had later become collaborationists--
had raised the scornful cry: "Why should we die for
Danzig?" Why, then, should Americans die for
Thailand, or for such outposts of British imperialism as Singapore or Hong Kong or of Dutch imperialism
in the East Indies...? Even if Roosevelt, through
diligent use of the Democratic party whip, could compel
the Congress to vote for war by a narrow margin
after weeks or months of demoralizing debate (during
which the Japanese would sweep ahead), what degree
of unity or of fighting spirit could the American
people achieve for the long and prodigious and
bloody effort that must be demanded of them?[150]

The Pearl Harbor attack, though a tactical disaster for

the United States, was a strategic escape from unsolvable

difficulties. The Japanese fired the first shot, opening

the war with a spectacular act of aggression which resolved

doubts and stilled debate.[151] As Sherwood shrewdly observes,

the Japanese attack saved the President:

There was just one thing that they could do to
get Roosevelt completely off the horns of the
dilemma, and that is precisely what they did,
at one stroke, in a manner so challenging, so
insulting and enraging, that the divided and
confused American people were instantly
rendered unanimous and certain.[152]

Although the Japanese completed the circle of justification

in the Pacific, the problem in the Atlantic remained. Decision

waited on Hitler's declaration of war. Here the President

was presented with another potential dilemma. Since

America's war plans were based on RAINBOW 5, calling for

immediate concentration of power against Germany and a

holding action against Japan, the United States was confronted

with a reversal of expectations. Unless Hitler honored his

pledge to Japan and declared war, the President would be

faced with another difficult choice. He would either

have to reverse American strategy, virtually abandoning his
allies; or conform to pre-arranged plans and declare war
against Germany, thereby challenging the isolationists and
the temper of the country.¹⁵³

4. Conclusion

The "first shot" presented the ultimate argument
justifying America's course of action in the prewar period.
Every step taken by the United States towards confrontation
had been defined as a defensive action against an insatiable,
unscrupulous foe: an enemy whose existence threatened
America's life. The final proof of this argument lay in
the aggression of the foe. Unless he directly attacked the
United States, justification would remain conjectural and
controversial, the nation still divided and uncertain. The
justifying arguments prepared the United States for
intervention; but they could not carry her over the
threshold of war. Only the enemy could accomplish that
end. Only the attack by the Japanese, followed by the
declaration of war by the European Axis, stilled doubt,
ended argment, and closed the circle of justification
by launching a full-scale crusade.

Chapter XII

A Time to Prepare for Time

Defense or offense? Production or participation? Stonewall or
Hemisphere defense? Direct or indirect approach? Political emphasis
or military preponderance? Just War or Crusade? Whatever war, whatever
means, whatever purposes, the basic need in the interwar period was for
time: time to prepare and to arm, to plan and to forge the implements
of war.

Month by month the Western Hemisphere drew closer to total
involvement, and though many hoped that American policy could avoid the
ordeal and postpone the final reckoning, most knew that war was inevitable.
All felt the terrible pressure, the relentless master who drove them
mercilessly towards the uncertain future, towards the ineluctable
accounting.

Basically this pressure was sharpened by the knowledge that time,
in the long run, favored the immense potential power of the United States.
But in the short run time was against her, the dangers of the present
threatening to cancel out the strength of the future. Her formidable
power was dormant, lulled to sleep by interwar isolationism, reinforced
first by prosperity and then by depression. Her energy lay unharnassed,
unprepared for combat. And before she knew it fully, before she was
psychologically and morally prepared, the danger was imminent, the threat
had materialized in the Far East and Europe. If the United States were
to save the future, she must primarily bridge the gap between aims and
means, balancing her forces against the strength of the enemy.

Time was short; time was urgent. The basic emphasis of the temporal
imperative in the prewar period was consistent. But the tempo varied,

shifting with the change of events, fluctuating with the attitudes of the participants, modulating with the periodic advance and retreat of danger. The United States prepared under the shadow of the Axis threat, whose strength shifted in pitch and intensity. The task of time grew as policy objectives expanded, as problems and pressures increased; but these were alleviated by the growth of American strength and the continued resistance of her allies.

It also varied simultaneously on several levels of interpretation: popular, presidential and military. Each could have a different sense of the urgency and pressure of time, and interpretation on one level could automatically influence and partially mold the attitudes of the others. The people's concern or indifference could liberate or hinder the President's initiative; but only his aggressive leadership could check or unleash the plans and preparations of the military and awaken the sluggish consciousness of the public.

One image summarizes the temporal imperative in the interwar period. The United States was a natural fortress, enclosed and protected by several advanced lines of fortification, each providing a vital interval of space and time, a buffer which would shield and protect her against the blows of any enemy. Four walls protected America from direct assault: the maintenance of peace, the French Army, the British Fleet and the geographical isolation of the Western Hemisphere. But while their strength would protect, their weaknesses would expose the garrison of the fortress to assault or penetration. The commander-in-chief, elected by the populace, depended ultimately on popular support. And the populace, absorbed in the routine of daily life, was unaware of the crumbling of the outermost ramparts. The members of the defending garrison--ill-paid, ill-equipped, unprepared to defend their fortress and its outer fortifications, totally dependent on the whim and will of the commander-in-chief--could neither plan nor prepare adequately without his consent or active support.

Previously we discussed the relationship of the temporal imperative to military, economic and psychological mobilization.[1] In the following two chapters we will study its relationship to and influence on public reaction, presidential initiative and military planning, tracing its shifting patterns and its basic consistency throughout the pre-Pearl Harbor period. We will use the alternation between the spur of urgency and the surrender to complacency as a gauge to measure the pressures of the temporal imperative on policy and strategy, following its rhythm on three levels: popular, governmental and military. We will explore the ways in which the temporal imperative molded presidential decisions and guided the hand of strategic planning, setting the tone for all wartime military thinking. We will also examine the influence which it exerted on American global strategic planning, reinforcing the policy decision that the Allies should concentrate their forces against Germany first while holding the Japanese at bay. In this connection the negotiations between the United States and Japan will be seen as tactical moves designed to gain time, as a temporal extension of priority selection.

1. Crisis and the Limits of Time

For most of the thirties, the American public slumbered. Although disturbed by the mounting crises in the Far East and Central Europe, most Americans did not relate these threats to their own security. They moved uneasily in their sleep, bothered by the sounds of the nightmare; but they did not awaken.[2] No sense of urgency made them relate the "rape of Nanking," the reoccupation of the Rhineland, the Anschluss, to the defense of the United States. These events, though provoking revulsion and indignation, took place far away, in the iniquitous Old World.

Then the tempo changed. From September, 1938, to December, 1941, from the Munich Conference to the attack on Pearl Harbor, the national sense of urgency mounted generally upward. Within this general pattern, however, the variations were frequent, fluctuating with the relative shifts of internal and external strength. The sense of urgency rose sharply during the Sudetan crisis; settled slowly after the opening of the Second World War in Europe; reached its nadir during the months of the Phony War; rose sharply and suddenly during the May-June 1940 crisis; sank perceptibly during the Presidential election; rose again over the Lend-Lease debate, remaining fairly keen until the German attack on the Soviet Union; finally oscillated violently in the last six months of 1941. It was a gradual awakening, marked by starts and shocks.

    a. From the Sudetan Crisis to the Beginning of the War.

    1) The Public: Apathy

The first awakening came in September, 1938, when the Sudetan crisis brought Europe to the edge of war and momentarily awakened Americans to their vulnerability. Since the event was massively covered by radio in Europe and newspapers at home,[3] its urgency and seriousness was apparent to the dullest minds. But little relation between the Munich deal and American security was noted. The isolationists denounced the transaction as indisputable evidence of the total corruption of the Old World powers.[4] The liberals and the radicals were appalled by its immorality.[5] Some realized "that Britain and France had, by their refusal to fight, let down America and betrayed the democratic cause."[6] But public consternation was unmarred by any concrete suggestion for either involvement or intervention.[7]

2) The Administration: Alarm

The President, however, had already sounded the alarm. He had already declared publicly that the deteriorating situation in Europe affected the interests and the safety of the United States. In a pre-Munich speech delivered at Queens University, Kingston, Ontario, on August 18, 1938, he stated the initial premise, the fundamental basis for the mounting sense of urgency throughout the remaining years of peace:

> We in the Americas are no longer a far away continent, to which the eddies of controversies beyond the seas could bring no interest or no harm. Instead, we in the Americas have become a consideration to every propaganda office and to every general staff beyond the seas. The vast amount of our resources, the vigor of our commerce and the strength of our men have made us vital factors in world peace whether we choose it or not.[8]

Only the belief that the fortunes of the New World were inextricably bound with those of the Old could evoke any sense of emergency or fear of time.

Although the solution of the Munich crisis brought some relief and hope to the Administration, all optimistic expectations were merely momentary.[9] A few days after the conclusion of the Munich Pact the President received discouraging reports from Europe. The crucially clarifying event, however, was the President's interview with Ambassador Bullitt on October 13, 1938.[10]

Mr. Bullitt began with the same initial premise as Roosevelt: the belief that any European conflict would vitally affect the interests of the United States even if the latter stayed out of war.[11] For such a struggle, Britain and France—America's first line of defense[12]—were obviously unprepared. And their weakness in airpower was exceptionally pronounced. From the Ambassador's report, the President realized that Hitler's success was partly due to his blatant use of military blackmail and the awe with which the French and British viewed German airpower:

> What impressed the French most was the existence of a German bomber fleet much larger than that of France and Britain

combined, and what the French military now wished ardently
was a rapid increase of French air resources of every kind,
for defense and for counter-offensive. They (and the British
as well) knew that a rapid increase could come about only from
American factories and they urged upon the United States a
development of American airplane production for Anglo-French
purchase.[13]

The logic was clear. If America's first line of defense in time of war

was weak and unreliable, then it should be reinforced and strengthened.

The uncertainty of Hitler's intentions and his present superiority in

military force lent urgency to this need.

The President knew the danger, felt its immediacy. The "momentous"
meeting of November 14, 1938,[14] in which American rearmament was initiated,

reflected his concern and realization that time was rapidly undercutting

American security. He began by citing the most recent intelligence

estimates of the relative air weakness of Britain and France.[15] He then

cited the frightening discrepancy in plane production between the Axis

and Allied powers, a discrepancy which showed little hope of improvement.[16]

Finally he came to the heart of the matter:

> 'The President then pointed out that the recrudescence of
> German power at Munich had completely reoriented our own
> international relations; that for the first time since the
> Holy Alliance in 1818 the United States now faced the
> possibility of an attack on the Atlantic side in both the
> Northern and the Southern Hemispheres. He said that this
> demanded our providing immediately a huge airforce so that
> we do not need to have a huge army to follow that airforce.
> He considered that sending a large army abroad was undesirable
> and politically out of the question.
> The President's next point was that in 1917 it took the United
> States thirteen months after its declaration of war to put the
> first plane on the battle front in Europe....hereafter there
> would be no such period of grace. We must have resources,
> plans and equipment for putting a large number of planes into
> actual operation at any time on short notice.
> He said there was a second reason why we had to have a large
> supply of planes...When I write to foreign countries I must
> have something to back up my words. Had we had this summer
> 5000 planes and the capacity immediately to produce 10,000
> per year, even though I might have had to ask Congress for
> authority to sell or lend them to the countries in Europe,
> Hitler would not have dared to take the stand he did." In a
> similar vein he elaborated the proposition that our foreign
> policy needs implementation.'[17]

The President's logic was fairly clear. Allied weakness in airpower would expose the West to diplomatic blackmail.[18] And a series of continued defeats, either diplomatic or military, would ultimately expose the New World to aggression. Moreover, America's lack of air power left Roosevelt powerless to counter or balance the growing strength of the German air force, either by diplomatic threat or by the massive sale of planes to the anti-Axis forces. Munich, by revealing the weakness of the British and French, had also exposed the vulnerability of the Americas. So, whether to bolster Allied strength or to guard the Western Hemisphere, the United States must arm rapidly, taking advantage of the brief "'period of grace.'"

3) The Military: Mounting Fears

Although the Army and Navy did not approve of the President's predominant emphasis on air power, preferring the development of a balanced force,[19] they agreed on the critical nature of time. Their sense of urgency was sharpened by the expanding immensity of their task and their consciousness of the inadequacy of their means. The threat was now rising with bewildering speed, thundering from both Europe and Asia. Two days before the President's November 14th meeting, the Joint Board indicated its concern and initiated the formulation of the RAINBOW plans.[20] As the Chief of Staff warned the Assistant Secretary of War, every problem was intensified by a drastic lack of means:

> The Army we have today is far below the strength contemplated by the National Defense Act and is totally inadequate to carry out these additional tasks without substantial increases in personnel and material. At present, it is actually not a serious deterrent to potential enemies; it lacks the necessary munitions; it cannot provide security for the homeland and at the same time provide the expeditionary forces necessary for the defense of the Western Hemisphere.[21]

The orthodox Army planner believed that the decisive unit, the

Infantry-Artillery team, must be strengthened. To one planner its
deficiency was glaring, dangerous and increasingly intolerable:

> The most serious weakness in our defense system is the
> shortage of mobile ground forces. Emphasis has been
> placed on the expansion of arms particularly dramatic in
> character while the less spectacular basic combat unit—
> the Infantry-Artillery team—the sole unit whose action
> is decisive, has almost escaped notice. Nations still
> measure military power in numbers of divisions (Infantry-
> Artillery teams)—units that are self-sustained and complete;
> that are trained; that are equipped with modern weapons; and
> that are prepared to undertake decisive operations on the
> instant. Germany has some 90 of these divisions, Italy 45,
> and Japan is now employing approximately 50 on the mainland
> of Asia. The United States has not a single complete division.[22]

After listing the rising Axis threats in Europe and Asia, and the penetration
of Axis agents into the Western Hemisphere,[23] the memorandum warned"...we
cannot close our eyes to the possibility of this nation becoming embroiled
in a war in the Atlantic, in the Pacific, or in both areas."[24]

It also asserted that the United States should have the means to
reinforce "any threatened area,"[25] delineating the danger that a hostile
power could entrench itself in the Western Hemisphere, threatening
such crucial areas as the Panama Canal:[26]

> The above mentioned contingencies will set up immediate demands
> for small, mobile, seasoned, hard-hitting, Infantry-Artillery
> teams—teams that can reinforce our overseas possessions and
> undertake the most difficult of military operations, landings
> on hostile shores. Such landings may be necessary to prevent
> extension of hostile activities; to destroy enemy bases that
> threaten our security; and to seize and hold bases of operation
> for our own naval, land, and air forces. Some of these
> operations may have to be undertaken before war becomes a fact.
> Our present Army cannot meet these demands...The War Department
> has no thought of aggression, nor does it desire to build up
> and maintain in peace the military forces that might be required
> to win a war. It believes that the very existence in peace of
> five complete and effective combat teams might serve as a
> preventive of war. It is firmly convinced that should war
> occur the need for these units will be immediate and imperative.[27]

Both the President and his military advisers, therefore, sought to
answer the threat to the Western Hemisphere. But they evolved different

solutions. The President, seeing the answer in production, emphasized
the creation of massive air power to reinforce the weak Allied air fleets.
The military advisers, thinking primarily, if not exclusively, of national
defense, saw the need and the answer in more conventional terms. They
emphasized the buildup of assault and expeditionary forces which could
be used to defeat or uproot any Axis move across the Atlantic. The
build-up of Infantry-Artillery divisions would bolster the striking force
of the Army and prepare it for hemispheric defense.[28] Both the President
and his planners agreed on three fundamentals: the multitude of dangers,
the scarcity of means, and the shortness of time.

    b. At the Opening of the War

        1) The Public: Sympathy and Complacency

    As the months slipped by, moving inexorably towards the outbreak
of the European war, the anxiety of the American people, the Administration,
and the military planners rose. The outbreak of war found the American
nation and its President united in sympathy and aim. Both hoped for the
victory of the Allies. Both wanted neutrality and peace for the United
States.[29] The ultimate incompatability of these two aims was ignored or
forgotten; and, therefore, urgency was temporarily muffled by over-
optimistic assumptions. Throughout the first month of the war the
temporal imperative vacillated, turning with every current estimate of
Allied capabilities, declining with every prediction of future Allied
success. Gradually the sense of urgency vanished. The Allied walls of
resistance—apparently formidable—still stood. Only their destruction
would finally shatter public complacency, fully awaken the nation and the
Administration to the mounting danger. At the beginning of the war the
possibility of a complete German victory was never formally considered.[30]

2) The Administration: Doubts and Fears

After the Polish campaign, American fears were almost totally stilled. But some of the more well-informed members of the Administration, cognizant of Allied weakness and appalled by the non-aggression pact between Germany and Soviet Russia,[31] had darker thoughts. Assistant Secretary of State, Berle, was one of them. He saw the future as immediately, almost inevitably, dangerous:

> "In this war...we cannot, so far as I can see, count on a military victory of Britain, France and Poland. Should they be on the eve of defeat, the square question would be presented to us whether to enter the war using them as our outlying defense posts; or whether to let them go, treble our navy, and meet the ultimate issue between us and a Russo-German Europe bent on dominating the world somewhere in the Middle Atlantic. My mind is rather running on the latter. This is brutal, and depends on a consideration of national interest. Matters may not get to this point. The Russian-German domination would be huge, impressive, and in appearance terribly powerful. Yet it reverses the processes of men's minds in a way which I do not believe can be permanent. Winning or losing, that combination must eventually break up. Even if it is victorious, we should be in a position to hold a powerful and almost impregnable line for a few years; and those years ought to see this tremendous combination tear itself to pieces internally; after which Europe will tend to re-emerge. But they will be ghastly years."[32]

Berle, therefore, envisioned the possible destruction of the Allied walls of resistance, the eventual challenge of the enemy coalition against the New World, and the ultimate internal dissolution of that coalition.

The President's attitude is more difficult to fathom. Even today, we cannot completely guage the thought processes or trace the logic of that extraordinary master of indirection. He knew, from the reports of his Ambassadors and attachés, that the Allies were militarily far weaker than they appeared.[33] If the worst happened, Allied resistance could crumble rapidly. But, despite his apprehensions, the President--first to sound the tocsin of alarm in 1938--proceeded as warily and furtively, as cautiously and as temperately as if the United States had unlimited

time in which to re-arm. His apprehensions about the strength of the
Allied nations were offset by his domestic worries, and his continued
fear of Congressional isolationism.[34] These pressing, more immediate
problems inevitably shackled the conduct of any foreign policy and
muffled the urgency of decision.

3) The Military: Public Silence

The President's immediate reaction to the outbreak of the European
war was to proclaim a "limited" national emergency and to issue an executive order permitting increases in the armed services.[35] But these increases,
considering the painful gap between ends and means, were unspectacular
and unsensational. On September 5, 1939, the President only authorized
a slight increase in personnel: 17,000 men,[36] leaving the military establishment far below the authorized goals of the National Defense Act of
1920 of a Regular Army of 280,000 men and a National Guard of 450,000 men.[37]
Although the increases did not meet the Chief of Staff's quotas, he publicly supported them and professionally made the best use he could out
of them.[38] So neither the President nor his chief strategic adviser spoke
with a clear voice, despite their awareness of weakness, despite the
continued need to plan and to prepare for the defense of the entire
Western Hemisphere. One was silenced by political necessity; the other,
by his military creed.[39]

c. The Phony War

1) The Public: Continued Lethargy

The indecision of the first period was followed by the lethargy
of the "phony war." The continued stillness on the western front throughout the remainder of the autumn and winter of 1939-1940, muted the sound
of danger, the cost of continued delay. The public slumbered, comfortable

in its belief that the Allies would win the war, that American involvement was neither necessary nor desirable.[40] And the insouciance of the masses was fed by the opiates of the experts:

> Prominent military commentators, like George Fielding Eliot, and Hanson Baldwin, appeared convinced that the Allies were bound to win in the end and that, consequently, the United States had nothing to fear. In some of the highest circles of the Army it was thought that the French and Belgian fortifications guaranteed those countries ample security and that in any case the French army was capable of taking care of itself in the face of any attack by the Germans. On the radio the ever-popular General Hugh S. Johnson declared that Hitler could not master sufficient sea power to threaten us even if he built warships for fifty years, and that furthermore, the combined fleets of any conceivable coalition could not land in either North or South America against a well-prepared defense.[41]

For the American people and their pundits time ran slowly, yielding the ultimate advantage to the Allies.

2) The Administration: Private Fears and Public Silence

For the President and his advisers the picture was neither hopeful nor reassuring. Well informed by the pessimistic reports of his Ambassadors, Joseph Kennedy in London and William Bullitt in Paris, the President knew the weaknesses of the Allies. Mr. Kennedy reported at length on British and French economic conditions, stressing their failure to outproduce Germany in either submarines or planes.[42] He drew a dark picture of the condition of morale: "The people of Britain and France...were low in spirit and yearned for an early peace."[43]

Ambassador Bullitt, who paid a visit to the front lines in December 1940, was convinced that French resistance might crumble under a German air assault.[44] Throughout the phony war period, he constantly reminded the President of Allied aerial vulnerability, stressing the imperative role which the United States could play in reinforcing the British and French.[45]

How seriously did the President take these warnings? How actively did he spot danger lurking in the lull on the Western Front? How strong was his sense of urgency in the pause before the tempest? Any answer is speculative and uncertain. But some sort of interpretation is imperative.

As distinguished and perceptive a biographer as Robert E. Sherwood believes that the President shared many of the wishful illusions of the general public, that he was unaware of the urgency until the fall of France fully awakened him:

> It is my belief--and this is pure speculation--that at this time and up to the fall of France, Roosevelt was wishfully hoping that Britain and France would prove indomitable in the West, that the Soviet Union would keep Germany contained in the East, that this stalemate would last until the German people would become fed up with "guns before butter" and revolt, thereby bursting the Nazi bubble so that peace would be restored without the need for American armed intervention. It seems quite evident that Roosevelt did not have full comprehension of the real, paralyzing force of the Nazi fury, nor of the imminence of the danger to the United States, until the Blitzkrieg was hurled into France in the spring of 1940.[46]

Probably these wishful thoughts did cross the President's mind repeatedly during the phony war, for they represented the ideal solution to the complexities of choice that lay before him. But he could hardly have been deluded by their easy promises. For, unlike the American public, he was well informed, well aware of the dangers and uncertainties of the situation. And later research shows that he was keenly sensitive to the potential disaster looming in Europe.[47] In a December 14, 1939, letter to William Allen White, the President expressed his fears, his concern with the prolonged indifference of the American people and his sense of urgency:

> Here is the thought for you to devote thought to. Taking things in their broadest aspect, the world situation seems to me to be getting rather progressively worse as the weeks go by. No human being, with the best of information, has the slightest idea how this war is going to come out. But the fact remains that there are four or five possibilities, each

leading to greater chaos or to the kind of truce which
could last only a very short period....[48]

After sketching the possible developments which could materialize

from the Russian–German combine—especially the possibility of a division

[49]

of the spoils of the world—the President lashed out at the source of

his frustration: the insouciance of the public:

> What worries me, especially, is that public opinion over here
> is patting itself on the back every morning and thanking God
> for the Atlantic Ocean (and the Pacific Ocean). We greatly
> underestimate the serious implications to our own future and
> I fear most people are merely going around saying "Thank God
> for Roosevelt and Hull—no matter what happens, they will
> keep us out of war." The Lord and you know perfectly well
> that Roosevelt and Hull fully expect to keep us out of war—
> but on the other hand, we are not going around thanking God
> for allowing us physical safety within our continental limits.
> Things move with such terrific speed these days that it is
> really essential for us to think in broader terms and, in
> effect, to warn the American people that they, too, should
> think of possible ultimate results in Europe and the Far East.[50]

Whatever the President's fears, whatever his anticipations, nothing

during the Phony War freed him from the paralysis of indecision which

followed the repeal of the Arms Embargo. And even the measures he ordered,

the preparations he allowed, did not touch the surface of the problem.

Everything was enacted at a leisurely pace; nothing sensational was

either decreed or discussed; every care was taken not to alarm, not to

awaken the anger of the isolationist watchdogs in the Senate and the House.

3) The Military: the Slow Pace of Mobilization

And no clear voice, no warning or protest, came from the military

planners of either service. They considered the possibility of Allied

defeat, but it remained an academic problem, a remote contingency. Plan-

ning still revolved around the defense of the United States and the

protection of the Western Hemisphere, even though the military were

still convinced that the Allied walls of resistance would stand, that

the dam would hold against the flood of Axis aggression.[51]

Discouraged by the President's apparent indifference and saddled with meager appropriations, the War Department planners were bound by the inadequacies of national defense. Neither military nor economic mobilization moved with any speed. There were no further increases in the size of the armed forces after the limited troop increase decreed by the President at the outbreak of war.[52] There was, however, one notable exception to the general unconcern about the future. During the Appropriations Hearings, General Marshall warned the members of the Committee that time might be shorter than anyone expected: "'If Europe blazes in the late spring or early summer, we must put our house in order before the sparks reach the Western Hemisphere.'"[53] Few listened.

And if the plans for military mobilization lagged, the plans for industrial mobilization hardly budged. In August, 1939, President Roosevelt had created the War Resources Board under the chairmanship of Edward M. Stettinius, Jr., to review the Industrial Mobilization Plan of the War Department.[54] Despite its purely limited aim, this board soon acquired a sinister reputation, being denounced in liberal circles as an extension of the interests and power of the Morgan banking empire.[55]

The Report of the War Resources Board was innocent and innocuous. Rejecting the proposal to create an economic superagency which would dictate the war effort at home, it merely recommended the creation of a War Resources Administration to command industrial mobilization "'coordinating America's productive capacity with the requirements of the Army and Navy and of the civilian populatic .'"[56] This insignificant document was treated with the secrecy and circumspection usually devoted to top flight intelligence reports. The Board was eliminated and its report exiled to the vaults for the duration.[57]

For the public, the President and the military, the Phony War was a period of "silence and slow time." If the President and some of his advisers anticipated the oncoming spring offensive in France with misgiving and trepidation, if General Marshall prophetically warned Congress that the war could explode suddenly, neither by action nor by public pronouncement did either the Chief Executive or his military advisers attack the general lethargy enveloping the entire country. They acted uniformly as if time were infinite.

This attitude contrasted sharply and surprisingly with the anxiety and urgency of the post-Munich period. Logically one would expect a sharper sense of emergency; but the rhythm of war carried its own logic, its own tempo. After the rapid conclusion of the Polish campaign, it settled down to a monotonous routine of patrol and counterpatrol along the Western Front. The phlegmatic expectations of the Allies infected our vision, dulled our anticipations. Their failure to order more planes, their neglect to adopt the stringent measures necessary for victory in total war, their dilatory conduct of operations, succeeded in offsetting any sense of emergency. To the public and to many military experts, it looked like a play without end. And this general indifference, combined with the President's natural cautiousness and the domestic situation, paralyzed effective action.

d. The Impact of the May-June 1940 Crisis

1) The Public: The Disintegration of Complacency

But a terrible awakening was at hand. The campaign which shattered the French Army swept aside the lethargy of the Phony War. Unprepared materially or psychologically, Americans saw the hand of darkness and terror descending over Europe and felt the roar of fear rise within their

own hearts.[58] The initial reaction was panic.[59] Danger was
imminent; menace, immediate.[60]

2). The Administration: Initiative and Action

Although the President had worried about the ability and
the preparedness of the Allies,[61] he never anticipated the speed
and momentum of the Nazi offensive. According to Langer and
Gleason:

> ...almost everyone, from the President down, was
> quite unprepared for a swift German victory in the
> West. What with the Maginot Line, the British Fleet
> and the industrial potential of the United States
> there seemed to be no reason why Britain and France
> should not at least hold their own.[62]

Not even the most pessimistic fears of the Administration
could match the 1940 cataclysm.[63]

As the crisis moved towards its climax, Roosevelt acted
to mobilize the energies of his people. He understood the
meaning of the May disaster. If the second and third walls
of resistance, the French Army and the British Navy, collapsed,
then the last wall of resistance, the distances of the
Atlantic and the Pacific, gave no protection. The President
knew that America's relative defenselessness and unpreparedness
mocked the illusions of geographical invulnerability.

Although the President drew his moral and dissected
the illusions of isolationism in his speeches of May 10 and
May 16 to the Pan American Scientific Congress[64] and to the
American Congress,[65] his fullest lecture on the implications
of modern warfare was delivered in his fireside chat of
May 26, 1940.[66] Here he excoriated the blindness that had
dominated the Phony War, a blindness which only the
onrush of events had finally cured:

> There are many among us who in the past closed their eyes to
> events abroad--because they believed in utter good faith what
> some of their fellow Americans told them--that what was taking
> place in Europe was none of our business; that no matter what
> happened over there, the United States could always pursue
> its peaceful and unique course in the world.
> There are many among us who closed their eyes, from lack of
> interest or lack of knowledge; honestly and sincerely thinking
> that the many hundreds of miles of salt water made the American
> Hemisphere so remote that the people of North and Central and
> South America could go on living in the midst of their vast
> resources without reference to, or danger from, other continents
> of the world.
> There are some among us who were persuaded by minority groups
> that we could maintain our physical safety by retiring within
> our continental boundaries--the Atlantic on the east, the
> Pacific on the west, Canada on the north, and Mexico on the
> south....
> To those who have closed their eyes for any of these many
> reasons, to those who would not admit the possibility of the
> approaching storm--to all of them the past two weeks have
> meant the shattering of many illusions. They have lost the
> illusion that we are remote and isolated and, therefore,
> secure against the dangers from which no other land is free.[67]

The final wall between the Old World and the New, isolation, was a

mere illusion, a phantom reduced to nothingness by modern technology

and its application to the art of war.

As the crisis mounted, so did the President's sense of danger.

After Dunkirk, he had little hope that the French could save the military

situation.[68] He saw clearly how closely the ultimate outcome of the

conflict in Europe would affect the fortunes of the United States, and

realized that time was of the essence.

On June 10th, a note of urgency was emphatically stressed in the

President's famous Charlottesville address, his announcement of a

double program of national rearmament and aid to the Allies.[69] He began

by stressing the unusual, critical nature of the present time, comparing

the 1940 crisis to the most decisive periods of American History.[70] The

nature of the crisis emphasized the need for speed:

> All roads leading to the accomplishment of these objectives
> must be kept clear of obstructions. We will not slow down
> or detour. Signs and signals call for speed--full speed
> ahead. Yes it is right that each new generation should ask
> questions. But in recent months the principal question has
> been somewhat simplified. Once more the future of the Nation,
> the future of the American people is at stake.[71]

But Roosevelt did not confine himself to proclamations. Filled

with the pressures of the moment, he implemented his eloquence with

measures designed to forestall the menace, build-up America's defenses,

and shore up Allied resistance in Europe. Rearmament was finally

launched in the President's May 16th message to Congress.[72] Although he

placed great emphasis upon the production of aircraft and the overall

build-up of air power,[73] his recommendations provided for the needs of

all the services.[74] And, most significantly, he made it absolutely clear

that neither the needs nor the requests of national defense would end

with this Congressional message:

> Defense cannot be static. Defense must grow and change
> from day to day. Defense must be dynamic and flexible,
> an expression of the vital forces of the Nation and of its
> resolute will to meet whatever challenges the future may hold.[75]

The previously sluggish Congress awoke to its responsibilities under

the impetus of the crisis and the President's leadership. By the end of

May it had passed appropriation bills calling for an expenditure of almost

$1,500,000,000 and authorizing contracts of approximately $260,000,000.[76]

But, as Roosevelt had warned, this appropriation merely marked the begin-

ning. On May 31, 1940, requesting supplimental appropriations, he

emphasized the danger of delay: "The one obvious lesson of the present

war in Europe is the value of speed. There is definite danger in waiting

to order the complete equipping and training of armies after a war begins."[77]

Again Congressional reaction was rapid and unequivocal. On June 26 the

necessary appropriations were passed.[78]

Under the impact of the disaster in France, moreover, the President sought to bolster Allied resistance, reinforcing the outer works to protect the inner fortress.[79] Anticipating the defeat of the French Army,[80] he hoped to salvage the French fleet[81] while strengthening the British Navy. Despite the formidable difficulties of aiding the United Kingdom in the summer of 1940, American supplies being so short, the President approved the British request for "500 field guns (75's) with ammunition,"[82] over the opposition of the General Staff.[83]

The President provided leadership and direction to the military mobilization of the country, but he persistently discouraged economic mobilization. The prophets, especially Bernard Baruch, were clamoring for the establishment of controls over war production and the initiation of the War Mobilization Plan.[84] The President ignored them.

Roosevelt temporized over any control agency; but paradoxically supported and implemented the 1940 Munitions Program.[85] This War Department proposal integrated military mobilization and industrial production, calling for sufficient equipment and reserves for a Protective Mobilization Force of 1,200,000 men by the autumn of 1941 and for a force of 2,000,000 men by the close of 1941.[86] The plan also promoted the build-up of the aircraft industry to the capacity of 18,000 planes a year.[87] Skirting the issue of control, Roosevelt nevertheless fully supported the demands of his military advisers, once they were trimmed to conform to political and budgetary necessity.[88]

3) The Military: Single Solution to Disaster

Often the military's sense of time ran ahead of their commander-in-chief. In the Phony War their materiel proposals had been conservative and undramatic; now, as the danger of a total Allied defeat loomed, they became radical and urgent, demanding full concentration on national rearmament.[89] On May 22, 1940, the War Plans Division drew the moral: "For at least a year, the United States Army and Navy would have to limit their activities to 'offensive-defensive operations in South America in defense of the Western Hemisphere and of our own vital interests;... possible preventive occupation of European possessions in the Western Hemisphere; and the defense of the continental United States and its overseas possessions East of the 180th Meridian.'"[90] Since American military forces were totally incapable of intervention either in Europe or the Far East,[91] and since the crisis was urgent, the United States should concentrate exclusively on limited tasks.

To defend the Americas from Axis attack, the United States would need expeditionary forces which could repel an invasion or uproot an occupation force. But by June, 1940, she had only a modicum of force to meet a maximum threat. The General Staff had merely earmarked the 1st and 3rd Infantry Divisions--respectively on the east and west coasts-- to form the nuclei of future emergency expeditionary forces.[92] Throughout 1940 their training and general fitness for combat remained appalling,[93] eminently unsuited to field operations, particularly to complex amphibious landings.

By the summer of 1940, however, the need for total mobilization was obvious to the American General Staff. A total Allied defeat seemed imminent and the loss of the French and British fleets was a distinct possibility.[94] Generally linked with the beginning of mobilization were

two other proposals: the adoption of a defensive line in the Pacific
and the cut-off of all Allied aid. Together these three measures would
help to allign needs with means. On June 17, 1940, a week before the
formal conclusion of the French-German armistice, General Strong
recommended this program to the Chief of Staff.[95] As he saw it the
third proposal would involve a variety of actions:

> 3d.--An immediate mobilization of national effort for
> Hemisphere Defense in order to meet the coming emergency.
> This involves an increase in naval strength in the Atlantic--
> an increase of strength in the Regular Army, and early mobili-
> zation of the National Guard, a marked increase of production
> of munitions, immediate preparations for protective seizure
> of key British and French possessions in the Western Hemisphere,
> preparation for immediate active military support of existing
> Governments in other American Republics and the furnishing them
> at the earliest possible date of means of defense on long term
> credits. It likewise involves a readjustment of our economic
> set-up to include other American Republics on a basis of
> approximating equality. [96]

Strong's program would allow the United States to concentrate in space
and time, ultimately strengthening hemispheric defense.

Perhaps echoing this warning, the Chief of Staff sent a memorandum
to Admiral Stark urging United States concentration on the Western Hemisphere.[97] After delineating the major tasks involved, he ended by weighing
the magnitude of the job and America's critical dependence on time:

> The essence of the problem is time. Consequently the
> definite suspension of French and British resistance should
> become the signal for the start of complete mobilization of
> all our national resources....[98]

Again the military leaders agreed with the President on the need
for speed, on the dangers of delay. But again their minds fastened on
a different objective. Whereas the President banked his policy and
decisions on the ability of the British to withstand the onslaught, to
hold the last wall of defense between the Axis and the Americas, the

military chiefs assumed the worst, planning for the total defeat of all Allied forces and for the consequent challenge to the security of the Western Hemisphere. To them there were no walls left. The task of protecting and arming the inner citadel could no longer be postponed. The enemy would soon be at the gates, and woe to those who had given away the arms necessary to defend the final fortress. But, though the President also realized the weakness of the inner citadel, he again drew the opposite conclusion. America's weakness could best be offset by shoring up the outer defenses with the frantic hope that they would hold, granting a necessary interval of time.

e. From the Battle of Britain to the Election of 1940

Time was short. But how short? Here interpretation turned on the outcome of the Battle of Britain. If the President's more optimistic prediction was correct, British resistance would hold. If the military planners were correct, British resistance would crumble; and the enemy would stand on America's threshold. The United States would merely have lost time while seeking to gain it.

1) The Public: A Lapse into Lethargy

By the opening of the Battle of Britain, the American people had recovered from the profound shock of the May, 1940, disaster. Although the public sympathized with the British, following the course of their struggle with intense interest, [99] most Americans felt that England was doomed to defeat. They felt that intervention was futile and that only [100] limited aid made any sense. [101] Moreover, the public sense of urgency, so keen during the May disasters, was gradually blunted by the familiarity and continuity of the crisis. [102]

2) The Administration: Unceasing Urgency

For the President no respite was possible. The Battle of Britain,
the assault on the final wall, had begun. Over England, in the Atlantic,
in southeast Europe, the menace of an Axis victory remained imminent.
If the Germans did not successfully invade Great Britain, they could
still strangle the British economy by the wholesale destruction of
Allied commerce in the Atlantic; or they could outflank Britain's
Mediterranean position by intervening in the Balkans.[103] The dangers
had increased.

But the problem of the war, and America's possible involvement,
was complicated by domestic politics. 1940 was an election year, and
political pressures abetted the urgencies of the international situation.
A continued emphasis upon urgency could have politically boomeranged
on the Democratic Administration. It would have given the Republican
party a chance to denounce the President for previous negligence, for
ignoring the state of America's defenses until the present crisis.
Although the President publicly pledged further aid to the Allies and
continued rearmament,[104] his major emphasis was on continuation, not
initiation.

He, therefore, hotly denounced Republican charges of neglect, lacing
into them in his Madison Square address on October 28, 1940:

> I now brand as false the statement being made by Republican
> campaign orators,...that the rearming of America is slow,
> that it is hamstrung and impeded, that it will never be able
> to meet threats from abroad.[105]

He then neatly turned the tables on his opponents:

> That particular misstatement has a history. It came into
> the world last June, just about the time of the Republican
> National Convention. Before that, the responsible Republican
> leasers had been singing an entirely different song. For
> almost seven years the Republican leaders in the Congress kept

on saying that I was placing too _much_ emphasis on national
defense. And now today these men of great vision have suddenly
discovered that there is a war going on in Europe and another
one in Asia. And so, now, always with their eyes on the good
old ballot box, they are charging that we have placed too
little emphasis on national defense.[106]

The rest of the speech followed naturally. It excoriated the Republican

leadership for its previous indifference to national defense and mocked

it for its latter-day wisdom, all to the refrain of "Martin, Barton and

Fish."[107]

The repudiation of Republican charges predetermined the President's

position on the military state of the Union. The argument ran as follows:

our forces need strengthening, but they are nevertheless stronger than

they ever were before thanks to this Administration's persistent and

consistent efforts to bolster national defense:

Year after year I asked for more and more defense appropriations.
In addition, I allocated hundreds of millions of dollars for
defense work from relief funds....Today our Navy is at the
peak of efficiency and fighting strength. Ship for ship,
man for man, it is as powerful and efficient as any single
navy that ever sailed the seas in history. But it is not as
powerful as combinations of other navies that might be put
together in an attack upon us. Our Army and our Air Forces
are now at the highest level that they have ever been in peacetime. But in the light of existing dangers they are not great
enough for the absolute safety of America at home.[108]

Another prominent concern mitigated the President's emphasis upon

urgency: the fear of entanglement and involvement in the European war.

Since he wanted to reassure the nation and convince the voters that the

United States could and would remain at peace, the President repeatedly

denounced and ridiculed the belief that he was planning to intervene

or involve us in "foreign wars."[109]

The note of emergency, so stridently proclaimed in the early summer

of 1940, was fairly muted by the fall. The exigencies of the election

calmed the urgencies of time. The next crisis--the British dollar

shortage[110]--did not come to a climax until after Roosevelt's re-election;
and, fortunately for him, his programs of rearmament and foreign aid were
already rolling under the impact of an earlier crisis. He could content
himself with implementation and avoid innovation.[111]

The field most afflicted by the election blight was economic mobilization, namely because the President persistently failed to provide any
centralized authority for rearmament. None of the existing agencies
answered this need. The theoretical apex, the Council of National
Defense, was an administrative phantom;[112] the Cabinet was more a discussion
group than a decision making body,[113] and the National Defense Advisory
Commission was a body without a head, an organization without a chief.
The extent and limit of the latter's authority was a well-kept secret,
a study in intricacy and ambiguity which the oracle of Delphi would have
envied.[114]

But the difficulties did not end with this headless wonder. The
lackadaisical attitude of the President towards industrial mobilization
expressed his determination to merely superimpose the war economy over
the peace economy. He deliberately refused to choose between "guns and
butter."[115] Obviously, any full-scale change entailed sacrifice and
scarcity--two unpopular words at election time.

The President only made two concessions to the urgencies of
mobilization: a partial adoption of a program proposed by Secretary
Stimson and the creation of the Priorities Board within the National
Defense Advisory Commission.[116] But these steps were merely limited moves
lost in the general tempo of indecision.

The President's actions--his limited use of executive prerogatives
and avoidance of radical proposals and extraordinary legislation--did

not and could not tally with his estimate of the situation, with the
mounting danger. He knew that the English were coming to the end of
their dollar resources,[117] and understood the threat that the Battle of
the Atlantic was already assuming.[118] Yet, in the interval between the
summer crisis and the presidential election, he postponed and delayed
vital decisions he knew to be pressing and imminent.

3) The Military: Optimism and Continued Caution

By the fall of 1940 the military planners were more optimistic than
they had been in the long summer months of unrelieved crisis. The chances
of Britain's survival were brighter; the anticipated attack on the Western
Hemisphere had lost its immediateness. Whereas RAINBOW 4--adopted in
the spring of 1940--assumed that the defeat of the Allies was imminent,[119]
the general military estimate of the fall months predicted that British
resistance would last at least six months.[120] And since the Axis fleet
would need at least this amount of time to equip and refit for any
expedition against the New World, the United States had a year's interval
of grace.[121] British resistance would allow her to prepare for the ultimate
confrontation.[122]

Part of the new optimism reflected the attitude of the Strong-Emmons
mission to England. After their late summer trip, the two emissaries
from the War Department returned to the United States, favorably
impressed by the prospects for continued British resistance.[123] Ultimately
their conclusions partly shaped and influenced the September 25, 1940,
estimate of the situation: "The Problem of the Production of Munitions in
Relation to the Ability of the United States to Cope with Its Defense
Problems in the Present World Situation."[124]

But this estimate, known as the Strong memorandum, did not reflect

the initial optimism of the Emmons-Strong mission. It was far more
guarded; and, like most sensible military documents, it anticipated the
worst. Time, it admitted, seemed to be working for the United States;
but then the future was always uncertain, always treacherous. All
optimism depended upon the continued resistance of the British Isles,
the preservation of the final European wall against the Axis flood.
Here hope remained and chances were constantly improving:

> Here time was an ally. With each day the likelihood of Nazi
> invasion of England decreased. Hitler's violent air attacks
> were not diminishing the high British morale, and the Italian
> offensive in the eastern Mediterranean was of such uncertain
> strength that the British might prove able to bottle up the
> Italian fleet indefinitely even if Gibraltar fell.[125]

But though time seemed reassuring, it could prove treacherous. The last
possibility, the fall of Gibraltar, posed a somber prospect. Accompanied
by the accession of Spain and Portugal to the Axis cause, by the control
or conquest of French North Africa and the Atlantic Islands, it would
pose a formidable challenge to Anglo-American control of the Atlantic.[126]
The consequent loss of Dakar would,[127] moreover, expose Latin America to
penetration and invasion.

The planners admitted, however, that these dangers might never
materialize; and if they should, were unlikely to occur at the same time.
Also, immunity against Axis attack was likely to continue for possibly
a year after the surrender or removal of the British Fleet.[128] But the
overall vulnerability of the United States could be drastically increased
by a Japanese attack against her possessions in the Pacific. If this
occurred, time could turn suddenly and dramatically against her. With
the Navy unable to withdraw from the Pacific, the shores of the Western

Hemisphere would be exposed to the conqueror.[129] The conclusions of the

first section of the Strong memorandum were, therefore, somber:

> As to the Pacific prospect...there could be no assurance that
> Japan would not shortly move against the Dutch East Indies or
> the Philippines or Guam, especially in view of the American
> embargoes on exports to Japan, and in the event that the
> American protests should be regarded as bluffs. Within the
> near future, then, the United States might be confronted with
> a demand in the Far East for a major effort for which WPD gave
> warning, "we are not now prepared and will not be prepared for
> several years to come." Along with this realistic discussion
> of Far East realities were further advices on the Atlantic.
> Thus, if it developed that the British Fleet might be lost,
> "from that very day, the United States must within 3 months
> securely occupy all Atlantic positions from Bahia...to...
> Greenland." And "at any time...the United States may be
> required to fulfill its commitments for the employment of...
> forces to prevent German-inspired upsets of Latin-American
> Governments." And "in order to safeguard our own security
> the United States may at any time, even before collapse of
> the British fleet, need to occupy preventively Dakar and the
> Azores." [130]

Obviously, continued British resistance merely offered a spell of time,

a brief interlude on whose prolongation the United States could hardly

base her plans or preparations.

The second section of the Strong Memorandum examined the discrepancy

between the ends of policy and available means, concluding that the

military capabilities of the United States were totally inadequate.

They were insufficient to protect the Western Hemisphere and too meager

to permit any active strategy or vigorous effort to save England.[131]

The concrete needs were obvious to the authors of the Strong

memorandum. The United States needed "as quickly as possible the

fully equipped, well-balanced Army of 1,400,000 men agreed upon the

previous summer."[132] At present the Army could only field a force of

55,000 men, and it could only accomplish this at the heavy price of

denuding the Selective Service personnel and the National Guard of their

equipment.[133] The other services varied. The Navy was ready for war.[134]

But the Army Air Corps was not.[135] The conclusion of the second part was,

therefore, inevitable and totally predictable. The United States did

not have the means to implement the minimum objectives of American
foreign policy.

The third section of the Strong memorandum, therefore, recommended
the remedies, proposed the solutions which would erase this imblaance.
The primary objective should be the acceleration of the American
production through increased work hours and additional labor shifts.[136]
But this goal would be futile if the Administration did not synchronize
American rearmament with foreign aid. "Henceforth...productive
capacity available to foreign powers should be rationed so as to prevent
hamstringing American rearmament."[137] Even the plant expansion financed
by the British should be subject to American control if national
security required it.[138] But these means would remain inadequate unless
economic mobilization was firmly controlled from above. The final
recommendation of the Strong Committee was for the establishment of a
high-level committee--composed of members of the War, Navy, and Treasury
Departments and of the Defense Advisory Commission. Its job would be
"the implementation of the recommendations contained in the report."[139]

So the top Army planners of the nation had examined the military
situation--its promises and its dangers--studied the available means
and recommended a number of sound, radical solutions. Since it was a
top secret report, they could express themselves freely and fully. To
them the urgencies of time were more apparent than ever. For the Battle
of Britain was merely a brief respite against the tide of disaster. The
possibilities of the future were disturbing signs, warnings of an
approaching danger which would fall upon an unprepared victim unless the
United States mobilized for a supreme effort, for the formidable test.
She was not prepared; and, therefore, the perils of time grew with its

passage.

 f. From Lend-Lease to the German Invasion of the Soviet Union

  1) The Public: Comparative Enlightenment

Although the leadership of both parties was committed to the defense of Great Britain, the election marked a watershed in the conversion of the American people to international reality.[140] The President's definitions and explanations of national policy had been marked by ambiguity and indirection. But the general course of his actions—their overall pattern and direction—was unmistakable. His re-election meant that Americans accepted his judgment, approved the trend of his policies. If the majority of the electorate had feared involvement more than a German victory, it probably would have voted for Wendell Wilkie, despite his announced internationalism. Though the American public still hoped to maintain peace, it knew that an Axis victory would preclude any possibility of avoiding war. And from the end of the election to the beginning of the Soviet-German conflict, public opinion increasingly favored a policy of more and more active aid to Great Britain.[141] Its sense of urgency reflected the realities of war, the dangerous challenges of the continuing crisis in the Atlantic. It was ready to accept Lend-Lease; and later to favor escort of convoy between the United States and England.

The comparatively advanced position of public and editorial opinion probably reflected the debate between the isolationists, the interventionists and the internationalists.[142] The American public had an unusual opportunity to hear every argument: for remaining out of the war totally, for intervening fully and for seeking to balance foreign aid to the Allies with the maintenance of pseudo-neutrality.

There was, therefore, no return to the lethargy and blindness of the phony war. The American public and its editorial representatives were comparatively enlightened about the dangers of the present situation. And this was fortunate, since the spring crisis of 1941 produced an emergency as serious as that of 1940. Not so obvious or dramatic, not so sudden or unexpected, it was, nevertheless, a decisive challenge and one which could submerge the British as completely as last year's blitzkrieg had overwhelmed the French. The British wall was menaced by four prominent dangers: supply shortage, dollar bankruptcy, continuing attrition in the Atlantic and deterioration in the Mediterranean. If these challenges were not swiftly and successfully met and checked, English resistance would crumble. Without supplies they could not equip their forces; without dollars they could not purchase supplies; without control of the Atlantic they could not ship munitions and food to the United Kingdom; without control of the Mediterranean, they could not defend the long lifeline stretching between the European and the Asiatic axes of their Empire. Supplies, dollars, shipping and the Mediterranean were all essential to continued resistance.

2) The Administration: the Uncertain Pattern

The President, well informed through his diplomatic contacts and especially through his correspondence with the Prime Minister, was fully aware of the exigencies of the moment, fully cognizant of the precariousness of the British position. He could gauge the crisis better than any of his advisers, better than the American public. And yet—despite the urgings of the bolder members of his administration, despite the comparative enlightenment of the American public—the President's course of action lagged behind the time sense of both public and interventionist. Occasionally, he seized the helm of the ship of state; usually he drifted

with the tides of the moment. He could fire the country
with enthusiasm; or he could disappoint his advisers,
leading them to feel that the Administration was drifting,
uninspired and untouched by any real sense of emergency.
At times, boldness and caution would follow one another so
closely that today's press conference would obliterate
yesterday's fireside chat.

Actually, the President's leadership falls into three
phases during this period: a short perod of drift after the
election; a long period of bold leadership during the Lend-
Lease debate; and a long period of half measures, punctuated
by a few bold speeches and a number of significant actions.
Throughout this time, Roosevelt's sense of urgency remained
sharp; but his public statements and official acts fluctuated
according to his assessment of the public and Congressional mood.

The first pause was tactical. The President, under the
strain of the campaign, had not yet devised the answer to the
problem of the British dollar shortage.[143] Therefore, on
December 2, 1940, he took his famous cruise of the _Tuscaloosa_
with an insouciance that jolted even his admirers. According
to Robert E. Sherwood: "It seemed to some alarmed British
officials that Roosevelt, following his victory at the polls,
had lost interest in the war situation--or, at any rate, was
blithely wasting the time that was running so short."[144]

This brief respite was followed by the dramatic
presentation of the Lend-Lease Program, the sense of
urgency pervading and motivating throughout. The
hour was already late. The continuing drain on the

British dollar supply was so serious that it threatened to cut off all supplies from the United States within a short period. And since England's demands for munitions were literally boundless, the problem could no longer be postponed. Delay meant disaster.

The Chief Executive's handling of the problem was fired by his conviction that the need for decisive action was imperative. The classic example of the garden hose and the burning house expressed it[145] clearly. For--as the President pointed out--there was no time for extensive legal and commercial agreements, for insisting that the obligations of both sides be clearly understood, clearly presented. The house was burning down and action must precede deliberation. The fire must be extinguished. Only then--if at all--would the question of return or renumeration arise.[146] There was no time for normal procedure.

Lend-Lease, therefore, was boldly conceived, boldly announced and quickly implemented. The President's leadership had matched the challenge of the situation; and his decision solved the first two problems of the British: supply and finance. However, the other two remaining problems--the attrition rate in the Atlantic and the deterioration of the British strategic hold on the Mediterranean-- became increasingly dangerous in the first six months of 1941. The rate of sinkings in the Atlantic rose;[147] the British were driven out of Greece, defeated in Crete,[148] swept back in Narth Africa by Rommel who dramatically ended their victorious advance against the unfortunate Italians.[149] Every- where disaster loomed. The emergency grew so keen that a good many inter- ventionists saw no hope for Great Britain unless the United States entered the war.[150]

But, despite this mounting crisis, the Lend-Lease debate was followed by a marked, prolonged slump into the "valley of doubt."[151] As the fire and daring seeped out of his leadership, the President reverted to the tempo of the Phony War. Despite the gravity of the world situation, he delivered no major speech to the American people until his May 27, 1941, proclamation of national emergency.[152] And even this speech which rang with boldness was followed by a press conference in which Roosevelt publicly retracted almost everything he had stressed the previous night.[153]

It was as if a strident call to arms had been immediately followed by a call to retreat. Unlimited national emergency followed by business as usual. The President's public statements moved on an uneven path; and his decisions on military and economic mobilization, on national rearmament and foreign aid were marked by ambiguity and uncertainty. After the uncompromising clarity of the Lend-Lease proposal came the half measures, the compromises with which Roosevelt sought to forestall a German victory in the Atlantic and the Mediterranean. Since all these measures fell within his executive province, he did not ask Congress for any major enactments after Lend-Lease.

The urgency of the situation in the Atlantic was a natural corollary to the urgency of the situation which led to the Lend-Lease proposal. If the latter called for immediate solution, so did the former. If the United States guaranteed the supply, she would also have to assure delivery. The natural answer was escort of convoy. There were two possible versions of this solution: full escort of convoy, covering all Allied shipping from the United States to the United Kingdom, and limited escort of convoy, protecting Allied shipping up to the oceanic

limits of the redefined Western Hemisphere. The outstanding champion
of the first proposal was Secretary of War Stimson. Convinced that the
United States was inevitably committed to eventual entry into the war,
he thought that the President should take a vigorous stand on principle
and, through the sheer power of his leadership, carry the country along.[154]
Stimson believed convoying was "the only solution",[155] and Knox, Ickes,
Morgenthau, Jackson and Hopkins agreed.[156] The alternative, limited escort
of convoy, was embodied in Hemisphere Defense Plan No. 1.[157]

The President, however, was not prepared to take the ultimate step,
full escort of convoy, which, he felt, would probably provoke a German
declaration of war. He was not even ready to adopt the more moderate
variant: full and open convoy within the limits of the Western Hemisphere.
Instead he chose a series of accommodating measures, hoping to bridge
the problem and to free himself from the necessity of intervention.
These were summarized for the British Prime Minister on April 11, 1941:

> "1. We propose immediately to take the following steps in
> relation to the security of the Western Hemisphere, which will
> favorably affect your shipping problem. It is important for
> domestic political reasons which you will readily understand
> that this action be taken by us unilaterally and not after
> diplomatic conversations between you and us. Therefore,
> before taking this unilateral action I want to tell you about
> the proposal.
> 2. This Government proposes to extend the present so-called
> security zone and patrol areas which have been in effect
> since very early in the war to a line covering all North
> Atlantic waters west of about west longitude twenty-five degrees.
> We propose to utilize our aircraft and naval vessels working out
> from Greenland, Newfoundland, Nova Scotia, the United States,
> Bermuda, and the West Indies, with possible later extension
> to Brazil if this can be arranged. We will want in great
> secrecy notification of movement of convoys so our patrol units
> can seek out any ships or planes of aggressor nations operating
> west of the new line of the security zone. We will immediately
> make public to you position aggressor ships or planes when
> located in our patrol area of west longitude twenty-five degrees.
> 3. We propose to refuel our ships at sea where advisable. We
> suggest your longer shipping hauls move as much as possible west
> of the new line up to latitude of the Northwest Approaches.
> We have declared Red Sea no longer a combat zone. We propose

sending all types of goods in unarmed American ships to Egypt
or any other nonbelligerent port via Red Sea or Persian Gulf.
We think we can work out sending wheat and other goods in
American ships to Greenland or Iceland through the next six
months.
We hope to make available for direct haul to England a large
amount of your present shipping which is now utilized for
other purposes. We expect to make use of Danish ships very
soon and Italian ships in about two months.
4. I believe advisable that when this new policy is
adopted here no statement be issued on your end. It is not
certain I would make specific announcement. I may decide to
issue necessary operations orders and let time bring out the
existence of the new patrol area." [158]

These measures were obviously designed to relieve both the Mediterranean

and Atlantic crises, and represented the ultimate[159] solution to Roosevelt.

The Chief Executive's caution was further shown by the means with

which he implemented his decisions.[160] On the weekend of April 19-20 he

rejected Hemisphere Defense Plan No. 1 which ordered full escort of

convoy within the extended limits of the Western Hemisphere, merely

deciding on an intensification of patrol.[161] He redefined the limits of

the Western Hemisphere to aid the British, but did not assert the

freedom of the seas in a definite and forceful manner. His sense of

danger was strong enough to lead him to action, but not to unequivocal

commitment.

But the threat in the Atlantic was reinforced and complicated by

the mounting danger to the British position in the Mediterranean. The

consequences of a German triumph in North Africa with its potential

menace to the southern approaches to the New World,[162] were almost as

serious as the slaughter of merchant shipping in the North Atlantic.

Therefore, under the impact of the May crisis--when rumors rose that

the Germans were preparing to seize the Atlantic Islands--the[163] President

prepared to dispatch an Expeditionary force, thereby anticipating and

frustrating the Nazi design.[164] But even these relatively bold plans were based on remote contingencies. After Lend-Lease, no

bold moves were initiated. There were no fundamental changes

in military mobilization, the President being content to let
165

the enacted measures roll along, and to allow the military
166

planners to recalculate the mounting mobilization needs of

the Army.

Roosevelt's economic mobilization measures were also geared

to the slow movement of a long war. Again he failed to create

an effective directing agency, to infuse urgency into the

economic mobilization program, to interfere with the prerogatives

of the labor movement, to create either the spirit or the

agencies essential to the time.

The President did create a new overall agency, the Office of

Production Management (OPM), to replace the ineffective Advisory

Commission. But the progressiveness of this step was illusory,

the President still refusing to appoint a production czar.

Policy making was now concentrated into the hands of a council:

the Director (Knudsen), the Assocaite Director (Hillman) and the
167

Secretaries of War and the Navy. The lack of an overall manager
168

left final decisions in the hands of the President. According

to Langer and Gleason, this vacuum soon fatally affected the

efficiency of the organization:

> Within three months of its birth OPM had already
> begun to manifest "the same overlapping of functions,
> multiplication of liaison groups, delays, contradictions,
> and general confusion" that had hastened the demise of
> the Advisory Commission.[169]

An ineffective organization could not resolve these problems.

Economic mobilization was a task totally incompatible with the

peacetime "'fiction that we can perform a miracle of industrial

transformation without hurting anybody.'" [170] And the momentum and the
incentive were not there. The objectives of the job were fully
recognized, but the steps necessary for their implementation were not
carried out.

After the enactment of Lend-Lease, the statisticians of OPM calculated the cost:

> ...the total cost of providing the armed forces of the
> United States, Britain, and other foreign beneficiaries the
> materiel they professed to require in the calender years
> 1941 and 1942 would amount to some fifty billion dollars.[171]

Since the achievement of this objective would place a fantastic load
on American industry, drastic measures would be essential. Billions
would be required "for the construction and expansion of defense plants";[172]
the labor force would have to be greatly expanded;[173] and, "finally, 'some
curtailment of consumer income or the production of durable non-defense
goods or both' was essential."[174] Obviously, the goals of the OPM estimate
could never be reached if the economy continued on the business as usual
basis, still favored by the President. Finally, the OPM estimate was
a mere beginning. By the end of May, Stimson and Knox advocated a
tripling of the earlier estimate,[175] a task totally impossible without
full and immediate conversion to total wartime economy.

But although the President shared the above estimate of the situation, he did little to handle the problem. He established a National
Defense Mediation Board to handle labor disputes inimical to national
defense;[176] he created the Office of Price Administration and Civilian
Supply and the Office of Civilian Defense.[177] But none of these organizational changes made any substantial difference or achieved any
startling progress.

The pattern of the entire period--with its alternation between bold and apathetic leadership--is marked with an almost schizophrenic quality. The mystery of the President's insouciance is not explicable either by the international situation or his estimate of it. As the tempo and momentum of war pitched to new heights, as dangers multiplied, Franklin Roosevelt's actions and speeches seldom rose to the occasion. His timing seemed incompatible with international reality, irrelevant to the deteriorating situation. But the President's sense of timing was nevertheless the governing factor in his decision to move cautiously after the enactment of Lend-Lease.

Despite the public opinion polls, the President remained profoundly skeptical. Naturally cautious, though he also delighted in bold and unorthodox action, Roosevelt felt that the American public and Congress were not yet ready for a drastic move, not prepared to go beyond a conservative "short of war" policy. Escort of convoy went too far too fast.[178]

Basically the President felt that most Americans did not comprehend modern war. They did not understand either its speed or the need for quick decision. In a letter to Norman Thomas who warned him against adopting escort of convoy and other measures which would precipitate America's entry into the war "'crabwise,'" the President pessimistically commented on the public's limited understanding:

> "The trouble with 99% of us Americans--who are not very different from other people in the world--is that we think of modern war in terms of the conduct of war in 1812, or in 1861, or in 1898. It takes several generations to understand the type of 'facts of life' to which I refer. Very few people really came to understand the lessons of the World War--even though twenty years went by.
> The lessons of this war constitute such a complete change from older methods that less than 1% of our people have understood.

I wish you could be here for a week sitting invisibly at my side. It would not be a pleasant experience for you because you would get a shock every ten minutes."[179]

Listening with his inner ear, President Roosevelt had decided that the American public was not ready for intervention or for any measure leading inevitably to it. But he also listened with an outer ear. And his inclination to postpone any major decision in the spring of 1941 was strengthened by increasing intelligence that Nazi Germany was preparing an assault against the U.S.S.R.[180] If Hitler turned towards the East, the entire strategic situation would be altered. Although the President could hardly have calculated the full revolutionary effect of such a decision,[181] he knew that it would postpone any German invasion of the British Isles and curtail Axis operations in the Mediterranean. Hitler's new adventure would not abet the crisis in the Atlantic, but it would allow the President to take further action without fear of retaliation. Any premature move, however, could trigger a German reaction which would threaten Great Britain, destroy her Mediterranean position and bring Axis forces to the southern shores of the Atlantic. It could also provoke Japanese intervention. As Langer and Gleason remark, uncertainty would dominate until Hitler made his next move:

> There was simply no knowing in what direction the Nazi conqueror would strike next. If Egypt were lost, that would be bad enough....From the American standpoint a German advance through Spain into North and West Africa, followed by seizure of the Atlantic Islands and possibly by a lunge at northeast Brazil, appeared as a greater threat and one which would be obviated only if and when Hitler turned his divisions against Soviet Russia. There were innumerable reports that the Fuehrer was planning to do so, but it was impossible to give full credence to this intelligence....The President's indecision probably stemmed from all these considerations, as well as from the realization that to go on with the naval escort program would involve great risk of conflict

with the Germans at sea. This in turn would draw their full
forces to the west against Eritain and the United States and
would, in all likelihood, provoke the intervention of the
Japanese. It was certainly the part of wisdom to avoid all
provocative moves, to hold the policy of supporting Britain
to established procedures, and at the same time to do everything possible to prepare defensively against all possible
to prepare defensively against all possible German moves in
western Europe and the Atlantic. [182]

The United States should hold and wait, hoping that the passage of time

would rescue her from the exigencies of the moment.

So the President's approach was not merely motivated by political

caution and domestic fears, but also by his estimate of the situation

and anticipation of the German course of action. If the United States

were patient and waited, the Fuhrer's own actions could rescue her from

the dilemmas of the present. In this sense the President was wiser than

his impatient advisers.

3) The Military: Continued Optimism, Continued Apprehension

Roosevelt's military advisers were also keenly aware of the existing

problems. All agreed on the progressive deterioration of the British

position; all feared that the Germans would successfully establish full

hegemony over continental Europe and Narth Africa by the end of 1941.

Even if England still remained unconquered, her position would be fairly

hopeless. General Arnold, for example, confided to Secretary Morgenthau

his fear of an imminent German victory:

> "Arnold says that through his Military Attache in Berlin he
> is informed that Hitler expects to clean up the whole situa-
> tion in Europe by December 1; that his general staff is 90%
> sure they can take England any time they want to, but that
> Hitler plans to capture and have under economic control
> everything in Europe up to the Russian border and the whole
> of North Africa." [183]

Gerow, then Acting Assistant Chief of Staff, WPD, saw the strategic

situation as currently dangerous, but potentially hopeful. If Germany

were to win the war, it would have to be within the present year. During

1942 time would begin to turn against her. But as long as the critical period lasted, the possibility of the invasion and conquest of Great Britain remained real and pressing:

> It is impossible to predict whether or not the British Isles will fall or if so when. The present views of War Plans Division on this subject are:
> It is believed that Germany has a complete and accurate knowledge of our actual and potential productive capacity of our ground and Air Forces. A fair assessment for Germany to make is that aid furnished by the United States to Great Britain cannot dangerously affect the existing relative strengths on land and in the air prior to the winter of 1941-42. However, should the war be prolonged into 1942, Germany will be faced with a progressively deteriorating situation with respect to relative strengths. It is, therefore, assumed that the greatest danger which the British Commonwealth must face during the present year is greatly intensified air, surface, and subsurface activity coincident with or followed by an attempted invasion. During this critical period, the United States cannot afford to base its military program on the assumption that the British Isles will not succumb as a result of blockade, or that they cannot be successfully invaded. The critical period is assumed to be from the present moment until November 1st 1941. [184]

Since 1941 was the critical period, the turning point which would decide the future of England, the United States could not afford to commit all her resources or aid to Great Britain's defense. She would have to balance the requirements of foreign aid with those of her own national security, holding back full strength until the outcome could be gauged.

Gerow's time estimate was mainly geared to his evaluation of the progressive effectiveness of American aid to the British cause. But there were other reasons. The American military chiefs--including General Marshall--were convinced that "the United States could not be ready for war before March 1942." [185] Certainly the rate of military mobilization and the failure of the United States to develop a first class force between December 1940 and June 1941 reinforced this calculation.

By the end of 1940, tremendous progress had been achieved.
The Army had grown from 264,118 at mid-year to 619,403 at the
[186]
end of the year, the overseas establishments growing from
64,500 to 92,000 men. With the federalization of the National
Guard and the initiation of selective service, the United States
[187]
was moving towards the creation of a large military force.
Finally, there was also progress in quality. Important steps
in the organization of the United States Army had been initiated.
The tactical and training organizations were separated from
the territorial organization for purposes of administration,
supply and housekeeping; the GHQ and the field armies were
[188]
split from the corps areas. However, as the Army logistical
historians point out, many of these improvements were not
immediately translatable into combat terms:

> ...the very substantial progress achieved in this
> six-month period was largely in the necessary preparatory
> work of defining policy, working out procedures and
> organization, placing contracts and "tooling up."
> The output of organized, trained and equipped troops
> was not impressive. The influx of selectees into the
> Army had a disrupting and retarding effect on training....
> Organization tables for the triangular division, the
> basic unit of the new army, were not completed until
> late in 1940. Six months of munitions production,
> moreover, had added relatively little to the Army's
> stock of weapons...The output included no medium tanks,
> no heavy caliber antiaircraft guns, no new standard
> 105 mm. anti-tank howitzers...and almost no new heavy
> artillery....The production of .50 caliber
> ammunition had been meager.[189]

This largely untrained and unequipped army was certainly
unprepared for any major military venture.

Time did not immediately resolve these problems. By the
middle of 1941, recruitment had reached the level planned in 1940:
1,455,565. But the process of equipping the Army had lagged.
A midsummer G-4 estimate was explicit: "the equipping of

the ground army was about 'a year behind the expectations of a year ago,' which meant presumably that another year's production would be needed to meet the objectives laid down in summer of 1940 for mid-1941."[190]

These weaknesses fatally affected the Army's ability to deploy its power, especially for an emergency expeditionary force. This ability could prove crucial since the need for rapid deployment could arise at any moment. The United States could not wait to be fully mobilized before encountering the Axis: As the President warned, "'we must be ready to act with what (is) available.'"[191]

2. To the Final Limit:From the Invasion of the Soviet Union to the German Declaration of War.

The spring crisis of 1941 was not ended by American initiative, but be Hitler's invasion of the Soviet Union on June 22, 1941. This formidable strategic decision shifted the entire Axis emphasis from west to east, inevitably and continually drawing the greater bulk of Germany's army into the empty endlessness of the Russian wastes. From then on--with the possible exception of the late fall and early winter of 1944--Adolf Hitler could not extricate sufficient forces to reach any firm conclusion in the western theater. The beginning of the German-Soviet war erected a new wall against the Axis hordes. But it did far more; it pulled the Nazi divisions towards another direction, towards another goal. The Allied powers and the United States received a free gift of invaluable time.

But although American leaders were cognizant of the gift, they neither calculated its proper value nor estimated its ultimate cost. For them it was merely another interval of grace.[192] No one estimated correctly the fantastic staying power of the Soviet Union, its ability to stave off defeat long enough to prepare for victory. Since the

present situation afforded only a temporary advantage, Roosevelt's
supporters felt that it must be quickly exploited. But how? By
intervention or by only a continuation of all methods short of war?
And should the United States aid the Soviet Union in its struggle?
Since this decision would commit America to the defense of Communist
Russia, it would pose a difficult problem in public persuasion. It was
far easier to see the defense of the United Kingdom as integral to the
security of the United States than to believe that Communist Russia,
alien in creed and sentiment, constituted an integral part in the
anti-Axis offensive.

This misreckoning reinforced the need for immediate action. The
defeat of the Soviet Union by Nazi Germany would leave the Axis powers
entrenched throughout the entire continent. Relieving Hitler of all
anxiety about his eastern front, it would liberate his forces--except
for occupation troops--for a concentrated effort against the west. Once
the present campaign ended, the danger to the United States and its
potential ally, Great Britain, would be greater than ever. This
borrowed time, therefore, afforded no release from the exigencies and
pressures of war.

The urgency of the situation still demanded total mobilization.
But the final stage of the prewar period continued to move in spasmodic
cycles: periods of intense crisis when the decks were cleared for action.[193]
Alternated with periods of relaxed tension when the pressures temporarily
abated and the fear of confrontation receded. Until the opening of the
war, the undeclared struggle between the United States and Germany was
like a play in which every climax was almost immediately followed by an
anticlimax. Something always seemed about to happen. Even the final
stroke, the German declaration of war against the United States, lacked

drama. It was not the sequel either to a daring American decision or
a military clash between major antagonists. It was merely the anticlimactic echo of an explosion in the Pacific.

The uneven pattern of the temporal imperative in this period was
not the result of any declension of urgency, any basic change in the
situation which, in the minds of American leaders, irrevocably altered
the balance of power. It was again the product of the conflicting needs
of internal and external mobilization, especially of the manner in which
these needs were reflected in the attitude, pronouncements and actions
of the President of the United States.

a. The Public: The Ebb and Flow of Opinion

The public pattern or commitment to the urgency of the situation
moved in a generally even direction. The Americans increasingly favored
bolder expedients, progressively realizing that security ultimately depended upon the defeat of Hitler. But although the pattern of American
public opinion was consistently upward, it was not persistently even.
It had its starts and stops, its ebb and flow. And this unevenness
confirmed the President's continued caution.

Should the United States use the opportunity provided by the
German-Soviet conflict to announce full-scale escort of convoy in the
Atlantic? Any such drastic action depended upon public approval. As
far as the President could see there was still no clear signal that the
American people and their representatives were prepared to accept this
move. Actually there were some fairly obvious danger signals. On
June 30th, eight days after the beginning of the assault on Russia,
Senator Wheeler had successfully "referred to the Naval Affairs Committee

a resolution instructing it to investigate rumors that American
ships were already" engaged in escort of convoy.[194] Also, as
Langer and Gleason remind us, anti-Soviet sentiment was powerful
and widespread:

> Mr. Roosevelt could have been under no illusion about
> the extent of opposition throughout the country to
> any proposal to aid Communist Russia, not only from
> the isolationist elements but also from the ranks of
> the so-called interventionists and especially from
> the Roman Catholic Church.[195]

Debate raged over the desirability of further involvement
and aid to the U.S.S.R. The isolationists were elated by the
news of the German invasion of Russia. This new war, as they
saw it, was a struggle between two ferocious dogs:[196] let them
consume one another.[197] Convinced that the German attack ended
the so-called emergency, they rejoiced that the Administration
had lost its case. As the Chicago Tribune trumpeted on June 23:
"'the news was hardly less welcome in this country than in
Britain, for it means that if there ever was any justification
of our intervention in arms, that justification no longer
exists.'"[198] Even isolationists who saw the danger of a Hitler
victory, felt that aid to Stalin would merely elevate another
dictator: "'If Germany wins, Russia will go fascist. If
Russia wins, Germany will go Communist. There is no chance
for us at all. The question now is, are we going to fight
to make Europe safe for Communism?'"[199]

Those who favored aid to the Soviet Union were hardly
Communist enthusiasts. Unlike the isolationists and many
prominent members of the Catholic hierarchy, they felt that
Hitlerism was the more pressing threat. They also underestimated
the chances of Soviet survival or quick recovery after the

war. To them, the present respite was a blessed interlude not to be neglected. Perhaps the <u>New York Herald Tribune</u> was most clearly explicit on the advantages of American aid to the Soviet Union:

> "A Hitler victory over Russia and Britain means, in the coldest calculation of probabilities, the triumph of totalitarian barbarism throughout the world. A victory of Great Britain, the United States and Communist Russia holds out no such prospect. Even if Communist totalitarianism survives the strain in Russia, the fact that it would only do so in association with victorious democracy in Britain and the United States would give it no such untrammeled prestige and power as success would bring to Nazi totalitarianism. An essentially democratic world would still be possible. This is not a matter of ethics or ideology or theory; it is a matter simply of the practical facts of the practical situation before us." [200]

Actually the above view was held by the majority. According to a Gallup poll 73% of those questioned preferred a Russian to a German victory. [201] Clearly the President had enough popular support--for whatever reason--to extend aid to the Soviet Union.

But was it sufficient to take full advantage of the present situation, extending American power and forces into the North Atlantic, committing naval strength to the preservation of the British lifeline, risking the almost inevitable clash which would precipitate the United States into war? The answer now seems fairly clear. The American public supported Mr. Roosevelt in every decision he made on the Battle of the Atlantic, in every half-measure he took to solve the maritime crisis. There is every reason to believe that they would have supported the President even if he had taken far more drastic measures, even if, by adopting escort of convoy, he had thrown the gage of challenge at the Nazi Fuhrer. Paradoxically, however, it probably would not have supported an outright demand for an American declaration of war. Like the President, it preferred the accidental to the deliberate.

The public reaction to the announcement of the Atlantic
Conference is a pertinent case. It was immediately apparent
to the supporters and foes of the Administration that the
Conference was not merely an oceanic chit-chat culminating in
the promulgation of the Atlantic Charter. Political and
strategic discussions were admittedly held.[202] However, despite
the suspicion that agreements were made, the American public
enthusiastically supported the President.[203]

But there were still limits to the American public's
involvement. Even in the autumn of 1941, feelings were ambiguous,
marked by incompatible objectives. Langer and Gleason evaluate
the public mood:

> By the autumn of 1941 the American public had gone
> far toward identifying itself with the opposition to
> Nazism and the Axis. It was united in its desire and
> determination to see Nazism destroyed and was all but
> unanimous in holding that Britain must be sustained,
> if only in the interests of American and hemisphere
> defense....But the American people, while willing to supply
> material aid and even prepared to accept measures
> for ensuring the safe arrival of munitions in Britain,
> still clung to the hope that material sacrifice would
> spare them the horror of full-fledged hostilities.
> Public opinion polls showed that some 75 to 80 percent
> still strenuosly opposed direct participation in the war.[204]

Paradoxically, public resitance against American military
involvement increased as the implications of the short of
war policy became apparent.[205]

Therefore, even on the eve of Pearl Harbor, American
public opinion still hampered the President from moving
openly against Germany. And Congressional opposition posed
an even greater obstacle. Long after escort of convoy was
accepted by the general public, it was blocked and
discouraged by Congress.[206]

b. The Administration: Increasing Commitment

The President's approach usually mirrored the inconsistencies of the public temper, either by design or conviction. But in the last six months of peace, he increasingly recognized the necessity for eventual intervention, expecting or hoping that his dilemmas would be solved by direct action from the enemy. And, although he apparently hoped late into the fall of 1941 that America's contribution to victory could be restricted to production rather than to full-scale involvement, he could not persistently ignore the conclusions of his planners that American participation was the sine qua non of Allied victory.

The pressures of the temporal imperative, however, largely depended on continued Russian resistance. Unlike most of his military advisers, the President was confident that the Soviet Union could hold out until the beginning of winter, thereby tying down German forces in a protracted eastern campaign and easing the pressures on the Atlantic front. As Mr. Welles reported to Lard Halifax, the President was fairly hopeful:

> "The President said that we would undertake to supply urgently
> to the Soviet Union such of the orders which the Soviet Govern-
> ment desired to place in the United States which it might find
> it possible to ship and that the President had emphasized the
> fact that whatever was sent of an urgent character should
> actually reach the Soviet Union before October 1 at the latest.
> I added that the President had made clear his own opinion that
> if the Russians could hold the Germans until October 1 that
> would be of great value in defeating Hitler since after that
> date no effective military operations with Russia could be
> carried on and the consequent tying up of a number of German
> troops and machines for that period of time would be of great
> practical value in assuring the ultimate defeat of Hitler.
> The President had also stressed his belief that the more
> machines the Germans were forced to use up in the Russian
> campaign, the more certain would be the rapidity with which
> Germany would be defeated, since he did not believe that the
> ability for replacement on the part of Germany was nearly as
> great as that which had been supposed." [207]

Roosevelt apparently calculated Russian resistance as a stable and
dependable element. America's overall strategic situation was temporarily
and ultimately improved by the German-Russian war.

As the year wore on and the Soviet armies--driven back, severely
mauled and badly battered--continued in the field, the President became
more and more confident that the Russians could fight on indefinitely if
supplied with the necessary equipment and aid.[208] The new wall of resistance
had proved its strength and demonstrated its value.

Soviet resistance allayed the crisis in the Atlantic and preserved
England from any immediate assault by German divisions. The sense of
danger in the Atlantic, so evident during the spring months of 1941,
receded. Throughout most of that summer, despite a series of incidents,
the maritime situation stabilized, the emergency subsided.

However, in September, with the attempted "torpedoing" of the Greer,[209]
it returned with swift and sudden force. Seizing his opportunity, the
President, in his September 11 speech on national defense,[210] cleverly manipulated this incident, citing it as conclusive proof of the imminence of the
Nazi threat:

> This attack on the Greer was no localized military operation
> in the North Atlantic. This was no mere episode in a struggle
> between two nations. This was one determined step toward
> creating a permanent world system based on force, on terror,
> and on murder.
> And I am sure that even now the Nazis are waiting to see
> whether the United States will by silence give them the green
> light to go ahead on this path of destruction.
> The Nazi danger to our Western world has lond ceased to be a
> mere possibility. The danger is here now--not only from a
> military enemy but from an enemy of all law, all liberty, all
> morality, all religion.
> There had come a time when you and I must see the cold, inexorable
> necessity of saying to these inhuman, unrestrained seekers of
> world conquest and permanent world domination by the sword: "You
> seek to throw our children and our children's children into your
> form of terrorism and slavery. You have now attacked our own
> safety. You shall go no further." [211]

Repeatedly using the word "now" the President crystallized his meaning [212]
with his famous image of imminent danger: "...when you see a rattlesnake
poised to strike, you do not wait until he has struck before you crush
him."[213]

Why did Roosevelt again interject a note of urgency into the Battle
of the Atlantic, a note silent since the spring crisis? There were specific
and general reasons. Specifically the President sought to justify his
adoption of escort of convoy within western waters; he also wanted to
revise the Neutrality Law to permit full escort of convoy from the
United States to the United Kingdom.[214] His emphasis on an imminent Nazi
threat to the Western Hemisphere was useful and convenient, but reflected
his conviction that the climax of the undeclared war was almost upon us.[215]
Despite his expectations, however, the anticipated never happened, the
climax never occurred.[216] The act stayed in suspension. Despite the caution
and ambiguity which veiled his decisions, the President moved increasingly
towards intervention. By the late fall of 1941 the choice which had been
materializing within the Administration since the beginning of the war
was clear. The President had decided that the preservation of Great
Britain was more important than the maintenance of peace. Although he
still left the final act to the enemy, he had adopted part of the
Stimson program. The United States would assure the delivery of supplies
to England even if it had to escort convoys across the Atlantic and fight
every inch of the way. Roosevelt's actions showed clearly the shift
in his attitude during the last six months of peace. His decision to
support Russia (officially made on August 2) was an attempt to gain more
time: to prepare, to shore up Britain's position and rectify the situation in the Atlantic. His decision (at the Atlantic Conference) to initiate
full escort of convoy within western waters was of a totally different

nature. It anticipated, not merely rectified; and was made only after the British had successfully checked and controlled the submarine threat in the North Atlantic.[217]

Superficially, it would seem that the new situation lacked the intense urgency of the spring crisis. But Roosevelt was well aware that the present lull concealed imminent pressures which would soon create new dangers, possibly worse than ever before. The ultimate tasks of the British Navy in the Atlantic were far beyond its capacity:

> It should be remembered...that the Nazi wolf packs had carried their attacks far into the western Atlantic and that, when effectively opposed there, they had begun to shift their operations to the vicinity of the Cape Verdes and the Canaries. In order to check their depredations in the North Atlantic the British Navy was obliged to employ all available destroyers and corvettes, many of which were badly needed elsewhere and would indeed be essential for countering the submarine menace off the African coasts. By the summer of 1941 yet another aspect of the situation had emerged: if supplies were to be sent to the Soviet Union, the British and other shipping required would have to be escorted northward along the Norwegian coast to Archangel and Murmansk. This additional mission would be beyond British naval capabilities unless some measure of relief were provided in the Atlantic. [218]

The true importance of the President's decision to adopt escort of convoy in Western waters lay in his timing. Previously, he had waited until a situation ripened, until a crisis was fully developed and clearly dangerous; now, anticipating a future crisis, he acted to forestall.

But Roosevelt's decision was accompanied by one equally significant: the decision to ask Congress for a repeal of the restrictive sections of the Neutrality Law.[219] Although repeal of only Section VI, prohibiting the arming of merchant ships,[220] was initially demanded, he clearly had a larger purpose in mind. He also wanted the repeal of all provisions barring the entry of American shipping into combat zones. In his October 9, 1941, speech, the President stressed the urgent need for revision:

> I cannot impress too strongly upon the Congress the seriousness
> of the military situation that confronts all of the Nations
> that are combating Hitler. We would be blind to the realities
> if we did not recognize that Hitler is now determined to expend
> all the resources and all the mechanical force and manpower
> at his command to crush both Russia and Britain. He knows that
> he is racing against time. He has heard the rumblings of revolt
> among the enslaved peoples--including the Germans and the
> Italians. He fears the mounting force of American aid. He
> knows that the days in which he may achieve total victory are
> numbered.
> Therefore, it is our duty, as never before, to extend more and
> more assistance and ever more swiftly to Britain, to Russia,
> to all peoples and individuals fighting slavery. We must do
> this without fear or favor. The ultimate fate of the Western
> Hemisphere lies in the balance.
> I say to you solemnly that if Hitler's present military plans
> are brought to successful fulfillment, we Americans shall be
> forced to fight in defense of our own homes and our own freedom
> in a war as costly and as devastating as that which now rages
> on the Russian front. Hitler has offered a challenge which
> we as Americans cannot and will not tolerate. [221]

The President's meaning was clear. If the United States wanted to win

the race against time, if she wanted to deny Hitler his opportunity for

total triumph, she should--she must--revoke the restrictive provisions

of the Neutrality Act hampering our policy of aid and, therefore, abetting

the efforts and ambitions of the enemy.

Though he saw a climax and a confrontation approaching in the Atlantic,

he still neglected full-scale military and economic mobilization. In the

field of military mobilization, he made no effort to build the type of Army

necessary for the defeat of Germany. He initiated the Victory Program

merely to calculate the production needs of the Allied powers and with no in-

tention of receiving a full analysis of American manpower requirements for

participation and intervention. He then still clung to the hope that the

United States could limit its contribution to production, avoiding the

need to send or commit a large expeditionary force. In late September

he even sought to limit the size of the American Army: [222] "It is certainly

worth noting that the President at no time prior to Pearl Harbor
suggested further increases of the Army which, according to the
existing program, was designed for national and hemisphere defense
rather than for overseas operations against Nazi Germany."[223]

If military mobilization were hidebound by originally limited aims,
economic mobilization was still constricted by the slow tempo and
emphasis of quieter days. The initial failure of the production and
aid policy was obviously embarassing:

> By the summer of 1941 it was common knowledge that the flow
> of munitions from American factories was far from satisfactory.
> Deliveries to Britain were still on a relatively modest scale
> and the new program of supporting Soviet Russia involved
> commitments which, under existing conditions, were impossible
> of fulfillment. [224]

Although individual logjams could be broken by Presidential action,
any full remedy depended upon full-scale economic mobilization. And
this conversion awaited an American declaration of war. As Secretaries
Stimson and Knox repeatedly stressed, America's economic mobilization
would lag as long as her production was geared to peacetime momentum:

> Secretary Stimson, like his Navy colleague and others, was
> convinced that many of these difficulties stemmed from lack
> of adequate psychological motivation: it was impossible to
> get the country to make the requisite effort and sacrifice,
> to act as though the nation were at war, so long as the
> American people was still hoping to escape involvement. In
> Mr. Stimson's opinion it would in any case prove impossible
> to defeat Hitler simply by supplying arms for the use of
> others. He therefore relentlessly urged the President to
> provide courageous leadership, that is, to declare the existence
> of a war which was inevitable anyway and thereby arouse the
> people to greater productive effort. [225]

But the President opposed any declaration of war; and American production
continued to move at an inadequate pace unstimulated by an unmistakable
and unavoidable emergency.

Stimson's proposal for the direction and control of the economy also fell on deaf ears. The Secretary of War urged President Roosevelt to appoint a production czar who could control the entire war production effort: a "'single responsible head.'"[226] But the President again showed his long-standing antipathy towards this favored proposal.

However, though American economic mobilization lacked the necessary emphasis and drive, though it lacked overall direction and a firm steering hand, it did accomplish one of its essential aims in the remaining months of peace. It set and established the objectives of wartime production. Both the studies of the newly created Supply Priorities and Allocation Board (SPAB) and the calculations and estimates of the Victory Program represented an attempt to forecast the ultimate cost of the war.

Judging, therefore, the President's actions and statements in the final six months before Pearl Harbor, we can evaluate the ways in which the temporal imperative affected and guided the commander-in-chief. Between June and December 1941 the President became convinced that our entry was inevitable. He could see the climax rising in the Atlantic as it mounted in the Pacific. But his sense of urgency was tactical rather that strategic. Believing that the German involvement in Russia was effectively blunting the German drive for world conquest, convinced that Soviet resistance could hold and check the Nazi horde, he still hoped that American intervention would be limited in scope. He still hoped that the United States could confine her efforts to production.[227] Since he envisioned a limited role for American military forces--a role confined largely to air and naval action--he failed to harness economic and military mobilization to their ultimate tasks. Even if the President had then envisioned full participation, he would probably have followed the same course of public action. Plans and preparations would possibly have been more thorough, but publicly he would have moved with the same caution and circumspection. Franklin Delano Roosevelt was primarily a superb and gifted politician; and a politician never allows what is strategically desirable to outpace and outrun what is tactically possible.

c. The Military: the Dangers of Time

His military advisers and planners, however, could move with a good deal more freedom in their estimate of the strategic situation and in their calculation of the ultimate cost. Whereas the President had to listen to a great many voices, to respond to a great many contradictory pressures, the military planners could simply proceed from their estimate of the situation and their understanding of national policy, logically and systematically calculating the requirements for victory. Their professionalism insulated them from many of the demands which bore heavily on the President.

By now the ultimate scope of American national policy was obvious even to the most obtuse: the United States was committed to the defeat of the Axis coalition. Responding to policy pressures, the perspectives of the military planners had widened considerably since the early 1920's. Although they never forgot their primary responsibility—emphasizing the security and protection of the continental United States—although they constantly warned their commander-in-chief that intervention should be postponed until all military forces were adequately prepared, the planners now accepted this objective with the same ease with which they had once accepted the aims of continental and hemispheric defense.[228]

The danger of frustration and possibly of defeat was apparent. The military planners were extremely pessimistic about the current war situation. Unlike the President, they considered the German involvement in Russia merely temporary. Their advice, therefore, closely paralleled that given at the time of the French defeat.[229] Then they had cautioned Mr. Roosevelt to concentrate on hemispheric defense and to limit rigidly, even end all aid to the Allies; now they advised him to concentrate on the defense of the North Atlantic and to avoid any aid commitment to the Soviet Union. Then they had predicted the speedy collapse and surrender of England under a massive German assault; now they foresaw the immediate crumbling of Russia under the triumphant stride of Hitler's victorious divisions. The pessimism of the War Department was succintly expressed in a memorandum sent by Secretary of War Stimson to President Roosevelt on June 23:

"For the past thirty hours I have done little but reflect upon the German-Russian war and its effect upon our immediate policy. To clarify my own views I have spent today in conference with the Chief of Staff and the men in the War Plans Division of the General Staff. I am glad to say that I find substantial unanimity upon the fundamental policy which they think should be followed by us. I am even more relieved that their views coincide so entirely with my own.
First: Here is their estimate of controlling facts:
1. Germany will be thoroughly occupied in beating Russia for a minimum of one month and a possible maximum of three months.
2. During this period Germany must give up or slack up on
   a. Any invasion of the British Isles.
   b. Any attempt to attack herself or prevent us from occupying Iceland.
   c. Her pressure on West Africa, Dakar and South America.
   d. Any attempt to envelop the British right flank in Egypt by way of Iraq, syria or Persia.
   e. Probably her pressure in Libya and the Mediterranean.
Second: They were unanimously of the belief that this precious and unforeseen period of respite should be used to push with the utmost vigor our movements in the Atlantic theater of operations. They were unanimously of the feeling that such pressure on our part was the right way to help Britain, to discourage Germany, and to strengthen our own position of defense against our most imminent danger.
As you know Marshall and I have been troubled by the fear lest

we be prematurely dragged into major operations in the Atlantic, one in the northeast and the other in Brazil, with an insufficiency of Atlantic Naval and shipping strength and an insufficient demonstrated superiority of American seapower to hold politics steady in South America. By getting into this war with Russia Germany has much relieved our anxiety, provided we act promptly and get the initial dangers over before Germany gets her legs disentangled from the Russian mire.... 'Germany's action seems like an almost providential occurrence. By this final demonstration of Nazi ambition and perfidy, the door is opened wide for you to lead directly towards the battle of the North Atlantic and the protection of our hemisphere in the South Atlantic, while at the same time your leadership is assured of success as fully as any future program can well be made.'" 230

The moral of the Secretary's consensus letter was apparent. The United States had been granted a respite which should be utilized to the fullest. Once this interval vanished, the danger would be almost overwhelming. The United States should prepare for the ultimate confrontation by securing her hemispheric positions and by achieving total domination over the North Atlantic—life line to the British Isles.

The Secretary's estimate and analysis reflected the assumptions and judgment of his military advisers. They, too, saw little chance of prolonged, effective Russian resistance. Almost three weeks after the German attack on the U.S.S.R., Sherman Miles—Assistant Chief of Staff, G-2—sent to the Assistant Chief of Staff of the War Plans Division, a summary on "the foreign situation," 231 as affected by the German-Soviet war. It began with a pessimistic assesment of the new conflict:

1. SUMMATION OF THE SITUATION
a. Germany possessing a central position and ground and air forces superior to any individual opponent, has exercised her initiative by attacking Russia. This attack will be at least so successful that, subsequent to the fall of 1941, Germany will have regained her ability to strike outwards from a central position.
b. The British Empire, widespread, with superior surface sea power, but deficient in man power, organization and battle leadership, is necessarily on the defensive. To her, the German attack on Russia affords a breathing spell in which she

can buttress her home and Middle Eastern defenses. Assumption
of the strategic offensive in any theater is beyond her power.
c. U.S.S.R., ill organized but formidable because of her size,
is exposed to the full vigor of German attack. The most that
can be expected of her is that she will remain in being in
her distant fastness after the German onslaught has been spent.
However, the German attack has cancelled out Russia as an Axis
source of supply from the short-term viewpoint.
d. The United States, with a superior navy in one ocean, but
without effective weapons and with but few combat organizations,
is committed to opposition to Germany, is providing limited
material support to the Axis' enemies, but lacks the means to
take over battle action against Germany in her own or anyone
else's behalf. [232]

In the second section of the summary, "SITUATION OF INDIVIDUAL POWERS,"

the author continued by estimating the number of German forces engaged

on the Russian front. He then traced the future course of German strategy,

highlighting the temporary advantages and ultimate dangers posed by this

new development:

(8) In consequence of this major offensive against Russia,
no German offensive operations are to be expected in any other
theaters of war in the immediate future. In particular, no
invasion of England, or of Iceland is probable during the
remainder of 1941. Germany's ground forces will, undoubtedly,
remain on the strategic defensive in both the Western European
and Mediterranean Theaters until she can spare troops and
aviation from Eastern Europe.
(9) In case of victory over Russia during this summer or fall
of 1941, one may expect as logical further German moves:
(a) The consolidation of the German hegemony in Europe (less
the British Isles).
(b) The expulsion of Britain from the Mediterranean.
(c) The continuance of the war of attrition against the British
seaborne commerce.
(10) The complete entry of the United States into the war
would probably not change the plans of the German High Command
nor affect for the present Germany's military, political and
economic position. It would undoubtedly depress somewhat the
war spirit and morale of the German people. It would so
stimulate the morale and hopes of Germany's subject populations
as to increase greatly the Reich's problems in controlling
them. On the other hand, our entry into war would cause
Germany to activate her existing fifth column arrangements
in Latin America. [233]

The report continued with an analysis of the military situation

in Japan, the British Empire, Italy, France, the Netherlands, the U.S.S.R.

and Latin America. Again it gave a pessimistic summary of Russian

chances and sounded the note of urgency. To Sherman Miles, the German-

Soviet war had not ended the Nazi threat; it had merely postponed it.

Now was the time for the United States to insist on the establishment

of military bases throughout Latin America to counter future Axis operations:

> (3) The necessity of U.S. bases in Latin America has become
> not only essential but urgent.
> (4) The establishment of bases requires, at least, several
> months.
> (5) The time has come when the United States must make specific
> requests for immediate concessions of bases at Natal, Brazil;
> the Galapagos Islands, Ecuador; Buenaventura, Colombia; and
> Acapulco, Mexico. Further postponements, particularly as
> regards Natal, might prove disastrous if the Germans seize
> the French naval base at Dakar. The American Republics must
> be shown that further delay in the concession of bases might
> not only be interpreted as an attitude of non-cooperation,
> but that it will also jeopardize the defense of the Western
> Hemisphere and the integrity and independence of their sovereignty. [234]

The conclusion of the G-2 chief was, therefore, inescapable. The opening

of the German-Soviet war had not fundamentally altered or transformed the

strategic situation. It had merely given the United States a tactical

interlude to prepare her defenses, to secure the Western Hemisphere.

The information gathered by G-2 went into a strategic estimate which

sketched the future timetable of events in dark colors, giving only a

faint flash of hope. Germany was pictured as becoming more powerful and

successful than ever, though it was also intimated that German morale

and internal cohesion would deteriorate by the summer of 1943:

> By July 1, 1942.
> (1) The following are envisaged:
> (a) German defeat of U.S.S.R. and re-establishment of German
> military initiative.
> (b) Participation of the U.S. in the war under Rainbow 5.
> (2) Under the foregoing the following are estimated to be
> the Axis disposition and capabilities:
> German occupation of the U.S.S.R. to Lake Baikel and possibly
> to the Pacific. Possible Japanese occupation of the Maritime
> Provinces of Siberia. Axis control of Africa, roughly north

of the line Fernando Po-Djibout is either accomplished or imminent. Continuation of the aerial and naval siege of the British Isles. German attempts to invade Great Britain or (more probable) a broad strategic movement through the Middle East toward the Indian Ocean, possibly in conjunction with a southward advance by Japan. The political consolidation of Europe under German leadership will have been accomplished, but the political cohesion of this entity will be low. Germany and Japan will be obviously war-weary. Economic exploitation of the U.S.S.R. will have barely begun. While still debarred physically, militarily and economically from Latin America, the Axis will have achieved a considerable amount of political disunion in that area by intrigue and propaganda. German propaganda will tend to have become less effective in India, the United States and the Mohammedan world.

c. By July 1, 1943, Axis dispositions and capabilities are estimated as follows: Germany will still possess superior ground forces. The invasion of the British Isles, if not already achieved, will now be impracticable. Germany will have extended her penetration southward in Africa and will still be able to renew the offensive in the Middle East. Japan, if not irrevocably committed to war on the side of the Axis, will tend to stand aloof. German economic exploitation of Russia will have progressed, but the general economic condition of Europe will be low. Axis morale will be generally low and war-weariness will be rifle. There will be no real political cohesion in Europe. The Axis propaganda effort, centered on Latin America will be losing ground. [235]

Neither the Secretary of War nor his military advisers believed that the Russian resistance would last very long; neither anticipated that it would become the fulcrum on which future Allied strategy would pivot. Therefore, they were merely concerned in exploiting their temporary, tactical advantage.

The President got the same estimate and similar proposals from his naval advisers. Both Secretary Knox and Admiral Stark were blunter than the Secretary of War, bolder than Sherman Miles. They felt that the moment for decisive intervention had arrived--that the United States should adopt escort of convoy and damn the consequences. The consequences of further delay could be deadly. [236]

The planners' belief in the fragility of Soviet resistance, continuing throughout the summer, became embedded within the Victory Program. Both the "Joint Board Estimate of United States Over-all Production

Requirements" and the "Ultimate Requirements Study"[237] predicted an early German victory in Russia. Neither foresaw a prolonged attritional conflict. The Joint Chiefs' warning that an anti-Axis victory was impossible without the intervention of the United States[238] was based on the belief that the present coalition could neither defeat nor stalemate Hitler's drive. Understandably, Section III of the Joint Board Estimate drew a fairly bleak picture predicting the "Probable Character of the Enemy's Major Strategy":

> "15. For Germany, the objective of the current phase of the war is the complete military and political domination of Europe, and probably of North and West Africa. If Germany is successful she may then seek a period of peaceful refreshment, during which she can reorganize Europe and prepare for further adventures. However, the possibility can not be dismissed that Germany might seek at once to continue into India, South Africa, or South America.
>
> 16. Germany's present major strategic objectives, and the means by which she seeks to attain them, seem to be some or all of the following:
>
> a. The conquest of European Russia, the destruction of the Russian Armies, and the overthrow of the Soviet regime. This is a task for the German army and air forces, and will doubtless absorb most of the energy available to these contingents for some months to come. Final success in this aim is still in the balance.
>
> b. The destruction of the power of resistance of the United Kingdom, through accelerated attrition of shipping, and continued bombing of British facilities. The forces employed will be surface raiders, submarines, and aircraft in the north-western approaches and down through the Middle Atlantic, operating from bases in Norway, France, Portugal, and French West Africa; and merchant-type raiders distributed throughout all oceans. Invasion of England may possibly not be attempted unless these other measures fail.
>
> c. The conquest of Egypt, Syria, Irak, and Iran. This may be undertaken. Large land and air forces must be employed, both German and Italian, aided by Italian naval forces in the Eastern Mediterranean and the Black Sea. Success may depend upon whether or not a large concentration of British and Russian defensive forces are available, and upon the continued military capacity of Italy, now an uncertain quantity.
>
> d. The occupation of Spain, Portugal, Morocco, French West Africa, Senegal, and the Atlantic Islands, for the purpose of strengthening the German offensive against British shipping,

and for denying these positions to Germany's enemies.
Considerable land, air, and naval forces will be required
for this offensive, though not so great as would be required
for conquest of the lands to the eastward of the Mediterranean."[239]

Although the final section of this strategic estimate recalled that

Germany's logistical problems would multiply as her military forces moved

away "'from the home base,'"[240] it was little comfort compared to the

possibility of a German victory in Europe. Triumph in Europe would be

a mere prelude to an assault upon the Western Hemisphere:

"8. Should Germany be successful in conquering all of Europe,
she might then wish to establish peace with the United States
for several years, for the purpose of organizing her gains,
restoring her economic situation, and increasing her military
establishment, with a view to the eventual conquest of South
America and the military defeat of the United States. During
such a period of "peace", it seems likely that Germany would
seek to undermine the economic and political stability of the
countries of South America, and to set up puppet regimes
favorable to the establishment on that continent of German
military power. In such circumstances, Germany would have
better chances to defeat the United States. This concept can
not be accepted as certain, because it is conceivable that
Germany might at once seek to gain footholds in the Western
Hemisphere."[241]

Either alternative—slow preparation followed by assault or immediate

attack—presented a dark prospect for the future.

The Victory Program estimates, moreover, presented a pessimistic

time table, predicting continued triumph for the Axis. By July, 1942,

the Soviet Union "would be 'substantially impotent,' with German air

power pulverizing at leisure the territories not yet conquered."[242]

The immediate sequel would be the elimination of the British power from

the Middle East and the securing of the Mediterranean.[243] By then Germany

would need to recover her strength. As the "Ultimate Requirements Study"[244]

carefully pointed out, the critical point, the last opportunity, would come in the middle of 1943. Then German recovery, if unchecked and unhampered, would evolve into an invincible power. "The Allied Powers could not afford to wait later than mid-1943...to take the offensive."[245]

But the race for time was a strategic one whose outcome ultimately depended upon economic mobilization, upon the full utilization of great potential strength. And, according to current estimates, it would take from eighteen months to two years[246] to build up the industrial power necessary to defeat the Axis. Unless the effort was made immediately, the opportunity would be permanently lost; American industrial power would develop too slowly, too late, to check the Axis march of conquest. As the "Ultimate Requirements Study" pointed out "time was running out"[247]:

> "It is mandatory that we reach an early appreciation of our stupendous task, and gain the whole-hearted support of the entire country in the production of trained men, ships, munitions and ample reserves. Otherwise, we will be confronted in the not distant future by a Germany strongly entrenched economically, supported by newly acquired sources of vital supplies and industries, with her military forces operating on internal lines, and in a position of hegemony in Europe which will be comparatively easy to defend and maintain...The urgency of speed and the desirability of employment of our present great economic and industrial advantage over our potential enemies cannot be over-emphasized."[248]

From the estimates of the Victory Program, it is obvious where the Army's sense of urgency arose. The planners felt that the present walls of resistance would not hold or contain the Axis drive. American intervention was necessary for victory and essential for survival. The strength of the enemy, the weakness of our allies, dictated an early intervention, a speedy commitment.

The Victory Program--predicated on the above time scheme--envisioned the creation of a massive American Army of 8,795,658 men: 215 divisions including 61 armored.[249] Army planners also envisioned a massive merchant fleet of more than 30 million tons as essential for the achievement of vital strategic tasks.[250] Only an Army backed by such a mass of force and power could win the war.

But the estimates of the Victory Program went far ahead of either the concepts or achievements of American military mobilization in the final months before Pearl Harbor. The forces then available were barely adequate "'to defend our military bases and outlying possessions, many of which were still well below their authorized, peacetime, garrison strengths."[251] They were "'wholly inadequate'" to defend the Western Hemisphere from attack.[252] And, of course, current mobilization plans, still based upon the concept of hemisphere defense, did not touch or approach the ambitious strategic concepts of the Victory Program.[253]

The late 1941 plans were modest indeed, as the Army would be expanded only be 10%, and the United States would plan for an overseas force of only sixteen divisions. There was little indication that the General Staff planned anything more ambitious or that General Wedemeyer's massive mobilization plans had had much impact. All subsequent proposals for military expansion were automatically rejected. In October, for example, Lt. General Lesley J. McNair—then Chief of Staff of GHQ— proposed "a program for 'mass production of trained divisions' on the assumption that the Army...had as its mission something 'more than passive hemispherical defense.'"[254] This proposal, echoing or paralleling the Victory Program, was rejected by the American General Staff.[255]

So mobilization continued largely along the lines of production rather than participation.[256] It followed the scope and scale set by the Navy Victory Program Estimate rather than that defined by the Army's plan.

Despite the Army's sense of urgency, despite the military planners'
realization that the situation was becoming increasingly dangerous,
the pace slackened in the last months before Pearl Harbor. For the
Army's size was merely a reflection of its purpose. And the aims now
envisioned went beyond the scope allowed by either public opinion or the
President. The larger objectives could not thrive or grow as long as
peace continued. Only war could create the proper tempo--the only tempo
which might answer the exigencies and pressures of time.

The Victory Program, however, did mark a new and prophetic point
of departure. Throughout the interwar period, the emphasis of the
temporal imperative had fallen upon the need to prepare and arm in restricted
time--arm against the hostile challenges of enemy power, prepare for
possible invasion of the Western Hemisphere by triumphant Axis forces. The
Victory Program, striking an entirely new note, gave the temporal imperative
a wide strategic cast. It carefully weighed the margin of time between
the possibility of victory and defeat. Emphasizing the necessity for
American military intervention, it implicitly raised the question of the
temporal relation between America's military mobilization for the offensive
and the limits of Axis power. It imperceptibly but emphatically marked a
shift of emphasis from American concern with the containment of the Axis
threat to a commitment to Allied victory. Formerly, the planners' emphasis
upon time had stressed the need to prepare for the defeat of an enemy invasion;
now they still emphasized the need for time, but the issue revolved around
the need to totally defeat and conquer an enemy nation. Even the temporal
imperative had shifted from defense to offense.

Chapter XIII

The Temporal Imperative: The Race against Time in the Pacific

During the immediate prewar years, America's Pacific policy was
primarily designed to gain time, to forestall and delay any showdown
with the Japanese "while everything in Europe was on the razor's edge."[1]
The United States shunned a two front war, fastening all her energies
and attention on the Atlantic. But it was difficult to disengage one
from the other, and she lived in perpetual danger that her actions and
counteractions could provoke an explosion in the Pacific.[2]

Although the developing crises in the Pacific greatly reflected the
pattern of events in the Atlantic, although Japanese and American plans
alternated with the shifting fortunes of the European war, the showdown
in the Pacific developed as a separate drama moving with its own momentum
towards a separate climax. Ironically, despite the anticipations of
American statesmen and planners, it was this crisis which provoked, almost
as an afterthought, the anticlimactic declaration of war between the
European Axis and the United States.

The Pacific drama did not have the spasmodic character of the
Atlantic drama where successive crises alternated with successive lulls,
where events moved unsteadily towards an uncertain, undefined climax
which never directly materialized, where the tempo of events and decisions
constantly shifted, alternately quickening and easing. Events in the Far
East moved at a different pace, followed a different pattern, always
heading inexorably, inevitably towards the inescapable climax of Pearl
Harbor.

There were several reasons for this difference in tempo.
First, although war began in Asia two years before it erupted
in Europe, it did not reach crisis proportions in the Pacific
until the summer of 1941. Second, by the time the United
States Government confronted the Japanese with the choice of
war and peace, American public opinion was united against
Japanese expansion. The doubts and controversies that harried
America's intervention in the Atlantic did not complicate the
debate over her Far Eastern stand. Third, once a decision
was made, the U.S. Government, which had previously steered
a cautious course, stood firm: an immovable object awaiting
an irresistable force. It would negotiate to gain time, not
to compromise its position.

In the Pacific, therefore, the aims of the temporal imperative
moved in diametrically opposed directions. The major antagonists were locked in a race against time which stemmed from
their totally incompatible objectives. Obviously, any
simultaneous attempt to accomplish these conflicting aims would
automatically lead to a showdown sealed by the conviction
of righteousness that gripped both sides.

Herbert Feis accurately dissects the conflict between the
two powers and their opposing sense of time.

The Japanese believed that they were the natural heirs to
power throughout East Asia. Their aim was expansionist: the
establishment of the East Asia Co-Prosperity Sphere. The
fulfillment of this dream was considered just and fitting:

> Japan, from its seat on the small island of
> Honshu, wanted to be arbiter of Asia and
> the Western Pacific. The wish throve

in poverty and pride, finding company in thoughts which made
it seem just. The Japanese people came to believe that the
extension of their control over this vast region was both
natural and destined; that the other people living there
needed the guardianship of Japan as much as Japan needed them.
The Japanese armies sailed across the China seas under a banner
which proclaimed peace, justice, and partnership for all. The
bayonets were merely to expel the devil who would not understand their "true intentions." [3]

But this dream was a nightmare to American leaders. It threatened
the destruction of all American interests in the Far East; it posed a
challenge to a policy pursued by the United States since the end of the
nineteenth century. Moreover, this Japanese "wish" presented a moral
question, contradicting the treasured precepts by which the United States
judged the conduct of foreign powers: the integrity of individual nations,
the legitimacy of persuasion and the illegality of force as a technique
for solving international disputes.

The Japanese-American conflict pivoted around the Open Door policy,
which so closely integrated American self-interest and morality. This
doctrine, protecting the trading and economic interests of the United
States, also defended the integrity of the Chinese nation against parti-
tion or conquest. Its maintenance, therefore, was a direct and complete
challenge to the pursuits and ambitions of Japanese imperialists and
militarists. Japan and the United States were deadlocked by their
incompatible aims. The course of conflict in the Pacific moved with
the inevitability of Greek tragedy.

The clash between the goals of America and Japan was more complex
than mere incompatability. The achievement of Japanese hegemony over
East Asia depended upon more than American acquiescence. It depended
upon American collaboration. The price of continued peace in the Far
East was high:

The United States would have been obliged, not only to end
aid to China, but to coerce it into accepting permanent
Japanese influence in its affairs. It would have been
pledged to provide Japan with the means of maintaining
whatever size army and navy it wanted. [4]

These converging aims provided the impetus and the momentum for the
conflicting attitudes of the two antagonists towards the temporal
imperative. For the United States more time meant more power. It
meant that she would be better prepared for the oncoming confrontation.
Her aim was to stall the Japanese, to delay direct conflict as long as
possible. For the Japanese more time meant less power. Any prolonged
delay would be seriously weakening and ultimately crippling, leaving them
totally incapable of challenging the power of the United States. After
July, 1941, it meant that their oil resources would be steadily drained
while America's military strength and power grew. "From now on the oil
gauge and the clock stood side by side. Each fall in the level brought
the hour of decision closer."[5] The Japanese had to strike quickly and
effectively, crippling American power in the Pacific before it could
be sufficiently strengthened, before their time of opportunity--created
largely by the involvements and distractions of the European war--passed.

The temporal imperatives of the two powers were, however, not simply
opposed. They were welded together, interlocked into one vast time bomb.
The actions and counteractions of the two powers were so intimately linked--
through their intricate prewar collaboration--that one power could not
press a button, release a spring, without accelerating the time mechanism
of both. Every action, every move, accelerated the momentum, the speed of
the approaching explosion.

This mounting pressure can be most clearly studied by examining its
impact and influence over public opinion, the President, his chief advisers

and the military planners. Here diversity of opinion was always matched
by a diversity of tempo, passing through three stages, mounting in
intensity towards the inevitable climax. The three stages were the
prelude, the decision and the confrontation.

The first stage, lasting from the opening of the Sino-Japanese
War in 1937 to the 1939 Tientsin crisis, was characterized by a series
of incidents, accompanied by mounting American disgust and distrust for
Japanese aims and methods. It was not marked by any strong sense of
public urgency; for the people remained innocent of the implications
of policy.

The second stage lasted from the denunciation of the Treaty of
Commerce and Navigation between the United States and Japan (July 26,
1939) to the freezing of all Japanese assets in the United States (July 26,
1941). Slowly but inevitably, America applied her economic sanctions on
the Japanese Empire, moving towards the final decision to forcibly resist
aggression and expansion in the Far East. Although America's sense of
urgency mounted as she approached the final choice, it never equaled
the accompanying sense of crisis in the Atlantic Theater. And the
public's understanding of the danger lagged far behind that of the Administration and the military.

The third stage lasted from the imposition of the embargo to the
declaration of war. It was characterized by an increasing realization
of the conflict of the two temporal imperatives and by growing apprehensions on the limits of time. This final stage was merely the inevitable
resolution of the second phase: The decision was already made; the
denouement was predetermined. Despite this mounting climax, the public
sense of urgency failed to match or measure the gravity of the situation.

The Administration and the military, however, could see events
as they moved towards their climactic resolution.

One word of warning. As we shall see, any awareness of
exigency was never consistent. Projections of hope alternated
with insights of despair. A feeling of urgency seems particularly
sharp now because we look at the climax building up between
the two powers sub species eternitatis. We know the outcome.
The chief participants in the drama of war and peace were not
so blessed. The patterns of time remained uncertain almost
to the end. Fate seemed reversible, the future redeemable.
Moreover, even within the "informed" circles of government,
variations were played on the theme of time. To the end,
passing perspectives veiled tragic inevitability.

1. The First Stage: Prelude

    a. Public Antipathy towards Japanese Aggression

From the beginning, American public opinion was united in
opposition to Japanese aggression and brutality. The opening
of the war in Asia found most Americans clear in their
sympathies and prepared to support policies which they would
shun in the European Theater. Even cooperative action with
the United Kingdom, as Langer and Gleason note, was not
unthinkable:

> Such cooperative action would certainly have been
> more acceptable to the American public in the Far
> East than in Europe, partly because American sympathy
> for China and dislike of Japan went far beyond material
> considerations and partly because Japanese aggression
> against China involved out-and-out violation of
> international agreements to which the United States
> was a party. To this should be added the fact
> that Japanese power was not held in high regard
> by Americans and that therefore it was thought
> that a strong stand would be less risky

than a firm attitude towards the European dictators. The
Japanese advance into China had evoked at once a vigorous
demand for an embargo on war supplies to Japan, by the
shipment of which, it was reiterated, the United States was
positively supporting the Japanese campaign. [6]

The major trend of American public opinion towards Japan is found
in this summary of the 1937 attitude: The image of the foe as a ruthless
lawbreaker whose aggression is fed by appeasement and the underestimation
of his power, leading to the comforting assumption that the United States
could impose her economic sanctions without fear of military retaliation.
Only this final illusion encouraged the American public to support every
measure short of war. Occasionally, as the country veered towards full-
scale conflict in the Pacific, the American people--shocked into
temporary awareness--fell into deep anxiety, temporarily seeking refuge
in political and military retrenchment.

The public attitude was also mirrored in the statements and stands
of the knowledgeable. In an October 7, 1937, letter to the New York Times,
former Secretary of State Henry L. Stimson also expressed the same low
estimate of Japan's strength. He, too, clearly underestimated the danger
of a Japanese reaction to an economic embargo. Continued restraint, he
claimed, would have the opposite effect than that intended by the Administration. It "'threatened to bring upon us in the future the very dangers
of war which we now are seeking to avoid.'" [7] To Stimson, the answer,
the course of policy, was obvious: the United States should impose an
embargo on all strategic materials, thereby attacking Japan's most vulnerable hinge: her "complete dependence on American and British Markets." [8]
Conversely, a continued policy of neutrality and appeasement would boomerang:

'In our recent efforts to avoid war we...are trying to put
peace above righteousness. We have thereby gone far toward
killing the influence of our country in the progress of the

world. At the same time, instead of protecting, we have
endangered our own peace.
Our recent neutrality legislation attempts to impose a dead
level of neutral conduct on the part of our Government between
right and wrong, between the aggressor and its victim, between
a breaker of the law of nations and the nations who are
endeavoring to uphold the law. It won't work. Such a policy
of amoral drift by such a safe and powerful nation as our own
will only set back the hands of progress. It will not save
us from entanglement. It will even make entanglement more
certain. History had already amply shown this last fact.' 9

Although Stimson was willing to fight for the above principles, he did

not foresee any necessity for war. Ultimately, strong measures would

effectively strengthen the chances for peace. 10

Despite his underestimation of Japanese strength and determination,

Stimson's position was built on a tough and consistent logic. He was

willing to face and accept the consequences of the failure of his premises,

willing to recognize that the pursuit of principle could lead to war.

But the rigor of his logic was hardly acceptable to the American public.

It favored the use of sanctions only because it had the same low estimate

of Japan's capacity and will as the former Secretary of State. It

embraced the contradictory objectives of peace and the embargo without

the slightest thought that one could destroy the other.

The course of events in Asia did not revolutionize American attitudes

towards Japan and China. They merely intensified and rigidified them

until they assumed the tenacity and the obduracy of dogma. Incident

after incident--as the war in China assumed an increasingly indiscrimi-

nate and brutal character--convinced the American public that its

assumptions were infallible.

This development was not totally clear in the beginning. The first

serious incident, the sinking of the United States _Panay_ on December 12,

1937, had been preceeded by a series of accumulating insults: "instances of Japanese bombing of undefended cities, towns, hospitals, missionary and educational establishments..." [11] In these attacks American property and lives had been destroyed despite flag markings and other protective devices. But these snowballing incidents did not have the dramatic impact and emphasis of the sinking of the _Panay_. This attack, clear, unprovoked, unnecessarily brutal and totally unambiguous, rang like the certain prelude to another _Maine_ crisis. [12]

But Japanese apologies and an indemnity settled the entire affair. [13] Apparently the blunt possibility of war temporarily silenced other deep revulsions and antipathies. The American public, greatly relieved by the settlement of the _Panay_ incident, strongly supported a policy of total withdrawal from Asia:

> In a Gallup poll conducted during the second week of January 1938, 70 percent of the American voters who were interviewed and had an opinion on the subject favored a policy of complete withdrawal from China—Asiatic Fleet, Marines, missionaries, and all. [14]

As Professor Morison remarked: "Apparently no American except Mr. Grew remembered the _Maine_." [15]

As incidents multiplied, their deliberateness became more and more obvious, and the depth of public feeling mounted. The brutal bombing attacks on Chungking, the blockading of the French and British concessions in Tientsin, the harsh treatment of British citizens, the close attack on the USS _Tutuila_: all these actions seemed like moves in a sinister plot to extend and consolidate Japanese power throughout the Far East. [16]

To most Americans the solution was painless and immediate. If the United States embargoed all war materials to the Japanese, aggression and its accompanying atrocities would cease. There was a deep desire to end the implicit collaboration between America and the Japanese Empire.

Since there was no realization that the curtailment of war
materials would move both countries over the brink of war,
this solution remained easy and complete. Langer and Gleason
evaluate these dominant illusions:

> American opinion, already much wrought up by the
> indiscriminate bombings of Chungking and other Chinese
> cities, was deeply outraged by the indignities visited
> on British subjects by the Japanese soldiery. Public
> protests were mingled with demands that the United
> States Government should, at the least, put an end
> to the selling of war materials to the Japanese.
> Since Japan was dependent on the United States for
> more than half its requirements of such materials,
> it was reasonable to ask why America should continue
> to aid and abet the brutal Japanese aggression against
> Chinese and Europeans....The popular reaction seems
> to have been that the Japanese were behaving just as
> badly as the Nazis and that it would be an easy
> matter to put a stop to Japanese atrocities simply
> by withholding American supplies.[17]

American sentiment during the 1939 Tientsin crisis, when the
Japanese humiliated British and French nationals, clearly
reveals the difference between the public's attitude towards
the European Axis and Japan. Although it condemned all
aggression, its attitude towards Japan was complicated by
America's greater involvement in the Pacific and by her
implicit though unwilling support of Japanese aggression through
the sale of war materials. In the Atlantic Theater, the steady
modification of neutrality increased the danger of war and
took the form of mounting commitments. In the Pacific Theater,
total disengagement would paradoxically strengthen American
involvement, heightening the danger of full-scale conflict.

    b. The Administration's Caution

    The schizophrenic attitude of the American public,
favoring action in the Pacific but strongly discouraging
involvement in the Atlantic, placed the United States

Administration in a difficult position. Releasing powerful pressures,
prodding Roosevelt to take provocative action, it ignored the effect
that a strong policy in Asia would ultimately have on our European
position.

The President, however, seeing only too clearly the relation between
the Pacific and the Atlantic,[18] could not easily disengage one theater
from another. Since his primary concern with the European Axis ultimately
inhibited his actions towards the Japanese Empire, his Administration
consistently lagged behind public sentiment. After an initial attempt
to awaken the nation to its danger, it then proceeded to follow a groping,
day to day policy combining general denunciations of Axis conduct with a
policy of unlimited sympathy, but limited aid to China.

Roosevelt's cautious course was initially determined by the failure
of his 1937 quarantine plan. This failure indicated to Roosevelt a deep
popular resistance to any provocative action against the Axis. He
proposed his plan at Chicago on October 5, 1937, in a famous speech in
which he denounced Axis aggression and advocated collective security.[19]
Although the speech was primarily directed against Japanese aggression
in China, the President drew his moral and defined his plan in general
terms. His speech bristled with urgency in tone and imagery, and
repudiated the isolationist premise that the United States could exist
like an independent island in a hostile sea. Interdependence, not
isolation, was the lesson of modern history.

His message centered around a single image: Axis aggression was
compared to the outbreak of an epidemic, the image of disease suggesting
the cure--quarantine:

> When an epidemic of physical disease starts to spread,
> the community approves and joins in   a quarantine of
> the patients in order to protect the health of the
> community against the spread of the disease....War is
> a contagion, whether it be declared or undeclared....
> We are adopting such measures as will minimize our
> risk of involvement, but we cannot have complete
> protection in a world of disorder in which confidence
> and security have broken down.[20]

Langer and Gleason speculate that to the President "quarantine"
meant "an extreme form of sanctions."[21]

The implications of the plan went beyond public tolerance.
Americans wanted to end economic aid to Japan; possibly, they
were willing to support limited cooperation with Great Britain
in the Far East. They were not prepared to support a program
of sanctions against all aggressors: European as well as
Asiatic. The reaction to F.D.R's proposal was, therefore,
predictably violent.[22]

The President's first attempt to impart his sense of
urgency to the nation went awry. It was diluted into an
innocuous program rejected by the other major powers who
needed the support of strong force rather than generous
generalities. The President had defined the mounting crisis
as a world-wide emergency, the Far Eastern situation being
merely the most blatant symptom of a general disease.
Not even Roosevelt, however, realized that the situation in
Japan was already more dangerous than anyone imagined. As
Herbert Feis correctly points out, the Western World had
by-passed "the last, lost good chance"[23] to preserve peace
in the Far East. Time was running out, the options were
disappearing, dissipated by ignorance and timidity:

> There was a lesson to be learned from the
> rout. The only way in which the war in
> China could have been well ended was

by firm collective action, action that would have offered
Japan an inducement for peace and met refusal with compulsion.
But this lesson was not learned, or even stated boldly, until
three years later--too late to prevent tragedy.[24]

From the start of the Sino-Japanese war to the early spring of 1939,
the moves of the American Government in the Far East followed a minimal
course. The Roosevelt Administration sought to aid China without
aggravating Japan.[25] However, even before the close of this period, the
attitude of the American Government was stiffening considerably. Although
the Administration still opposed economic sanctions, it began to study
means and ends to counter and punish Japanese actions and ambitions:

> ...the larger question of retaliation on Japan for the viola-
> tion of American rights and interests continued to receive
> attention in the State Department. Every possible method of
> economic pressure was carefully analyzed, but after much
> deliberation it was decided that a comprehansive and thorough-
> going program of reprisal was not desirable at the time,
> though it might be advisable to frame such a program for
> future use and to consider the denunciation of the commercial
> treaty of 1911 as an indispensable preliminary step....For
> the time being nothing concrete was done, chiefly, as the
> records show, for fear of going too far, provoking Japanese
> counteraction, and possibly becoming involved in hostilities.
> The concluding months of the year 1938 nevertheless marked a
> stiffening of the American attitude towards Japan, a firm
> and explicit statement of position with respect to Tokyo's
> pretensions, and at least the serious contemplation of practical
> measures to secure respect for American rights and interests in
> China. Though the skirmish was still largely one of words, the
> issue had been joined and the ground prepared for a more posi-
> tive American policy.[26]

So the American Government prepared for the worst and waited for
the course of events and the moods of public opinion before reaching
its decisions. Although filled with revulsion at Japanese conduct and
uneasy over the dual threat in the Atlantic and the Pacific, its
concern was still vague and general. There was not the same oppressive
feeling of urgency over Japan's future moves as that which hung over
Germany's every play for power. The threat in the Pacific was largely

considered insofar as it complicated the position in the Atlantic.
Throughout this period it seemed a subsidiary and contributory threat,
not a major menace.

c. The Military: A Profound Sense of Urgency

During this first stage, the President's military advisers, especially
his Army planners, were far more alarmed than Roosevelt or the American
public over the Far Eastern situation.[27] They had measured America's
capabilities as opposed to those of the enemy; and they knew that her
Pacific position was strategically insupportable, tactically undefendable.[28]
Their sense of urgency, therefore, can be measured by the intensity with
which they advocated a withdrawal to the strategic triangle, a retreat
which would help to realign ends with means.[29] The dangers of time were
mounting and complicating America's overall position; but, as far as her
military planners could see, no sensible retrenchment was imminent.

2. The Second Stage: Decision

The second stage was a time of decision, for within this period
the United States moved away from her implicit collaboration with the
Japanese Empire, severing the economic bonds which tied her to Japan's
military war effort. Finally, the United States decided to resist
further Japanese aggression with every means of peaceful coercion at
her command. As she moved towards her choice, the exigency of the
Pacific situation increased, leaving only a slight interval of time to
prepare for the inevitable.

The breakaway from economic collaboration with Japan that dominated
this period passed through seven progressive steps: 1) July 26, 1939: the
termination of the Treaty of Commerce and Navigation between the United
States and Japan; 2) July 2, 1940: the first Presidential act restricting

exports, excluding both scrap iron and oil; 3) July 25, 1940: the
establishment of liscensing for all exports of aviation gasoline and
top grade scrap iron; 4) September 26, 1940: the application of
controls over all grades of iron and steel scrap; 5) December 10, 1940:
the broadening of the liscensing system to include iron ore, pig iron,
steel; 6) June 20, 1941: the restriction of all oil products from
eastern ports; and 7) July 26, 1941: the freezing of all Japanese
assets by the United States Government.[30] These steps progressively
tightened the noose around the Japanese Empire, threatening its economic
survival while systematically disassociating the United States from
collaborative commitments.

    a. Public Pressure for the Imposition of Economic Sanctions

    As the United States severed its connections with Japanese aggression
and moved towards the application of economic sanctions, public opinion
steadily, unwaveringly supported an increasingly restrictive policy.
Always it rode ahead of official action; always its clear boldness
contrasted rather sharply with the deliberate caution of the American
Government.

    Even the first step--the denunciation of the Treaty of Commerce and
Navigation--was partly a response to public clamor, to public demand for
retaliatory action against Japanese conduct at Tientsin, Chungking and
throughout China.[31] It was enthusiastically acclaimed:

> The public applauded and even Senator Borah expressed
> approval. As ever, the country was much more ready to take
> a strong stand against Japan than against Germany. In the
> words of Mr. Berle: "It is a curious fact that the United
> States, which bolts like a frightened rabbit from even
> remote contact with Europe, will enthusiastically take a
> step which might very well be a material day's march on
> the road to a Far Eastern War." [32]

    Ironically, the role of the leader and the people was totally
reversed. While the Administration moved with measured, hesitant steps,

the American public clamored for bolder action. Although the American
Government had reassured the Japanese that the expiration of the treaty
on January 26, 1940, did not necessarily mean the end of all commercial
relations between the two countries and did not automatically evoke the
imposition of economic sanctions,[33] the American public apparently interpreted
it as the prelude to a total interdiction of Japanese-American commerce
in strategic goods:

> To make matters worse, it seemed for a time that the American
> people would not accept the decision of the President and his
> advisers. Sentiment against Japan ran high and the demand
> for economic action was insistent. The termination of the
> commercial treaty seemed to many Americans the ideal moment
> for ending the export of essential materials to Japan, which,
> it was argued, was tantamount to aiding Tokyo's aggression
> against innocent and friendly China.[34]

This belief was still strengthened by the conviction that the
termination of exports would not provoke any military confrontation with
Japan, a belief fully expressed and exploited by Henry L. Stimson. In
his January 11, 1940, letter to the New York Times, Mr. Stimson castigated
those who thought that only appeasement could prevent general war in
the Pacific.[35] As he saw it, there was no real danger; the Japanese would
not pick up the challenge. An American embargo on essential materials
would bring peace, not war, to the Far East.

Mr. Stimson began his letter by denouncing the American record of
appeasement and collaboration:

> For three years the great resources of our country to a major
> degree have been thrown continuously to the aid of wrongdoing
> in the Far East. They have been used not only to assist
> unprovoked aggression against China but also to facilitate
> acts of inexcusable cruelty towards unoffending Chinese
> civilians, women and children. They have been used to promote
> the violation of treaties which we initiated and which repre-
> sent the hope of modern civilization in the Far East. They
> have been used to destroy the humanitarian work carried on
> in China by American churches, missionaries and educators.

The evil which we have assisted in China has been much more
widespread and brutal than anything which has yet happened
in Europe, but American responsibility in dealing with it is
somewhat different. [36]

This unholy traffic was the achievement of a "small number of Americans" [37]

who profited directly from continued trade with Japan. After condemning

these new "merchants of death," the former Secretary of State ridiculed

the belief that strong American action would precipitate war in the Pacific:

Experienced observers have promptly recognized and publicly
stated that such a fear was without foundation; that the very
last thing which the Japanese Government desires is a war with
the United States; and that on the contrary every act and word
of our government in respect to the Orient is followed with
most anxious solicitude in Japan. Admiral Yarnell in a discussion in the New York Town Hall radio forum was one of the
most recent of such observers, and certainly his authority is
outstanding. [38]

As additional proof of Japan's reluctance to challenge American power,

Mr. Stimson cited the conciliatory actions of the Japanese Government

since the denunciation of the commercial treaty: "These leaders desire

strongly to subjugate China, but they also clearly recognize that a

head-on quarrel with us would be fatal to that project." [39]

The reasons for opposing Japanese expansion in the Far East were

not merely moral; they were also political. The conquest of China by

the Japanese would merely spread more chaos, destroying the stability

and security of the Far East while sweeping away American interests.

Only a show of force could salvage the situation and redeem the tragedy:

...we have a strong feeling that it is highly desirable in
the interests of the United States that the Japanese military
organization should be discredited in the eyes of the Japanese
people. We know that the Japanese people are highly patriotic
and that until they themselves become convinced that their
army has embarked on a venture which is a failure and which
also has brought severe burdens and hardships upon the Japanese
people, it will be unlikely that the people will cease to support it. [40]

Only an embargo would shock the Japanese people back to reality and force them to repudiate their military leaders.

As the extensive analysis of American public opinion by Langer and Gleason shows, Stimson's opinions reflected the widespread dissatisfaction of public spokesmen with any continued collaboration with Japan.

The New York Times sanctioned Stimson's logic as "'unanswerable.'"[41] And the Congress seethed with proposals for economic retaliation: "...there were oft-repeated demands 'get out of the Japanese-Chinese War' by imposing an embargo."[42] This phrasing reveals that the embargo advocates saw economic sanctions as a means of disengagement. The emphasis was more on disassociating the United States from her complicity with the Japanese than on aiding the Chinese.

This semi-belligerent mood was temporarily stilled by the impact of Hitler's victory over France. The first Japanese moves into French Indo-China, the July 19, 1940 ultimatum demanding termination of trade to China and the admission of a Japanese control commission into Indo-China, brought an anguished recognition of the relation between Far Eastern and European affairs. Public ardor was dampened:

> The first moves of Japan brought popular attention
> back to the Far East with an abrupt shock. Despite
> the fact that the American people had for some time
> been inclined to favor a strong line against Japan,
> they were momentarily so thoroughly alarmed by
> Hitler's victories that they would surely have
> objected to any commitment in the Far East that
> might have led to war with Japan.[43]

For once, positions were reversed. The attitude of the American public helped to check the President's initial impulse in July 1940, to impose full controls over all oil and metals going to Japan.[44]

This moderation did not last. The increasing depredations of the
Japanese Government and the conclusion of the Tripartite Pact[45] evoked
anger and determination, not fear and restraint as the Japanese
militarists[46] hoped. Consequently, the anticipatory countermoves of the
American Government—the iron and steel embargo and the new loan to
China—evoked strong support:

> ...commentators and newspaper editors generally adopted a stiff
> line. The country, which had openly defied Hitler by committing
> itself to all-out support of Britain, was in no mood to cringe
> before Japan, or to be frightened by what Senator Claude Pepper
> termed an 'international squeeze play.' News of the additional
> loan to China and of the imposition of an embargo on the ship-
> ment of scrap to Japan evoked strong popular support; a public
> opinion poll of September 30, 1940, indicated that 57 percent
> of those queried thought the United States should take steps
> to keep Japan from becoming more powerful, even if it meant
> the risk of war. Public sentiment in general took the line
> that if the dictators of Europe and Asia were going to
> cooperate, that was all the more reason for the United States
> to stand by Britain and perhaps conclude an out-and-out
> alliance with that power.[47]

The passage of time and the increasingly severe restrictions placed
by the American Government upon Japanese-American trade did not weaken
or alarm the nation. On the eve of the final decision, which would strip
the Japanese of their oil markets and push them towards war, the American
public was totally opposed to any continued appeasement in Asia.[48] On
July 26, 1941, the President ordered the freezing of all Japanese assets
in the United States.[49] Although the application and the consequences
of this act would open the gates of war in the Far East, the American
public enthusiastically welcomed it as an unequivocal stand, the final
blow to continuing oil traffic. They did not measure the consequences,
certain that the Japanese would sensibly yield rather than obstinately
resist:

> To the American public the new measures did not come as a sur-
> prise, for the deliberation of the Government had leaked to

the press on July 22. The popular response was generally
favorable, even to the extent of approving a complete embargo
on trade with Japan. The New York Times (July 24) had called
for a stiff line: 'The Japanese Government must be made to
understand clearly that aggressive action on its part in any
one of three possible areas...Siberia, the Netherlands East
Indies, or Indo-China...will be met by prompt retaliation on
the part of the United States. We have a direct and legitimate
interest in each of these three areas....Any action by Japan
that threatens a legitimate American interest in the Far East
should be met at once by efforts on our part to deal Japanese
finance and industry and trade a deadly blow.' 50

The freezing order fell, therefore, on receptive ground:

Other newspapers, which had long since been agitating for an
embargo, were jubilant over the new orders, assuming that they
meant the end of all trade with Japan. They hailed the end
of "appeasement" and rejoiced that their Government at last
meant business. "Let there be no mistake," wrote the New
York Post , "the United States must relentlessly apply its
crushing strength." "The noose is around Japan's neck at last,"
crowed a writer in PM, pointing out that it was now in America's
power to decide how fast Japan should be strangled: "For a
time it may bluster and retaliate, but in the end it can only
whimper and capitulate." 51

Like a bad boy, soundly whipped, soundly taught, the Japanese Government

would retreat and possibly recant. The American people were relieved

and delighted to free themselves from the burden of collaboration. They

were so convinced of the effectiveness of the solution that they did not

see the fatefulness of the decision: "...they did not yet understand,

and of course the Administration could not tell them, that shutting off

oil made one of two things inevitable: war with Japan, or an easy

Japanese conquest of areas which would make that nation well-nigh

invincible." 52

In summary, except for a brief spasm which passed rapidly during

the spring 1940 crisis, there was no public sense of urgency throughout

the period of decision. The Americans did not understand the consequences

of the anti-Japanese measures which it advocated so liberally. They were

thought of as cures, solutions. It was not realized that they could provoke problems more monumental than those they allayed. The United States sought to clear herself of guilt, with little thought of future consequences.

But the American belief that an economic embargo provided the perfect solution was also bolstered by innocent assumptions of Japanese power. Whereas the public was sold on the dangers of Nazi Germany and recognized the extent of the European Axis threat, it simply could not appreciate the formidable strength of the Japanese in the Pacific, nor did it grasp America's temporary strategic impotence. And its misunderstanding of the balance of power in the Far East was underlined and emphasized by its complete innocence of the strength and determination of Japan's will. Otherwise the American public would have understood that a challenge to Japanese economic power must provoke a confrontation.

But if public innocence was an incentive to action, it was also a brake. The public's eagerness for economic sanctions was totally dependent on its failure to measure the consequences. If the sanctions were imposed and the Japanese went to war, sweeping away British and Dutch possessions in the Far East, isolating the Philippines without touching a foot of American soil, how would Americans react? Would they accept the consequences and calmly disassociate themselves from them? Or would they recognize the serious menace to American interests and support a declaration of war? The United States Government could, therefore, find itself in a more tragic bind than collaboration. It could suddenly discover that it had provoked war between Japan and America's potential Allies, imperiled, if not lost, the entire strategic position in the western Pacific, and left the British and Dutch to pay the price for American folly. The United States would incite the fight, but stand on

the sidelines while the enemy destroyed the interests and resources of
her Allies, sweeping away any possible defense in the Far East.

b. The Great Debate

Though the problems of American policy were complicated by public
naivety, they were also hampered by the internal split or debate between
the advocates of the hard line and the champions of moderation. This
debate dominated the policy scene until the imposition of the freezing
order in July 1941. During this period of decision, the President
stayed behind the scenes, sometimes sympathizing with the hard-line group,
usually favoring the moderates, masking his intentions and his aims
behind the screen of their conflict. The factions of the Administration
dominated the foreground, the President stepping on stage only before
the final minute of decision.

1) The Logic of the Hard Line

The advocates of the hard line--Stimson, Morgenthau, Ickes, Knox
and Hornbeck--fervently believed that the Japanese lacked the will to
wage war against the United States. Tenaciously confident that their
image of the enemy--outwardly bullying, inwardly timid--was accurate,[53]
these men shared the general assumptions of the American public. Until
the end of the second phase, they did not agree with the prevalent
pessimism of the State Department and the military planners. A hard
line would soon bring Japan to terms and reveal their basic weakness.
The emergency in the Far East would last only until the United States
confronted the enemy. The hard-line advocates, therefore, firmly felt
that a continued policy of appeasement and implicit collaboration in
the Far East was losing, not gaining time. By failing to take a firm

stand, the United States was encouraging military aggression, thereby
increasing the chances of war by miscalculation. The half-measures by
which the American government inexorably restricted the flow of economic
goods to Japan seemed a case of "too little, too late."[54] Characteristic
was the Secretary of the Treasury's attitude towards the scrap iron
embargo announced by the Administration on September 26, 1940:

> 'My own opinion is that the time to put pressure on Japan
> was before she went into Indo-China and not after and I
> think it's too late and I think the Japanese and the rest
> of the dictators are just going to laugh at us. The time
> to have done it was months ago and then maybe Japan would
> have stopped, looked and listened.'[55]

The time for bold action was running out. The more the United
States delayed her decision, the greater the danger. As Stimson's
October 2, 1940, memorandum summarized: "'For the United States now
to indicate either by soft words or inconsistent actions that she has
no...clear and definite policy towards the Far East will only encourage
Japan to bolder action.'"[56] Time was only an enemy if America became
stalemated in indecision.

2) The Logic of the Moderates

The logic of the moderates differed totally in its assumptions and
conclusions. It issued from an entirely different image of the enemy.
Whereas the Japanese seemed ruthless but basically cautious to the
advocates of the hard line, they seemed ruthless and determined to
the moderates. The Secretary of State and the President's chief military
advisers thought that a tough policy would merely trigger a Far Eastern
War, for the enemy could not be deterred by any show of strength. Therefore, they sought to postpone a showdown so as to gain time.

For the Secretary of State the temporal imperative meant two things:
tactical time, which would allow the United States military to prepare,
and strategic time, which would permit the Japanese Government to change
its aims, to modify its ambitions.

> We realized that the danger in the Far East was constantly
> growing. We appreciated the gravity of the situation in
> Europe and on the Atlantic. We knew that the territory we
> had to defend was vast, that our armaments had to be built
> up, that at the same time we had to supply war materials
> for the defense of the Western Hemisphere, the British Isles,
> the Near East, and the Far East. We took cognizance of the
> fact that our own public opinion was divided on the issues
> confronting us in Europe and the Orient. We had in the
> forefront of our minds the advice repeatedly given us by
> our highest military officers that they needed time to prepare
> the defenses vital to ourselves as well as to the countries
> resisting aggression. We had before us the statements made
> to us by the British, Australian, and Netherlands Governments
> that they were dangerously vulnerable in the Far East. We
> foresaw the far-reaching consequences to the whole world that
> would follow the outbreak of war in the Pacific.
> Consequently, the President and I agreed that we would do what-
> ever we could to bring about a peaceful, fair, and stabilizing
> settlement of the whole Pacific question. We knew we would
> have to be patient, because the Japanese Government could not,
> even if it wished, abruptly put into reverse Japan's march of
> aggression. Implementation of promises Japan might make in
> any peaceful agreement would demand much time. But we also
> agreed that, while carrying no chip on our shoulders in our
> negotiations with Japan, we could not sacrifice basic principles
> without which peace would be illusory. [57]

As negotiations continued, prolonging themselves indefinitely, strategic
possibilities faded. Increasingly the moderates realized that even time
would bring few changes in Japanese intentions, but it could, however,
still give the United States the opportunity to prepare for the inevitable.

If the advice of the hard-line advocates were adopted, the natural
and almost immediate consequence would be war--any change of heart would
become impossible and the American government would be caught militarily
unprepared. As one of the leading advocates of the moderate approach,
Ambassador Joseph C. Grew predicted that the imposition of sanctions

would start an inevitable slide:

> One course envisages complete intransigence. Unless and until
> Japan reorientates her policy and actions, both as regards her
> commitments under the Nine Power Treaty (until modified by
> orderly processes) and her respect of American rights and
> interests in China, we would refuse to negotiate a new treaty
> of commerce and navigation and would, if public demand in the
> United States calls for it, impose an embargo next winter.
> This course would set Japanese-American relations moving on
> a downward slope to a point from which it would be difficult
> to bring them back to normal for a long time to come; a treaty-
> less situation, with its attending handicaps to Japanese trade,
> would start the movement; the imposition of an embargo would
> greatly accelerate it. [58]

The sequel insured a disastrous course of events:

> The Japanese are so constituted and are just now in such a
> mood and temper that sanctions, far from intimidating, would
> almost certainly bring retaliation which in turn, would lead
> to counteraction. Japan would not stop to weigh ultimate con-
> sequences. [59]

As the Ambassador concluded, the imposition of sanctions would turn time

against the United States, destroying any possibility of the moderates'

restraining the will and hand of the militarists:

> The argument is often advanced that Japan should and can be
> brought to terms through isolation. The corollary is further-
> more advanced that unless isolated and reduced by economic and
> financial attrition to the rank of a second or third rate power,
> it is only a question of time before Japan continues her con-
> tinental and overseas expansion, involving the Philippines,
> the Netherlands East Indies and other western possessions in
> the Far East; that the time to restrain her expansion is now.
> With regard to this thesis, I submit the following considera-
> tions. The resort to methods calculated to bring about the
> isolation of delinquent nations must presuppose in the final
> analysis the use of force. Sanctions commenced but not carried
> through bring in their wake a loss of prestige and influence
> to the nation declaring them. Sanctions carried through to
> the end may lead to war. This statement seems to me to be
> axiomatic and hardly open to controversy. In my view the use
> of force, except in defense of a nation's sovereignty, can
> only constitute an admission of a lack first, of good-will,
> and, second, of resourceful, imaginative, constructive
> statesmanship. To those who hold, with regard to the specific

> situation with which we are dealing, that it is not enough
> for good-will and statesmanship to exist only on one side,
> my rejoinder would be that these factors exist also in Japan,
> albeit in latent form until now, and that one of the functions
> of diplomacy is to bring those factors into full vigor.
> Shidehara diplomacy has existed; it can exist again. [60]

Only patience and restraint could engender an amenable Japanese Government, the change necessary to ultimately end the tragic situation in
the Far East.

Hull and his supporters never adopted the logic of the hard-line
advocates; they never believed that a policy of forceful opposition
and economic sanctions would bring peace to the Pacific. Yet,
increasingly, their resistance to the measures recommended by Stimson
and Morgenthau weakened.

This shift in position accompanied the realization that the hands
of the moderates were bound by the desires and ambitions of the extreme
militarists. As time became progressively tactical and the hope for
strategic change declined, the resistance of the State Department to
the imposition of economic sanctions faltered.

Since this shift from strategic hope to tactical convenience was
never absolute or complete, the wish for compromise and adjustment
never totally disappeared. The State Department never despaired of
securing some agreement, temporary or permanent, with Japan.

During the period of decision, strategic hope and tactical
reasoning were essentially inseparable. The United States would play
for time, hoping that in the meanwhile the ambitions and nature of the
Japanese Government might change. Since it was widely recognized that
Japan's opportunity emerged out of the European War, there was good
reason to hope that her aims would moderate, would bend, if it became

obvious that the Allies were defeating the Axis powers. If
America waited long enough, time could bring its own
solution. All tactical reasoning prior to the imposition of
the freezing order carried some hope of escape.

    3) The Evolution of Tactical Time

    Since moderate opinion dominated American policy throughout
the period of decision, we can trace the emergence of her
uncompromising stand against Japan by showing how moderate
thinking gradually converted to economic resistance. At the
opening of the European war, the moderates could feel satisfaction
at the neutral position assumed by the Japanese Government.
As Herbert Feis points out, they could feel that their
policy of bargaining for time was justified:

> The President and the State Department could feel
> roughly pleased with the way in which their recent
> handling of Japan had worked out. At least Britain
> and France would not have at once to divide their
> forces to protect their colonies and sea routes in
> the Far East. The United States would not have to
> decide at once whether to let Japan run loose or
> risk war....Time remained to test further the results
> of a firm but unaggressive policy of opposition.
> The temper of the American people and the state of
> our armed forces made it expedient, if not compulsory,
> to go on that way.[61]

At first this policy of watchful delay worked. The Japanese
looked for the outcome in Europe, hoping for some portent,
foretelling the winner. The United States waited for the
expiration of the commercial treaty denounced on
July 26, 1939:

> Between 'will' and 'won't,' the President and
> Hull thought, the time for decision had not come.
> Let matters between us and Japan take their course,
> opinion form as it took the further measure of them.
> They would not foretell what ought or must be done
> when January 26, 1940, came round, and the treaty
> with Japan expired.[62]

The Secretary of State followed, therefore, a policy of calculated uncertainty. Throughout the months of the phony war in Europe, he deliberately refused to define American policy in the Far East, or to state under what conditions the United States would impose sanctions, under what conditions she would fight:

> Hull decided that the best course for the time being was merely to prolong the uncertainty. To refrain from the use of sanctions which might produce a crisis, but also to refuse to give Japan any guarantee as to what the United States might do in the future. [63]

But it became more and more difficult for the State Department to resist the arguments of the hard-line advocates. Delay could postpone the outbreak of war in the Far East, but could it prevent it? And if war came after the Japanese were well supplied with strategic materials, they would be far stronger than if an immediate and total embargo had been imposed.[64] As long as the leisurely pace of the phony war prevailed, choice could be postponed; for the Japanese remained fairly quiescent. But once the tide of conquest descended upon western Europe, all the dangers of watchful delay became glaringly apparent. Now the temptations of the moment were irresistable to the Japanese expansionists. France's defeat and the apparently imminent conquest of Great Britain opened the opportunity for the realization of the East Asia Co-Prosperity Sphere, an opportunity which might never recur.[65] Continued delay could no longer insure effective or prolonged deterrence.

Hull, however, was still anxious to continue his policy until its bankruptcy became an infallible certainty rather than a strong possibility. In May, 1940, he told his chief advisers:

> 'I can't think of anything we have overlooked in trying to arrive at working relations with Japan. But I want you to take a fine-tooth comb and a microscope and go back over our relations with Japan and see if it is humanly possible to find something additional with which to approach them and prevail upon them not to gallop off on a wild horse.' [66]

But the temptation to grab while the grabbing was good was too much. The Japanese made their first moves toward establishing their hegemony over Indo-China and shutting off all supplies from Southeast Asia to China almost immediately after the German triumph in the West.[67] They stationed their military observers in Indo-China and forced Great Britain to close the Burma Road for three months.[68] The image of the enemy hardened; the possibility of a strategic change in the composition or nature of the Japanese Government faded. Now the moderates could merely hope that Japan would remember the potential power of the United States and delay its showdown in the Pacific.[69]

The continuing dilemma of the moderate policy was expressed by Secretary Hull in his postwar memoirs:

> ...neither should we make concessions so sweeping that Japan would accept them as a basis for agreement and then bide her time to make further demands or take further steps, nor should we embark upon military or economic action so drastic as to provoke immediate war with Japan. I did not believe Japan was yet ready to make war on Britain and the United States. She would make her moves towards further expansion but, as long as Britain stoutly resisted Germany and at the same time the American fleet remained in the Pacific, she would try to nibble off what she could without engaging in a major conflict.[70]

The middle-road advocates now hoped that they could restrict Japan to discreet aggression. The facts of power still gave some promise that a tactical delay could be achieved. The Japanese would still not dare to challenge America's major interests or provoke her into war.

Consequently, the Secretary of State opposed all hard-line proposals for an economic blockade. When the Secretary of the Treasury, on July 18, 1940, proposed an embargo on all oil shipments to Japan,[71] Sumner Welles, then Acting Secretary of State, reacted vigorously. In his conferences with the President, he stressed the dangers of provoking Japan into an immediate attack by a sudden dramatic act. Japanese aggression in Indo-China would have to be countered, but America would have to select "with care the scope, time, and form of action."[72] Obviously, the only result of such a policy, ironically seeking to deter aggression by not forbidding it, would "be time--time to prepare for defense in a world of enemies."[73]

But despite Welles' success in restricting the embargo to aviation gasoline and top grade scrap iron, the first clear step towards the imposition cf an economic blockade had been taken. Further Japanese incursions into Indo-China would provoke a further tightening of restrictions. Until late in September, 1940, Secretary of State Hull still wanted to wait, hoping that a successful outcome to the Battle of Britain might deter the Japanese, or at least prevent our taking action "in the dark".[74]

Hull's inhibitions and doubts against further motions against the Japanese were stilled by three developments: the defeat of the Luftwaffe in the Battle of Britain,[75] the occupation of northern Indo-China by the Japanese, and the confirmation of previous reports that Japan was forming an alliance with the European Axis.[76] But although Hull assented to the imposition of controls over the export of all grades of iron and steel scrap,[77] he still opposed the most vital and decisive step: an oil embargo. Unlike the hard-line advocates, he was certain that its imposition would provoke an outright declaration of war.[78]

Hull's resistance to this final step continued throughout the balance of 1940 and into the first half of 1941. The tactical reasons for delay were still strong, though any hope for strategic change was faint. So he persuaded the President to follow a middle course policy which would avoid direct provocation, indicate our opposition to aggression and gain time. As he summarizes in his Memoirs:

As the President and I, in various discussions following the
announcement of the Axis alliance, developed American policy
in the Far East, we fixed on these points:
(1) Avoid an open struggle in the Pacific so as to bend all
efforts to aiding Britain and strengthening ourselves.
(2) Maintain as to Japan all our rights and principles, continue
our economic pressure, and aid China, but not push Japan to the
point where her military elements would demand war.
(3) Let Japan realize that we were strong in the Pacific, and
gaining in general strength.
(4) Never let her gain the impression that we would not use
our strength, if required, but at the same time refrain from
quarreling with her and leave the door open for discussion
and agreement, always in conformity with our basic principles.[79]

This policy left the initiative for further action and counteraction

to the Japanese. By refraining from extreme economic measures, the United

States could prevent a premature attack; fundamentally, she could neither

convert or restrain the enemy.[80] Long-range strategic hope was dead; only

short-ranged—in the sequel short-lived—tactical convenience remained.

So Hull strongly resisted the proposals of the hard-line advocates

who saw salvation in a show of strength. By now the moderates knew that

confrontation with Japan was inevitable. It was no longer a question

of whether, but when. The major reason for restraint beyond hope lay

in American military unpreparedness. Hull saw the Navy chiefs frequently,

and was constantly warned about America's military vulnerability and

totally exposed position in the Pacific.[81] Therefore, he stubbornly

resisted the pressure of his critics, repeatedly asserting that there

would be no oil embargo until the Navy assured him that the fleet was

ready and stationed for action.[82]

The answer to the question "when?" remained indeterminate. Moreover,

it was fused with an equally undefined and important question "under what

conditions?" Hull remained deliberately enigmatic:

> ...in dealing with lawless governments, it was
> important to lead them to do a bit of guessing,
> without making any threats. I believed in letting
> them guess as to when and in what set of circumstances
> we would fight. While Japan continued to guess, we
> continued to get ready for anything she might do.[83]

There were reasons why the Secretary would not reply to the

questions of "when" and "under what conditions." First of all,

he was not certain of the answer. Until the attack at Pearl

Harbor, the conditions under which the U.S. would go to war in

the Pacific were speculative. It was dangerous for any public

official to define them too precisely since so much depended

on the uncontrollable actions of the enemy and the unpredictable

reactions of the American public. Also, practical ends were

served by this policy. An undefined approach which would keep

the enemy guessing would more likely inhibit Japanese aggression

than a clearly articulated stand. It would also gain a maximum

amount of time. For a clear stand would either encourage the

enemy to act in the belief that he could strike with impunity

or else drive him to desperate action in the knowledge that

no settlement with the United States was possible. Uncertainty

could deter where certainty would seduce or incite.

The effectiveness of this policy depended upon whether

the Japanese Government had already opted for war. Through

the maze of uncertainty, the State Department sought to deter

Japan by flashing ambiguous signals: signals to the foe that
[84]
American patience was neither inexhaustible nor short-lived.

The Japanese were to guess where the line lay, when patience

would end and retaliation begin.

But while the Secretary still cautioned delay and care,

the patience of the Department was rapidly vanishing. By

February 1941, it was drawing closer and closer to the position
supported by the hard-liners, favoring an embargo even at the
risk of offending the Japanese.[85]

The conversations between Hull and Nomura, from March 1941
to the Pearl Harbor attack, were tactical in intent. The
Secretary of State knew that the aims of the two powers were
incompatible, that the chances of a change of heart in Tokyo
were improbable; but he hoped that the Japanese would not
realize that agreement was impossible. Or he hoped that they
would draw this conclusion too late to halt the buildup of
Allied power in the Pacific. Feis summarizes Hull's strategy:

> ...no purpose, Hull thought, would be served by an
> unqualified rejection of this child of chance. It
> was wise to keep the opinion alive within the Japan-
> ese government that the issues dividing the two
> nations might be settled by talk. It was essential
> to ward off the conclusion that no path except that
> of war could take Japan towards its ends. Who knew
> what turn of battle or new estimate of chances might
> change the outlook?[86]

Time gained through deception could alter the balance of power
in the Pacific, thereby preventing what now seemed unavoidable.
For delay could mean new strength, and new strength could
deter the Japanese.

Throughout the first half of 1941, Hull maintained his
opposition to the embargo and to any freezing order, knowing
they could trigger a time bomb:

> Nomura in every talk cited the existing denials of
> vital materials as the prod which might set Japan
> off for the south. If, Hull said over and over
> to his more impatient colleagues, the American
> government stopped oil, any remaining influence
> of the Japanese advocates of peace would
> vanish.[87]

Essentially he was waiting for the Japanese to act, hoping they would delay their decision until it was too late for them to implement it effectively.

Japan did not wait long. Her July 2, 1941, decision to move southward into Indo-China and Thailand sealed the course of fate, buried the cause of peace. Destroying the last argument with which the moderates could counter the champions of the hard line, the Japanese convinced the State Department that moderation was futile, and that their course of action would be chosen without regard to American reaction. Hull now felt that the decision had been made and that America could no longer wait; she could no longer equip her future foe with the implements of war:

> When Welles telephoned me, I said to him that the invasion of
> Southern Indo-China looked like Japan's last step before
> jumping off for a full-scale attack in the Southwest Pacific.
> Since it came in the midst of the conversations we were
> holding with Japan, I said I could see no basis for pursuing
> the conversations further. [88]

Believing that the Japanese were now on the brink, the Secretary of State agreed to the freezing order. [89] Now the hope for peace was largely recognized as a mirage, and the necessity for mounting military preparations was paramount. Though strategic time had totally vanished, tactical time still held the stage and dominated the action:

> The first act of the drama of our dialogue with Japan ended
> in failure, just as the second act was destined to end. It
> showed us, however, what we had to face. Japan would readily
> and instantly have signed a straight nonaggression pact with
> the United States. She would as readily have signed a general
> agreement with us on the basis of her own proposals. But
> neither pact would have given us peace for more than a short
> time. And either one would have meant a betrayal of China,
> Britain, Russia, and the Netherlands, and of our own future
> security.
> From now on our major objective with regard to Japan was to
> give ourselves more time to prepare our defenses. We were

still ready--and eager--to do everything possible toward
keeping the United States out of war; but it was our con-
current duty to concentrate on trying to make the country
ready to defend itself effectively in the event of war
being thrust upon us. [90]

4) The President's Muted Role

During the entire debate, the President watched the conflict of
opinions and the clash of wills from the wings, allowing his Secretary
of State to direct the course of decision and action. He moved to the
fore only when the final decision was announced. Then he firmly and
clearly alligned himself with the policy of total resistance, a complete
economic break with the Japanese Government. His role was totally
different now than it was in the formulation of Atlantic diplomacy.
Since he considered the Pacific a holding theater, he was content to
leave the conduct of negotiations and the control of policy to the
State Department, only intervening when he felt it was absolutely
necessary. The President could let Hull work for him.

The care with which Roosevelt publicly disassociated himself from
Pacific policy in this second phase is shown by the few references to
Japanese aggression in his speeches. Moreover, since Hull was seeking
to negotiate, to heal the issues dividing the two countries, the
President did not emphasize the urgency of the situation. His emphasis
was always on Nazi aggression, Nazi brutality, Nazi tyranny. He treated
Japanese conquests and atrocities as an adjunct to Hitler's world scheme. [91]

Each public step taken to counter Germany was accompanied by a
careful explanation of public policy, an elaborate analysis of the reasons
for decision. Far Eastern affairs were handled on a lower key. [92] Even
the final step--the freezing order--was not preceded by any oratorical
prelude. Ironically, however, only two days before the imposition of
the order, the President extemporaneously explained the core of our

policy towards Japan to a volunteer committee of the Office of Civilian

Defense. In a style of Sunday school simplicity the President lectured

his audience on the realities of Far Eastern politics, giving no indication that he had already decided to freeze Japanese assets.[93] Any listener

could have interpreted the speech as a defense of existing policy, rather

than a new departure:

> All right. Now the answer is a very simple one. There is
> a world war going on, and has been for some time--nearly two
> years. One of our efforts, from the very beginning, was to
> prevent the spread of that world war in certain areas where
> it hadn't started. One of those areas is a place called the
> Pacific Ocean--one of the largest areas of the earth. There
> happened to be a place in the South Pacific where we had to
> get a lot of things--rubber--tin--and so forth and so on--
> down in the Dutch Indies, the Straits Settlements, and
> Indo-China. And we had to help get the Australian surplus
> of meat and wheat, and corn, for England.
> It was very essential from our own selfish point of view of
> defense to prevent a war from starting in the South Pacific.
> So our foreign policy was--trying to stop a war from breaking
> out down there. At the same time, from the point of view of
> even France at that time--of course France still had her head
> above water--we wanted to keep that line of supplies from
> Australia and New Zealand going to the Near East--all their
> troops, all their supplies that they have maintained in
> Syria, North Africa, and Palestine. So it was essential for
> Great Britain that we try to keep the peace down there in
> the South Pacific.
> All right. And now here is a Nation called Japan. Whether
> they had at that time aggressive purposes to enlarge their
> empire southward, they didn't have any oil of their own up
> in the north. Now, if we cut the oil off, they probably would
> have gone down to the Dutch East Indies a year ago, and you
> would have had war.
> Therefore, there was--you might call--a method in letting
> this oil go to Japan, with the hope--and it has worked for
> two years--of keeping war out of the South Pacific for our
> own good, for the good of the defense of Great Britain, and
> the freedom of the seas.
> You people can help to enlighten the average citizen who
> wouldn't hear of that, or doesn't read the papers carefully,
> or listen to the radio carefully--to understand what some of
> these apparent anomalies mean. So, on the information end,
> I think you have got just as great a task as you have in the
> actual organization work.[94]

Despite its irritatingly condescending simplicity, the lecture achieved

its main objective. It taught the American people the facts of power and

their relation to American policy in the western Pacific. Two days later
the President signed the freezing order, liquidating the very policy he
had so carefully defended.

Therefore, before taking the most momentous step in American–Japanese
relations since 1857, the President did not resort to either exhortation
or validiction for his new policy. Instead he defended his now discarded
stand. The bow to the past swept in the future. Of course, those who
recalled his message after the imposition of the freezing order would
realize that clearly, though guardedly, the President had shown that the
new alternative policy could easily trigger war in the Far East.[95]

But on July 24, 1941, Roosevelt's approach towards the problem of
Japanese expansion was still circumspect and quiet. The President--like
his Secretary of State--knew that he did not have to arouse American public
opinion. He knew that psychological mobilization was complete. Like
Hull, he preferred to hold back the tide, to discourage public excitement
as long as possible. Dealing with the European Axis, the President had
put all emphasis and exhortation on the pressures of time and the urgency
of the situation. The people had to be psychologically mobilized, convinced and converted to an active policy in the Atlantic; but where Pacific
policy was at stake, it needed no persuasion. Moreover, European policy
required a positive commitment, a definite involvement. Pacific policy
was far more passive; it required only America's withdrawal from her
commitment to Japanese trade and a disassociation from past appeasement.

c. Military Caution

The cautious policy of the President and the Secretary of State
was largely guided and moved by the careful advice of the military planners.
Their approach was consistent:

> In contrast to...civilian leaders, the military advisers of
> the President were firmly opposed to all measures of retalia-
> tion likely to provoke the Japanese to make war. General
> Marshall and Admiral Stark recognized that a conflict with
> Japan in the near future was altogether probable, but they
> insisted that the United States was as yet unprepared for
> hostilities in the Pacific and that in any event it was
> more in the American interest to arm against Hitler and
> support Britain than to devote a major effort against Japan.[96]

During the period before the imposition of the freezing order, the

military chiefs were consistently opposed to any embargo upon Japan.

Their opposition had two sources, both embedded in all prewar planning:

the general military unpreparedness of the United States and the primacy

of the Atlantic front. Since they were convinced that the threat from

Nazi Germany was far greater than that from imperial Japan, they rejected

any policy, opposed any measures, which would ultimately challenge the

principle of concentration, involving the United States in the wrong war,

at the wrong time, in the wrong place.[97]

Even though Admiral Stark, for example, thought that a declaration

of war against Germany was essential in the late spring and early summer

of 1941, he opposed the decision to impose severe sanctions upon Japan

to the end. In a letter to Admiral Kimmel at Pearl Harbor, dated July 24,

1941--two days before the freeze order was announced--Stark clearly

revealed his opposition to any embargo policy and his belief that the

Japanese Government would not attack the Netherlands East Indies unless

provoked by American sanctions. The Chief of Naval Operations began by

describing his recent talks with Japanese Ambassador Nomura:

> We have had very plain talk. I like him, and as you know,
> he has many friends in our Navy. Nomura dwelt at length on
> his country's need for the rice and minerals of Indo-China.
> My guess is that with the establishment of bases in Indo-China,
> they will stop for the time being, consolidate their positions,
> and await world reaction to their latest move. No doubt they
> will use their Indo-China bases from which to take early action

> against the Burma Road. Of course, there is the possibility
> that they will strike at Borneo. I doubt that this will be
> done in the near future, <u>unless</u> we embargo oil shipments to
> them....The question of embargo has been up many times and
> I have consistently opposed it just as strongly as I could. [98]

Since further Japanese policy was still a mystery, the Admiral felt that

the United States should continue to forebear and wait on the future

course of events. [99] To him, though perhaps not to General Marshall, time [100]

could still be gained in the Pacific.

Even after the decision was made, Admiral Stark and other top

military planners were fearful of the embargo. [101] It represented the

danger of easily provoking a Japanese attack which the United States was

not prepared to meet and which would upset all her strategic plans. Once

the decision was sealed, therefore, the military maintained their effort

to gain the maximum amount of time for preparing American defenses in

the Far East, concentrating especially on this objective during the final

period preceding the Pearl Harbor attack.

3. The Third Stage: Confrontation

The third stage was dominated by a mounting sense of tension and

exigency. As the inevitable confrontation approached, it became obvious

to the civilian leaders and military planners alike that time was becoming

very short, that the interval of grace was uncertain and increasingly

tenuous. Of course there were still advisers and planners who optimistically

predicted that the Japanese would wait, would not strike until the defeat

of the Soviet Union and Great Britain were certain. There were also

moments when even the wisest thought that the confrontation with Japan

could be avoided. But these views and moments were merely deceptive

eddies of calm in an increasingly threatening sea. Except in an

academic sense, the debate was stilled, the decision made. The final

stage was merely the concluding act of a predetermined drama.

Despite all the facts to the contrary, there was still some hope left that America could build up her military forces and deploy her B-17's in sufficient numbers so as to paralyze Japanese power. It was also hoped that the United States could gain enough tactical time to revolutionize the strategic situation in the western Pacific. If she could avoid a showdown until the spring of 1942, America would be ready.

The need for time was also accentuated by the demands of policy. Appeasement of Japan had not yet been replaced by full-scale collaboration with America's potential Allies against Japan. The United States was drawing a line of defense throughout the Pacific, formulating joint plans and preparations. But her definitions and moves were indefinite and only partially formulated. The battle line had been drawn, but no one knew exactly where it fell. Only time could firm plans and fill preparations.

a. The Ambiguities of Public Opinion

The entire problem was complicated by American public opinion. Could the President and his advisers still depend on its support? For this question was now marked by curious ambiguities. Most Americans still favored a bold and inflexible stand against Japanese aggression. Their opinion still operated as a major pressure on the Administration, urging and supporting a tough policy. But the people who had clamored for an end to appeasement hesitated to support the increasingly necessary, still undeclared and only partially defined policy of association with the British and the Dutch. As the President realized, he would need overwhelming support to lead the nation into war; otherwise continued division would hamper the conduct of the war and marr the unity of the country.

The attitude of the American public towards economic sanctions was still reinforced by persistent contempt for Japanese military power and a failure to clearly grasp the fateful complications of the hard line. On August 1, 1941, the President strengthened the freezing order by prohibiting the export to Japan of certain strategic materials, including petroleum products convertible into gasoline.[102] The public reacted enthusiastically. Langer and Gleason analyze the effect of this belligerent temper:

> The more ardent newspapers proclaimed that Japan was now bound hand and foot, that Japan would either have to put up or shut up. A survey of opinion on the West Coast reported the general sentiment to be: 'They are asking for it, let's let them have it.' According to public opinion polls at least half of those questioned expressed willingness to risk war in order to keep Japan from becoming more powerful.... It can hardly be denied that with respect to sanctions against Japan, American public opinion was running well ahead of the President and his Administration.[103]

This belligerent tone, with its curious insouciance, was an obstacle to any compromise, modus vivendi or stopgap measure like the proposed Konoye-Roosevelt meeting.[104] The public mood sealed the conflict between the two powers:

> Spiritually as well as economically the United States was already at war and already exulting in its easy successes. 'Japan,' wrote one influential editor, 'is encircled by the consequences of her own outrages and she is getting desperate....'
> It need not be maintained that this was the universal American attitude, but it was certainly the prevelant one. If the Administration had already decided to take a strong stand, most of the press clamored for an even stronger one. If the Japanese press was bellicose, so was the American. The truth of the matter was that the policies of the two powers were no longer reconcilable.[105]

A simple formula dominated the American mind: appeasement feeds aggression; firmness thwarts expansionism.

The public mood made any settlement other than a complete reversal of Japanese policy totally unacceptable. By the end of September, the pressure of the major newspapers had become an immovable block against negotiation. No agreement which did not fully insure the complete independence of China was

possible. As the <u>New York Times</u> declared: "'Such a "settlement"
would be a flat betrayal of our best friend in Asia. It
would ridicule our moral position in the war.'"[106]

The problem of public support remained vital to the end.
For while the news media and Congress clamored against
appeasement, the isolationists remained adamant, set against
any alignment between the United States, Britain and Holland
in the Far East. They felt that America should avoid commitment
to any war resulting from Japanese attacks on foreign colonies
in Asia.[107]

As the climax became increasingly unmistakable and the
Pacific powers teetered on the brink of catastrophe, public
uncertainty swelled. The crisis was no longer theoretical
or distant. Now, as Langer and Gleason point out, it was real
and imminent:

> As to the state of American public opinion on the
> eve of the conflict, it is difficult to generalize
> with any assurance. The press, always inclined to
> to treat Japan in a cavalier fashion, grew somewhat
> more circumspect as the crisis deepened. While
> still overwhelmingly opposed to any form of appease-
> ment, most editors were reluctant to renounce all
> hope of a peaceful settlement. Tabulations of
> public reaction, submitted to the President,
> revealed the usual inconsistencies....
> It is not much easier to form a judgment on the
> vitally important factor of Congressional opinion.
> Secretary Hull was evidently worried to the end
> by the strength of isolationist sentiment in
> Congress. The President, too, had not forgotten
> the heated debates of recent months. Although
> Representative May, Chairman of the Armed Services
> Committee, declared publicly on December 2 that
> Congress would 'support a declaration of war
> now if Japan moves southward,' Mr. Roosevelt
> knew that there were few member of Congress as
> bellicose as Mr. May.[108]

Public opinion, therefore, closed the door to appeasement, but did not open the gate to full and open cooperation between the United States and its potential Allies. Americans still did not take the Japanese menace as seriously as the threat of the European Axis. They still failed to understand that the July 1941 decision meant war. Time moved inexorably towards the inevitable, but most were deaf to its ticking.

   b. The Administration: Perspectives before Disaster

   The Roosevelt Administration saw the developments in the Far East far more clearly than the American people. Through the medium of MAGIC, the Japanese diplomatic code, the United States could read intentions and predict plans.[109] But even with this unique window into the mind of the enemy, the perception of the Administration was blinded by uncertainty. It could feel the mounting urgency, spot the oncoming crisis, but could not measure the intensity or predict the climactic nature of the crisis. It did not know the direction of the enemy's blow until one month before the attack. Even then it could not definitely identify Japan's specific objectives.

   The inevitability of war depended directly on the course of direction and the choice of objectives. There were only two ways Japanese aggression could move: north or south, into Siberia or into the South Pacific. In the former case, the objective was certain, obviously predictable. If the Japanese Army attacked north, it would assault the Soviet Union.[110] In the latter contingency, however, the objectives were far more indeterminate; the Japanese having a multitude of geographic goals and a wealth. of enemies. They could attack Thailand, leaving British, Dutch and American possessions alone for the moment.[111] Or they could assault Singapore, Malaya and the Netherlands East Indies, encircling the Philippine Islands without

touching American soil. Finally, they could assault all positions in
the South Pacific, sweeping away American and European Empires in the
fury of their advance. They had multiple options.

Any attack on either the Soviet Union or Thailand would present a
serious problem. One would threaten the Russian armies with a two front
war, presenting them with the formidable problem of feeding two theaters,
connected only by tenuous lines of communication which stretched over
infinite distances. The other would give the Japanese another platform
for an air, sea and land attack on Malaya and the fortress of Singapore.
But neither of these two possibilities would confront the United States
with the immediate and inescapable choice between war and peace.[112] Any
attack on British and Dutch possessions, however, would pose an imminent
and dangerous menace to American interests in the Far East, threatening
the "Germany First" premise of Allied strategy. It would create a far
greater emergency which would demand, though not necessarily secure, an
American declaration of war. It would give the United States almost as
little time, as little choice, as a direct attack upon her possessions
in the Far East.

The degree of urgency, therefore, depended upon the chosen
objective of Japanese policy, upon whether their decision would involve
or invoke a declaration of war. Paradoxically, however, this choice,
this objective, ultimately turned upon the effect of American policy.
Would the adoption of the hard line drive the Japanese to attack, or
would it deter them? Would it make them desperate or cautious? Although
the debate between the moderates and the hard-line advocates was now
academic, finally being settled by the freezing order, it still continued
in a new form. The clash was no longer over whether this decision should

be made, but rather over the effect the decision <u>would</u> have,
now that it was made. As Barbara Wohlstetter remarks:

> There was great conflict of opinion on the wisdom
> of imposing an embargo on Japan; the conflict continued
> after July 26 and was reflected in the elastic
> wording of the Embargo Act itself. Calculations about
> what the Japanese might do if and when the United
> States imposed an embargo varied between two extremes:
> from the belief that they would thereby be deterred
> from further aggression to the belief that they would
> retaliate by an immediate attack on U.S. possessions.[113]

Once the decision was sealed, surprising shifts took place.
Some who had consistently opposed the embargo as dangerous
and provocative became convinced of its effectiveness. Others
who had seen a simple solution to policy problems through the
application of force, had second thoughts.

Until the last hours before the Japanese attack, the
State Department remained in command of the negotiations.
By July 1941, Hull and his chief associates were disgusted
with Japanese conduct, doubtful that the issues dividing
the two countries could be resolved. By November, Hull was
merely dragging out the negotiations, hoping to hedge his
position against the inevitable. As Wohlstetter notes,
he was tired, pessimistic but still cautious:

> By November, Hull was more than anything else--weary.
> Again and again the private accounts from government
> circles describe him with this adjective. He had
> gone, in his own words, 'around and around the same
> circle' for so long that he no longer hoped for a
> peaceful settlement with Japan or the imposition of
> some kind of restraint on her military aggressions.
> He could only use his remaining energy to try to gain
> more time for the U.S. military, and this meant a
> constant balance between severity and patience with
> the Japanese delegates....But minimum and maximum
> concessions for each side had been pretty rigidly
> defined by then, and the possibilities of diplomatic
> manoeuvering were consequently restricted. Even within
> these confines Hull persisted in his efforts to
> maintain peace in the Pacific and to keep the President
> firmly persuaded of this goal.[114]

Hull had abandoned his previous convictions but not his approach.

He was, however, a man of stubborn moral convictions. He believed implicitly in a policy of morality, feeling that nations should follow certain eternal principles in their relationships to others. He reproved mere expediency and denounced predatory conduct. The moral position of China as opposed to the immoral conduct of the Japanese was indelibly etched in his mind. And this commitment of the Secretary of State made any long-range solution impossible:

> We could easily have had an agreement with the Konoye Government at any time by signing on the dotted line. Mr. Roosevelt and Konoye could have met, and from their meeting might have flowed vague generalities on undying peace. But we should have negated principles on which we had built our foreign policy and without which the world could not live at peace. We should have betrayed China and the Philippines and abandoned Britain and Holland. Japan might have gone into Russia and so weakened her that Hitler might have won over Stalin. And on the ladder of an agreement such as the Japanese demanded, a mightier Japan would have climbed to become a greater danger to us than ever before. [115]

Since such an agreement was a violation of American principles, as well as a threat to security, it was totally unthinkable. And the impossibility of long-range salvation placed clear limits on the time the Secretary of State could gain for the military to complete their preparations. The practical uses of time were restricted by the moral imperatives of international conduct.

Hull finally lost all hope in the last weeks of negotiations. Tactical time was at last running out. His conviction of the hopelessness of any agreement and that confrontation was rapidly approaching was heightened and underlined by his reading of MAGIC. From October, from Tojo's accession to power until the attack on Pearl Harbor, the Secretary of State could perceive a rising sense of urgency in the Japanese Government:

> ...I began to note a sense of urgency in Tojo's and Togo's attitude towards our conversations. Konoye had pressed us

to move rapidly in accepting his terms; but one of his
purposes had been to continue himself in office, with the
help of an agreement with us. Tojo wanted something done
quickly, but it was apparent that his purpose was different
from Konoye's. If an agreement were not reached he was prepared,
I believed, to take action that would mean war.
This sense of urgency, this almost frantic effort to push us
into an agreement that would give Tokyo all it wanted, continued
up to Pearl Harbor. We noted it a few days after Tojo came
to power when the translation of an intercepted message from
Togo to Nomura dated October 21 came to my desk. It said,
in part: 'Our country has said practically all she can say
in the way of expressing of opinions and setting forth our
stand. We feel that we have now reached a point where no
further positive action can be taken by us except to urge
the United States to reconsider her views....We urge, therefore,
that, choosing an opportune moment, either you or Wakasugi
(Chancellor of the Embassy) let it be known to the United
States by indirection that our country is not in a position
to spend much more time discussing this matter.' [116]

He knew that the impossibility of agreement made a military collision

inevitable.

Moreover, convinced that the Japanese would attack the Philippines,

Hull anticipated that any Pacific war would immediately involve the United

States. [117] At a War Council meeting on November 28, he was ominous, even

pessimistic in his assesment:

'The Japanese were likely to break out any time with new acts
of conquest and that the matter of safeguarding our national
security was in the hands of the Army and Navy...any plans
for our military defense should include an assumption that
the Japanese might make the element of surprise a central
point in their strategy and also might attack at various
points simultaneously with a view to demoralizing efforts of
defense and of coordination.' [118]

Hull made a fairly accurate prediction of Japanese plans, having probably

caught the tone of their urgency more acutely than others, and having

dealt for so long a time with their negotiators.

Surprisingly, however, the Secretary of State still tried, toiling

with persistence but without hope. He pushed for a modus vivendi, only

abandoning it with considerable reluctance and continued regret when it
was apparent that this proposal would shake the foundations of any potential
Pacific Alliance.[119] He persistently protested against any clear definition
of America's defensive line in the Pacific,[120] and opposed any firm warning to
Japan, seeking to postpone any Presidential address to Congress on the
Far Eastern crisis and any final appeal to the Japanese Emperor.[121] Why
did he continue this obviously unrenumerative labor even to the last fatal
stroke of the clock?

There are several reasons. Primarily, and most obviously, was the
nature of his job, the essence of his role. A negotiator never ceases
to negotiate. As long as the guns are still silent, he will try to avoid
the inevitable even when he recognizes its inevitability. The second
reason centers around the special situation governing America's relations
with Japan. Since her potential enemy held the initiative, since--for
purposes of justification--it was extremely important to allow her to
strike the first blow--the Secretary of State could only insist on
continued caution and persistent patience.

Hull, of course, had always feared that the imposition of an
embargo would mean war. But the advocates of the hard line had always
maintained that the Japanese would back down and avoid any final confrontation. With the freezing order and the subsequent tightening of restrictions
closing the economic ring around Japan, their proposals became official
policy.[122] But, though their program was adopted, their prophecy remained
unfulfilled. How did their sense of urgency compare with that of the
Secretary of State whose policies they had so tenaciously criticized and
opposed before July 1941?

Stimson had once castigated America's cautious policy towards Japan
as "akin to the 'appeasement of Neville Chamberlain.'"[123] He had always

felt that with the Japanese, force--not prolonged diplomacy--was the real answer.[124] Yet, in the remaining months of peace, the Secretary of War consistently backed Hull, persistently urged the continuation of Japanese-American negotiations, stressing that the United States needed more time to prepare its defenses in the Far East and to steady its forces. Stimson now spoke as an ally, not a critic, of the Secretary of State.

There were several factors at work here. First, the Stimson proposals had been adopted in July, 1941, when the freezing order had ended all strategic trade with Japan. And yet, as only too evident from the MAGIC intercepts, the Japanese had not modified their plans nor changed their purposes. The potential threat expressed by America's formidable economic resources and her inherent ability to economically strangle the Japanese had failed altogether.

The second reason for Stimson's shift derived from the one remaining hope, the reinforcement of the Philippine Islands. Now that the United States could strengthen its previously vulnerable position in the Western Pacific with a powerful force of B-17's, the possibility existed that "this new and concrete threat might do what a merely potential threat had failed to do."[125] Although the Japanese could possibly "be persuaded not to force the issue,"[126] the Secretary of War knew that the race against time was close. By November he knew that we were losing, that "a showdown could not be long delayed."[127]

In the final conferences of the last two weeks before Pearl Harbor, Stimson's sense of urgency fully matched that of Hull. He could see the confrontation moving rapidly like an approaching tornado. War was inescapable. And, like the Secretary of State, Stimson felt that any conflict in the Western Pacific would inevitably involve the United States. His position

at the November 25 meeting of the War Council was unmistakably revealed in
his reaction to the President's reminder that despite the desperateness of
the situation and the clear threat to our interests, the United States
could never initiate hostilities:

> 'The question was how we should maneuver them into the position
> of firing the first shot without allowing too much danger to
> ourselves. It was d difficult proposition. Hull laid out his
> general propositions on which the thing should be rested--the
> freedom of the seas and the fact that Japan was in alliance
> with Hitler and was carrying out his policy of world aggression.
> The others brought out the fact that any such expedition to
> the South as the Japanese were likely to take would be an
> encirclement of our interests in the Philippines and cutting
> into our vital supplies of rubber from Malaysia. I pointed
> out to the President that he had already taken the first steps
> towards an ultimatum in notifying Japan way back last summer
> that if she crossed the border into Thailand she was violating
> our safety and that therefore he had only to point out (to Japan)
> that to follow any such expedition was a violation of a warning
> we had already given. So Hull is to go to work on preparing
> that.' [128]

Since war was inevitable, the only problem that remained was justification.
And this problem would only become serious if the Japanese forces avoided
any direct attack on American possessions. To the Secretary of War,
however, the decision had already been made to contain the Japanese at
any cost.

The Secretary of the Treasury, Henry Morgenthau, had also been one
of the outstanding champions of the hard line, repeatedly chiding the
Administration because it did too little too late. [129] Like Stimson, he had
advocated an early end to appeasement and the full imposition of an
embargo on Japan. And with Stimson he was resolved to oppose any "'let
up on the economic pressure on Japan.'" [130] But now, in late October,
as he felt the drift towards war and the mounting urgency of the situation,
the Secretary of the Treasury hoped desperately that the oncoming
confrontation could be avoided. Unlike Hull and Stimson, he still felt

that a strategic settlement in the Pacific was possible. Morgenthau was
not as close to the developing situation as the other two Secretaries:
"...he was ignorant of the hardness of Japan's position as expressed in
negotiations with Hull and ignorant, too, of the Japanese staging for a
southwestward offensive, as revealed by MAGIC."[131]

What was the President's reaction to the mounting crisis? Was his
sense of exigency as sharp as the Secretary of State's? Did he share
some of the hopes and illusions of the remaining hard-line advocates?
Actually, his state of mind was an enigma, unfathomed by even his closest
advisers. Listening to all views, harboring no final answer, Roosevelt
largely waited upon the developing course of events, allowing Hull to
dominate the scene.[132] Until the last week in November, moreover, he remained
uncertain, unsure of the degree of danger, doubtful as to the seriousness
of Japanese intentions. As he remarked to Harold Ickes on November 21:

> ...he wished he knew whether Japan was playing poker or not.
> He was not sure whether or not Japan had a gun up its sleeve.
> My reply was that I had no doubt that sooner or later, depend-
> ing upon the progress of Germany, Japan would be at our throats;
> as for me, when I knew that I was going to be attacked, I
> preferred to choose my own time and occasion. I asked the
> President whether he had any doubt that Japan would attack
> Siberia if the Germans overcame the Russians. He said that
> he hadn't. I felt that by going to war with Japan now we
> would soon be in a position where a large part of our Navy,
> as well as of the British Navy and of the Dutch East Indies
> Navy, could be released for service in the Atlantic. The
> President's feeling was that Japan would draw herself in and
> that she was too far away to be attacked. It seemed to me
> that the President had not yet reached the state of mind
> where he is willing to be aggressive as to Japan. [133]

There were two major reasons for the President's continued caution. Unlike
Ickes, he knew the ambiguities of the American people and the need for a
public consensus for the waging of total war. And like Hull, Roosevelt,
confronted by the united desire of his military advisers, probably agreed
that no attempt to gain time should be neglected. His initial interest

in the modus vivendi was based on his conviction that the United States
should negotiate beyond any reasonable hope. He agreed with Hull that
they should work "to gain time to 'the last split second.'" [134]

Gradually, however, the feeling of inevitability closed around him.
The concentration of Japanese forces around Indo-China, the obvious
preparations in the Far East for a new act of aggression, sealed his
convictions. The moment of illumination came on the morning of November
26, when Secretary of War Stimson informed the President:

> '...about the Japanese having started a new expedition from
> Shanghai down toward Indo-China. He fairly blew up--jumped
> up into the air, so to speak, and said he hadn't seen it and
> that that changed the whole situation because it was an
> evidence of bad faith on the part of the Japanese that while
> they were negotiating for an entire truce--an entire with-
> drawal...they should be sending an expedition down there to
> Indo-China.' [135]

The Japanese action led to the abandonment of the modus vivendi. The
purpose of temporizing had obviously ended and the danger of a clash was
inescapable. In a Presidential message to the High Commissioner of the
Philippines sent on the 26th, Roosevelt underlined the threatening
nature of recent Japanese moves and directly connected them with a possible attack upon the Philippine Islands. His strongest note revealed the
full impact of the crisis: "'I consider it possible that this next
Japanese aggression might cause an outbreak of hostilities between the
U.S. and Japan....'" [136] His opinion was confirmed by the final 14-part
message of the Japanese Government, decoded in the last hours before
Pearl Harbor's attack. For, after reading 13 of the 14 parts, the
President turned to Hopkins and quickly remarked: "'This means war.'" [137]

c. The Military's Continued Demand for Time

During the entire third phase, Hull and Roosevelt had sought to
gain time, to prolong their negotiations despite their loss of any hope,

despite their realization that Japanese aggression was tenacious and
insistent. These negotiations were largely continued because of the
constant and persistent demand of the military for more time to prepare
for the inevitable.[138] There were two major reasons for this request.
First, there was the constant drain of the Battle of the Atlantic, where
the United States was increasingly throwing its military emphasis. Any
Pacific crisis would disrupt accepted military plans and arrangements
for a concentration of forces against Germany.

Second, our Far Eastern positions were obviously, but no longer
hopelessly, vulnerable. The special urgency of the military planners
largely turned on this final possibility. If America's positions in the
Western Pacific were totally indefensible, the planners would have re-
gretfully reconciled themselves to their loss. But, since they were not,
since they could be saved by a proper deployment of an existing weapon
system, their salvation largely depended upon time. If the United States
could forestall the blow long enough, she could improve her strategic
position throughout the Pacific and turn the Philippines into an invulnerable fortress. Then if the Japanese struck, they would strike at their
own cost. If they refrained, awed by the might of our deployed force,
new possibilities would open. Command of tactical time could reopen the
possibility of a strategic change in the Pacific.

But here even the military were governed by a sense of limits.
They wanted more time, but they were not willing to pay any price for it.
They were convinced that the loss of the Malay Barrier or the Netherlands
East Indies was totally unacceptable.[139] Their loss would doom the
Philippines and destroy any possibly viable defense in the Western Pacific.

These interlinking attitudes can be followed by studying
the military chiefs' emphasis upon the defense of the Philippines
throughout this final act. Now, though diplomacy still
dominated the foreground, it was merely the mock play behind
whose moves the real drams was enacted. As Herbert Feis notes:

> ...from now on, these talks were turns in front of
> the footlights, while the real play went on behind.
> The curtain of diplomacy was becoming more and more
> transparent. Less and less it concealed the military
> preparations made by each side to cause the other
> to yield, before or in battle.[140]

We have already studied the reasons for the decision to
reinforce the Philippines.[141] Here we shall concentrate on the
role played by time. The success of the policy of reinforcement,
begun on July 31, 1941, depended on America's ability to build-up
a strategic fleet of B-17's in the Archipelago, a deterrent
force like the battle fleet at Pearl Harbor. Along with more
conventional reinforcements, this buildup would secure the
U.S. position throughout the Western Pacific, anchoring the
Archipelago to the strengthened Malay Barrier.[142] But success
or failure depended upon the fall of time.

The problems were multitudinous. If the Philippines
were to become a bastion, the United States would have to
overcome tough obstacles. There were seven problems: 1) the
small number of available B-17's; 2) the slow development
of pursuit units, essential for interception and the protection
of the big bombers; 3) the shortage of anti-aircraft artillery,
essential for the protection of the airfields; 4) the shortage
of bombs and ammunition; 5) the lack of sufficient radar sets
and the inadequacy of the early warning system; 6) the inevitable
delays in moving supplies to the Philippines and organizing them;

and 7) the vulnerability of the line of communications to the
Philippines which necessitated the construction of a new line
of bases along the less exposed South Pacific route.[143]

Despite these obvious difficulties, however, optimism
grew throughout the summer and fall. Military planners became
convinced that the United States could succeed. The target[144]
date was March 1942. If the Japanese did not attack before
then, American positions could be secured against assault.
If they struck earlier, the United States would be caught
unprepared, physically and psychologically. As Secretary
Stimson explained to President Roosevelt on October 21, 1941:

> 'A strategic opportunity of the utmost importance has
> suddenly arisen in the southwestern Pacific....From
> being impotent to influence events in that area, we
> suddenly find ourselves vested with the possibility
> of great effective power....even this imperfect
> threat, if not promptly called by the Japanese, bids
> fair to stop Japan's march to the south and secure
> the safety of Singapore.'[145]

Not surprisingly, therefore, Army and Navy leaders were
anxious to gain as much time as possible. The Army's reasons
were, as noted above, centered around the needs of Philippine
defense. As Herbert Feis remarks, the Navy's reasons were
more global:

> It wanted neither to spare nor risk warships and
> merchant ships in a fight in the Pacific. Besides,
> it was worried by the lack of tankers, the vulnerability
> of its lines of communication, the inadequacy of
> repair facilities in Manila and Singapore and of anti-
> aircraft protection at the Far Eastern bases.[146]

But though the military chiefs wanted more time, they did not
want a truce which would immobilize their forces, leaving them
exposed once the truce expired;[147] and they were not willing to
relinquish Allied positions in the Far East. These conflicting
objectives were explored at the November 3 Joint Board meeting.

This meeting mainly revolved around the question of whether or not the United States should warn Japan against any military advance into Yunnan, a move which could cut off the Burma Road, isolating China from the outside world. The problem was posed by Captain Schuirmann of the U.S. Navy Office of Naval Operations:

> At the request of Admiral Stark, Captain Schuirmann gave a statement of the action taken at the State Department meeting on Saturday morning, November 1, at which a discussion was held on the Far Eastern situation. Captain Schuirmann states that the meeting was occasioned by messages from Chiang Kai-Shek and General Magruder, urging the United States to warn Japan against making an attack on China through Yunnan and suggesting that the United States urge Great Britain to support more fully opposition to Japan. He pointed out that on August 17, following the President's return from the meeting at sea with Mr. Churchill, the President had issued an ultimatum to Japan that it would be necessary for the United States to take action in case of further Japanese aggression. He further stated that Mr. Hull was of the opinion that there was no use to issue any additional warnings to Japan if we can't back them up, and he desired to know if the military authorities would be prepared to support further warnings by the State Department. [148]

This State Department request evoked a personal review of the situation by Admiral Ingersoll, then Assistant Chief of Naval Operations. He listed the Navy's objections to the pursuit of any provocative policy in the Far East. He pointed out that a Pacific war would drain shipping from the Atlantic, weaken our policy of aid to England and create a serious oil shortage throughout the United States because of the fantastic demands of the Pacific Theater. He also noted the inadequacy and incompleteness of American preparations throughout the Far East. [149] He then came to the heart of the matter: where and when should the United States resist Japanese aggression?

> This review pointed out that Japan is capable of launching an attack in five directions; viz, against Russia, the Philippines, into Yunnan, Thailand and against Malaya. Considering that

Japan might initiate one or more of these five operations, United States' action should be: In case of
Japanese attack against either the Philippines or
British and Dutch positions the United States should
resist the attack. In case of Japanese attack against
Siberia, Thailand or China through Yunnan the United
States should not declare war. The study concludes
that the United States should defer offensive action
in the Far East until the augmentation of United States
military strength in the Philippines, particularly
as to the increase in submarines and army forces
becomes available.[150]

General Marshall also stressed the value of additional
time for preparation and deployment. After supporting Ingersoll's
contention that a Pacific war would infinitely complicate the
task in the Atlantic,[151] he reasserted his faith in the ultimate
effectiveness of the reinforcement policy:

General Marshall emphasized the point that Japan could
hardly take the risk of military operations with a
powerful air and submarine forces directly on the flank
of their supply lines, and that when United States
power is sufficiently developed in the Philippines,
we would then have something to back up our statements....
It appeared that the basis of U.S. policy should be
to make certain minor concessions which the Japanese
could use in saving face.[152]

The discussions and recommendations of the November 3
conference were embodied in a War and Navy Department estimate,
conveyed to the President on November 5. Marshall and Stark's
letter began by rejecting the Chinese bid for an American pledge
for the defense of Yunnan. After delineating the difficulties
which the Japanese would encounter if they initiated a Yunnan
campaign, they warned that American operations in the defense
of Yunnan, "however well disguised, would lead to war."[153] Then,
the letter delineated America's current strategic situation:

At the present time the United States Fleet in the
Pacific is inferior to the Japanese Fleet and cannot
undertake an unlimited strategic offensive in the
Western Pacific. In order to be able to do so, it
would have to be strengthened by withdrawing all naval
vessels from the Atlantic except those assigned to

local defense forces. An unlimited offensive by the Pacific
Fleet would require tremendous merchant tonnage, which could
only be withdrawn from services now considered essential.
The result of withdrawals from the Atlantic of naval and merchant strength might well cause the United Kingdom to lose
the Battle of the Atlantic in the near future.
The only existing plans for war against Japan in the Far East
are to conduct defensive war, in cooperation with the British
and Dutch, for the defense of the Philippines and the British
and Dutch East Indies. The Philippines are now being reinforced.
The present combined naval, air and ground forces will make
attack on the islands a hazardous undertaking. By about the
middle of December, 1941, United States air and submarine
strength in the Philippines will have become a positive threat
to any Japanese operations south of Formosa. The U.S. Army
air forces in the Philippines will have reached the projected
strength by February or March 1942. The potency of this threat
will have then increased to a point where it might well be a
deciding factor in deterring Japan in operations in the areas
south and west of the Philippines. By this time, additional
British naval and air reinforcements to Singapore will have
arrived. The general defensive strength of the entire southern
area against possible Japanese operations will then have reached
impressive proportions. [154]

This optimistic delineation of future prospects was followed by an

admonition that our aid to China should be closely confined to those

measures which would not provoke a Japanese attack. The Chiefs concluded

their analysis by interweaving America's delaying tactics with the

objectives of her military policy:

The Chief of Naval Operations and the Chief of Staff are in
accord in the following conclusions:
(a) The basic military policies and strategy agreed to in the
United States--British Staff conversations remain sound. The
primary objective of the two nations is the defeat of Germany.
If Japan be defeated and Germany remain undefeated, decision
will still have not been reached. In any case, an unlimited-
offensive war should not be undertaken against Japan, since
such a war would greatly weaken the combined effort in the
Atlantic against Germany, the most dangerous enemy.
(b) War between the United States and Japan should be
avoided while building up defensive forces in the Far East,
until such time as Japan attacks or directly threatens territories whose security to the United States is of very great
importance. Military action against Japan should be undertaken only in one or more of the following contingencies:
(1) A direct act of war by Japanese armed forces against the
territory or mandated territory of the United States, the
British Commonwealth, or the Netherlands East Indies;

(2) The movement of Japanese forces into Thailand to the west
of 100 East or South of 10 North; or into Portugese Timor, New
Caladonia, or the Loyalty Islands.
(c) If war with Japan can not be avoided, it should follow
the strategic lines of existing war plans; i.e. military
operations should be primarily defensive, with the object of
holding territory, and weakening Japan's economic position.
(d) Considering world strategy, a Japanese advance against
Kumming, into Thailand except as previously indicated, or an
attack on Russia, would not justify intervention by the United
States against Japan. [155]

Bearing in mind all the dangers of the world situation, the Navy and Army

Chiefs recommended a continuation of the policy of tactical delay. They

ended their letter by advising "that no ultimatum be delivered to Japan."[156]

One month before the attack at Pearl Harbor, the logic of the mili-

tary chiefs ran along the following lines: until the Japanese directly

threatened or attacked the undeclared but vital defensive line in the

Pacific, the United States should continue her policy of delay, gaining

every possible moment. With time defensive positions could be reinforced

until eventually any attack could be deterred. The success of this

tactic would ultimately guarantee and protect the foundations of military

policy, while failure would undermine and perhaps overthrow them, entrapping

the United States into an unlimited conflict with her weaker foe, while

being forced to ignore the menace of her most formidable opponent.